Solutions for Sustainability Through Peri-Urbanization Processes

Vasco Barbosa
University Polytechnic of Viana do Castelo, Portugal & Faculties of Humanities, University of Johannesburg, South Africa

Mónica Marcela Suárez Pradilla
Julio Garavito Colombian School of Engineering University, Colombia

IGI Global Scientific Publishing
Publishing Tomorrow's Research Today

Vice President of Editorial	Melissa Wagner
Director of Acquisitions	Mikaela Felty
Director of Book Development	Jocelynn Hessler
Production Manager	Mike Brehm
Cover Design	Jose Rosado

Published in the United States of America by
IGI Global Scientific Publishing
701 East Chocolate Avenue
Hershey, PA, 17033, USA
Tel: 717-533-8845
Fax: 717-533-7115
Website: https://www.igi-global.com E-mail: cust@igi-global.com

Library of Congress Cataloging-in-Publication Data

LCCN: 2024053577 (CIP Data Pending)
ISBN13: 9798369360897
Isbn13Softcover: 9798369360903
EISBN13: 9798369360910

British Cataloguing in Publication Data
A Cataloguing in Publication record for this book is available from the British Library.

Editorial Advisory Board

Table of Contents

Detailed Table of Contents

The aim of this chapter is to compare two case studies, that of Mérida in Mexico and that of Rosario in Argentina, based on the legal instruments that regulate real estate developments owned by condominium regime, as well as their impacts on the urban form. This interest arises every time that the city of Mérida is experiencing a boom in private developments, preferably in the northern periphery, while in Rosario a municipal by-law that prohibits them has been in force since 2010. Both the cities of Rosario and Mérida have common points regarding the temporality of legal instruments, although their positions regarding condominium property have been opposite.

This study intends to analyze the conceptual, theoretical and empirical interconnections between the sustainable innovation and the new urban green innovation agenda. It departs from the assumption that sustainable innovation is at the core of the new urban green innovation agenda. The method employed is the meta-analytical, reflective and descriptive based on the conceptual, theoretical and empirical literature review.

The study concludes that there are clear evidences that sustainable innovation is at the center of the new urban green innovation agenda.

This chapter focuses on how Brazil's national urban policy has affected peri-urbanization in São Paulo. Since the Federal Constitution of 1988, the idea of property social function was established, leading to the development of the City Statute. This law includes instruments related to informal settlements, such as collective adverse possession. The REURB Law of 2017 further modified this instrument and guaranteed security of tenure through the formal possession of properties. Within the city of São Paulo, the chapter aims to highlight how the 2014 Master Plan implemented these policies. For this purpose, the research relies on a case study design, employing an inductive and qualitative approach supported by bibliographic and documentary research. The chapter emphasizes some critical issues related to the application of the REURB Law in peri-urban areas, thus identifying pathways to enhance policy implementation through community-driven actions. Additionally, it seeks to provide a theoretical framework that can serve as a panoramic basis for future scientific research in the field.

The northern metropolitan area of Bogotá is characterized by a dispersed urban growth, caused primarily by processes of decentralization of the population and economic activities relocated from the metropolitan center. This chapter reviews the case of the Chicú River basin — in the north of the city —in accordance with the hypothesis that the processes of anthropization of the non-urbanized metropolitan territory — caused by patterns of dispersed urban growth and changes in land use into productive economic activities — are transforming the ecosystem services provided by the area and putting the environmental sustainability of the region at risk. Using GIS tools, satellite images, and census data from 2005 and 2018, changes in land use cover were analyzed. The results allowed us to generate scenarios informed by public policy decision-making that are useful to harmonize territorial growth processes and to mitigate negative externalities, in order to safeguard the existing ecosystem services.

Women's political and community action, particularly in informal urban-rural border territories sustained from processes of social reproduction, offer other dimensions from intersectional feminisms to rethink wellbeing and sustainability. Intersectionality accounts for the intertwined action between capitalism, patriarchy and colonialism in the construction of an extractivist relationship with the land and women's bodies, feminized and racialized, reproducing impoverishment, subordination and naturalization of violence. Other dimensions of welfare and sustainability are related both to the extractivist logics of the land and bodies, as well as to the agenciamientos (agency) motivated by the personal, political and community desire to defend the territory-body-land. In this context, this chapter discusses the processes of social reproduction in informal or popular urbanization and the search for wellbeing and sustainability from intersectionality, taking as a case study the Alto Fucha Ecoterritory, an urban-rural border territory in Bogotá

The phenomena of peri-urbanization in the cities of the Global South are closely linked to the implementation of transport infrastructures, which facilitate urban expansion beyond the limits of consolidated areas. This study aims to assess how the dynamics of transport infrastructures contribute to socio-spatial fragmentation, generating exclusion and inequality in peripheral areas. For this purpose, the locality of Suba has been selected, one of the largest peripheral areas of Bogota, where approximately 1.2 million people live and where different economic strata coexist, with an unequal supply of infrastructure and transportation. The 2023 mobility survey conducted by the District Mobility Secretariat of Bogota was used to evaluate economic, time, accessibility and transportation mode indicators, as well as the characteristics of the transportation infrastructure. A composite indicator was obtained by applying an entropy model. The results reveal that economic inequality is the main cause of spatial fragmentation in the Suba locality.

The act of walking is becoming not just a means of transportation but a crucial to creation of sustainable cities. This transformation is significant in cities that are more vulnerable to impacts of climate change. The study focuses on pedestrian mobility in peri-urban areas so, increasing pedestrian mobility in these areas is an important role as climate change impacts will gradually increase in cities. Also, it focuses on importance of pedestrian mobility to develop sustainable urban areas. This micro-scale model, which can use the proposed quantitative and qualitative urban design factors to measure walkability, offers a different approach to sustainability for the peri-urbans. Furthermore, it provides an opportunity for spatial evaluation to increase the sustainability of peri-urban areas. As a case study, it focuses on the urban margin: Gratosoglio which is located south of Milan, a major Italian city. The main conclusion illustrate how walkability is affected by urban design elements and the importance of walkability in developing sustainable and climate-sensitive areas.

Interpreting the benefits derived from urban ecosystem services is crucial for managing lake landscapes, enabling the simultaneous achievement of multiple objectives in urban landscape conservation. This study focuses on the assessment of the capacity of the ecological infrastructure of the San José de Uzuña dam in Arequipa, Peru. This assessment uses the zoning criteria proposed by the ECOTERR environmental tool, complemented by semi-structured interviews with users of the dam. The methodological-logical framework developed constitutes a valuable resource in the urban discourse on eco-system services and the management of urban landscapes. Consequently, this research provides significant data that can be used for specific interventions to improve ecosystem services in similar contexts.

Indoor air quality (IAQ) in peri-urban areas of a fast-developing South Indian metropolis, Hyderabad, has deteriorated due to growth in urbanization, industrialization, and emissions from vehicular traffic. This paper examines the effectiveness of green infrastructure (GI) measures on IAQ in Hyderabad, particularly emphasizing urban design strategies and low-VOC paints for reducing indoor pollution. A literature review was conducted on previous IAQ research in Hyderabad, emphasizing urban design and VOC emissions from paints. The chapter also evaluated interventions concerning GI in peri-urban Hyderabad to determine their efficiency in enhancing IAQ. It has been found that poor urban design and the use of high-VOC paints are two primary causes of indoor air pollution in Hyderabad. Some interventions, like urban forests, green roofs, and green walls, have demonstrated the capability of improving IAQ by controlling particulate matter, volatile organic compounds, and carbon dioxide.

Ensuring access to potable water, basic sanitation, and hygiene (WASH) in Latin America, particularly in rural areas, remains challenging. In 2022, 8.4% of the population lacked safe drinking water, while 74.6% had basic sanitation. Regulatory approaches vary but are generally nascent, facing significant water quality challenges from agricultural runoff, industrial discharges, and mining activities. Inadequate wastewater treatment leads to bacteriological pollution. Over-extraction of groundwater, unplanned urban growth, and limited resources exacerbate pollution and water stress. Monitoring and enforcement are hindered by outdated infrastructure and inadequate training. Critical water quality parameters are inconsistently measured,

Foreword

As an urban planner, I am honoured to present this amazing book, which is a collection of scholarly insights that together reimagine the changing urban landscapes of Latin America and the Global South through the lenses of peri-urban growth, sustainability, resilience, and urban policy transformation. This book covers a wide range of topics, including the legal issues surrounding urban growth in Mexico and Argentina, the potential for green infrastructure to change things in India, the social and spatial effects of transport infrastructure in Bogotá, and the gendered dynamics of informal urbanisation from feminist and intersectional points of view. The chapters critically look at important urban issues like climate change, walkability, indoor air quality, access to clean water, and ecosystem degradation. They do this by using real-world data, local contexts, and inclusive planning. What binds these diverse contributions is a shared commitment to redefining the way cities grow, prioritizing equity, ecological sensitivity, and participatory governance.

As a foreword author, I find this collection to be both intellectually enriching and practically relevant, offering a timely and necessary intervention into urban discourse. It serves as a vital resource for urban planners, policymakers, researchers, and students committed to shaping cities that are not only resilient and sustainable but also just and inclusive for all. I commend the editors and authors for this thoughtful, interdisciplinary, and impactful contribution.

Manpreet Singh Saini
Lovely Professional University, Phagwara, India

Preface

DESCRIPTION OF THE TOPIC

Peri-urbanization is a complex and dynamic process that challenges conventional paradigms of urban and rural development. It refers to the spatial, functional, and socio-environmental transformations occurring at the fringes of cities, where the urban and rural realms intersect and interweave. Far from being transitional or marginal areas, peri-urban territories have emerged as strategic zones where diverse pressures—demographic, economic, political, ecological—converge, creating hybrid landscapes that reflect both the promises and contradictions of contemporary urbanization.

This book explores peri-urbanization not merely as a spatial expansion of cities, but as a multilayered phenomenon shaped by governance structures, infrastructure development, land use conflicts, environmental transformations, and socio-spatial inequalities. In this sense, peri-urban areas become laboratories of innovation and conflict, where the sustainability of urban systems is tested and redefined.

Recent decades have shown that the traditional binary between urban and rural no longer captures the complexity of territorial dynamics. As cities expand outward, driven by population growth, housing demands, transportation networks, and changing economic logics, peri-urban areas absorb these forces in uneven and often unsustainable ways. The absence or weakness of institutional frameworks, environmental regulations, and integrated planning approaches exacerbates fragmentation, vulnerability, and exclusion in these territories.

At the same time, peri-urban zones hold unique opportunities for rethinking urban resilience, sustainability transitions, and inclusive development. They are critical in shaping ecological corridors, protecting water sources and agricultural land, and creating new forms of urban governance that are adaptive, participatory, and equity-oriented.

This book is the result of a collective academic effort within the CYTED network *"Diretrizes, planos e ações em áreas periurbanas: ecossistemas num desenvolvimento equitativo (DPAAPU)"*, involving researchers from multiple countries in Latin America and beyond. By documenting diverse case studies and methodological innovations, the volume contributes to a more situated and critical understanding of peri-urbanization as a key arena for sustainable territorial transformation.

The Place of the Topic in Today's World

In the contemporary global context, peri-urbanization occupies a critical and increasingly visible position within the debates on sustainable development, climate change adaptation, urban inequality, and territorial governance. The rapid growth of cities—especially in the Global South—has extended urban processes beyond the traditional limits of built-up areas, generating vast peri-urban zones characterized by land-use heterogeneity, environmental degradation, and social fragmentation. These areas are no longer peripheral in functional or strategic terms; they are central to understanding how urbanization shapes ecological systems, affects social justice, and defines the sustainability of future cities.

As urban expansion intensifies, peri-urban territories are often caught between institutional neglect and speculative pressures. They are subject to informal urbanization, infrastructure deficits, conflicting land uses, and precarious governance structures. However, they also represent spaces of opportunity for rethinking spatial planning, climate resilience, food systems, and access to basic services. These tensions are particularly relevant as governments and international agencies increasingly acknowledge the need to address urban sustainability through integrated territorial strategies.

The topic of peri-urbanization is particularly urgent in light of the 2030 Agenda for Sustainable Development and the New Urban Agenda, which call for inclusive, safe, resilient, and sustainable cities. Achieving these goals requires attention not only to dense urban cores but also to the complex transitions occurring in peri-urban and rural-urban interface zones. These are the very spaces where infrastructure investment, land protection, housing, and mobility policies must be reconciled with ecological sustainability and equity.

Moreover, global phenomena such as climate change, pandemics, and geopolitical crises have made clear the vulnerability of urban peripheries. The COVID-19 crisis, in particular, exposed the fragile conditions of informal settlements and under-serviced peri-urban communities, further reinforcing the importance of spatial justice and territorial integration.

In this context, the study of peri-urban processes is no longer a niche or peripheral concern. It has become essential to urban theory and practice, with implications for public policy, environmental stewardship, and socio-technical innovation. This book situates itself within this urgent conversation, offering a multi-scalar, multi-disciplinary, and comparative perspective on peri-urbanization processes and their potential to shape more sustainable and inclusive futures.

Target Audience

This book is intended for a diverse and interdisciplinary audience of scholars, practitioners, policymakers, and students interested in the dynamics of urban development, sustainability, and territorial transformation, particularly in the context of peri-urbanization. Given the complex and multifaceted nature of peri-urban territories, the volume offers valuable insights for those working at the intersection of urban planning, transportation, environmental studies, sociology, geography, political science, and public administration.

First and foremost, the book serves as a key reference for researchers and academic institutions engaged in the study of urban expansion, land use change, socio-spatial inequality, and the governance of transitional spaces. The comparative and empirical focus on Latin American, African, and Southern European contexts enriches current academic debates by offering grounded, situated perspectives from regions often underrepresented in mainstream urban theory.

Urban planners, designers, and architects will find the book relevant for its analysis of spatial configuration, infrastructure provision, walkability, and green infrastructure as tools for promoting more inclusive and resilient urban forms. Similarly, transportation engineers and mobility specialists will benefit from chapters that highlight the role of transport systems in shaping access, fragmentation, and integration within expanding urban regions.

In addition, the book is tailored to *public policymakers, decision-makers, and development agencies* who are responsible for designing and implementing urban and territorial strategies. It provides them with evidence-based case studies, legal and institutional analyses, and methodological tools that can guide more effective policy-making in peri-urban environments, where traditional urban models often fall short.

Importantly, *civil society organizations, grassroots collectives, and community leaders* involved in territorial defense, housing, and environmental justice will also find resonance in the book's attention to intersectionality, informality, and bottom-up planning approaches. By highlighting the lived experiences of communities at the urban fringe, the book encourages more participatory and equitable planning frameworks.

Finally, *graduate and postgraduate students* in urban studies, environmental science, political ecology, and related fields will find in this volume a comprehensive and accessible collection of case studies, theoretical frameworks, and methodological reflections that can inform both their academic formation and their future professional practice.

CHAPTER DESCRIPTIONS

Chapter 1. Legal Framework of Urban Expansion in Two Latin American Cities: The Cases of Mérida (Mexico) and Rosario (Argentina).

This chapter provides a comparative analysis of two contrasting legal approaches to urban expansion through condominium regimes in Mérida, Mexico, and Rosario, Argentina. While Mérida is experiencing a rapid proliferation of privately driven real estate developments in its northern periphery, Rosario has enforced a municipal by-law prohibiting such developments since 2010. The chapter critically examines how legal instruments influence urban morphology and governance. It highlights the tension between market-led development and planning regulations, revealing important insights into how legal and institutional frameworks shape peri-urban growth across different national contexts.

Chapter 2. Sustainable Innovation and the New Urban Green Innovation Agenda

This chapter explores the interrelationship between sustainable innovation and the emerging green urban innovation agenda. Drawing on a meta-analytical review of conceptual and empirical literature, the authors argue that sustainable innovation lies at the heart of future-oriented urban strategies. The chapter proposes a theoretical model that integrates economic, environmental, and institutional dimensions to guide urban transformation. By shedding light on innovation processes in green urbanism, the chapter contributes to rethinking how cities can adopt regenerative and circular practices to foster sustainability in peri-urban areas.

Chapter 3. Unveiling the Urban Fringe: Brazilian National Urban Policy's Impact on Peri-Urban Informal Settlements in São Paulo

Focusing on the city of São Paulo, this chapter analyzes the effects of Brazil's national urban policies—especially the City Statute and REURB Law—on informal peri-urban settlements. Through an in-depth case study and qualitative analysis, the chapter reveals both the transformative and contradictory effects of these policies. It examines how the legal recognition of collective adverse possession and the 2014 Master Plan have impacted land tenure and urban governance. By highlighting gaps between formal frameworks and grassroots practices, the chapter underscores the critical role of policy adaptation in supporting equitable peri-urban development.

Chapter 4. Urban Expansion and Transformation of the Ecosystem Value of the Territory: The Case of the Northern Metropolitan Border of Bogotá

This chapter investigates how dispersed urban growth in Bogotá's northern periphery affects ecological systems and territorial sustainability. Using GIS tools, satellite imagery, and census data from 2005 to 2018, the authors analyze land use changes in the Chicú River basin. Their findings indicate that urbanization processes, driven by population decentralization and land use conversion, are degrading ecosystem services. The chapter proposes decision-making scenarios to harmonize territorial expansion with environmental preservation, offering actionable strategies for integrating ecological value into urban planning processes.

Chapter 5. Popular Urbanization in Bogotá: An Intersectional Reading in Search of Wellbeing and Sustainability – Case Study of Alto Fucha Ecoterritory

By exploring the role of women's political and community engagement in informal urbanization processes, this chapter introduces an intersectional feminist perspective on wellbeing and sustainability. Focusing on the Alto Fucha Ecoterritory, the authors examine how gender, class, and race intersect with territorial and environmental struggles in peri-urban areas. The chapter critiques extractivist dynamics imposed on land and bodies and proposes alternative, community-driven frameworks of territorial care. This innovative lens broadens the discourse on sustainability by emphasizing socio-political agency and ecological justice.

Chapter 6. Impact of Transportation Infrastructure on Socio-Spatial Fragmentation in Bogotá's Peri-Urban Area: A Case Study of Suba Locality

This chapter explores the link between transport infrastructure and socio-spatial fragmentation in Bogotá's periphery, using Suba as a case study. Through data from Bogotá's 2023 mobility survey and a composite indicator based on entropy modeling, the authors assess inequality in transport access and infrastructure provision. The findings reveal how economic disparities are reinforced by mobility limitations, contributing to exclusion and fragmentation. The chapter offers a robust methodological approach to analyzing mobility justice in urban peripheries and highlights policy opportunities to improve transport equity.

Chapter 7. Evaluating Walkability in Peri-Urban Areas for Enhanced Urban Sustainability: A Case Study of Milan's Southern Margin

Focusing on Gratosoglio, a peri-urban district in southern Milan, this chapter assesses walkability as a key factor in sustainable urban design. It presents a hybrid methodology combining quantitative and qualitative spatial indicators to evaluate pedestrian accessibility and urban form. By linking walkability to resilience and climate adaptation, the authors argue for a paradigm shift in peri-urban planning. Their findings suggest that integrating walkable infrastructure into peripheral urban areas can significantly improve liveability, health outcomes, and climate responsiveness.

Chapter 8. Development of a Methodology to Identify Urban Ecosystem Services by Applying Tools for Intervening and Planning Lake Landscapes: The San José de Uzuña Dam in Arequipa

This chapter introduces a novel methodological framework to assess urban ecosystem services in lake landscapes, using the San José de Uzuña dam in Peru as a case study. The framework combines ECOTERR zoning tools with user interviews to evaluate ecological and social functions. The results offer critical insights for designing interventions that balance environmental conservation with urban growth. This work significantly contributes to urban landscape planning and strengthens the dialogue between ecosystem management and spatial development in peri-urban contexts.

Chapter 9. Transforming Peri-Urban Resilience through Green Infrastructure for Healthier Communities: A Case Study on Indoor Air Quality in Hyderabad

Addressing the pressing issue of indoor air pollution in Hyderabad's peri-urban zones, this chapter investigates the role of green infrastructure (GI) in improving air quality. The study evaluates the effectiveness of urban design interventions—such as green roofs, walls, and low-VOC materials—against rising pollution from traffic and industrial sources. By integrating IAQ considerations into urban planning, the authors provide valuable guidelines for sustainable and health-focused peri-urban development, especially in rapidly urbanizing and vulnerable contexts.

Chapter 10. Management and Challenges in Access and Diagnosis of Drinking Water Services in Rural Areas of Latin America.

This chapter offers a comprehensive overview of water access challenges in Latin America's rural and peri-urban areas. Drawing from cross-country data and regulatory analysis, the authors explore how pollution, poor infrastructure, and weak institutional capacity hinder the achievement of SDG 6. The chapter also examines the links between unplanned urban expansion and water stress, advocating for targeted investments in training, monitoring systems, and infrastructure. Its contribution lies in highlighting the multifaceted nature of water insecurity and proposing integrated responses.

Chapter 11. Reframing Urban Resilience: Integrating Climate Adaptation with Sustainable Development

The final chapter redefines urban resilience by linking it with climate adaptation strategies and long-term urban sustainability. Through a critical review of adaptive planning, green infrastructure, and governance models, the author presents a comprehensive vision for integrating resilience into urban policy. The chapter discusses both technological innovations (e.g., cool roofs, permeable pavements) and institutional challenges. It calls for flexible, multilevel governance frameworks that embed resilience thinking into spatial planning, particularly in peri-urban areas vulnerable to environmental shocks.

CONCLUSION AND CONTRIBUTION TO THE FIELD

The contributions compiled in this volume underscore a critical and timely rethinking of peri-urbanization as a multidimensional process, not merely a stage of physical expansion, but a strategic arena where urgent questions of sustainability, equity, governance, and resilience intersect. By spanning diverse geographies—from the Andean highlands to the Italian periphery and the South Asian metropolis—the book exposes the uneven patterns, systemic vulnerabilities, and emergent opportunities that define the contemporary peri-urban condition.

A recurring insight throughout the chapters is that peri-urban territories are not marginal by default, but made peripheral through planning omissions, policy blind spots, and extractive development logics. These zones are also sites of vibrant innovation, where communities experiment with grassroots sustainability, gender-inclusive governance, mobility justice, and ecosystem stewardship in ways that often precede or challenge formal planning.

Methodologically, the volume contributes to advancing interdisciplinary frameworks that blend spatial analysis, legal critique, socio-ecological valuation, participatory diagnostics, and design-based interventions. This pluralism not only reflects the complexity of peri-urban realities but also signals a methodological shift in urban studies—one that acknowledges the epistemological value of local knowledge, intersectional perspectives, and multi-scalar governance.

Thematically, the book reinforces the imperative of integrating environmental sustainability and social justice in all discussions of urban expansion. From the role of women in co-producing ecoterritories, to the implications of green infrastructure for health equity, to the inclusion of informal settlements in resilience frameworks, each chapter pushes the boundaries of conventional urban theory by foregrounding the peri-urban as both a challenge and a laboratory for transformative solutions.

In doing so, the volume provides a critical knowledge base for scholars, practitioners, and policy-makers working on the frontlines of urban and regional transitions. It equips them with theoretical tools, comparative insights, and methodological innovations to respond to the pressing demands of sustainable territorial development in a context marked by planetary urbanization and socio-ecological crisis.

Ultimately, this book makes a substantial contribution to the emerging field of peri-urban studies. It strengthens the analytical and policy-oriented foundations necessary for reframing peri-urban territories not as zones of neglect, but as frontiers of innovation, sustainability, and inclusion. Through this lens, peri-urbanization is revealed not just as a byproduct of metropolitan growth, but as a key terrain for reimagining the future of urban life in the Global South and beyond.

This collective endeavor has also been made possible thanks to the generous support of the Ibero-American Science and Technology for Development Programme (CYTED) and the strategic efforts of the thematic network DPAAPU – "Sustainable Development and Planning of Peri-Urban Areas." CYTED has provided not only funding but a collaborative platform that fosters South-South and South-North dialogue, enabling academic exchange, joint research, and capacity building across the Ibero-American region. The DPAAPU network, in particular, has served as a catalyst for knowledge co-production, methodological innovation, and the formation of a scholarly community committed to sustainable, inclusive, and equitable territorial transformations. In this sense, the book also stands as a testimony to the power of regional cooperation in addressing complex socio-territorial challenges through collective intelligence and shared commitment.

Acknowledgments

We would like to express our deepest gratitude to all the authors who generously contributed chapters to this book. Your commitment, expert knowledge, and valuable perspectives have been fundamental to the collective construction of this volume, which seeks to offer sustainable solutions to the contemporary challenges of peri-urbanization processes.

This work is the result of a collaborative effort carried out within the framework of the CYTED Network: Guidelines, Plans, and Actions in Peri-Urban Areas: Ecosystems for Equitable Development (DPAAPU). We especially acknowledge and thank the Ibero-American Programme for Science and Technology for Development (CYTED) for the institutional and financial support that has made this academic, interdisciplinary, and regional dialogue among researchers across Ibero-America possible. CYTED's support has been essential in consolidating a committed working network focused on equitable development in peri-urban territories.

We also extend our sincere thanks to IGI Global for welcoming this publication and to the editorial and peer review teams for their rigorous and professional support throughout the editing process.

In particular, we would like to recognize the institutional support provided by the Polytechnic Institute of Viana do Castelo (Portugal) and the Universidad Escuela Colombiana de Ingeniería Julio Garavito (Colombia), whose contributions have been instrumental to the editorial and academic coordination of this book. We also extend our appreciation to all the universities and research centers that have supported the researchers of the DPAAPU network, making the production and dissemination of critical, sustainability-oriented knowledge possible.

Finally, as editors of this volume, Vasco Barbosa and Mónica Suárez Pradilla, we are grateful for the opportunity to contribute to this collective initiative.

Being part of a network where critical thinking and transformative action are nurtured in peri-urban territories throughout our region has been experienced as a profound privilege.

Chapter 1
Legal Framework of Urban Expansion in Two Latin American Cities:
The Cases of Mérida in México and Rosario in Argentina

Oscar Bragos
Universidad Nacional de Rosario, Argentina

Yolanda Fernández Martínez
Universidad Autónoma de Yucatán, Mexico

ABSTRACT

The aim of this chapter is to compare two case studies, that of Mérida in Mexico and that of Rosario in Argentina, based on the legal instruments that regulate real estate developments owned by condominium regime, as well as their impacts on the urban form. This interest arises every time that the city of Mérida is experiencing a boom in private developments, preferably in the northern periphery, while in Rosario a municipal by-law that prohibits them has been in force since 2010. Both the cities of Rosario and Mérida have common points regarding the temporality of legal instruments, although their positions regarding condominium property have been opposite.

DOI: 10.4018/979-8-3693-6089-7.ch001

THE TEMPORAL CONTEXT OF THE CASE STUDIES

In the case of Mérida, we have slightly over a decade of data to evaluate the impacts of legal instruments on the territory. This period began in December 2010 with the enactment of the *Ley de Desarrollos Inmobiliarios del Estado de Yucatán* (Real Estate Development Law of the State of Yucatán) and its corresponding regulations introduced in May 2012. Additionally, it includes the publication of the new *Ley sobre el Régimen de Propiedad en Condominio del Estado de Yucatán* (Law on the Condominium Property Regime of the State of Yucatán), as well as the subsequent amendment of the Real Estate Development Law in October 2014.

It is important to highlight that in 2023, Yucatán underwent significant reforms regarding regulatory instruments associated with real estate development. Therefore, conducting a comparative analysis between these newer instruments and the earlier ones becomes essential, especially considering that the timing of the earlier regulations coincides precisely with the enactment of Ordinance No. 8725 by the Municipal Council of Rosario in December 2010.

In the case of Rosario (Santa Fe Province), the Ordinance *Supresión de la figura de barrio privado o cerrado en todo el suelo del ejido municipal de la ciudad de Rosario* (Suppression of the figure of private or gated neighborhood for all the land in the municipal ejido of the city of Rosario) marks an intermediate point in the most recent expansion process of the urbanized areas. Process that begins to arise from the middle of the last decade of the 20th Century and continues to the present. A period of changes in the provincial government's requirements for the approval of new development projects and changes in the national government's housing policy. The policies of the three states (nation, province, municipality), initiatives without a comprehensive vision of planning in a metropolitan area, affect the territorial transformation process of those last decades. More recently, the COVID pandemic also influenced the consolidation of this expansive process of urbanized areas in peri-urban territories.

In relation to the figure of gated community, it is interesting to highlight in the case of Rosario two different and contemporary processes that take place in the central city, on the one hand, and in the localities of the metropolitan region, on the other.

THEORETICAL AND METHODOLOGICAL APPROACH

The theoretical approach for this comparative study is precisely grounded in the arguments underpinning the Rosario Ordinance. These arguments align with the principles later articulated, in 2016, within the New Urban Agenda and the Right to the City—central themes of the UN-Habitat III Summit held in Quito, Ecuador.

Moreover, this vision of the city forms part of a broader set of rights (access to infrastructure land and to affordable housing, among others) that should be guaranteed to the population, yet it contrasts with the current urban situation resulting from land consumption and real estate activities.

In this sense, Gilles Lipovetsky's (2014) perspective on *Los tiempos hipermodernos* (Hypermodern Times) enables us to approach this emerging urban phenomenon, which is driven more by lifestyle and patterns of land consumption than by the city's long-term needs. Consequently, addressing the Right to the City remains a priority for analyzing current urban manifestations, as well as generating critical and alternative interpretations of legal instruments that theoretically emphasize the primacy of collective interests.

Likewise, it is relevant to address the emergence of a city model about which international organizations and academia were already warning. The configuration of a diffuse, dispersed, and extensive city, of mono-functional fragments united by the main routes that link the central city with the nearby towns, results in a model far from a sustainable urban development. The waste of land resource and the use of the private automobile as a practically exclusive mean of mobility are the main features of this model. The "fading" of the concept of the traditional city as proposed at the time by Oriol Nel-lo (1998) is complemented by the critical vision of Javier Monclús (1998), focused on the economic, social, and ecological costs of the from then "new suburbanization" that continues today. A territory with conditions of inequity and inequality that latter was summarized by Bernardo Secchi (2015) in his book *Città dei ricchi, città dei poveri* (City of the rich, city of the poor).

Starting from a first theoretical discussion that arises from that the same regulatory instruments declare; we move on to the urban analysis of the study areas where condominium ownership takes place. The main variables to establish the comparative analysis between Rosario and Mérida are divided into three groups. The first group refers to the external conditions of the condominium property such as accessibility, proximity, and urban structure. The second group refers to their internal conditions, such as their morphology, typology, and soil values. The third group refers to establishing the relationship between the total real estate developments owned by condominium regime with respect to each of the cities and determining the impacts on the efficiency of the urban structure and on the transformation of that portion of the territory that begins to be identified as peri-urban land.

According with the above, it is relevant to establish relationships on these two cities, where the legal framework of Rosario could become a starting point for Mérida to take the pertinent measures to evaluate the impacts that the fragmented urban structure is having on efficiency and quality of life, from the perspective of the New Urban Agenda and the Right to the City.

Likewise, it should be noted that the arguments that support the normative action carried out in Rosario in 2010 were anticipatory of what was proclaimed in the New Urban Agenda of the UN-Habitat III Summit six years later. And according to this, it will be a priority to analyze the foundations that gave rise to the recent modifications in the regulatory instruments of Mérida in terms of condominium property. That is, to what extent matters relating to the Right to the City have been decisive for reformulating these regulatory instruments.

MEXICO. URBAN PLANS BY MARIO PANI AND CONDOMINIUM PROPERTY IN THE SECOND HALF OF THE 20TH CENTURY

Institutional planning in Mexico can be understood from two perspectives. The first relates to the visions of prominent academics who, since the mid-20th century, have driven legal reforms and developed planning instruments that shaped Mexican cities in response to the specific needs and contexts of their time—a chronotopic reflection. The second perspective corresponds to the governmental stance, through which national-level institutions influenced urban public policies at state and municipal levels.

In the first case, we refer to the architect Mario Pani (1953), who stood out prominently in two aspects directly relevant to this study. Firstly, he was a pioneer in urban planning in Mexico, thus being responsible for developing Mérida's first urban plan. Secondly, he actively promoted Mexico's Condominium Property Law, approved in 1954 (Cebey, 2014, para. 2), which subsequently led to the enactment of a corresponding law in the State of Yucatán in 1962 (Government of the State of Yucatán, 1962).

Regarding the government's role in urban development in Mexico, four key aspects should be contextualized to better explain the contemporary phenomenon of condominium property and its impacts on processes of urban expansion, fragmentation, segregation, and polarization. These four aspects relate to the establishment of two governmental structures: one dedicated to promoting workers' housing, and another focused-on land tenure regularization. The remaining two aspects concern land management practices aimed at providing urban infrastructure and services.

As mentioned earlier, urban planning in Mexico was strongly influenced by regulatory plans, in which architect Mario Pani played a significant role, both nationally and specifically within the state of Yucatán. His principal contribution to Mérida was the formulation of the city's first regulatory plan in 1953. Notably, the Ninth Proposition titled "Regulating the Growth of the City" (Pani et al., 1953, p. 39) includes the following key aspects:

Land Speculation and Urban Expansion: Pani identified land speculation occurring on the urban periphery and highlighted the associated challenges of regulating city expansion. He anticipated what is currently known as "land banking," emphasizing the necessity for the city itself to benefit from the strategic location of these lands. He advocated for acquiring such plots before private owners could resell them exclusively for profit, thus safeguarding broader urban interests.

Land Acquisition for Urban Growth Control: Consequently, Pani proposed to state and municipal governments the essential strategy of acquiring land reserves to manage and control urban growth effectively. Such acquisitions should carefully consider population needs, strategic location, and appropriate distances aligned with different residential typologies.

Autonomous Future Cities: Finally, Pani clearly stated that "future neighboring cities or satellite cities would have an autonomous regime for their services and would not impose additional burdens on the local municipality" (Pani et al., 1953, p. 39).

Through his forward-looking approach to the city's future via the concept of satellite cities operating autonomously—thereby avoiding overloading municipal governance—Pani set the foundational ideas that now characterize Mérida's northern periphery, particularly in the form of gated communities. This development will be analyzed further in the forthcoming section concerning urban planning and condominium property in Mérida. Reflecting on the evolution and lasting impacts of this urban model conceptualization over the 70 years since its introduction in Mexico remains crucial.

However, it is important to highlight that Pani's vision was aimed at equipping the municipality with effective tools to manage land use, thereby addressing two critical issues: speculation and uncontrolled, unnecessary urban expansion. Additionally, he prioritized the urban structure to guarantee continuity in the hierarchical road network and to encourage the "transformation and regeneration of specific areas into a system of 'superblocks,' featuring differentiated circulation systems, zoning, educational facilities, and sports parks" (Pani et al., 1953, p. 34).

In this respect, Pani's proposal from the early part of the second half of the 20th century established a clear relationship among the fundamental components of urban settlements, such as housing, educational, and recreational facilities. From this perspective, the road network was consolidated as the foundational element for structuring human activities, and superblocks were conceived as autonomous units interconnected within the broader urban system.

It is also noteworthy that, a year after his contribution to Mérida's urban planning, Mexico's National Condominium Law (*Ley Nacional de Condominios*, Secretaría de Gobernación, 1954)—also actively promoted by architect Mario Pani—was enacted. This legislation facilitated some of the era's most significant housing developments in Mexico City, strongly influenced by the Modern Movement and Le Corbusier's architectural principles, such as the Miguel Alemán Multifamily Complex and the Nonoalco Tlatelolco housing complex. Additionally, Pani collaborated with other architects on emblematic and influential projects both for Mexico City and for the country, including Ciudad Universitaria (University City), home to the National Autonomous University of Mexico (UNAM), and Ciudad Satélite (Levi & Guzmán, 2019, p. 9).

The social context and urban complexity that emerged in Mexico City during the mid-20th century corresponded to a significant period of urban expansion from the 1940s through the 1970s, aligning with the economic phase known as the "stabilizing development." During this period, the population of the Federal District—now Mexico City—increased dramatically, growing from 1.2 million inhabitants in 1930 to approximately 6.9 million in 1970 (Levi & Guzmán, 2019, p. 8). In response to this substantial migratory phenomenon, Pani (1957) articulated a vision that led to the development of Ciudad Satélite:

> *"We are already many who think that, until the supreme decision of statesmen provides a remedy for the formidable migratory phenomenon causing these issues, the problems of the modern city have only one solution capable of successfully confronting them. That solution has a name: the city outside the city" (Pani, 1957, p. 211).*

Thus, the concept of Ciudad Satélite as "a city outside the city" emerged as an appealing alternative for Mexico's middle classes (Alcantar García, 2020). On January 9, 1957, construction of Ciudad Satélite in Naucalpan, State of Mexico, was approved, driven by private-sector initiatives aligned with Pani's Master Plan. This plan was pioneering, as it was the first in Mexico to implement advanced functionalist urban planning techniques for the design of commercial subdivisions (Garay, 2010, p. 18).

This urban proposal, located on Mexico City's northwestern periphery, encompassed approximately 800 hectares (Pani, 1957, p. 216). It featured a superblock layout, and a road network explicitly designed to accommodate automobile use. Pani (1957) emphasized the following point clearly: "The most advanced contemporary road organization distinguishes three forms of access: communication arteries, penetration arteries, and distribution arteries" (p. 222).

In this way, the peri-urban vision that emerged in Mexico during the second half of the 20th century promoted the development of autonomous suburban areas. In one of his early proposals, architect Mario Pani envisioned combining multifamily housing with single-family lots, thereby implying higher density and greater building heights. However, the commercial interests of investors were primarily focused on the idea of a "residential suburb." To support this model, a standardized lot size was established to prevent two specific outcomes: the purchase of large land parcels and the subsequent subdivision of these lots for resale (Alcantar García, 2020, p. 184).

Within the city, the Miguel Alemán Multifamily Complex and the Nonoalco Tlatelolco Housing Unit represented key manifestations of condominium property as tools for urban regeneration, increased residential density, and the strategic use of internal infrastructure. The Tlatelolco Housing Unit, inaugurated in 1964, was developed on a 100-hectare site to accommodate 102 buildings and 12,016 apartments, with a planned density of 1,000 inhabitants per hectare and 75% designated as green space. The project included "sports centers, clinics, schools, nurseries, offices, and theaters, enabling residents to meet their basic needs within the complex and fostering an environment of constant interaction and internal circulation" (Martínez & Reza, 2020).

Mario Pani's vision involved the use of regulatory plans as instruments to guide urban development, ensuring that essential services and facilities were fully integrated into the urban fabric. His concept of *superblocks* —which combined residential, educational, recreational, and commercial functions within a clearly defined area— was intended to foster self-sufficient communities. This approach aimed to reduce travel distances, enhance quality of life, and encourage social interaction.

Pani's urban planning principles emphasize the following core ideas:

Functionalist Zoning: Dividing urban space into distinct zones—residential, commercial, industrial, and recreational—to ensure the orderly, efficient, and purposeful use of land.

Strategic Location: Locating urban infrastructure and facilities where accessibility and utility for the population would be maximized, based on comprehensive and forward-looking regulatory plans.

State Ownership: Preserving state ownership of key urban facilities to guarantee their long-term availability and accessibility for public use.

Integration of Services: Designing urban areas so that essential services—such as schools, markets, and parks—are within proximity to residential neighborhoods, thereby fostering community cohesion and minimizing the need for long-distance commuting.

Deep Reforms in Mexico

In this section, we contextualize the final three decades of the 20th century by examining four key governmental actions in Mexico that significantly shaped urban expansion and were particularly decisive for land management. These include the establishment of two governmental institutions, the formulation of a regulatory guide for the provision of urban infrastructure, its subsequent transformation into an Official Mexican Standard, and the implementation of Agrarian Reform.

The first institutional action was the creation of the Institute of the National Housing Fund for Workers (INFONAVIT) in 1972 (*Historia del Infonavit*, n.d.; Cerdán, 2006), an institution that remains active to this day. INFONAVIT has been one of the most influential forces driving both the expansion and consolidation of urban areas in Mexico. Over the past five decades, it has played a central role in mass housing production, and land management has often depended on the federal government's ability to acquire land and respond to housing demands.

As a result, INFONAVIT emerged as an alternative financing institution for populations excluded from conventional banking systems, primarily by channeling subsidies to construction companies. However, in recent years, this support has declined, contributing to the bankruptcy of several major construction firms during the 2012–2018 federal administration (Salinas Arreortua, 2022, p. 8).

These developments reveal two fundamental challenges in the processes of urban growth. On one hand, strategic land management is essential for guiding housing development in both intra-urban and peri-urban areas. On the other hand, effective subsidy programs are critical for financing the infrastructure, urban facilities, and housing required to ensure accessibility for underserved populations.

The other governmental institution that played a significant role in Mexico's urban development was the Commission for the Regularization of Land Tenure (CORETT), established on November 8, 1974. Its purpose was to "contribute to reducing patrimonial poverty by providing legal certainty, incorporating human settlements into territorial planning and sustainable urban development through land tenure regularization" (INSUS, 2023, p. 3).

After nearly four decades, CORETT was transformed—by presidential decree on December 16, 2016—into the National Institute of Sustainable Land (INSUS). This new entity was tasked with "planning, designing, directing, promoting, coordinating, and implementing programs, projects, strategies, actions, works, and investments related to land management and regulation, following principles of planned and sustainable territorial development" (Ídem).

A critical aspect of these urban transformation processes is the implementation of public policy aimed at the strategic distribution of spaces designated for infrastructure. Housing provision and land management are closely linked to securing the legal certainty of citizens' assets through land tenure regularization. Accordingly, a broader planning vision became necessary—one in which schools, health clinics, sports areas, and marketplaces, among other facilities, were allocated based on service scale and the size of the population they would serve.

Beginning in 1981, the Secretariat of Human Settlements and Public Works (SAHOP) designed and published the *Urban Equipment Normative System: Basic Norms* (SAHOP, 1981). This regulatory guide was later adopted and adapted by successive federal agencies overseeing territorial matters: first by the Secretariat of Urban Development and Ecology (SEDUE) starting in 1985 (*Diario Oficial de la Federación*, 1985); then by the Secretariat of Social Development (SEDESOL) in 1999; and finally, by the Secretariat of Agrarian, Territorial, and Urban Development (SEDATU), established on January 2, 2013.

The original guide later evolved into an Official Mexican Standard, becoming NOM-002-SEDATU-2022, titled *"Urban Facilities in the Instruments that Make Up the General System of Territorial Planning: Classification, Terminology, and Application"*. This standard is directly linked to NOM-001-SEDATU-2021, titled *"Public Spaces in Human Settlements"*, both published in the *Official Journal of the Federation* on February 22, 2022 (SEDATU, 2022).

According to NOM-002-SEDATU-2022, Urban Facility is defined as: *"the set of buildings, installations, constructions, and furniture used to provide urban services to the population for the development of economic, social, cultural, sports, educational, transport, and supply activities"* (Ídem).

The conceptual foundation of Urban Facility originated from two fundamental criteria: first, its location was determined by a regulatory plan; and second, the facilities were built on state-owned land. Therefore, cities were expected to strategically and hierarchically allocate land for urban functions that complemented and supported daily life.

As a result, Urban Facility served both public and social functions, precisely because it was situated on public land. This condition guaranteed both legal and social certainty, ensuring that such facilities would remain part of the city's public patrimony. Consequently, residents of any neighborhood or subdivision would always have access to basic services such as schools, markets, or parks—facilities that, as public property, could not be transferred to private ownership.

This concept of state participation in the formation of community life was clearly articulated by Mario Pani in his regulatory plans and superblock proposals, both within central urban areas and on their outskirts. His approach was grounded in the basic principles of functionalist zoning, emphasizing the relationship between land use, spatial distance, and the provision of infrastructure to support the population's fundamental activities.

However, the new NOM-002-SEDATU-2022 establishes that Urban Facilities may be either public or private, making it essential to critically examine this perspective, particularly in relation to condominium property within both intra-urban and peri-urban contexts. Urban planning must prioritize the common good over private interests, land speculation, and the monopolization of strategic areas, as these practices undermine urban continuity, permeability, and equitable access to services.

The distinction between public and private Urban Facility in NOM-002-SEDATU-2022 underscores the need to assess their respective impacts on urban dynamics. Public infrastructure ensures accessibility, inclusivity, and collective benefit, whereas private amenities often cater to closed or exclusive communities, potentially reinforcing patterns of social segregation. In contrast, Mario Pani's vision emphasized public ownership and the strategic distribution of urban facilities as essential to strengthening community life and preventing speculative land practices.

The implementation of these foundational principles has been reflected in a range of urban development policies and regulatory frameworks over the past decades. The adoption of standards such as NOM-002-SEDATU-2022 codifies these principles into actionable planning guidelines, ensuring that contemporary urban development adheres to the strategic and hierarchical allocation of land for public functions. This planning approach not only preserves the public character of essential services, but also fosters sustainable urban growth by integrating social, economic, and environmental considerations into territorial decision-making.

The strategic distribution of Urban Facilities, as envisioned by Mario Pani and formalized through regulatory frameworks such as NOM-002-SEDATU-2022, plays a crucial role in shaping Mexico's urban landscape. By ensuring that essential services are accessible, well-located, and publicly owned, these policies contribute to the development of livable, equitable, and sustainable urban environments. The foundational principles of functionalist zoning, strategic location, state ownership, and integration of services continue to guide urban development, enabling cities to meet the evolving needs of their populations while advancing social equity and environmental sustainability.

Furthermore, the structured distribution of infrastructure through coherent public policies and normative guidelines has been instrumental in molding Mexico's urban development over recent decades. By ensuring that infrastructure is systematically planned and implemented, these instruments have promoted legal certainty, spatial order, and equitable access to essential services. The evolution of technical guides into Official Mexican Standards reflects the state's ongoing commitment to organized, inclusive, and sustainable urban growth, aligned with a broader vision of integrated territorial planning.

In the state of Yucatán, however, investors developing condominium properties are not required to allocate land for public facilities. Instead, they design private common areas, or so-called "amenities," within the gated perimeters of their developments. These are marketed as secure, exclusive, and high-value environments for residents, offering communal spaces and experiences that are often inaccessible outside these private enclaves. This scenario calls for a deeper examination of the impact of condominium property on the city, particularly the balance between public and private spaces. Such analysis is especially relevant considering Mario Pani's 1953 Regulatory Plan for Mérida, which proposed state land reservation as a tool to control urban growth and guarantee the equitable distribution of infrastructure and services.

The establishment of SEDATU in 2013—through the merger of the Secretariat of Agrarian Reform and the Secretariat of Social Development—marked the institutionalization of a comprehensive territorial vision that integrates both urban and rural dimensions (Meyer Falcón, 2023). Understanding the historical background of Agrarian Reform is essential, particularly the constitutional amendments of December 1991, which brought an end to agrarian land redistribution and opened the door to the privatization of ejido and indigenous community lands (Mackinlay, 1993, p. 99). This reform enabled peasants to gain land ownership through both social and private property mechanisms (Ídem).

The impacts of the 1992 Agrarian Reform led to the reformulation of the General Law of Human Settlements, published on July 21, 1993. In the case of Mérida, urban effects began to materialize in the early 21st century, indicating that the 1990s were a transitional period in which land ownership shifted from ejido to private property. Although *ejidatarios* were granted ownership rights, the value of their land increased significantly once it entered the real estate market, which in turn accelerated processes of urban expansion.

In summary, the reforms and institutional actions undertaken by the Mexican government during the final three decades of the 20th century had a profound influence on urban expansion and land management. The creation of INFONAVIT and CORETT, the formulation of regulatory frameworks for urban infrastructure, and the implementation of Agrarian Reform were pivotal in reshaping the urban landscape and responding to the housing demands of the Mexican population.

The Delayed Institutionalization of Urban Planning in Mexico: From Curitiba to León and Mérida

The institutionalization of urban planning in Mexico through decentralized public bodies with citizen participation has been notably delayed. It was not until 1994 that the first Municipal Planning Institute (IMPLAN) was established in León, Guanajuato. Its objective is "to generate and establish the foundations of urban planning that guide and advise the Municipality of León in its short-, medium-, and long-term development" (IMPLAN León, n.d.).

This Institute was inspired by the Institute for Urban Planning and Research of Curitiba (IPPUC), founded in 1965 to implement the Curitiba Master Plan. The plan focused on "land use, road systems, public transport," and integrated environmental, economic, and social considerations (Fukuda-Hayakawa, 2010, pp. 56–57).

In the case of Mérida, on August 4, 2014, the City Council officially approved the creation of its own Municipal Planning Institute (IMPLAN) (Municipality of Mérida, 2014). A decade has since passed with this institution dedicated exclusively to the municipality's planning processes. Two of the most significant outcomes include:

The update of the Urban Development Program in August 2017, following the previous version from September 2012.

The creation of the Strategic-Level Comprehensive Urban Mobility Plan, Vision 2040 (PIMUS), which aims:

"(...) to meet the mobility needs of people, goods, and services in cities and their surroundings. It is based on planning methodologies and practices to improve the quality of life, considering the principles of integration, participation, and evaluation." (IMPLAN Mérida, 2019)

However, it is important to note that while Mérida now has these two instruments for urban planning and mobility, they are not legally binding or interdependent. In other words, mobility strategies do not condition or influence territorial planning strategies, which limit integrated decision-making.

Furthermore, condominium ownership (*propiedad en condominio*) is not incorporated into the strategic components of the municipal planning instruments. This means that no specific public policies exist to regulate or guide the urban expansion process as it relates to gated communities. As a result, this form of urban development continues to grow without clear integration into the city's broader planning framework.

URBAN PLANNING AND CONDOMINIUM PROPERTY IN MÉRIDA: 1962-2014, HYPERMODERNITY, REAL ESTATE BOOM, AND THE 2024 REAL ESTATE REFORM

What is the main problem with gated communities? They represent a significant trend in Latin American urban development. While the reasons for their rise may vary, Pfannenstein (2019) argues that it primarily stems from "(...) the increasing sense of insecurity within the urban environment, which motivated the real estate sector to offer fortified housing as a response to the public administration's inability to address urban problems." (p. 1088)

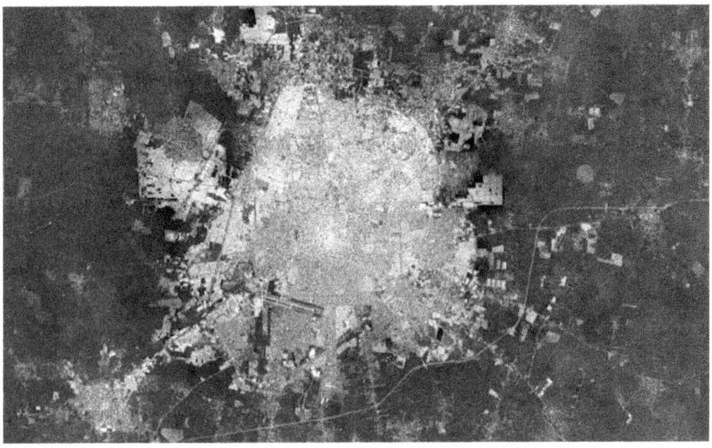

However, Mérida presents a different urban phenomenon. Known as one of the safest cities in the country—and internationally recognized as a desirable place to live and invest—the prevalence of gated communities in Mérida is not necessarily a response to security concerns, but rather to aspirations related to status, exclusivity, and privacy. These features are characteristic of what can be described as spaces of hypermodernity, linked to lifestyles and consumption patterns that give rise to hyperreal urban spaces (Lipovetsky & Sébastien, 2006). This sociological lens invites an inquiry into why residents of one of Mexico's safest cities choose to live in enclosed communities on the urban periphery.

From a legal perspective, condominium property in Yucatán began to be regulated in 1962, through the *Law on the Regime of Property and Condominium Real Estate* (*Gobierno del Estado de Yucatán*, 1962). However, this law was not updated to reflect the growing urban complexity that emerged after the year 2000. It was not until 2014 that the 1962 legislation was repealed and replaced by the *Law on the Regime of Property in Condominiums* (*Gobierno del Estado de Yucatán*, 2014).

This new law was enacted in a context shaped by two significant regulatory moments. The first corresponds to the renewal of legal instruments governing the real estate sector, particularly in relation to housing development. In this context, the Law of Subdivisions of 1985 (*Gobierno del Estado de Yucatán*, 1985) was repealed and replaced by the Law of Real Estate Developments in 2010 (*Gobierno del Estado de Yucatán*, 2010), followed by the publication of its regulatory provisions in 2012 (*Gobierno del Estado de Yucatán*, 2012).

The second phase corresponds to the emergence of gated communities on the northern periphery of Mérida. It is particularly noteworthy that in the Fourth Explanatory Statement of the new *Law on the Condominium Property Regime*, one of its key objectives is explicitly stated as promoting increased urban density, preventing urban sprawl, and encouraging vertical real estate development (pp. 7–8). This is especially relevant given that the law's stated purpose is to "regulate the establishment, modification, and termination of the condominium property regime, and to lay the foundation for its organization and operation" (p. 13).

However, over the past decade, since the enactment of this new condominium law, Mérida has lacked an integrated legal framework, as the law has not been binding with the *Real Estate Development Law* or with the *Municipal Urban Development Program of Mérida* (2017). This disconnect is critical, as the law fails to specify key planning criteria—such as the maximum surface area permitted for gated communities or the requirements for connectivity and continuity with the broader urban structure. This omission is particularly significant given the prevalence of this real estate model in peripheral areas of the city. Moreover, under the current regulatory framework, developers are not required to allocate a portion of their land for public facilities, such as parks, schools, or community centers, further weakening the capacity of public planning instruments to shape inclusive and connected urban environments.

It is important to note that on January 3, 2024, a set of real estate reforms was published (UN-Habitat, 2023). Among the most notable changes is the amendment to the *Real Estate Development Law*, which now formally recognizes both Public and Private Real Estate Developments. In the case of private developments, these are now classified into vertical, horizontal, and mixed-use typologies. One of the most significant advances in this reform is the following provision: "For private horizontal real estate developments, the area to be ceded for public use shall be 7% of the gross area." (*Government of the State of Yucatán*, 2024, p. 19).

Within this new legal framework, there is now an opportunity for municipal governments to acquire land from each new private horizontal development in order to equip it with public facilities and infrastructure. However, it remains essential to evaluate whether 7% of the gross area is sufficient to meet the requirements established in Official Mexican Standards regarding public space and urban equipment.

Balancing public and private urban infrastructure require a nuanced, context-sensitive approach that considers broader social, spatial, and equity-based implications. By revisiting Mario Pani's regulatory principles and understanding the long-term effects of agrarian and real estate reforms, urban planners and policymakers can work toward building inclusive and sustainable urban environments. Ensuring public ownership and the strategic distribution of urban equipment is key to promoting equitable urban development and preventing the harmful consequences of privatization, exclusion, and land speculation.

The evolving legal framework and sociocultural dynamics in Mérida highlights a complex interplay between legal reforms, societal perceptions of safety and exclusivity, and the practical realities of urban development. This interplay shapes not only the physical landscape of the city but also its social fabric and governance, emphasizing the need for ongoing evaluation and adjustment of policies to address in a better way, the unique urban challenges faced by Mérida and similar cities in Latin America.

ARGENTINA. ROSARIO PLANS AND TOOLS TO GUIDE URBAN GROWTH

This section will address the emergence of the figure of the urban plan (*plan regulador*), the concern for environmental issues in urban planning and the emergence of peri urban as a theme of urban plans. For this purpose, three issues are considered: planning in the city of Rosario, the provisions of the provincial government regarding rules to be fulfilled by the new urbanization projects and the planning proposals for the metropolitan territory. The first and second issue of legal force, the third only indicative.

In Argentina, there is no national framework law regarding general issues on land use planning, and planning tools. This missing law could have served the provinces as a base to define their own laws on the matter. This absence explains why not all provinces yet have a specific law on these issues. Santa Fe is one of those provinces where the lack of such legislation is significant. Although there is no comprehensive law at the provincial level, there are a series of tools that define rules regarding land use planning. It is a set of laws and regulations from ministries and other agencies that must be observed when planning the territory.

Planning Tools. The Institutionalization of the Urban Plan

At the origins of Urbanism in Argentina, urban plans were proposed as the appropriated tools to get a harmonious city development. Along with it, the urban code was the most widespread and used tool by local governments. A tool that, in simple terms, established the organization of the city by identifying the structural road network and the different internal zones as the basic and necessary components for such organization.

The purpose of the plan was to solve present problems and anticipate future needs, according to a city model with a time horizon (the city within fifty years) or a dimensional horizon (the city of one million inhabitants). In those times, Urbanism was understood as the discipline that analyzes the city, diagnoses its problems, and proposes a solution. A solution that was none other than the urban plan or *plan regulador*. At that time, during the first three decades of the 20th Century, several cities had already proposed their urban plans since it was understood that a great and modern city had to have its urban plan.

In 1935, Law No. 2,439 -Organic Law of Communes- was enacted in Santa Fe Province, establishing the obligation for communal governments (localities with less than ten thousand inhabitants) to prepare an urban plan indicating the urban and suburban or orchard zones along with simple and basic criteria to be taken into account in the internal organization of a small locality (layouts and minimum street widths, types of blocks, bypass roads, location of squares and parks, and towpaths for towns located on the banks of navigable rivers).

Four years later, in 1939, Law No. 2,756 -Organic Law of Municipalities- was enacted, referring to local governments of towns with more than ten thousand inhabitants. It established that municipalities had to prepare their urban plans, which would contain the necessary provisions for the organization and future development of the city, including indications regarding public works, construction, protection of public buildings, conditions for social housing, regulation of public transport, among other issues.

Thirty years later, in 1967, concerns about urban planning were revisited by the provincial government. The then *de facto* military government issued Decree No. 7,317, referring to the "Norms for Preliminary Projects of Structural Urban Development Plans," known as "minimum norms." Its purpose was to protect land, water, landscape, and the health of the inhabitants from pollution. To this end, it established the conditions to be considered in planning the extension of urbanized areas (land uses classification, standard regulations for new urbanizations, minimum construction regulations, and banning urbanization in flood areas).

Years later, in 1978, under another *de facto* military government, the provincial government issued Decree No. 0563, establishing the conditions to be considered in the preparation of urban plans: a) local authorities must adhere to the guidelines established by the General Secretariat of Communal Action, which, once completed, had to be approved by the provincial government; b) local governments that did not had their urban plans should use the indications of the "minimum norms" Decree.

Urban-Territorial Planning, Environmental Issues, And the Control of New Urban Developments

It was only in the late 20th and early 21st Centuries that the provincial government began to pay more attention to territorial planning issues. In 1999, Law No. 11,717 on "environment and sustainable development" was enacted, with the purpose of preserving, conserving, improving, and recovering the environment. This law included urbanization rules, economic decentralization, and sustainable development. It also mandates the coordination between different public agencies, communes, and municipalities for the implementation of norms related to urban sustainable development.

This law is regulated by Decree No. 0101/03, which establishes, among other things, the ranking of urbanization projects according to their environmental impact (low or negligible impact, medium impact, high impact). Projects with medium and high impact must submit an environmental impact study -EIS- along with an environmental suitability certificate. Development projects (gated communities, private neighborhoods, simple subdivisions, residential / sports / educational complexes, cemeteries, botanical gardens, zoos, ecological reserves, shopping centers) are considered to have medium impact. On the other hand, those categorized as having a high impact include industrial parks and areas.

Considering the accelerated process of expansion of urbanized areas in the Rosario metropolitan region registered at the end of the 20th century and the beginning of the 21st century, the provincial government decided to launch new initiatives aimed to a greater control of the urban expansion processes. In 2014, through Decree No. 638, the Interministerial Committee on Territorial Planning (CIOT, Spanish acronym for *Comité Interministerial de Ordenamiento Territorial*) was created as a "cross-sectoral coordinating body for actions related to the Territorial Planning process." This decree establishes that the provincial government must maintain a registry of Territorial Planning Plans in the province, training municipalities and communes on territorial planning issues to be able to do the plans.

In 2017, the Ministry of Environment of Santa Fe Province advanced in the classification of new urbanization projects, with the purpose of establishing the mandatory requirement for an environmental impact assessment study. Through Resolution No. 350, two types of new urbanization projects are considered: simple urbanization subdivisions (within the urbanized area) and real estate complexes (residential enclaves: country clubs, gated communities).

In Annex II of Resolution No. 350/17, a “Categorization Formula for land subdivisions and subdivisions for simple urbanization and real estate complexes” was established. The results of the formula determine which category the new urbanization project belongs to (null/low impact, medium impact) or if the project is considered unfeasible, categorizing it as "non-urbanized." This new categorization considers various aspects (location and dimensions of the new development, flood risk, and available services).

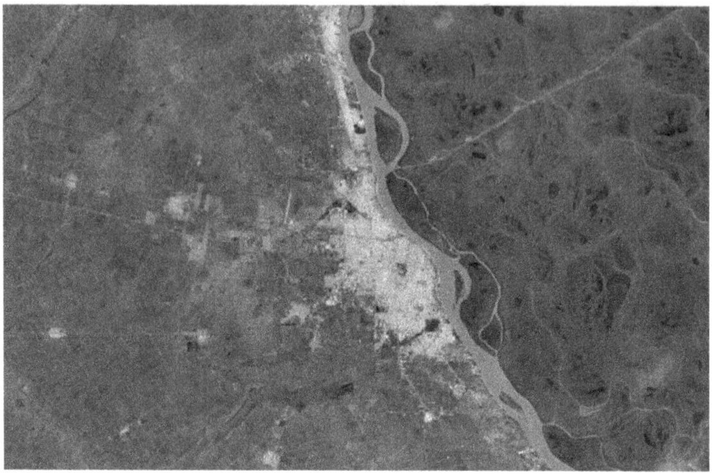

Metropolitan Territory Planning

Since 2012, the Rosario Metropolitan Coordination Authority Rosario -ECOM- (Spanish acronym of Ente de Coordinación Metropolitana), has been operating, considering the metropolitan territory: the city of Rosario and about twenty-six neighboring towns. This organization was later recognized as a non-state public entity by Provincial Law No. 13,532 of 2016. Regarding territorial policies, the first task of ECOM was to develop the Territorial Planning Guidelines -DOTs- (Spanish acronym of *Directrices de Ordenamiento Territorial*) between 2012 and 2014. The DOTs were developed during the peak of new urbanization initiatives in the metropolitan area localities, so they arrived too late to contain the uncontrolled process of urban expansion in the metropolitan region.

These guidelines are "common organizing principles, agreed upon by the set of communes and municipalities of the Rosario Metropolitan Area, that facilitate and guide the drafting of local urban plans." The first of the seven DOTs aim for the "definition of sustainable urbanization and land use patterns."

Subsequently (between 2016 and 2019), planning for each of the twenty-six localities integrated into the ECOM was carried out: the local urban plans -PULs- (Spanish acronym of *Plan Urbano Local*). Although these plans were jointly developed with local technical teams, the central idea of organizing the PULs, their contents, and many of the projects were conceived from the planning approach that then prevailed in Rosario. Two documents were prepared for each locality: proposals and preliminary diagnosis, and the corresponding local urban plan.

Some of the innovations proposed, those to manage of new urban land, are related to defining the category of "peri-urban area" differentiating it from "rural" land (policy of "promotion of peri-urban spaces"), "urban expansion land and special projects" (policy of "integration of local structure"), and "riverfronts" (policy of "revaluation of watercourses").

The recognition of peri-urban areas goes hand in hand with the ordinances regulating the application of phytosanitary products that many of the towns in Santa Fe have been approving in recent years, establishing restriction areas for the aerial and terrestrial application of highly toxic products.

Urban Planning in the City of Rosario

During the period when minimum urbanization standards were in effect, some cities and towns in the province developed their own urban plans (also known as *planes reguladores* or master plans, depending on the time). For example, Rosario has a *Plan Regulador* from 1968 approved by municipal and provincial decrees. In 1991, a new plan, known as the Master Plan (*Plan Director*), was submitted to the Municipal Council for approval, but it was never addressed by that governing body. The same fate befell the 2001 plan (Rosario Master Plan: Bases for Agreement – *Plan Director Rosario: bases para el acuerdo*) and the 2008 plan (Rosario Plan 2007 – 2017). The 1991, 2001, and 2008 plans were all presented to the Municipal Council for consideration and subsequent approval, but they were not addressed and, therefore, not approved. Despite this these plans became the reference for urban regulation and for public works in the city. On the other hand, urban regulation in Rosario (land subdivision, building, and land use and density zoning) are considered by the Urban Planning Standards (formerly the Urban Code).

Gated Communities and Country Clubs

The concept of residential enclaves, which in Argentine cities are gated communities and country clubs, first appeared in Rosario in 1997 with the enactment of Ordinance No. 6,492, which modified the Third Section of the then Urban Code and with Decree No. 1,542 of 2000. The Article 3 of Ordinance No. 6,492 established the figure of "Urban Agreement Programs on Urbanized Land," which are urbanization or land subdivision operations carried out by public, private, or mixed entities. This article sets the minimum area of the development according to the location, the percentage of land to be ceded to the Municipality, conditions regarding access to public roads, and internal common areas. These developments had to be exclusively for family housing.

Finally, three years later, the Municipality issued Decree No. 1,542 of 2000, which regulates Article 3 of Ordinance No. 6,492. For the first time in a document of urban planning regulation, this decree introduced the figure of "private neighborhood," indicating the conditions to carry out such a project: dimensions of the development according to location, integration with the urban environment, complementary works, access, infrastructure, continuity of the urban and traffic grid, minimum accesses from public roads, perimeter fencing, cession of the perimeter streets to the Municipality, location of for green spaces and equipment outside the project area.

Ten years later, in 2010, the Municipal Council passed Ordinance No. 8,727, which eliminates the figure of private or gated neighborhood throughout the municipal area of Rosario (Article 1) and prohibits the figure of country club (Article 2). This ordinance prohibiting the figure of a gated neighborhood wanted to avoid the problems of the expansive process of urbanized areas in the metropolitan region: insufficient provision of services, increased car mobility (use of private cars), soil impermeabilization that hinders the free drainage of water in the basins of the two streams, Saladillo and Ludueña.

Ordinance No. 8,727 of 2010 is the result of a long conflict between developing companies and land occupants in the northwestern sector of the city known as Nuevo Alberdi Oeste. The group GIROS played a prominent role in organizing and defending the residents of the area. This group became later the party *Ciudad Futura*, which today has representatives at City Council.

Real Estate Complexes

On August 1, 2015, the new Civil and Commercial Code of the Nation came into effect. It includes the figure of "real estate complex," which particularly refers to a type of urbanization, closed enclaves such as "country clubs, gated or private neighborhoods, industrial, business, or nautical parks, or any other urban development regardless of its residential, labor, commercial or business purpose, including those that contemplate mixed uses, in accordance with the provisions of local administrative regulations." (Article No. 2073)

The figure of "real estate complexes" thus represents recognition from the Civil and Commercial Code of these types of "residential enclave" developments that were already recognized in the urban regulations of cities or provincial legislation. In Rosario's case, the impact was felt more by the inability to continue such developments than by the recognition of the real estate complex figure. This impact is particularly felt in neighboring localities, where various types of urbanizations, "open" or "closed," appear to satisfy a demand originated in Rosario and that could not find offers in its city.

The effect of Rosario's urban regulations on neighboring localities has been significant: on one hand, the regulation banning gated neighborhoods accelerated the supply of this type of urbanization in other locations in the region. On the other hand, the introduction of the figure of Integrated Housing Park in the city determined that this type of urbanization was carried out only by large real estate companies. Consequently, the available land for urbanization and building family housing became scarce and expensive. The demand originating from Rosario was then met in other neighboring localities.

With the launch of national government's ProCreAr Program, which consisted of providing mortgage loans for the construction of housing to families who already owned a lot, the demands for land to access credit skyrocketed. Rosario had practically all the developable land divided into different Integrated Housing Parks -PHI- (Spanish Acronym of *Parque Habitacional Integrado*), based on an agreement established between the large developers and the municipal government. This policy of the local authorities failed, making it impossible for new urbanization projects to appear to satisfy the growing demand for land for the construction of family housing.

CONCLUSIONS

Considering all the above, this represents an initial exploration of urban extension processes related to regulatory planning visions, land management methods, and the ways in which condominium ownership has been addressed in both Mérida and Rosario. This sets the groundwork for further research and enables a deeper analysis of the urban impacts in terms of spatial efficiency and fragmentation, as well as the comparison of indicators of urban fragmentation and socio-spatial segregation.

In this context, and emphasizing the role of regulatory tools, it is evident that Rosario has developed a robust and consolidated legal framework for managing gated communities and private real estate developments. Since 1997, these typologies have been recognized in municipal ordinances, and by 2010, they were formally banned due to their impact on urban expansion, automobile dependency, and—most notably—their implications for the Right to the City.

In contrast, Mérida's trajectory unfolded differently. Precisely during the period when Rosario acknowledged and later abolished gated communities (1997–2010), Mérida began to experience urban expansion because of the 1992 Agrarian Reform. From 2010 onwards, adjustments to real estate and condominium legislation sought to justify densification and discourage urban sprawl, but without establishing clear guidelines—such as maximum surface areas—for gated communities. Although the

2024 real estate reform introduced a requirement for developers to donate 7% of the gross area for public facilities, the law still does not address the critical issue of limiting the total area that horizontal private real estate developments may occupy.

This leads to a pressing question: What is the maximum area that gated communities should occupy to ensure urban efficiency and quality of life, in alignment with the principles of the New Urban Agenda and the Right to the City? Rosario's response was to prohibit such developments outright while partially displacing the problem to other jurisdictions. In contrast, Mexico has a historical precedent: 70 years ago, Mario Pani proposed the concept of superblocks—autonomous yet integrated units within the urban system—as a visionary alternative to unregulated suburbanization.

From this perspective, Mérida appears to be attempting to justify the continued expansion of gated communities by requiring a 7% land donation, rather than confronting their structural implications. It is therefore urgent and relevant to deepen the understanding of horizontal condominium models and to analyze their urban, social, and environmental impacts more comprehensively.

Urban land development, and the tools used to regulate it, are not only local matters but are deeply embedded in the dynamics of metropolitan regions. In conclusion, while the Real Estate Development Law in Mérida facilitated the proliferation of new horizontal and vertical developments outside the urban core, Rosario's prohibition of gated enclaves during the same period also contributed to the displacement of urban growth to peripheral areas—albeit through a different legal rationale. Both trajectories raise critical questions about how to balance regulation, inclusion, and sustainability in the governance of urban expansion.

ACKNOWLEDGMENTS

The authors wish to express their gratitude to the project "Guidelines, plans, actions in peri-urban areas: ecosystems in equitable development" (DPAAPU – CYTED) for its support in undertaking the writing of this chapter.

REFERENCES

Alcantar García, É. (2020). Ciudad Satélite: El habitar moderno de las clases medias mexicanas. *Academia XXII*, *11*(22), 22. Advance online publication. DOI: 10.22201/fa.2007252Xp.2020.22.77411

Ayuntamiento de Mérida. (2014). *Acuerdo en el que el Ayuntamiento de Mérida aprueba crear el Instituto Municipal de Planeación*. IMPLAN.

https://isla.merida.gob.mx/serviciosinternet/normatividad/files/Acuerdos/ACUERDO_IMPLAN.pdf

Bragos, O., Latour, M., Mazzaro, P., & Ochoa, A. (2016): Suburban sprawl in the metropolitan region of Rosario. And sustainable urban development? En: NALARs Jurnalarsitektur, Vol. 15, Nº 3.

Cebey, G. (2016, mayo 9). Insurgentes 300: Un fantasma de la modernidad. Letras Libres. https://letraslibres.com/revista-espana/insurgentes-300-un-fantasma-de-la-modernidad/

Cerdán Verástegui, A., González Arreola, M. A., & Velasco Sánchez, E. (2006). IV. La reforma en marcha, 2001-2006. In *El proceso de modernización en el INFONAVIT, 2001-2006: Estrategia, redes y liderazgo* (pp. 101–266). El Colegio de México.

Decreto por el que se reestructura la Comisión para la Regularización de la Tenencia de la Tierra para transformarse en el Instituto Nacional del Suelo Sustentable. (2016). https://www.dof.gob.mx/nota_detalle.php?codigo=5465842&fecha=16/12/2016#gsc.tab=0

Diario Oficial de la Federación. (1985, agosto 19). Reglamento Interior de la Secretaria de Desarrollo Urbano y Ecología. https://www.dof.gob.mx/nota_detalle.php?codigo=4758477&fecha=19/08/1985#gsc.tab=0

Fukuda-Hayakawa, I. (2010). Planeación urbana en Curitiba. Quivera Revista de Estudios Territoriales, 12(1), Article 1.

de Garay, G. (2010). Recordando el futuro de la Ciudad de México. Testimonios orales de sus arquitectos, 1940-1990. *Alteridades (El Parque)*, *20*(39), 11–28.

Gobierno del Estado de Yucatán. (1962). Ley Sobre el Régimen de Propiedad y Condominio Inmobiliario del Estado de Yucatán. https://docs.mexico.justia.com/estatales/yucatan/ley-sobre-el-regimen-de-propiedad-y-condominio-inmobiliario-del-estado-de-yucatan.pdf

Gobierno del Estado de Yucatán. (1985). Ley de Fraccionamientos del Estado de Yucatán. https://www.poderjudicialyucatan.gob.mx/digestum/marcoLegal/02/2012/DIGESTUM02073.pdf

Gobierno del Estado de Yucatán. (2010, diciembre 7). Ley de Desarrollos Inmobiliarios del Estado de Yucatán. https://www.poderjudicialyucatan.gob.mx/digestum/marcoLegal/02/2012/DIGESTUM02098.pdf

Gobierno del Estado de Yucatán. (2012). Reglamento de la Ley de Desarrollos Inmobiliarios del Estado de Yucatán. https://www.poderjudicialyucatan.gob.mx/digestum/marcoLegal/05/2012/DIGESTUM05044.pdf

Gobierno del Estado de Yucatán. (2014). Ley sobre el Régimen de Propiedad en Condominio del Estado de Yucatán. https://www.congresoyucatan.gob.mx/storage/legislacion/leyes/45e8dfc61af9521fa5b579bce956a7d7_2024-01-17.pdf

Historia_del_Infonavit.pdf. (s. f.). Recuperado 22 de junio de 2024, de https://portalmx.infonavit.org.mx/wps/wcm/connect/7cf006d4-1466-48fe-88eb-78bc920a0624/Historia_del_Infonavit.pdf?MOD=AJPERES&CONVERT_TO=url&CACHEID=ROOTWORKSPACE-7cf006d4-1466-48fe-88eb-78bc920a0624-naAruF

León, I. M. P. L. A. N. (s. f.). ¿Quiénes somos? - Somos Implan, un puente que construye León hacia el futuro. Recuperado 23 de junio de 2024, de https://www.implan.gob.mx/quienes-somos.php

Mérida, I. M. P. L. A. N. (2019). Plan Integral de Movilidad Urbana Sustentable, Nivel Estrategia. *Vision (Basel)*, *2040*, •••. https://isla.merida.gob.mx/serviciosinternet/ordenamientoterritorial/docs/PIMUS_2040.pdf

INSUS. (2023). Manual de procedimientos para la integración y actualización del inventario nacional de suelo del INSUs. SEDATU. http://insus.gob.mx/transparencia/Normateca/nis/Manual-integracion-acutalizacion-INS.pdf

Levi, L. L., & Guzmán, E. R. (2019). Mario Pani: De la ciudad imaginada a la ciudad habitada. TOPOFILIA, 18, Article 18.

Lipovetsky, G., & Sébastien, C. (2006). Los tiempos hipermodernos (Primera). Anagrama. https://cursoshistoriavdemexico.wordpress.com/wp-content/uploads/2019/07/lipovetsky-gilles-y-sc3a9bastien-charles-los-tiempos-hipermodernos.pdf

Mackinlay, H. (1993). Las reformas de 1992 a la legislación agraria. El fin de la Reforma Agraria mexicana y la privatización del ejido. *Polis (Bologna)*, *1*(1), 1.

Martínez, J. G., & Reza, C. M. (2020). Tlatelolco. Decadencia urbana y arquitectónica de un proyecto simbólico del Modernismo – Editorial Restauro Compás y Canto. Revista Gremium. https://editorialrestauro.com.mx/tlatelolco-decadencia-urbana-y-arquitectonica-de-un-proyecto-simbolico-del-modernismo/

Meyer Falcón, R. (2023, enero 12). 10 años de Sedatu, el reflejo de una transformación. Medium. https://meyerfalcon.medium.com/10-a%C3%B1os-de-sedatu-el-reflejo-de-una-transformaci%C3%B3n-9b81c7a0a909

Monclus, j. Ed. (1998): La ciudad disperas. Suburbanizacion y nuevas periferias. Barcelona, CCCB.

MXCity. (2023, febrero 7). Ciudad Satélite, la historia de un suburbio que se proyectó como la ciudad del futuro. MXCity. https://mxcity.mx/2023/02/ciudad-satelite-la-historia-de-un-suburbio-que-se-proyecto-como-la-ciudad-del-futuro/

Nel.lo. O. (1998): Los confines de la ciudad sin confines. Estructura urbana y límites administrativos de la ciudad difusa. En: Monclús, J. (editor) La ciudad dispersa. Centre de Cultura Contemporània de Barcelona.

ONU-Hábitat. (2023, diciembre 4). Yucatán, México, reforma leyes en ordenamiento territorial. https://onuhabitat.org.mx/index.php/yucatan-mexico-actualiza-su-normativa-territorial-y-urbana

Pani, M. (1957). México, un problema, una solución. Ciudad Satélite. *Arquitectura México*, *XIII*(60), 198–226.

Pani, Mario, Cuevas, José Luis, Ramos, García, & Domingo, Vila, Victor, & Manero Peón, Enrique. (1953, March). Estudios de planificación sobre Yucatán. *Arquitectura México*, *41*, 5–39.

Pfannenstein, B., Martínez Jaramillo, J. O., Anacleto Herrera, E. E., Sevilla Villalobos, S., Pfannenstein, B., Martínez Jaramillo, J. O., Anacleto Herrera, E. E., & Sevilla Villalobos, S. (2019). Planificación urbana y la influencia de las urbanizaciones cerradas: El Área Metropolitana de Guadalajara, México. *Economía, Sociedad y Territorio*, *19*(59), 1087–1117. DOI: 10.22136/est20191278

Ramírez, A. (2003, December). Comisión para la Regularización de la Tenencia de la Tierra (CORETT). Podium Notarial. *Revista Digital de Derecho del Colegio de Notarios de Jalisco, México.*, *28*, 130–133.

SAHOP. (1981). *Sistema Normativo de Equipamiento Urbano*. Normas Básicas. Secretaría de Asentamientos Humanos y Obras Públicas.

Salinas Arreortua, L. A. (2022). Financiarización subordinada. El mercado hipotecario de la vivienda social en México. *Investigaciones Geográficas*, *107*, 1–13. DOI: 10.14350/rig.60458

Secretaría de Gobernación. (1954). *Ley sobre el Régimen de propiedad y Condominio de las Edificaciones Divididas en Pisos, Departamentos, Viviendas o Locales*. Diario Oficial.

SEDATU. (2022). NOM-002-SEDATU-2022, Equipamiento en los instrumentos que conforman el Sistema General de Planeación Territorial. Clasificación, terminología y aplicación. https://www.dof.gob.mx/nota_detalle.php?codigo=5662152&fecha=23/08/2022#gsc.tab=0

Chapter 2
Sustainable Innovation and the New Urban Green Innovation Agenda

José G. Vargas-Hernandez
https://orcid.org/0000-0003-0938-4197
Financial Literacy Research Center, Universidad Cristóbal Colón, Mexico & Tecnológico Nacional de México, Mexico

Elsa Patricia Orozco-Quijano
https://orcid.org/0000-0002-6616-3174
Laurentian University, Canada

Omar C. Vargas-González
https://orcid.org/0000-0002-6089-956X
Ecnológico Nacional de Mexico, Ciudad Guzmán, Mexico

Absalón J. Salmerón-Zapata
https://orcid.org/0009-0002-2621-2426
Universidad Cristóbal Colón, Mexico

ABSTRACT

This study intends to analyze the conceptual, theoretical and empirical interconnections between the sustainable innovation and the new urban green innovation agenda. It departs from the assumption that sustainable innovation is at the core of the new urban green innovation agenda. The method employed is the meta-analytical, reflective and descriptive based on the conceptual, theoretical and empirical literature review. The study concludes that there are clear evidences that sustainable innovation is at the center of the new urban green innovation agenda.

DOI: 10.4018/979-8-3693-6089-7.ch002

INTRODUCTION

The pandemic crisis significantly impacted organizational sustainable performance, prompting many firms to adopt sustainable practices as a strategic response (Block et al., 2021; Fitriasari, 2020). In particular, small and medium-sized enterprises (SMEs) faced a critical choice: to embrace sustainability or risk closure. During this period, many SME managers opted for sustainability-oriented operations as a pathway to survival.

Sustainable development was originally defined by the Brundtland Commission in 1987 as the ability to meet the needs of the present without compromising the ability of future generations to meet their own needs (WCED, 1987). This foundational concept continues to underpin contemporary approaches to sustainability.

A considerable body of research is currently focused on the Sustainable Development Goals (SDGs), especially from the perspective of environmental sciences (Sukma & Leelasantitham, 2022a). The ongoing debate around sustainable development centers on achieving these goals. Among them, sustainable urbanization has emerged as a key driver of inclusive development, emphasizing the principle of leaving no one and no place behind by improving living conditions in alignment with the SDGs.

Global frameworks such as the Sustainable Development Goals and the Paris Agreement on greenhouse gas emissions serve as guiding strategies for both public and private sectors. Within this context, resource mobilization plays a crucial role in advancing the new urban green innovation agenda. Efforts to improve local financing mechanisms, access to development funds, and fiscal decentralization instruments are vital. Notably, Sustainable Development Goal 11 highlights the importance of inclusive urban planning, including equitable access to transportation and public spaces for persons with disabilities.

The development of a holistic sustainable development framework integrates diverse factors aimed at achieving long-term organizational sustainable performance. This framework is grounded in the implementation of technological, scientific, and political practices that account for the regenerative and absorptive capacities of energy and materials. These practices are essential to maintaining output growth while ensuring global sustainability (Gladwin et al., 1995). Organizations are increasingly calibrating their sustainability ambitions based on realistic capabilities. In particular, firms that invest in advanced energy technology tend to demonstrate high sustainability ambition, thereby expanding their innovation potential. Conversely, firms lacking such ambition often operate within constrained innovation spaces, leading to low-impact strategies and increased innovation costs.

The concept of green identity has emerged as a catalyst that enhances organizational capacity for green creativity, sustainable growth, and long-term environmental development. This is particularly relevant in the context of global development, which necessitates the evolution of organizational management models oriented toward sustainability (Kneipp *et al.,* 2019).

This research contributes by introducing multiple constructs within the broader context of green and sustainable environmental development. Specifically, it explores the determinants of innovation crucial for long-term organizational survival, the key drivers and barriers to sustainable innovation, and the resultant innovation outcomes within the context of sustainability-oriented innovation (SOI) (Díaz-García, González-Moreno, & Sáez-Martínez, 2015; Kiefer, Del Río González, & Carrillo-Hermosilla, 2018; March, 1991; Tidd & Bessant, 2009; Álvarez Jaramillo, Zartha Sossa, & Orozco Mendoza, 2018; Bos-Brouwers, 2009).

Furthermore, the study examines how innovation factors directly influence organizational sustainability. Research on business model innovation in conjunction with sustainability efforts has contributed to the identification and characterization of sustainable business models (Teece, 2010; Amit & Zott, 2012; Spieth *et al.,* 2014; Hellström, 2007; Adams *et al.,* 2012; Boons *et al.,* 2013). However, there remains a need for greater clarity in understanding the relationship between sustainability initiatives and financial performance.

In addition, emerging research in sustainable urbanization has underscored its transformative potential by revealing the interrelated dynamics between various urban domains. These studies also highlight the growing importance of new technologies in reshaping urban systems to align with sustainability principles.

This study begins by analyzing the core tenets of sustainable innovation, thereby establishing a foundation for the formulation of the new urban green innovation agenda. The paper concludes with a set of final observations and insights that encapsulate the strategic relevance of sustainability-oriented innovation in shaping future organizational and urban trajectories.

SUSTAINABILITY INNOVATION

Sustainability is commonly defined as the ability to meet the needs of the present without compromising the ability of future generations to meet their own needs (United Nations, 1987). Within the context of strategic change, the integration of sustainability and green technologies by firms has emerged as a means of capturing new business opportunities (Noci & Verganti, 1999; Hart *et al.,* 2003). This shift in strategic focus underscores the increasing relevance of sustainability in addressing systemic issues such as climate change, resource depletion, and socioeconomic inequality. Urban sustainable development, in particular, emphasizes mitigation measures and resilience strategies aimed at enhancing livability and fostering inclusive economic growth. The transfer and adaptation of scientific and technical knowledge for sustainable urban planning have become essential, especially for addressing the needs of low-income and vulnerable populations. Sustainable urban environments thus encompass targeted efforts to strengthen climate action, including reducing greenhouse gas emissions and improving resource efficiency.

It is important to recognize, however, that sustainability does not always depend on innovation to deliver added value. For some technology-independent firms, sustainability may be pursued without the active development of innovative practices. These firms can achieve basic sustainability outcomes without generating additional value through innovation. Nevertheless, sustainable innovation—defined through eco-innovation constructs—plays a crucial role in linking sustainability with long-term competitiveness and transformation (Bossle *et al.,* 2016). In environments marked by volatility and uncertainty, corrective actions such as green process and product innovations become necessary to address sustainability-related challenges, particularly in energy sectors (Awan *et al.,* 2020). New generations of high-efficiency energy technologies are examples of areas where sustainability ambition can be significantly elevated.

From a theoretical standpoint, the resource-based view (RBV) posits that a firm's internal capabilities and sustainability practices are critical drivers of sustainable performance and competitive advantage (Alshehhi *et al.,* 2018). Achieving environmental sustainability thus requires the adoption of organizational practices that leverage unique resource configurations (Tseng, Tan, & Siriban-Manalang, 2013). Human capital, organizational assets, and dynamic capabilities together form the foundation of sustainable performance by enabling firms to use resources innovatively and maintain competitiveness (Galbreath, 2019). According to RBV theory, it is the uniqueness of both tangible and intangible resources that sustains competitive advantage in environmentally conscious business models (Barney, 1991).

Organizational innovation also serves as a powerful mechanism for improving environmental performance, expanding industrial exports, and achieving excellence in sustainable development (Li *et al.,* 2020; Wu *et al.,* 2019). At the strategic level, top management's innovative capabilities enable the acquisition and deployment of sustainable resources in pursuit of high performance (Smith & Tushman, 2005). Executives actively seek new applications for existing core technologies, particularly in emerging markets where sustainability is increasingly becoming a driver of innovation (Baumard & Starbuck, 2005; Taylor & Helfat, 2009). One such example is the role of green supply chain management, which enhances organizational sustainability through eco-efficient practices across the value chain (Fatoki, 2019).

Collaboration management among stakeholders throughout the value chain is equally critical in fostering sustainable innovation. In this regard, green innovation not only enhances firm performance but also contributes to solving broader societal issues (Hansen, Große-Dunker, & Reichwald, 2009; Hart *et al.,* 2003). Firms that adopt innovation-led approaches to green technology development position themselves as active agents of sustainable development (Scheyvens, Banks, & Hughes, 2016). These firms engage in diversification strategies complemented by clean technology initiatives, which collectively strengthen their competitive advantage and deliver long-term value (Hart, 1997; Jenkins, 2009).

The exploration of green technologies by firms represents a strategic opportunity to define early-stage innovation trajectories. By leveraging core competencies, organizations can create sustainable value in emerging green markets. This process is often supported by exploration-based strategies and the strategic management of technology-driven firms, particularly those with strong technological foundations (Ansoff, 1957; Voss & Voss, 2013; Kiefer *et al.,* 2018; Taylor & Helfat, 2009). Moreover, the sustainable management of natural resources in urban contexts plays a critical role in protecting and enhancing environmental services and ecosystems, leading to the reduction of greenhouse gas emissions, improved air quality, and enhanced disaster risk mitigation.

Sustainability aspects are inherently linked to the characteristics of green technologies and markets. The concept of core competence in sustainability enables the identification of technologies that contribute meaningfully to green markets. However, firms must navigate trade-offs between the scope of innovation and the level of sustainability ambition. This tension demands a learning process that allows organizations to engage with the complex dynamics of green markets while bridging cognitive gaps between traditional and emerging green approaches. Notably, sustainable markets often require increased regulatory interventions, particularly in the renewable energy sector (Luethi, 2010).

Within this context, the concept of the innovation space becomes crucial. Organizations continuously adjust their innovation strategies to balance sustainability ambitions with feasible outcomes. The innovation space represents this balance—expanding as firms increase their commitment to sustainability and develop components that improve the efficiency of sustainable technologies (Wicki *et al.,* 2015). The broader the innovation space, the greater the firm's ability to realize transformative green technologies.

Collaboration along the value chain is essential in scaling up green innovation. When actors cooperate effectively, they can drive the development and implementation of green innovations at scale. However, failure to foster collaboration may instead produce competitive tensions that hinder progress (Huhtala *et al.,* 2014).

Value chain actors who prioritize sustainability contribute to generating organizational value and promoting broader societal benefits through innovation.

Sustainability innovation also improves production processes, product offerings, and services while influencing both market dynamics and sociopolitical structures (Schaltegger & Wagner, 2011). The adoption of green product labeling enhances both individual and organizational behavior toward sustainable production and consumption. Consumers and producers demonstrate stronger intentions to engage with environmentally responsible products when such labeling is present (Ma *et al.,* 2017). Additionally, operational procedures surrounding production and delivery are crucial for driving firms toward enhanced sustainability performance (Chen, 2008; Chiou *et al.,* 2011; Muisyo & Qin, 2021).

Green marketing practices further support sustainable production and consumption, playing a pivotal role in advancing sustainable development (Fatoki, 2019). Yet, persistent patterns of unsustainable consumption and production—alongside biodiversity loss, pollution, ecosystem degradation, natural disasters, and climate change—continue to threaten the viability of cities and human settlements. Policymakers recognize that reversing these patterns is essential for safeguarding sustainability outcomes. Although the concept of green marketing is increasingly tested in relation to sustainability performance, it still requires deeper theoretical refinement (Hasan & Ali, 2015; Kinoti, 2011; Lam & Li, 2019). Environmental awareness and conservation efforts shape individual intentions toward green behavior, including sustainable consumption choices like opting for biodegradable packaging (Choi & Johnson, 2019).

True sustainability innovation calls for an integrated, systems-thinking approach. It involves the reconfiguration of knowledge management systems, organizational capabilities, stakeholder relationships, leadership styles, and corporate culture (Adams *et al.,* 2012). The development of localized knowledge management systems can inform regional policy frameworks through partnerships with sustainability-focused organizations. In doing so, organizations contribute not only to their internal transformation but also to normative developments, best practices, and international sustainability guidelines. Ultimately, these efforts support organizational transitions aligned with the Sustainable Development Goals (SDGs) and strengthen regional contributions through policy integration and knowledge dissemination.

The leadership role of youth in advancing the Sustainable Development Goals (SDGs) is central to guiding sustainable urban development. This vision is strongly reflected in the new urban green innovation agenda, which positions young people as agents of transformation. The advancement of infrastructure-related information technology resources, their automation, and their integration into organizational processes are key to developing sustainable capabilities. In particular, Information Systems (IS) play a pivotal role in facilitating organizational transformation by enabling hybrid physical–digital solutions that support green technologies. These systems directly contribute to enhanced organizational performance and foster the adoption of sustainable operational practices (Hanelt *et al.,* 2016).

Organizational transformation toward sustainability involves comprehensive restructuring, leading to more agile, efficient, and inclusive institutional configurations. This transformation promotes accountability, trust, and transparency—essential for implementing strategic sustainable development plans. However, transitioning to sustainable operations is inherently complex due to numerous uncertainties and institutional barriers (Han & Chen, 2021). The "firework innovation" model offers a process-based framework to analyze the complexities inherent in green technology innovation, shedding light on how sustainability-driven innovations evolve over time (Fichter *et al.,* 2007; Van de Ven *et al.,* 2000/1989; Van de Ven, Polley, Garud, & Venkataraman, 2008).

The adoption of green technology is increasingly informed by consolidated models that account for multiple determinants, such as sustainable innovativeness, perceived compatibility, environmental values, and household-level green technologies (Al-Saedi *et al.,* 2020; Ahn *et al.,* 2016). These models help identify the conditions under which sustainable technologies are embraced and diffused.

Within this context, innovation configurations differ significantly. Systemic innovations led by proactive organizations generate synergistic benefits, whereas technology-independent firms may adapt existing processes without a focus on innovation, as such efforts may not yield immediate value. Therefore, green technological adoption models must be validated through decision-making frameworks that incorporate green attributes and sustainability outcomes.

Sustainable innovation is inherently proactive, offering a strategic pathway for scaling up emerging technologies aligned with the broader sustainability agenda. While the prevalence of ecological, green, and sustainable innovations has increased, the innovation processes within greening organizations remain largely marginal (Hansen *et al.,* 2009; Schiederig, Tietze, & Herstatt, 2012; Klewitz & Hansen, 2014). Among key enablers of these innovations are material manufacturers and suppliers along the value chain, who act as proactive agents in the dissemination of sustainable technologies. These actors collectively shape the innovation landscape by configuring multiple innovation strategies—systemic, process-oriented, and product-based—to scale up technologies that contribute to sustainability.

In some cases, sustainable technologies are introduced without any direct innovation activities. Technology-independent firms, for example, may adopt existing solutions using current capabilities, thereby bypassing the need for additional innovation. These firms typically adjust their practices to accommodate green technologies without developing new processes or knowledge systems. This approach is particularly prevalent in less-developed countries, which often exhibit lower levels of innovation and are disproportionately vulnerable to climate change impacts, thus heightening the urgency of adopting sustainable technologies (Lee *et al.,* 2021; Global Innovation Index, 2018).

Evidence increasingly shows that sustainable urbanization accelerates progress toward the SDGs. Facilitating green innovation in this domain requires the involvement of intermediaries—including design consultants, advisory firms, niche platforms, and other stakeholders—who co-innovate by generating novel ideas and collaborative opportunities.

This process involves a form of normative work that encompasses foundational research, knowledge dissemination, and capacity-building. Such efforts help establish principles, norms, and standards that inform the formulation of urban policies and foster institutional collaboration. In particular, capacity building within local governments is critical for achieving environmental sustainability. This includes efforts to implement smart city planning strategies that rely on frontier technologies to regenerate urban environments and create technology-driven opportunities for long-term sustainable development.

Capacity building for strategic urban sustainable planning equips both organizations and individuals with the tools necessary for effective policy implementation, institutional reform, and transformative action. The integration of frontier technologies further expands innovation pathways in the realm of sustainable urban development, particularly through the empowerment of local governments. These technologies can be applied to address sustainability challenges in underserved populations by mitigating social and spatial inequalities.

Urban development must be closely aligned with the broader sustainable development agenda, linking specific urban targets to the overarching Sustainable Development Goals (SDGs). However, urbanization models often present structural and implementation challenges that may undermine the realization of SDGs. In this context, operational strategies—such as technical assistance derived from expert knowledge and crisis response mechanisms—play a vital role. This study aims to analyze the conceptual, theoretical, and empirical interconnections between sustainable innovation and the evolving urban green innovation agenda.

Sustainable urban transformation requires deliberate engagement with communities that have historically been excluded from mainstream development initiatives. A significant proportion of these marginalized populations live in poverty. To advance poverty reduction goals, sustainable urban development must adopt inclusive decision-making frameworks that actively support access to rights and resources. This includes addressing systemic discrimination based on gender, ethnicity, migration status, and other factors that limit the participation of individuals in urban development processes. The United Nations General Assembly has prioritized this approach by promoting strategies for sustainable urban development and human settlements through coordinated action across country teams.

The new urban green innovation agenda emphasizes gender equality, responsiveness, and empowerment across all dimensions of sustainable urban development. Particular attention must be given to displaced populations affected by conflict or crisis. The SDG framework acknowledges the specific needs and vulnerabilities of marginalized and excluded groups by including targeted goals to address their challenges.

A forward-looking approach to sustainable urbanization involves the adoption and development of frontier and digital technologies. These tools facilitate the collection and analysis of urban data, enhance spatial planning capabilities, and enable smart city strategies. These strategies often target critical sectors such as mobility, environmental sustainability, energy efficiency, and public service delivery. Long-term urban sustainability relies on leveraging these technological advances to create dynamic, responsive, and resilient cities.

A holistic approach to urban development is required—one that connects human settlements and cities through inclusive strategies that account for all segments of society. In doing so, urbanization can become a primary driver of the Sustainable Development Goals by improving living standards and promoting equity. Strategic urban planning, when grounded in principles of sustainability, plays a critical role in catalyzing developmental change and ensuring that urban growth contributes positively to environmental, economic, and social well-being.

The objective of strategic planning for sustainable urbanization is to serve as a catalyst for development and peace, aligning closely with the core principles of the Sustainable Development Goals (SDGs). This process aims to improve living conditions by fostering cities that are more inclusive, resilient, and environmentally sustainable, thereby ensuring that no one is left behind. Equitable and sustainable urbanization must address risks associated with natural hazards as well as the root causes of instability and conflict.

Implementing strategic plans for sustainable urbanization necessitates organizational change supported by a robust and adaptable financial sustainability model. This model must ensure the appropriate allocation of resources while embracing innovative financial strategies, investment mechanisms, and project financing tools tailored to urban development. Integrated city development strategies should also incorporate urban poverty reduction measures. The mobilization of financial resources is essential and requires coordinated strategic partnerships between public and private sectors. In many cases, sustainable urbanization projects rely on extra-budgetary resources to finance technical assistance and implementation support.

Strategic planning for sustainable urbanization evolves in parallel with the implementation of the SDGs. A key institutional challenge, particularly for UN-Habitat, lies in ensuring predictability, role clarity, and long-term resource sustainability. To address this challenge, a comprehensive financial sustainability framework is required. Such a framework should build institutional financial capacity, align budgetary resources with strategic goals, increase revenue streams, and eliminate inefficiencies in spending.

Financing mechanisms are pivotal in driving national and local strategic planning efforts, enabling governments and institutions to mobilize financial resources, instruments, and schemes that align with the broader sustainable development agenda. Urban sustainable development increasingly relies on innovative financial frameworks, including financing facilities, international funds, and hybrid mechanisms that support long-term infrastructure and service delivery needs.

Strategic organizational planning must also integrate dimensions of social inclusion and disability rights, embedding human rights considerations across all areas, including resilience and safety. This inclusive approach is essential to ensure that all individuals benefit from sustainable urbanization processes. Safety and security, as integral components of the SDG agenda, must intersect with efforts to promote equitable access to mobility, public space, and essential services. These intersections foster greater social inclusion, cohesion, and overall well-being in urban environments.

UN-Habitat advocates for sustainable urbanization through the implementation of innovative operational projects tailored to local conditions. As a global authority on sustainable urban innovation and development, UN-Habitat plays a critical role in repositioning strategic planning by focusing on specialized programs that define agendas, influence political discourse, generate and disseminate knowledge, and shape technical principles, norms, and standards informed by global best practices.

The body of knowledge developed around smart and sustainable urban development includes technical expertise supported by governments, particularly in areas such as the circular economy and smart city initiatives. Technical support in these domains enhances the competitiveness and innovativeness of cities, creating comparative advantages through increased productivity, reduced negative externalities, improved transit systems, and more reliable public services. These efforts are integral to aligning global agendas with the evolving needs of sustainable urban development.

UN-Habitat is uniquely positioned to address the complex challenges posed by sustainable urbanization. Its mandate includes seizing opportunities to strengthen urban sustainability by leveraging institutional knowledge and innovation capacity. This capacity enables the development of both normative and operational solutions rooted in evidence and best practices. The deployment of frontier technologies and cutting-edge innovations is essential to ensuring inclusive prosperity across individuals, cities, and regions.

To address regional diversity and emerging urbanization trends, UN-Habitat is reconfiguring its organizational structures. These adjustments align with broader international commitments to sustainable development and enable more responsive programming. By focusing on priority areas and streamlining processes, UN-Habitat supports the rationalization of development programs undertaken in partnership with other global institutions.

The organization's contribution to sustainable urbanization is further reinforced by its strategic use of knowledge and innovation to transform urban settlements. Strategic planning for organizational change within sustainable urbanization acts as a catalyst for integrated solutions that span multiple scales, sectors, stakeholders, and human settlement contexts. These efforts are aligned with the Sustainable Development Goals (SDGs) and aim to amplify collective action toward their achievement.

Furthermore, reforming systems and procedures within organizational structures is essential to improving financial and resource management in urban development processes. Such reforms ensure that sustainable urbanization programs and services are delivered efficiently and effectively, thereby enhancing overall organizational performance and accountability.

ransformative organizational change in sustainable urbanization development is guided by a deliberate paradigm shift. This shift enables the creation of a framework for implementing meaningful change through strategies such as repositioning innovation priorities, leveraging strategic partnerships, focusing on context-specific solutions, and enhancing collaborative delivery mechanisms. The emerging agendas for urban and sustainable development aim to make human settlements more inclusive, resilient, safe, and sustainable, particularly in the pursuit of gender equality and social inclusiveness.

THE NEW URBAN GREEN INNOVATION AGENDA

The new urban green innovation agenda facilitates a transition toward the sustainable management of natural resources within a circular economy. This transition supports ecosystem conservation, restoration, and the regeneration of resilience. Urban resilience, in this context, refers to the measurable capacity of urban systems to maintain continuity amid natural and anthropogenic stresses, including earthquakes, demographic shifts, and sustainability-related transformations.

There has been significant growth in sustainable and responsible investment, particularly through private-sector funds focused on climate change. However, to ensure that these investments have widespread impact, it is essential to strengthen both innovative funding mechanisms and the institutional capacities of local governments. Frontier technologies for urban sustainability must be implemented to promote shared prosperity across individuals, cities, and regions. Climate-related projects, particularly in regions with limited innovation capacity, must balance local needs with scientific rigor and evidence-based planning. Urban sprawl, which fragments city functions, exacerbates climate warming and underscores the need for climate-neutral urban growth strategies.

Concerns over commodity prices have pushed organizations to adopt the latest environmentally friendly technologies. These innovations help reduce costs, minimize waste, and provide firms with a competitive advantage (Ahn *et al.,* 2016; Anser *et al.,* 2020).

Recent advances in digital technology are increasingly being integrated into organizations and their environmental strategies. These integrations drive green innovation and contribute to sustainable development (Wen *et al.,* 2021; Sukma & Leelasantitham, 2022b). Green innovation serves as a key response to environmental challenges, enabling organizations to develop new processes that add value. Often, this occurs through reactive adaptation to changes in supply chains involving sustainable materials.

Established firms with traditional product lines are increasingly exploring sustainable opportunities by developing green technologies and diversifying into niche markets. This stands in contrast to entrepreneurial firms that are founded with a green mission at their core (Hart, Milstein, & Caggiano, 2003; Jenkins, 2009; Schaltegger, Lüdeke-Freund, & Hansen, 2012). The development trajectory of sustainable green technology markets differs significantly between emerging and mature markets (Suurs et al., 2010). Organizational digitalization enhances transparency, fosters shared commitment and trust, and promotes innovation—each of which is essential for sustainable development (Dong *et al.,* 2021; Sukma & Leelasantitham, 2022a).

Eco-innovation is increasingly recognized as a foundational element in emerging sustainable manufacturing systems and green supply chains (Dubey *et al.,* 2015). Successful implementation of sustainable green practices requires alignment between technological innovations and enabling technologies that facilitate adoption and diffusion (Etzion, 2007; Lin & Ho, 2011; Thomas *et al.,* 2016). The influence of sustainability drivers varies by geographic location, yet internal organizational factors—such as leadership, structure, and culture—remain critical. These internal dynamics motivate firms to redesign their processes to enhance environmentally sustainable manufacturing and operations management (Galbreath, 2019; El-Kassar & Singh, 2019).

Technological factors strongly influence the adoption of green marketing practices that support sustainability objectives (Karjaluoto & Vaccaro, 2009). In this regard, frontier technologies and sustainable urban development must be leveraged to bridge existing social and spatial inequalities, particularly in underserved communities. Innovations in end-of-pipe technologies—both additive and curative—are particularly important for firms exporting to international markets, where alignment with global sustainability norms is increasingly demanded (Hojnik & Ruzzier, 2016). Trade barriers designed to exclude environmentally harmful producers reinforce these expectations and support the transition to greener global supply chains.

Despite their potential, the implementation of environmental technology innovations presents challenges for many organizations, particularly in managing technological control processes (Elkington, 1994; Kemp, 2010). Adoption is further shaped by motivation: individuals' willingness to engage with smart technologies influences their sustainable consumption behaviors and their household-level sustainability practices (Ahn *et al.,* 2016).

Organizational support is critical for the successful adoption of sustainable green practices (Lin & Ho, 2011). Among various initiatives, green human resources (GHR) practices show the most significant positive impact on sustainable organizational performance, whereas the impact of green supply chain practices is less pronounced. As sustainable urbanization becomes a focal point of global development agendas, the quality of human resources management plays a crucial role in the implementation and success of these green practices (Lin & Ho, 2011; Singh, Khamba, *et al.,* 2017; Singh, Tan, *et al.,* 2017). Furthermore, ongoing reassessment of innovation is required to maintain and improve sustainability performance outcomes.

Management innovation represents a significant source of competitive advantage and plays an essential role in achieving sustainable performance (Hamel, 2006). Firms that adopt innovative management systems, supported by diverse policies and strategic approaches, are better positioned to optimize resource use and secure long-term sustainability gains (Hinterhuber & Liozu, 2017). These innovations offer unique value, particularly in emerging markets, where management innovation is a vital driver of corporate sustainability (Kraśnicka *et al.,* 2018). Nevertheless, management may remain unaware of the broader positive outcomes their decisions generate within ecosystem contexts.

Sustainable green practices are closely linked to improved organizational performance, including financial gains in emerging markets. Investments in sustainable technologies and project-based approaches yield both financial and operational benefits. These improvements also support the diffusion of green innovation across sectors. Organizational sustainability is further enhanced through green human resource management (HRM) practices (El-Kassar & Singh, 2019; Mousa & Othman, 2020).

Firms increasingly recognize that engaging in sustainable practices can lead to higher profitability (Eccles *et al.,* 2014). Many companies publicly share their experiences with green supply chain initiatives to demonstrate their contributions to sustainability and promote ethical practices (Geng et al., 2017). Sustainability is achieved through transformation—firms evolve into more responsible organizations through intentional, continuous change (Zollo, Cennamo, & Neumann, 2013).

Despite growing interest, terms such as "business model innovation" and "sustainable business models" often lack clear definitions. There is no broad agreement on how these models should be characterized, classified, or bounded, which has led to conceptual fragmentation (Magretta, 2002; Osterwalder & Pigneur, 2005; Boons & Lüdeke-Freund, 2013; Spieth *et al.,* 2014; Zott *et al.*, 2011). In practice, business model innovations for sustainability are often ad hoc rather than systematic and integrated (Stubbs & Cocklin, 2008). Process innovations within value chains, however, have shown strong potential for enhancing business sustainability when internalized as part of an organization's strategy.

Network analysis of value flows reveals that sustainability outcomes are significantly influenced by stakeholder satisfaction and engagement (Shaw, 2010). Intermediaries—such as local governments, facilitators, and consultants—play a pivotal role in supporting sustainability-oriented innovation processes (Goodman et al., 2017; Klewitz *et al.,* 2012).

The life cycle concept is foundational for designing sustainable, holistic product–service systems. It enables organizations to evaluate and manage environmental impacts across all stages of a product's lifespan (Aurich *et al.,* 2006; Linder & Williander, 2015).

Entrepreneurship plays a crucial role in implementing sustainable practices, especially among small and medium-sized enterprises (SMEs). While many SMEs have adopted environmental practices, they often require customized tools that reflect their resource constraints and knowledge profiles. Unfortunately, modeling tools and methods used in practice rarely emphasize sustainability (Osterwalder & Pigneur, 2010; Johnson et al., 2008).

Evidence shows that SMEs adopt technological innovations and green practices more actively during times of crisis (Chege & Wang, 2020a; Omri, 2020; Ryoo & Koo, 2013). Proactive SMEs—whether resource-rich or resource-constrained—often develop radical innovations to address sustainability challenges (Aragón-Correa, Hurtado-Torres, Sharma, & Garcia-Morales, 2008; Halme & Korpela, 2014). Even in unsupportive contexts, radical innovations among SMEs follow similar process patterns (Klewitz & Hansen, 2014; Cooper, 1983; Van de Ven et al., 2008).

Biodiversity conservation and the promotion of sustainable food systems are essential for ensuring equitable distribution of high-quality protein to populations (Nadathur, 2017; FAO, 2014; Aiking & de Boer, 2020; Chardigny & Walrand, 2016). System innovation is a critical pathway for transforming food systems toward sustainability.

However, sustainable agricultural systems face several challenges—including resource scarcity, climate change, limited food access, rising demand, food waste, and global supply chain complexity (United Nations, 2016). In this context, digital agricultural technologies and innovation breakthroughs are needed to mitigate these risks and support transformation. These technologies play a critical role in training, cost optimization, and system resilience across diverse agricultural sectors. Digital sustainable agriculture thus represents a major innovation frontier in addressing food system challenges globally (Maletic, 2015; Anwar, 2018).

Transformational innovation in sustainable food systems can directly contribute to achieving the Sustainable Development Goals. Key enablers of food system sustainability include access to fertile land, favorable climate conditions, clean water, energy, and fertilizer. Discussions on food alternatives increasingly center on the integration of sustainability and food safety frameworks. Nonetheless, food systems remain under pressure due to demographic trends, global population growth, rising food demand, and stress on energy and water supplies.

Lastly, adaptive capacity, novelty, creativity, and innovation are fundamental to sustainable business evolution (Winn *et al.,* 2011; Hall & Wagner, 2012). Notably, factors such as age and education do not significantly influence an individual's sustainability orientation, indicating the broader systemic nature of sustainable practice adoption.

Governmental and non-governmental policies, along with shifting consumer preferences, increasingly support the integration of plant-based proteins into daily diets. This shift has encouraged the exploration of sustainable alternative protein sources such as grains, leafy vegetables, seeds, legumes, and others (Fasolin *et al.,* 2019; Henchion *et al.,* 2017). In parallel, urban policy implementation now emphasizes national and local multi-stakeholder partnerships designed to foster integrated urban systems. These partnerships promote cross-sectoral cooperation to enable sustainable and inclusive urban development. Collaborative approaches also strengthen investment flows into sustainable urban projects. In this context, evidence-based policymaking—supported by robust scientific data—enhances the quality and effectiveness of decision-making.

The integration of sustainability networks, aimed at achieving both individual and collective goals, is enhanced through effective governance mechanisms. These mechanisms are instrumental in creating value networks and enabling innovation. Strengthening urban sustainability programs requires access to seed capital, financial support, and technical assistance. These resources are essential for mobilizing both internal and external funding to advance the implementation of sustainable development objectives. In many cases, local governments rely on international cooperation to support sustainable urban planning initiatives, particularly in building climate resilience and implementing clean air actions. Localized efforts are vital to overcoming challenges and accelerating progress on the Sustainable Development Goals (SDGs), treating urban development as an evolving continuum of knowledge generation, implementation, and monitoring.

Strategic sustainable urban planning leverages expertise, partnership-building, advocacy, and technical collaboration to scale impact across domains of change. A core requirement of next-generation strategic planning is the dismantling of bureaucratic silos at various levels of governance. This includes fostering coherent engagement across systems of development, improving organizational performance, and integrating planning processes across intersecting domains of change.

Partnerships play a critical role in advocacy and resource mobilization, which are necessary for scaling the impact of sustainable urban development programs. Strong partnerships contribute to transparency, accountability, national ownership, and the inclusion of communities—particularly vulnerable groups—in implementing the new urban green innovation agenda aligned with the SDGs. A comprehensive and effective communication strategy is essential to raise awareness about both the challenges and opportunities of sustainable urbanization, while also strengthening commitments to resource mobilization.

Urban planning and design must prioritize transparency as a cornerstone of modern governance, thereby reinforcing principles of local democracy, citizen inclusion, and participatory planning. Ensuring spatially just and sustainable urbanization depends on amplifying the voices of diverse stakeholders—including residents, decision-makers, grassroots organizations, and civil society partners.

Participatory urban governance that is accountable, transparent, equitable, environmentally conscious, and inclusive has been shown to significantly enhance the outcomes of sustainable development initiatives. Transparent and coordinated governance requires the creation of institutional frameworks capable of empowering urban stakeholders and providing coherence and predictability. These mechanisms are critical to supporting inclusive economic growth, advancing social cohesion, and promoting environmental protection.

Finally, the evaluation of strategic sustainable urban development plans must consider three core performance dimensions: efficiency, effectiveness, and sustainability. These criteria ensure that planning efforts are not only actionable and impactful but also aligned with long-term sustainable development objectives.

CONCLUSIONS

This study has examined the conceptual, theoretical, and empirical interconnections between sustainable innovation and the new urban green innovation agenda, departing from the foundational assumption that sustainable innovation constitutes the core of this agenda. The analysis confirms that there is robust evidence positioning sustainable innovation as a central mechanism driving the urban green innovation framework.

The integration of the Technology–Organization–Environment (TOE) framework has proven effective in supporting green practices and in identifying positive determinants of organizational sustainable performance. Emerging innovations, rooted in new knowledge development, offer transformative possibilities to accelerate the achievement of Sustainable Development Goals (SDGs), particularly those focused on climate change mitigation and the deployment of innovative technologies. Furthermore, systematic reviews of scientific literature clarify the relationship between eco-innovation and sustainable performance, emphasizing the mediating role of service innovation.

Sustainable development has the capacity to mobilize collective responsibility to sustain peace, reduce disaster risk, and address conflict and humanitarian crises. In the context of urban environments, the complexity of crises affecting people and systems demands targeted strategies to enhance resilience, stability, and sustainable development. Humanitarian responses, when built on a shared understanding of urban crises, can empower local stakeholders and governments to facilitate rapid recovery and foster more resilient, inclusive, and sustainable urban futures.

Organizational change emerges as a strategic driver for fostering innovation, improving the monitoring of sustainability indicators, and enhancing performance outcomes aligned with the SDGs. Within this transformation, the new urban green innovation agenda advances inclusive sustainable urban development through commitments to poverty reduction, urban prosperity, and enhanced resilience.

A critical aspect of implementing this agenda lies in addressing social inequalities through resource allocation across urban systems. This includes eliminating discrimination within and between urban areas and strengthening urban–rural linkages as mutually reinforcing processes for sustainable development. The effective mobilization of financial, technological, and human resources is essential to the success of this agenda. Its implementation depends on sustained partnerships and the strategic application of knowledge, innovation, and data.

Lastly, the development of sustainable organizations must be grounded in a human rights-based approach. This entails not only responding to symptoms of poverty but also addressing the structural economic, social, and spatial causes. Discretionary policies and targeted measures must aim to improve living conditions, promote social inclusion, and ensure that urban development remains equitable, just, and sustainable.

REFERENCES

Adams, R., Jeanrenaud, S., Bessant, J., Overy, P., & Denyer, D. (2012). *Innovating for Sustainability. A Systematic Review of the Body of Knowledge*. Network for Business Sustainability.

Ahn, M., Kang, J., & Hustvedt, G. (2016). A model of sustainable household technology acceptance. *International Journal of Consumer Studies*, *40*(1), 83–91. DOI: 10.1111/ijcs.12217

Aiking, H., & de Boer, J. (2020). The next protein transition. *Trends in Food Science & Technology*, *105*, 515–522. DOI: 10.1016/j.tifs.2018.07.008 PMID: 38620223

Al-Saedi, K., Al-Emran, M., Ramayah, T., & Abusham, E. (2020). Developing a general extended UTAUT model for M-payment adoption. *Technology in Society*, *62*, 101293. DOI: 10.1016/j.techsoc.2020.101293

Alshehhi, A., Nobanee, H., & Khare, N. (2018). The impact of sustainability practices on corporate financial performance: Literature trends and future research potential. *Sustainability (Basel)*, *10*(2), 494. DOI: 10.3390/su10020494

Álvarez Jaramillo, J., Zartha Sossa, J. W., & Orozco Mendoza, G. L. (2018). Barriers to sustainability for small and medium enterprises in the framework of sustainable development—Literature review. *Business Strategy and the Environment*, *10*(1), 1.

Amit, R., & Zott, C. (2012). Creating value through business model innovation. *MIT Sloan Management Review*, *53*(3), 41–49.

Anser, M. K., Yousaf, Z., & Zaman, K. (2020). Green technology acceptance model and green logistics operations: To see which way the wind is blowing. *Frontiers in Sustainability*, *1*(3), 1–9. DOI: 10.3389/frsus.2020.00003

Ansoff, H. I. (1957). Strategies for diversification. *Harvard Business Review*, *35*(5), 113–124.

Anwar, M., Shah, S. Z. A., & Khan, S. Z. (2018). The role of personality in SMEs internationalization: Empirical evidence. *Rev. Int. Bus. Strategy*, *28*(2), 258–282. DOI: 10.1108/RIBS-12-2017-0113

Aragón-Correa, J. A., Hurtado-Torres, N., Sharma, S., & Garcia-Morales, V. J. (2008). Environmental strategy and performance in small firms: A resource-based perspective. *Journal of Environmental Management*, *86*(1), 88–103. DOI: 10.1016/j.jenvman.2006.11.022 PMID: 17239519

Aurich, J. C., Fuchs, C., & Wagenknecht, C. (2006). Life cycle oriented design of technical product–service systems. *Journal of Cleaner Production, 14*(17), 1480–1494. DOI: 10.1016/j.jclepro.2006.01.019

Awan, U., Arnold, M. G., & Golgeci, I. (2020). Enhancing green product and process innovation: Towards an integrative framework of knowledge acquisition and environmental investment. *Business Strategy and the Environment*, •••, 1–13. DOI: 10.1002/bse.2684

Barney, J. (1991). Firm resources and sustained competitive advantage. *J. Manag.*, 17, 99–120. Baumard, P., & Starbuck, W. H. (2005). Learning from failures: Why it may not happen. *Long Range Planning, 38*(3), 281–298. DOI: 10.1016/j.lrp.2005.03.004

Block, A., Gellrich, M., & Russ, C. (2021). Effects of the COVID-19 Pandemic on SME sustainability: Case study of car dealerships in Switzerland | Block | European Journal of Applied Business and Management. *European Journal of Applied Business and Management, 7*(1). Retrieved April 24, 2021, from https://nidisag.isag.pt/index.php/IJAM/article/view/547

Boons, F., & Lüdeke-Freund, F. (2013). Business models for sustainable innovation: State-of-the-art and steps towards a research agenda. *Journal of Cleaner Production, 45*, 9–19. DOI: 10.1016/j.jclepro.2012.07.007

Bos-Brouwers, H. (2009). Corporate sustainability and innovation in SMEs: Evidence of themes and activities in practice. *Business Strategy and the Environment, 19*(7), 417–435. DOI: 10.1002/bse.652

Bossle, M.B., De Barcellos, M.D., Vieira, L.M. and Sauvee, L. (2016), The drivers for adoption of eco-innovation, *Journal of Cleaner Production*, Vol. 113 No. 2014, pp. 861-872.

Chardigny, J.-M., & Walrand, S. (2016). Plant protein for food: Opportunities and bottlenecks. OCL *Oilseeds Fats Crop. Lipids* 23, 6p

Chege, S. M., & Wang, D. (2020a). The influence of technology innovation on SME performance through environmental sustainability practices in Kenya. *Technology in Society, 60*, 101210. DOI: 10.1016/j.techsoc.2019.101210

Chen, Y. S. (2008). The driver of green innovation and green image - Green core competence. *Journal of Business Ethics, 81*(3), 531–543. DOI: 10.1007/s10551-007-9522-1

Chiou, T. Y., Chan, H. K., Lettice, F., & Chung, S. H. (2011). The influence of greening the suppliers and green innovation on environmental performance and competitive advantage in Taiwan. *Transportation Research Part E, Logistics and Transportation Review*, *47*(6), 822–836. DOI: 10.1016/j.tre.2011.05.016

Choi, D., & Johnson, K. K. P. (2019). Influences of environmental and hedonic motivations on intention to purchase green products: An extension of the theory of planned behavior. *Sustainable Production and Consumption*, *18*, 145–155. DOI: 10.1016/j.spc.2019.02.001

Díaz-García, C., González-Moreno, Á., & Sáez-Martínez, F. J. (2015). Eco-innovation: Insights from a literature review. *Innovation (North Sydney, N.S.W.)*, *17*(1), 6–23. DOI: 10.1080/14479338.2015.1011060

Dong, J. Q., Karhade, P. P., Rai, A., & Xu, S. X. (2021). How firms make information technology investment decisions: Toward a behavioral agency theory. *Journal of Management Information Systems*, *38*(1), 29–58. DOI: 10.1080/07421222.2021.1870382

Dubey, R., Gunasekaran, A., & Samar Ali, S. (2015). Exploring the relationship between leadership, operational practices, institutional pressures and environmental performance: A framework for green supply chain. *International Journal of Production Economics*, *160*, 120–132. DOI: 10.1016/j.ijpe.2014.10.001

Eccles, R. G., Ioannou, I., & Serafeim, G. (2014). The impact of corporate sustainability on organizational processes and performance. *Management Science*, *60*(11), 2835–2857. DOI: 10.1287/mnsc.2014.1984

El-Kassar, A. N., & Singh, S. K. (2019). Green innovation and organizational performance: The influence of big data and the moderating role of management commitment and HR practices. *Technological Forecasting and Social Change*, *144*, 483–498. DOI: 10.1016/j.techfore.2017.12.016

Elkington, J. (1994). Towards the Sustainable Corporation: Win–win–win Business Strategies for Sustainable Development. *California Management Review*, *36*(2), 90–100. DOI: 10.2307/41165746

Etzion, D. (2007). Research on organizations and the natural environment, 1992-Present: A review. *Journal of Management*, *33*(4), 637–664. DOI: 10.1177/0149206307302553

FAO. (2014). Conference outcome document: Rome declaration on nutrition. In Proceedings of the Second International Conference on Nutrition, Rome, Italy, 19–21 November 2014.

Fasolin, L. H., Pereira, R. N., Pinheiro, A. C., Martins, J. T., Andrade, C., Ramos, O., & Vicente, A. (2019). Emergent food proteins–Towards sustainability, health and innovation. *Food Research International, 125*, 108586. DOI: 10.1016/j.foodres.2019.108586 PMID: 31554037

Fatoki, O. (2019). Green marketing orientation and environmental and social performance of hospitality firms in South Africa. *Foundations of Management, 11*(1), 277–290. DOI: 10.2478/fman-2019-0023

Fichter, K., Beucker, S., Noack, T., & Springer, S. (2007). Entstehungspfade von Nachhaltigkeitsinnovationen. *Fallstudien und Szenarien zu Einflussfaktoren, Schlüsselakteuren und Internetunterstützung* [Development pathways of sustainable innovation: Case studies and scenarios of influencing factors]. Stuttgart: Fraunhofer IRB-Verlag (nova-net Werkstattreihe).

Fitriasari, F. (2020). How do small and medium enterprise (SME) survive the COVID-19 outbreak? *Jurnal Inovasi Ekonomi, 5*(02). Advance online publication. DOI: 10.22219/jiko.v5i3.11838

Galbreath, J. (2019). Drivers of green innovations: The impact of export intensity, women leaders, and absorptive capacity. *Journal of Business Ethics, 158*(1), 47–61. DOI: 10.1007/s10551-017-3715-z

Geng, R., Mansouri, S. A., & Aktas, E. (2017). The relationship between green supply chain management and performance: A meta-analysis of empirical evidences in Asian emerging economies. *International Journal of Production Economics, 183*, 245–258. DOI: 10.1016/j.ijpe.2016.10.008

Gladwin, T. N., Kennelly, J. J., & Krause, T. S. (1995). Shifting Paradigms for Sustainable Development: Implications for Management Theory and Research. *Academy of Management Review, 20*(4), 874–907. DOI: 10.2307/258959

Global Innovation Index. (2018). *Key findings report*. https://www.globalinnovationindex.org/about-gii#keyfindings

Goodman, J., Korsunova, A., & Halme, M. (2017). Our collaborative future: Activities and roles of stakeholders in sustainability-oriented innovation. *Business Strategy and the Environment, 26*(6), 731–753. DOI: 10.1002/bse.1941

Hall, J., & Wagner, M. (2012). Integrating sustainability into firms' processes: Performance effects and the moderating role of business models and innovation. *Business Strategy and the Environment, 21*(3), 183–196. DOI: 10.1002/bse.728

Halme, M., & Korpela, M. (2014). Responsible innovation toward sustainable development in small and medium-sized enterprises. A resource perspective. *Business Strategy and the Environment, 23*(8), 547–566. DOI: 10.1002/bse.1801

Han & Chen (2021) 800 Survey TRA To uncover the antecedents of eco-innovation adoption by SMEs in Myanmar Customer demands, Environmental concerns and regulations, Rivalry pressures, Eco-innovation adoption, and Firm innovation capabilities.

Hanelt, A., Busse, S., & Kolbe, L. M. (2016). Driving business transformation toward sustainability: Exploring the impact of supporting IS on the performance contribution of eco-innovations. *Information Systems Journal, 27*(4), 463–502. DOI: 10.1111/isj.12130

Hansen, E., Große-Dunker, F., & Reichwald, R. (2009). Sustainable innovation cube—A framework to evaluate sustainability-oriented innovations. *International Journal of Innovation Management, 13*(4), 683–713. DOI: 10.1142/S1363919609002479

Hart, S. L., Milstein, M. B., & Caggiano, J. (2003). Creating sustainable value [and executive commentary]. *The Academy of Management Executive (1993–2005)*, 17(2), 56.

Hasan, Z., & Ali, N. A. (2015). The impact of green marketing strategy on the firm's performance in Malaysia. *Procedia: Social and Behavioral Sciences, 172*, 463–470. DOI: 10.1016/j.sbspro.2015.01.382

Hellström, T. (2007). Dimensions of environmentally sustainable innovation: The structure of eco-innovation concepts. *Sustainable Development (Bradford), 15*(3), 148–159. DOI: 10.1002/sd.309

Henchion, M., Hayes, M., Mullen, A. M., Fenelon, M., & Tiwari, B. (2017). Future protein supply and demand: Strategies and factors influencing a sustainable equilibrium. *Foods, 6*(7), 53. DOI: 10.3390/foods6070053 PMID: 28726744

Hojnik, J., & Ruzzier, M. (2016). The Driving Forces of Process Eco-innovation and Its Impact on Performance: Insights from Slovenia. *Journal of Cleaner Production, 133*, 812–825. DOI: 10.1016/j.jclepro.2016.06.002

Huhtala, J., Mattila, P., Sihvonen, A., & Tikkanen, H. (2014). Barriers to innovation diffusion in industrial networks – a systematic combining approach. In Woodside, A., Pattison, H., & Marshall, R. (Eds.), *Field Guide For Business-To-Business Case Study Research (Advances in Business Marketing and Management)* (Vol. 21). Emerald. DOI: 10.1108/S1069-096420140000021002

Jenkins, H. (2009). A 'business opportunity' model of corporate social responsibility for small- and medium-sized enterprises. *Business Ethics (Oxford, England)*, *18*(1), 21–36. DOI: 10.1111/j.1467-8608.2009.01546.x

Johnson, M. W., Christensen, C. M., & Kagermann, H. (2008). Reinventing your business model. *Harvard Business Review*, *86*(12), 51–59.

Karjaluoto, H., & Vaccaro, V. L. (2009). B2B green marketing and innovation theory for competitive advantage. *Journal of Systems and Information Technology*, *11*(4), 315–330. DOI: 10.1108/13287260911002477

Kemp, R. (2010). Eco-innovation: Definition, Measurement and Open Research Issues. *Economics and Politics*, *27*(3), 397–420.

Kiefer, C. P., Del Río González, P., & Carrillo-Hermosilla, J. (2018). Drivers and barriers of eco-innovation types for sustainable transitions: A quantitative perspective. *Business Strategy and the Environment*, *107*, 103.

Kinoti, M. (2011). Green marketing intervention strategies and sustainable development: A conceptual paper. *International Journal of Business and Social Science*, *2*(23), 263–273.

Klewitz, J., & Hansen, E. (2014). Sustainability-oriented innovation in SMEs: A systematic literature review. *Journal of Cleaner Production*, *65*, 57–75. DOI: 10.1016/j.jclepro.2013.07.017

Klewitz, J., Zeyen, A., & Hansen, E. G. (2012). Intermediaries driving eco-innovation in SMEs: A qualitative investigation. *European Journal of Innovation Management*, *15*(4), 442–467. DOI: 10.1108/14601061211272376

Kneipp, J. M., Gomes, C. M., Bichueti, R. S., Frizzo, K., & Perlin, A. P. (2019). Sustainable innovation practices and their relationship with the performance of industrial companies, *Rev. Gest˜ao*, *26*(2), 94–111. DOI: 10.1108/REGE-01-2018-0005

Kraśnicka, T., Głód, W., & Wronka-Pośpiech, M. (2018). Management innovation, pro-innovation organisational culture and enterprise performance: Testing the mediation effect. *Review of Managerial Science*, *12*(3), 737–769. DOI: 10.1007/s11846-017-0229-0

Lam, J. S. L., & Li, K. X. (2019). Green port marketing for sustainable growth and development. *Transport Policy*, *84*, 73–81. DOI: 10.1016/j.tranpol.2019.04.011

Lee, J., Baig, F., Talpur, M. A. H., & Shaikh, S. (2021). Public intentions to purchase electric vehicles in Pakistan. *Sustainability (Basel)*, *13*(10), 1–18. DOI: 10.3390/su13105523

Li, L., Msaad, H., Sun, H., Tan, M. X., Lu, Y., & Lau, A. K. W. (2020). Green innovation and business sustainability: New evidence from energy intensive industry in China. *International Journal of Environmental Research and Public Health, 17*(21), 1–18. DOI: 10.3390/ijerph17217826 PMID: 33114610

Lin, C. Y., & Ho, Y. H. (2011). Determinants of green practice adoption for logistics companies in China. *Journal of Business Ethics, 98*(1), 67–83. DOI: 10.1007/s10551-010-0535-9

Linder, M., & Williander, M. (2015). Circular business model innovation: Inherent uncertainties. *Business Strategy and the Environment*. Advance online publication. DOI: 10.1002/bse.1906

Liozu, S. M., & Hinterhuber, A. (2017). Is innovation in pricing your next source of competitive advantage? In *Innovation in Pricing* (pp. 29–46). Routledge.

Luethi, S. (2010). Effective deployment of photovoltaics in the Mediterranean countries: Balancing policy risk and return. *Solar Energy, 84*(6), 1059–1071. DOI: 10.1016/j.solener.2010.03.014

Ma, Y. J., Gam, H. J., & Banning, J. (2017). *Perceived ease of use and usefulness of sus-tainability labels on apparel products: Application of the technology acceptance model*. Fashion and Textiles., DOI: 10.1186/s40691-017-0093-1

Magretta, J. (2002). Why business models matter. *Harvard Business Review, 80*(5), 86–92. PMID: 12024761

Maletic, M., Maletic, D., Dahlgaard, J., Dahlgaard-Park, S. M., & Gomišcek, B. (2015). Do corporate sustainability practices enhance organizational economic performance? *International Journal of Quality and Service Sciences, 2015*(7), 184–200. DOI: 10.1108/IJQSS-02-2015-0025

March, J. G. (1991). Exploration and exploitation in organizational learning. *Organization Science, 2*(1), 71–87. DOI: 10.1287/orsc.2.1.71

Mousa, S. K., & Othman, M. (2020). The impact of green human resource management practices on sustainable performance in healthcare organisations: A conceptual framework. *Journal of Cleaner Production, 243*, 118595. DOI: 10.1016/j.jclepro.2019.118595

Muisyo, P. K., & Qin, S. (2021). Enhancing the FIRM'S green performance through green HRM: The moderating role of green innovation culture. *Journal of Cleaner Production, 289*, 125720. DOI: 10.1016/j.jclepro.2020.125720

Nadathur, S., Wanasundara, J., & Scanlin, L. (2017). Proteins in the diet: Challenges in feeding the global population. In *Sustainable Protein Sources* (pp. 1–19). Elsevier. DOI: 10.1016/B978-0-12-802778-3.00001-9

Noci, G., & Verganti, R. (1999). Managing 'green' product innovation in small firms. *R & D Management*, *29*(1), 3–15. DOI: 10.1111/1467-9310.00112

Omri, A. (2020). Technological innovation and sustainable development : Does the stage of development matter? *Environmental Impact Assessment Review*, *83*, 106398. DOI: 10.1016/j.eiar.2020.106398

Osterwalder, A., Pigneur, Y., & Tucci, C. L. (2005). Clarifying business models: Origins, present, and future of the concept. *Communications of the Association for Information Systems*, *15*, 1–25. DOI: 10.17705/1CAIS.01601

Ryoo, S. Y., & Koo, C. (2013). Green practices-IS alignment and environmental performance: The mediating effects of coordination. *Information Systems Frontiers*, *15*(5), 799–814. DOI: 10.1007/s10796-013-9422-0

Schaltegger, S., Lüdeke-Freund, F., & Hansen, E. (2012). Business cases for sustainability: The role of business model innovation for corporate sustainability. *International Journal of Innovation and Sustainable Development*, *6*(2), 95–119. DOI: 10.1504/IJISD.2012.046944

Schaltegger, S., & Wagner, M. (2011). Sustainable entrepreneurship and sustainability innovation: Categories and interactions. *Business Strategy and the Environment*, *20*(4), 222–237. DOI: 10.1002/bse.682

Scheyvens, R., Banks, G., & Hughes, E. (2016). The private sector and the SDGs: The need to move beyond 'business as usual. *Sustainable Development (Bradford)*, *24*(6), 371–382. DOI: 10.1002/sd.1623

Schiederig, T., Tietze, F., & Herstatt, C. (2012). Green innovation in technology and innovation management—An exploratory literature review. *R & D Management*, *42*(2), 180–192. DOI: 10.1111/j.1467-9310.2011.00672.x

Shaw, D. R. (2010). Value creation in multi-level networks: a development of business model theory. In *PACIS 2010 Proceedings*; 25–36.

Singh, S., Tan, B. C., & Khan, N. (2017). Driving green practice adoption in restaurant sector: Restaurant operator's perspectives - MMU institutional repository. In *Proceedings of the 5th International Conference on Innovation and Entrepreneurship (ICIE 2017)* (pp. 219–226). Academic Conferences and Publishing International Limited. https://shdl.mmu.edu.my/7108/. Accessed 24 April 2021.

Smith, W. K., & Tushman, M. L. (2005). Managing strategic contradictions: A top management model for managing innovation streams. *Organization Science*, *16*(5), 522–536. DOI: 10.1287/orsc.1050.0134

Spieth, P., Schneckenberg, D., & Ricart, J. E. (2014). Business model innovation – state of the art and future challenges for the field. *R & D Management*, *44*(3), 237–247. DOI: 10.1111/radm.12071

Stubbs, W., & Cocklin, C. (2008). Conceptualizing a 'sustainability business model'. *Organization & Environment*, *21*(2), 103–127. DOI: 10.1177/1086026608318042

Sukma, N., & Leelasantitham, A. (2022a). A community sustainability ecosystem modeling for water supply business in Thailand. *Frontiers in Environmental Science*, *10*, 940955. DOI: 10.3389/fenvs.2022.940955

Sukma, N., & Leelasantitham, A. (2022b). From conceptual model to conceptual framework: A sustainable business framework for community water supply businesses. *Frontiers in Environmental Science*, *10*, 1013153. DOI: 10.3389/fenvs.2022.1013153

Taylor, A., & Helfat, C. E. (2009). Organizational linkages for surviving technological change: Complementary assets, middle management, and ambidexterity. *Organization Science*, *20*(4), 718–739. DOI: 10.1287/orsc.1090.0429

Teece, D. J. (2010). Business models, business strategy and innovation. *Long Range Planning*, *43*(2/3), 172–194. DOI: 10.1016/j.lrp.2009.07.003

Thomas, M., Costa, D., & Oliveira, T. (2016). Assessing the role of IT-enabled process virtualization on green IT adoption. *Information Systems Frontiers*, *18*(4), 693–710. DOI: 10.1007/s10796-015-9556-3

Tidd, J., & Bessant, J. R. (2009). *Managing innovation. Integrating technological, market and organizational change* (4th ed.). Wiley.

Tseng, M. L., Tan, R. R., & Siriban-Manalang, A. B. (2013). Sustainable consumption and production for Asia: Sustainability through green design and practice. *Journal of Cleaner Production*, *40*, 1–5. DOI: 10.1016/j.jclepro.2012.07.015

United Nations. (1987). Report of the World Commission on Environment and Development: Our Common Future; UN Documents; United Nations: New York, NY, USA.

United Nations. (2016). *New urban green innovation agenda. Draft Resolution Submitted by the President of the General Assembly*. Available online: https://habitat3.org/wp-content/uploads/N1639668-English.pdf (accessed on 24 May 2020).

Van de Ven. Angle, H. L., & Poole, M. S. (Eds.) (2000/1989). *Research on the Management of Innovations: The Minnesota Studies*. Oxford, New York: Oxford University Press.

Van de Ven. Polley, D., Garud, S., & Venkataraman, S. (2008). *The innovation journey* (2nd ed.). New York: Oxford University Press.

Voss, G. B., & Voss, Z. G. (2013). Strategic ambidexterity in small and medium-sized enterprises: Implementing exploration and exploitation in product and market domains. *Organization Science*, *24*(5), 1459–1477. DOI: 10.1287/orsc.1120.0790

Wen, H., Lee, C. C., & Song, Z. (2021). Digitalization and environment: How does ICT affect enterprise environmental performance? *Environmental Science and Pollution Research International*, *28*(39), 54826–54841. DOI: 10.1007/s11356-021-14474-5 PMID: 34014481

Wicki, S., Hansen, E. G., & Schaltegger, S. (2015). Exploration of Green Technologies in SMEs: the Role of Ambidexterity, Domain Separation and Commercialization, *XXVI ISPIM Innovation Conference*, 14-17 June 2015, Budapest, Hungary.

Winn, M., & Kirchgeorg, M. (2005). The siesta is over: a rude awakening from sustainability myopia. In Sharma, S., & Starik, M. (Eds.), *Corporate Environmental Strategy and Competitive Advantage* (pp. 232–258). Elgar. DOI: 10.4337/9781845426859.00017

World Commission on Environment and Development (WCED). (1987). *Report of the World Commission on Environment and Development: Our Common Future*. WCED, United Nations.

Wu, J., Liao, H., Wang, J. W., & Chen, T. (2019). The role of environmental concern in the public acceptance of autonomous electric vehicles: A survey from China. *Transportation Research Part F: Traffic Psychology and Behaviour*, *60*, 37–46. DOI: 10.1016/j.trf.2018.09.029

Zollo, M., Cennamo, C., & Neumann, K. (2013). Beyond what and why: Understanding organizational evolution towards sustainable enterprise models. [https://do]. *Organization & Environment*, *26*(3), 241–259. DOI: 10.1177/1086026613496433

Zott, C., Amit, R., & Massa, L. (2011). The business model: Recent developments and future research. *Journal of Management*, *37*(4), 1019–1042. DOI: 10.1177/0149206311406265

Chapter 3
Unveiling the Urban Fringe:
Brazilian National Urban Policy's Impact on Peri-Urban Informal Settlements in São Paulo

Milena Albrecht Silveira
http://orcid.org/0000-0001-6132-084X
Politecnico di Milano, Italy

Thaís Maria Rossetto
https://orcid.org/0000-0003-2670-6223
Universidade Estadual de Campinas, Brazil

ABSTRACT

This chapter focuses on how Brazil's national urban policy has affected peri-urbanization in São Paulo. Since the Federal Constitution of 1988, the idea of property social function was established, leading to the development of the City Statute. This law includes instruments related to informal settlements, such as collective adverse possession. The REURB Law of 2017 further modified this instrument and guaranteed security of tenure through the formal possession of properties. Within the city of São Paulo, the chapter aims to highlight how the 2014 Master Plan implemented these policies. For this purpose, the research relies on a case study design, employing an inductive and qualitative approach supported by bibliographic and documentary research. The chapter emphasizes some critical issues related to the application of the REURB Law in peri-urban areas, thus identifying pathways to enhance policy implementation through community-driven actions. Additionally, it seeks to provide a theoretical framework that can serve as a panoramic basis for future scientific research in the field.

DOI: 10.4018/979-8-3693-6089-7.ch003

1. INTRODUCTION

With more than 11 million inhabitants (IBGE, 2022), the urban sprawl phenomenon is no news to Brazil's biggest city. Sao Paulo's rapid growth has been an emblematic urbanization trend shaping the Global South scenario. Amidst this context, a national urban agenda has been gradually implemented to address social demands arising from decades of massive rural-urban migration, unbridled urban growth, profound social and economic inequality, and environmental conflicts (Pioletti & Dalla Vecchia, 2022). The demographic explosion resulting from this process led to the deepening of the social abyss and the precariousness of urban life for the lower classes.

The compilation of social issues with the exclusionary development processes of the neoliberal city reflects the expansion of the "informal city", where informal processes and irregular occupation become the most plausible alternative for economically marginalized citizens to access urban land. Informal settlements reflect Brazilian socioeconomic segregation by being established in peri-urban areas of the city, where environmentally fragile areas are often found and, therefore, not targeted by the speculative real estate market (Fernandes, 2018).

Starting from this current scenario, the objective is to provide a comprehensive and realistic assessment through case study analysis in a selected neighbourhood within the scope of the São Paulo Master Plan (2014) and recent legislation. This chapter examines the impact of Brazilian urban policy on peri-urbanization in the city of São Paulo, focusing on the evolution of political instruments and proposed community approaches. The discussion proposed regarding the recognition of advancements and/or setbacks imposed by the implementation of urban legislation in São Paulo is considered of utmost importance.

1.1. Conceptualising blurred notions

Understanding and unblurring the concept of peri-urban areas is crucial before delving into the chapter. Buxton (2022) states that peri-urban areas are non-urban landscapes adjacent to or surrounding metropolitan settlements. These regions are defined by their spatial relationships with metropolitan areas on their inner boundary and rural areas on their outer boundary. As mega-urban regions continue to expand, particularly in the Global South, they consume the rural areas surrounding cities, making peri-urban regions some of the fastest-growing areas globally.

According to Rajendran et al. (2024), the term "peri-urban" is used loosely with no consensus on its definition. However, by acknowledging that this concept was developed in the European context, it is possible to recognize the inherent and embedded Western approach to knowledge production concerning urbanity and rurality. This Eurocentric perspective presents issues because it fails to consider its geographical implications.

This chapter will explore and use the concept of peri-urban in the Brazilian context, which is closely related to urban sprawl and the formation of what can be termed "informal settlements." Specifically, within the São Paulo metropolis, these areas are not yet regularized by legislation and, therefore, excluded from the discourse of the right to the city. Fedeli posits that

"We are experiencing a phase under which the distinction between urban and non-urban is less evident. Not only because the physical boundaries between urbanised and non-urbanised areas are more eroded than ever, within processes of agglomeration and interconnections. But because urban and non-urban lifestyles are more than ever hybridised, with severe consequences for how the traditional right to the city is conceived and expressed". (Fedeli, 2022, p.280)

In the Brazilian context, Rolnik (2015, p.177) discusses self-produced popular neighbourhoods (or "informal settlements") through the plurality of orders. Still referred to as clandestine or irregular subdivisions, it is common in Brazil to "purchase small plots of land from small landowners and farmers on the outskirts of urban areas, which is one of the most widespread forms of urban settlement production (...)". Often, this transaction is done in a notary's office, in front of witnesses, making it legal. However, even if an individual possesses a document proving the legality of the purchase, "the subdivision is illegal because it violates zoning and land subdivision legislation or because the landowner did not apply for (or did not receive) a permit to subdivide." In the aforementioned example, illegality and legality are interconnected on different levels, whether they are urban, environmental, or civil orders.

Although acknowledging that language does matter (Gilbert, 2007) and that the term 'informal' has been discussed and problematised by some authors (Rolnik, 2015; Roy, 2005) due to the fact that it implies that informality is not an integral part of the urbanisation process, this particular term will be pertinent to the discussion specifically concerning the legality of the settlements presented here, as a way to facilitated the understanding and avoiding the use of terms like slums, illegal city, squatters or impermanent communities that had already been so indelicately oversimplified and spread in the academic community.

Thus, this study contributes to the ongoing discourse on urban policy and planning in peri-urban areas, especially regarding their treatment and implementation of national policies. It delves into the São Paulo context, however it can offer valuable lessons for other similar urban contexts.

2. METHODOLOGY

The research employs an inductive method and qualitative approach, incorporating bibliographic and documentary research. Connections were drawn between relevant concepts and federal and municipal laws and instruments governing the spatial planning of urban areas in São Paulo, Brazil. This scope was applied through a case study of Cidade Tiradentes, a neighbourhood situated in the eastern periphery of São Paulo (Figure 1). The study timeline spans from 2014, marking the establishment of the current Master Plan, through the end of 2023.

Figure 1. Map of the study's location. From left to right, in red, São Paulo State, São Paulo City, and Cidade Tiradentes

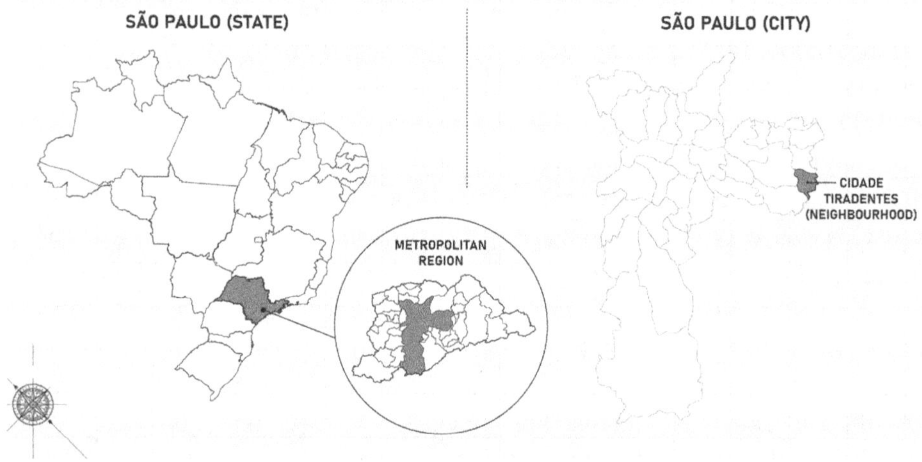

Source: elaborated by the authors.

The neighbourhood was characterized and analyzed using tools provided by the São Paulo Municipal Government, such as "GeoSampa," a georeferencing data website, and the Regional Plans of the Subprefectures, which include diagnostic reports, analysis, and action perimeters of public policies in each neighbourhood. These documents and thematic maps were crucial tools for understanding urban dynamics influenced by implemented public policies in the area. Based on this framework, critical aspects such as urban infrastructure, housing, access to public services, and socio-environmental characteristics were taken into consideration. The selection of these aspects aligns with the "Guide for the Mapping and Characterization of Informal Settlements" published by the Ministry of Cities, where they are presented as important variables in the characterization and intervention in informal settlements, "with the aim of ensuring housing, as well as land tenure regularization and a basic level of infrastructure, accessibility, and socio-spatial inclusion" (Brasil, 2010, p. 8).

By analyzing urban infrastructure and public services, the goal was to assess whether the area is underserved. This determination was guided by studies on deprivation (D'Ambrosio & Rodrigues, 2008), which provided a structured approach to evaluating the level of service provision in the neighbourhood. Housing is a crucial element in this study to determine the living conditions, and the configuration of an 'informal settlement', either because of the self-produced nature of architecture or for the legal status of the land (Rolnik, 2015), and also to consider the presence of ZEIS and public housing in the area. Socio-environmental characteristics involve taking into consideration the demographics and environmentally sensitive zones. This dual focus helps to identify where social factors such as poverty and inequality may be exacerbating environmental issues.

This approach enabled documentation of the planned and executed interventions under the municipal master plan between 2014 and 2023, aimed at evaluating their effectiveness in improving residents' quality of life in Cidade Tiradentes. By integrating spatial analysis with the aforementioned qualitative aspects that represent important variables in the urban and social characterization of a given area, as well as quantitative data such as social and demographic indicators, access to services and housing, and land use, present in the Subprefecture Booklet for Cidade Tiradentes. The study aims to provide substantial insights by identifying faced challenges and emerging opportunities through the application of municipal policies and instruments.

3. RESULTS AND DISCUSSION: IMPACT OF URBAN POLICY ON INFORMAL SETTLEMENTS

3.1. Brief Overview of Brazil's National Urban Policy

It is important to note that social movements have demanded access to housing, welfare and urban services and equality as priorities since the 60s. (Pioletti & Dalla Vecchia, 2022). However, this section will briefly discuss national urban policies post-democratization.

In 1987, The National Urban Reform Forum (Fórum Nacional de Reforma Urbana) was established, unifying more than 40 movements that tackled urban issues (Maricato, 1988) through the Constitutional Amendment of Popular Initiative (Popular Amendment No.63 of 1987). Even though only partially approved, the amendment could be considered the very first step towards this new legal urban order. It included important advancements, such as the universal right to decent urban living conditions, and proposed instruments like the special 'usucapiao' for housing purposes, a form of adverse possession. Considerations that had been ignored in the previous constitution, drawn up during the military regime in 1969, which "had failed to acknowledge the predominantly urban nature of modern Brazil." (Bassul, 2010) A fact that led 'land' to be a major concern in the urban reform since it has been left out of the agenda so far, being regulated by the market. At this point, real estate speculation had driven the expansion of peri-urban areas and urban sprawl in major cities like São Paulo, fueled by rising land values in city centers, often caused by the practice of leaving land vacant to sell at a higher price later on.

The Federal Constitution (FC) of 1988 was a significant milestone in the Brazilian urban agenda, featuring two chapters on urban development policies. It adopted decent housing as a fundamental right, drawing attention to problems such as the precariousness of the living conditions in informal dwellers. In addition, it addressed the 'land' concern by establishing the social function of properties, as explicitly stated in Article 5, XXIII. However, the principle of social function of property was made subject to a federal provision (Pioletti & Dalla Vecchia, 2022) and must be regulated by the issuance of municipal Master Plans.

In 2001, the federal government set out urban policy guidelines, namely the City Statute (CS), to regulate the innovations introduced by the FC. The CS consisted of a legal framework in the form of guidelines, setting tools for the municipalities to deal with urban issues, which recognised more autonomy to local governments since their application must be regulated by municipal legislation.

Despite the constraints and drawbacks of its application, the CS represented a significant step towards combating the country's social inequalities. It included several instruments regarding the regularization of land tenure in low-income neighbourhoods and informal settlements, which will be explained in detail in the following sections of this chapter.

Another important step, considering the global attention to the urban question, was the establishment of the Ministry of Cities in 2003. The Ministry was tasked with the creation, oversight, and funding of urban development policies, as well as specific policies related to housing, environmental sanitation, and urban transportation (Pioletti & Dalla Vecchia, 2022) under one umbrella, facilitating more cohesive and effective governance. Several sectoral programs followed its creation, such as the institutionalization of the National Cities Council and the creation of the National Programme of Land Tenure Regularization in 2004, as well as the Minha Casa, Minha Vida (Law nº 11.977) federal programme introduced in 2009. This characterized a period of great excitement and expectations for the urban scenario in Brazil.

"Participation was considered the main driver of the democratization of public policies. It dealt with social inclusion and reduction of inequalities and resulted in some participatory budgeting experiences, municipal conferences and partici-

patory master plan definition, but also public debates and public audiences. For the first time, the elaboration of municipal master plans was made compulsory in municipalities with more than 20,000 inhabitants". (Pioletti & Dalla Vecchia, 2022, p.198)

Between 2004 and 2016, many other essential policies and frameworks were proposed and introduced, strengthening the Brazilian urban agenda and aiming to tackle pressing issues like climate change, metropolization, basic infrastructure, etc. However, political instability and changes in governance imposed drawbacks on implementing reforms and the continuity of national programs. The Ministry of Cities was dissolved (only to be re-established in 2023), and well-established programs were changed (Minha Casa, Minha Vida changed to Minha Casa Verde Amarela beneficiating upper-level housing categories that are more profitable for the real estate business).

Land tenure regularization has been provided for in art. 2o of the CS as follows:

"Article 2. The objective of urban policy is to regulate the full development of the social functions of the city and urban property through the following general guidelines: [...] XIV – land regularization and urbanization of areas occupied by low-income populations through the establishment of special regulations for urbanization, land use and occupation, and building standards, taking into account the socioeconomic situation of the population and environmental regulations;" (Brasil, 2001).

With the introduction of the Urban Land Regularization Law (Reurb), Law No. 13.465/2017, the process of urban land regularization changed from the methods established by Law No. 11.977/2009[1], focusing particularly on the social function of the properties being regularized (Pereira, 2023). It also introduced the legal institution of land legitimization in Article 23, which consists of a formal process. "Land legitimization" involves gaining legal ownership rights for individuals who have built or own a building with urban use in either public or private areas within an informal urban area established before December 22, 2016 (Pioletti & Dalla Vecchia, 2022).

Criticism arose regarding the mechanisms altering the process of disposing of federal buildings. The Reurb Law allowed the sale of public lands, including those where settlements have occurred since the Agrarian Reform and encompassing urban areas occupied by low-income families. According to Article 22, municipalities have taken on the responsibility of managing land division, but local governments often face influence from landlords, making it difficult to achieve a land division that aligns with the equality principles of the Agrarian Reform. This had a direct impact on informal settlements, which, in the Brazilian context, often emerged from occupation processes.

It is understood that one of the main factors contributing to the appearance of these settlements is speculative land markets. Real estate speculation drives up urban land prices rapidly, making housing unaffordable for low-income populations. As a result, access to urban land and, consequently, adequate housing is hindered. Additionally, clientelism within political systems exacerbates the issue, as in such systems, land access is often controlled by political groups or influential individuals who distribute land in a non-transparent manner based on personal relationships and political favours, perpetuating an unjust distribution of land.

Elitist legal regimes also contribute to the lack of access to land and adequate housing for the most vulnerable. Laws and regulations are often designed to favor the interests of the economic and political elite, making it difficult for low-income populations to access legally recognized land with basic services. In summary, the proliferation of informal settlements in peri-urban areas is intrinsically linked to speculative land markets, clientelism-based political systems, and elitist legal regimes (Fernandes, 2018).

In this unequal and exclusionary context of Brazilian society, structurally ingrained limitations are evident in the process of ensuring minimal conditions for decent housing for the population. Although they are slowly incorporated into the city through specific urbanization and regularization actions, there is a lack of incisive measures aiming to eliminate precariousness by addressing underlying issues. The dynamic between legal and illegal orders complexifies the issue of peri-urban areas occupied by informal settlements. Holston (2013, cited in Rolnik, 2015, p.179) conceptualizes the

> *"legal and bureaucratic irresolution" that permeates these areas, which develop "as an arena of conflicts over land where the distinctions between legal and illegal occupation are temporary and the relationships between them, dangerously unstable. In this context, the law often produces unsolvable procedural and substantive complexities; this legal-bureaucratic irresolution always leads to extrajudicial solutions [...]. Thus, land legislation promotes conflicts, not resolutions."*

Fernandes (2018, p.17) acknowledges the importance of policies such as land regularization but warns of the need to address the issue as a whole through "the construction of alternatives to expand the formal market and, on the other hand, to rethink the ways of formulating legislation, avoiding translating forms into law but building practices/proposals that respond to our reality." In other words, regularization programs become merely mitigating when dissociated from broader guidelines of planning, management, and public policies that aim to deeply intervene and reverse the exclusionary and unequal dynamics of urban development. Fernandes (2018) concludes that regularization should have as its primary objective not only the recognition of legal security of tenure for occupants but also the promotion of socio-spatial integration of informal settlements. In this context, regularization seeks not only to legitimize individual property but also to foster social and spatial inclusion of the residents in these areas.

3.2. Specific policies for informal settlements

Among national policies and programs, this section will explain in more detail those that include instruments that directly affect informal urban settlements, specifically in peri-urban areas. Within the City Statute, the most influential instruments include Collective Adverse Possession, allowing communities residing in informal settlements to acquire legal ownership of the land they occupy, Social Interest Zones (ZEIS), corresponding to designated areas where informal settlements are located prioritizing their regularization and provision of basic infrastructure and services, and Joint Urban Operations (OUC), public-private partnerships designed to regenerate degraded urban areas by leveraging anticipated future value gains from private sector investments to fund current development projects. In addition, it is also worth mentioning the mandatory implementation of the Master Plans (Plano Diretor) in cities with more than 20,000.

3.2.1. Collective Adverse Possession and the Reurb Law

The REURB Law, or Law No. 13.465/2017, has been fundamental in addressing issues regarding informal settlements since it facilitates the legalization of land tenure in consolidated areas.

The REURB Law establishes two distinct types of urban land regularization processes for informal settlements: REURB-S (Regularização Fundiária Urbana de Interesse Social) and REURB-E (Regularização Fundiária Urbana de Interesse Específico). The former benefits low-income populations living in informal settlements by providing the proper legalization. The law contributes to the social inclusion of the residents, who become more empowered to participate actively in economic, social, and political life. The latter is designed for settlements that do not fall under the social interest category.

An important advance is establishing the municipality's duty to work towards regularization in the appropriate cases (REURB-S), especially considering that often, individuals entitled to the benefits of collective adverse possession are unaware of this right or the measures to request its protection (Pereira, 2023).

The importance of the aforementioned regularization actions is understood; however, various weaknesses are identified in producing more effective impacts against socio-spatial and economic inequality. It is acknowledged that by properly legalizing irregular peri-urban areas, the law contributes to including residents in the formal city. However, when applied in isolation and only mitigatively, "the regulation of urban land does not necessarily guarantee access to certain urban infrastructure and the integration of residents into the city in practice" (Castro, 2022, p. 72). This proposition indicates the relevance of articulating regularization programs with other public policies, strategies, and urban guidelines that act against the intrinsic inequality and exclusion inherent in the growth of Brazilian cities.

3.2.2. Social Interest Zones (ZEIS)

In the 1980s, the demarcation of Special Zones of Social Interest (ZEIS) was initially conceived as a response to the demand from irregular settlements for recognition and urban integration. Since then, it has emerged as a fundamental instrument in Urban Development Plans and municipal laws governing land use and occupation in Brazil. Subsequently incorporated into the Statute of Cities, this strategy has become a cornerstone of municipal land policies, focusing on implementing housing projects and programs targeted at low-income populations.

Generally, ZEIS are areas designated in urban zoning for priority allocation to Social Interest Housing. These areas may encompass locations characterized by informal and precarious settlements, often involving some form of irregularity, as well as vacant areas, preferably situated in regions with adequate infrastructure. By signalling the recognition of these informally occupied areas, this approach facilitates land and urban regularization, functioning as a strategic tool for land management aimed at providing land for the construction of new social housing units (Rolnik & Santoro, 2014).

The inclusion of ZEIS in urban planning is recognized as a systematic attempt to address urban challenges related to precarious housing and the unplanned expansion of Brazilian cities. However, Ribeiro, Daniel & Abiko (2016)[2] indicate that the "property regularization efforts within land registry offices indicate a lack of political prioritization and scant provision of public amenities. Evidently, as a zoning tool, ZEIS has yet to facilitate the most equitable processes of occupation". To achieve greater effectiveness, the path indicated by the authors emphasizes the importance of integrating ZEIS with other innovative and realistic strategies concerning Brazil's housing issues.

3.2.3. Joint Urban Operations (OUC)

According to the definition contained in the City Statute, the Joint Urban Operations (OUC) consists of a municipal law constituted as the integrated set of measures and interventions organized by the Municipal Public Authority aimed at achieving "structural urban transformations, social improvements, and environmental valorization" within a designated area (article 32, BRASIL, 2001). This instrument highlights the importance of the participation of "owners, residents, permanent users, and private investors" throughout the entire process. In São Paulo, according to the Article 138 of the Strategic Master Plan (PDE), in general terms, Joint Urban Operations were implemented with the purpose of

> *I - optimizing the use of underutilized areas through urban interventions; II - implementing strategic facilities for urban development; III - expanding and improving the public transportation system, infrastructure networks, and structural road system; IV - promoting environmental recovery of contaminated areas and flood-prone areas; V - establishing social public facilities, public spaces, and green areas; VI - promoting Social Interest Housing Projects and urbanizing and regularizing precarious settlements; VII - protecting, recovering, and enhancing environmental, historical, and cultural heritage; VIII - promoting economic development and revitalizing areas to generate jobs (SÃO PAULO, 2014).*

Despite the scope presented emphasizing concerns regarding improvements for the most vulnerable segments of the population, its implementation has been strongly influenced by the financialization of the city. Broadly speaking, these operations followed the existing logic of benefiting private actors, but what sets them apart is their "fragmented vision of the city," creating conditions of exceptionality in specific locations deemed key to altering processes of urban decline, concentrating all efforts and investments there while neglecting a holistic urban vision and the most precarious areas. Nobre (2018) highlights the problematic freedom of decision granted to private initiatives, as public authorities relinquish their role in planning and coordinating the entire process.

3.3. Role of the 2014 São Paulo Strategic Master Plan and Additional Municipal Laws

São Paulo's 2014 Strategic Master Plan (PDE) was developed as a revision of the Master Plan approved in 2002, following the requirements and guidelines of the CS. It presents a strong focus on "ways of fighting the widespread practice of speculation of land by real estate developers, which results in huge unoccupied private areas waiting to obtain the best value" (Anelli, 2018, p.18).

One of the main tools set out by the PDE is the definition of eight Macrozones that determine priorities and regulate which instruments can be used to tackle the most pressing challenges in these defined areas. In the case of peri-urban informal settlements, many of those were included in the border of two or more zones, such as the Macro Areas for the Reduction of Urban Vulnerability (MRVU), Macro Areas for the Reduction of Urban Vulnerability and Environmental Recovery (MRVURA).

This aspect increased the complexity with conflicts between the general guidelines for each zone and local specificities.

While acknowledging the strides made in the PDE, various scholars (Silva, 2021; Ribeiro, Daniel, & Abiko, 2016) highlight the partial fulfilment of the plan's objectives. They note that there persists an overlap of areas and, consequently, a certain conflict of standards.

Regarding informal settlements, the plan also aims to regulate the aforementioned instruments provided by the CS, establishing mechanisms for the regularization of land in peri-urban areas. The Strategic Master Plan foresees the creation of The Urban Development Fund (FUNDURB) from which 30% of the funds would be allocated to the acquisition of well-located land for the development of social housing and providing subsidies for housing programs. In addition, it addresses the Joint Urban Operations (OUC) and Urban Intervention Area (AIU) with also 25% of resources for promoting housing of social interest. The PDE also regulated the forms of local participation in the OUCs (Anelli, 2018).

However, the main instrument that "highlighted the city government's intention to designate available land for social housing construction" (Ribeiro, Daniel, & Abiko, 2016) was the demarcation of ZEIS, already present in the previous plan from 2002.

The need to establish a legislative foundation for the municipality's housing policy arose in 1992, with several municipal decrees in the following years. After the 2014 PDE, changes were needed to incorporate its proposals and boost housing production by the private market. This was achieved through the relaxation of regulations, the creation of ZEIS 5[3], and the promotion of Social Interest Housing (HIS) and Market-Rate Housing (HMP) along Urban Transformation Axes near major public transport networks (Teixeira, 2018).

The Municipal Decree n° 56.759 from 2016 (São Paulo,2016c) provides several changes aligned with the objectives of the PDE. For instance, it stimulates the density of areas designated as ZEIS by increasing the floor area ratio (coeficiente de aproveitamento C.A.) from 2.5 to 4 in ZEIS 2 areas. The Occupancy Rate (T.O.) was also relaxed from 0.50 to 0.80. The incentive to increase density in ZEIS 2 areas results in a concentration within the MRVU and the MRVURA, where most of these plots are located. In previous decrees, the parameters used to define urban planning indices referred to the typology[4]. Decree 56.759 uses the PDE's macro zones to define the urban planning parameters regardless of the type of housing typology (Teixeira, 2018).

In the same year, another Municipal Decree regulating ZEIS was established (DM nº 57.377/16). The changes between both regulations are slight and point to legislative fragmentation and weak compliance with the ZEIS as instruments for urban regularization and promotion of social housing. In this scenario, the mechanisms for confronting socio-spatial inequality are directed towards fiscal and urban planning permissiveness in favour of the private sector and profitability, such as the regulation of the Joint Urban Operations (OUC) that brings market interests closer to neoliberal ideals.

In his research on São Paulo's urban planning, Nobre (2018, p. 229-230) links the direct rise of neoliberalism through Strategic Urban Planning with implementing major urban operations as manifestations of urban entrepreneurship and financialization. The author also points out the regressive and exclusionary fiscal outcomes resulting from using the OUCs in São Paulo, evidenced by the significant concentration of investments in specific areas of real estate and elitist interest. Concurrently, there is a process of gentrification through the spontaneous or forced 'expulsion' of the most vulnerable and low-income populations.

The 2014 São Paulo Strategic Plan and the additional municipal degrees play a crucial role in shaping the city's peri-urban areas, as they define the priorities, axes, and implementation of the guidelines established by the CS. There is an emphasis on substantial, dense developments in ZEIS 2, located mainly in these peripheral areas, alongside areas experiencing financial capital expansion, like Joint Urban Operations and Urban Structuring and Transformation Axes. Furthermore, it is noted that the revision of the decrees gradually shifted focus away from being an instrument intended for an inclusive public policy, as in the first version, to making room for the expansion of the real estate and construction sectors (Teixeira, 2018).

3.3.1. Local Impacts of Urban Policies and Proposed Approaches: The Case of Cidade Tiradentes

With 74% of its territory composed of ZEIS-1 and ZEIS-2, the Cidade Tiradentes neighbourhood in the east urban periphery of São Paulo will be discussed in this section as a study case. This area presents itself as of interest for this study because it has been marked 'rural' by some scholars (D'Ambrosio & Rodrigues, 2008), being located in the extreme east of the municipality's administrative boundaries. It is an area that fits the aforementioned concepts of peri-urban, in the Brazilian context, and informal settlement with the emergence of self-produced housing. This characterization has been evidenced with qualitative and quantitative data. D'Ambrosio & Rodrigues's (2008) studies on deprivation show that Cidade Tiradentes ranked as one of the last on the index, meaning that the neighbourhood does not have quality access to basic services.

The neighbourhood is divided into two in the PDE, the majority of it being included in the Environmental Protection and Recovery Macrozone, with only a small portion of the region to the north of the territory being designated as the Urban Structuring and Qualification Macrozone, namely the areas with the Prestes Maia, Inácio Monteiro, and Juscelino Kubitschek complexes (São Paulo, 2016b).

This aspect itself already increases the complexity presenting conflictive objectives for different areas in the same administrative boundary (in this case, the Cidade Tiradentes Subprefecture). Furthermore, the Macrozones are yet divided into Macroareas, as shown in Figure 2, with the former being divided into three different ones, namely the Macroarea for Reduction of Urban Vulnerability and Environmental Recovery, the Macroarea for Urban and Environmental Control and Qualification and the Macroarea for Preservation of Natural Ecosystems (MRVURA, MCQUA and MPEN), and the latter composed of the MRVU.

Figure 2. Map of the Macroares in Cidade Tiradentes

Source: São Paulo, 2016, adapted by the authors.

With a combination of two types of ZEIS and four Macroareas, and considering that urban planning indices are now defined according to the PDE areas rather than housing typology (Teixeira, 2018), with significant encouragement of density increase, these areas face potential risks. Increasing density in peri-urban zones can be particularly problematic due to insufficient investment in critical infrastructure such as sewage systems, transportation, and adequate housing. Moreover, this push for higher density might undermine the objectives of the Macroareas that aim to protect the environment, resulting in conflicting goals within the same Subprefecture, complicating effective implementation. "The lack of public and private investments, combined with the irregularity of land occupation, results in the impairment of environmental service provision in the area" (São Paulo, 2016b, p.7).

Most of the neighbourhood has irregular land tenure. The current housing situation in Cidade Tiradentes is partly constituted by unplanned urban growth, which occurs mainly through the occupation of green and open areas, usually environmentally sensitive. As a result, the Municipal Housing Secretariat (SEHAB), through the Lot Regularization Program of the Department of Land Regularization (RESOLO), conducted various land regularization projects in the following years, for instance, the Vila Yolanda plots, Vila Paulista I e II, Vila Santa Luzia, Jardim Pérola III and the housing complexes built by the SEHAB, the Metropolitan Housing Company of São Paulo (COHAB), and the Housing and Urban Development Company of the State of São Paulo (CDHU), the latter was only made possible thanks to the enactment of Municipal Law 17.859/22, which enabled Urban Land Regularization - REURB for this type of housing developments.

In the process of regularizing these lots, improvements were made in paving, stream channelization, construction of retaining walls, and the implementation of sewerage and drainage networks. Despite the positive impacts generated, these actions are perceived as superficial when applied as remediation for broader issues, while these areas remain segmented from the urban fabric and distant from the services provided within them. Due to their complexity, the issues in these peri-urban areas call for larger-scale actions and investments, such as the comprehensive renewal achieved through OUCs. This approach would enhance the effectiveness of regularization efforts by ensuring that the returns on investment are continuously directed toward the upgrading and ongoing maintenance of areas with high social vulnerability, thereby ensuring substantial social and economic changes.

To support these large-scale actions, fostering community involvement is essential. Integrating residents into the planning process through participatory mechanisms ensures that interventions are tailored to local needs. The Support Material for Participatory Revision of the Regional Plans of the Subprefectures (São Paulo, 2016b), specifically the Subprefecture Booklets, consists of a quantitative diagnosis of socio-economic and territorial indicators designed to assist in the participatory process. As stated in the document, "the citizen will have sufficient content, combined with their knowledge of the territory, to actively contribute to the re-elaboration of their subprefecture's plan." However, given the socio-economic constraints faced by low-income populations, which corresponds to a significant parcel of Cidade Tiradentes' inhabitants, including limited access to information, digital resources, and legal knowledge, laypersons frequently encounter difficulties in interpreting the provided material. Furthermore, the diagnostic process must be grounded in bottom-up approaches, incorporating qualitative data and being developed collaboratively with the community.

As long as planning for these multi-faceted peri-urban areas, such as Cidade Tiradentes, remains rooted in top-down, zoning-focused approaches criticized by numerous scholars (Lindblom, 1959; Sclavi & Buraschi, 2022; Friedmann, 1987) there will persist inherent risks of planning errors and the emergence of conflicting objectives. In this sense, social innovation can offer a promising avenue to enhance inclusivity in the urban planning process. When applied as a bottom-up transcalar approach, it can emphasise initiatives emerging from the community, escaping the 'local trap' (Busacca, 2022), fostering not only urban renewal but also the creation and formalization of jobs and professional development opportunities.

As Busacca (2022, p.335) notes, social innovation "emerges as a policy idea based on social activation as a way of dealing with complex and/or emerging social problems". However, it is crucial to acknowledge that social innovation does not substitute the intervention and responsibilities of the state. It is not a panacea but a complementary mechanism that can work alongside traditional state functions. The concept's vagueness has been one of its strengths, allowing for its adaptation across diverse contexts and meanings. Thus, implementing a transcalar approach in São Paulo requires recognizing the territory as a dynamic space of interaction, ensuring that social innovation initiatives are informed by and responsive to the specific needs and conditions of the communities they aim to serve (Busacca, 2022).

4. CONCLUSIONS

Through critical investigation into the impact of public policies on the informal peri-urban area of São Paulo, this chapter draws parallels between identified issues and contrasts them with innovative approaches and encouragement of bottom-up movements. In assessing the impact of Brazilian national urban policies on informal peri-urban settlements, the findings highlight direct and explicit (D'Albergo, 2010) efforts, such as the establishment of the City Statute and the Reurb Law. Those have provided municipalities with instruments to combat social inequalities and regulate land use. However, the study revealed that despite the progress made through the implementation of national policies in the São Paulo PDE, there remain deep-seated structural limitations and socio-spatial exclusions within Brazilian urban development. By defining eight Macrozones, the PDE aimed to address pressing urban challenges and reduce socio-spatial inequalities. However, the overlapping zones and conflicting guidelines have complicated implementation, particularly in informal settlements. In addition, regularization programs, while beneficial, have not been sufficient on their own. The effectiveness of these policies and regulations is limited by the lack of integration and the overarching influence of market-driven development. This influence is evident in regulatory changes, such as increasing density allowances in ZEIS 2 areas and the relaxation of occupancy rates.

Scholars such as Silva (2021) and Nobre (2018) have critiqued this transition, noting that while the PDE's intentions were to mitigate land speculation and enhance social housing, the implementation has often favoured financial capital and urban entrepreneurship. Ribeiro, Daniel, and Abiko (2016) also highlight that this has led to regressive outcomes, such as gentrification and the marginalization of low-income populations, undermining the plan's original inclusive vision.

The complex interplay of zoning regulations, urban planning indices, and land tenure issues in Cidade Tiradentes highlights the challenges faced in peri-urban development. The encouragement of density increases in ZEIS and Macroareas, without commensurate investment in infrastructure, risks exacerbating existing vulnerabilities. This can lead to environmental degradation and inadequate service provision, further marginalizing already disadvantaged communities. While land regularization efforts by SEHAB and other agencies have led to some improvements, these actions, much like the PDE's implementation, often fail to address the deeper, systemic issues of urban fragmentation and socio-economic exclusion.

Therefore, to achieve the proposed improvements, broader coordination must be attained while addressing the root causes of inequality and promoting inclusive urban development through bottom-up initiatives.

Conflicts of Interest: The authors declare no conflicts of interest. The funders had no role in the design of the study; in the collection, analyses, or interpretation of data; in the writing of the manuscript; or in the decision to publish the results.

REFERENCES

Anelli, R. L. S. (2018). Planning São Paulo. Planum The Journal of Urbanism, 36(1).

Bassul, J. R. (2010). City statute: Building a law. In *The city statute: A commentary* (pp. 71–90). Ministry of Cities, Cities Alliance.

. Brasil. (2001). Lei nº 10.257, de 10 de julho de 2001. Estatuto da Cidade. Brasília, DF: Presidência da República.

Buxton, M. (2022). Connecting peri-urban theory with policy: Implications for practice. In P. Pereira, E. Gomes, & J. Rocha (Eds.), Mapping and Forecasting Land Use (pp. 55-94). Elsevier. https://doi.org/DOI: 10.1016/B978-0-323-90947-1.00005-3

. Castro, P. R. (2022). A luta pelo solo urbano: avanços e limites da regularização fundiária de interesse social [Master's thesis, Faculdade de Engenharia Civil, Arquitetura e Urbanismo, UNICAMP].

D'Albergo, E. (2010). Urban issues in nation-state agendas: A comparison in Western Europe. *Urban Research & Practice*, *3*(2), 138–158. DOI: 10.1080/17535069.2010.481220

D'Ambrosio, C., & Rodrigues, R. I. (2008). Deprivation in the São Paulo Districts: Evidence from 2000. *World Development*, *36*(6), 1094–1112. DOI: 10.1016/j.worlddev.2007.10.007

Fedeli, V. (2022). National Urban Policies in Europe, a Contrasted and Fragmented Picture or a Shared Social Construction? In Gelli, F., & Basso, M. (Eds.), *Identifying Models of National Urban Agendas, Comparative Studies of Political Agendas.* Springer Nature Switzerland AG., DOI: 10.1007/978-3-031-08388-4_10

Fernandes, E. (2018). A Produção Socioeconômica, Política e Jurídica da Informalidade Urbana. Instituto Polis. Retrieved from https://abrir.link/hNfgq

Friedmann, J. (1987). *Planning in the Public Domain: From Knowledge to Action.* Princeton University Press.

Gilbert, A. (2007). The Return of the Slum: Does Language Matter? *International Journal of Urban and Regional Research*, *31*(4), 697–713. DOI: 10.1111/j.1468-2427.2007.00754.x

IBGE. (2022). *Brazilian Census of 2022*. IBGE.

Lindblom, C. E. (1959). The Science of "Muddling Through". *Public Administration Review*, *19*(2), 79–88. DOI: 10.2307/973677

Macedo, J. (2008). Urban land policy and new land tenure paradigms: Legitimacy vs. legality in Brazilian cities. *Land Use Policy*, *25*(2), 259–270. DOI: 10.1016/j.landusepol.2007.08.001

Maricato, E. (1988). The urban reform movement in Brazil. *International Journal of Urban and Regional Research*, *12*(1), 137–138. DOI: 10.1111/j.1468-2427.1988.tb00079.x

Maricato, E. (2010). The statute of the peripheral city. In *The city statute: A commentary*. Ministry of Cities, Cities Alliance.

Nobre, E. A. C. (2018). *Do plano diretor às operações urbanas consorciadas: a ascensão do discurso neoliberal e dos grandes projetos urbanos no planejamento paulistano. Livre Docência*. Faculdade de Arquitetura e Urbanismo/USP., DOI: 10.11606/T.16.2018.tde-27012022-090358

Pereira, K. C. (2023). O impacto da Lei Federal 13.465 de 2017 sobre usucapião coletivo urbano no tribunal federal da 1ª região: Uma análise dos processos do Estado do Tocantins, Research. *Social Development*, *12*(4), 1–15.

Pioletti, M., & Dalla Vecchia, V. (2022). The Federal Urban Agenda in Brazil: Democratization and Politicization of Planning Practice. In Gelli, F., & Basso, M. (Eds.), *Identifying Models of National Urban Agendas: A View to the Global Transition* (pp. 189–211). Springer Nature Switzerland AG. DOI: 10.1007/978-3-031-08388-4_7

Rajendran, L. P., Raúl, L., Chen, M., Guerrero Andrade, J. C., Akhtar, R., Mngumi, L. E., Chander, S., Srinivas, S., & Roy, M. R. (2024). The 'peri-urban turn': A systems thinking approach for a paradigm shift in reconceptualising urban-rural futures in the global South. *Habitat International*, *146*, 103041. DOI: 10.1016/j.habitatint.2024.103041

Ribeiro, S. C. L., Daniel, M. N., & Abiko, A. (2016). ZEIS maps: Comparing areas to be earmarked exclusively for social housing in São Paulo city. *Land Use Policy*, *58*, 445–455. DOI: 10.1016/j.landusepol.2016.08.010

Rolnik, R. (2009). Democracia no fio da navalha: Limites e possibilidades para a implementação de uma agenda de reforma urbana no Brasil. *Revista Brasileira de Estudos Urbanos e Regionais*, *11*(2), 31. DOI: 10.22296/2317-1529.2009v11n2p31

Rolnik, R. (2015). *Guerra dos lugares: a colonização da terra e da moradia na era das finanças*. Boitempo.

Rolnik, R., & Santoro, P. F. (2014). *Zonas Especiais de Interesse Social (ZEIS) em Cidades Brasileiras: Trajetória Recente de Implementação de um Instrumento de Política Fundiária*. Lincoln Institute., https://www.lincolninst.edu/pt-br/publicacoes-recursos/

Roy, A. (2005). Urban Informality: Toward an Epistemology of Planning. *Journal of the American Planning Association*, *71*(2), 147–158. DOI: 10.1080/01944360508976689

. São Paulo. Câmara Municipal. (2014). Lei Municipal nº 16.050 - Plano Diretor de São Paulo, de 31 de julho de 2014.

São Paulo. (2016a). Cadernos das Subprefeituras: Material de apoio para Revisão Participativa dos Planos Regionais das Subprefeituras - Cidade Tiradentes. Secretaria Municipal de Desenvolvimento Urbano. Retrieved from gestaourbana.prefeitura.sp.gov.br

São Paulo. (2016b). Caderno de Propostas dos Planos Regionais das Subprefeituras: Quadro Analítico. Secretaria Municipal de Desenvolvimento Urbano. Retrieved from gestaourbana.prefeitura.sp.gov.br

São Paulo. (2016c). Decreto nº 56.759, de 7 de janeiro de 2016. São Paulo, SP. Retrieved from https://legislacao.prefeitura.sp.gov.br/leis/decreto-56759-de-07-de-janeiro-de-2016/detalhe

São Paulo. (2016d). Decreto nº 57.377, de 11 de outubro de 2016. São Paulo, SP. Retrieved from https://legislacao.prefeitura.sp.gov.br/leis/decreto-57377-de-11-de-outubro-de-2016/

. São Paulo. Câmara Municipal. (2022a). Lei Municipal nº 17.734, de 11 de janeiro de 2022.

. São Paulo. Câmara Municipal. (2022b). Lei Municipal nº 17.859, de 16 de dezembro de 2022.

Sclavi, M., & Buraschi, D. (2022). Participative Democracy and the Art of Listening. Ascolto Attivo srl, Milan.

Silva, S. U. A. (2021). As ZEIS no planejamento de São Paulo: Regulações urbanas e assentamentos informais. *Revista Brasileira de Direito Urbanístico*, *7*(12), 43–84. DOI: 10.55663/rbdu.v7i12.303

Teixeira, C. C. (2018). Os decretos de Habitação de Interesse Social e a flexibilização de parâmetros de uso e ocupação do solo na cidade de São Paulo no período de 1992 a 2016. *PosFAUUSP*, *25*(45), 86–101. DOI: 10.11606/issn.2317-2762.v25i45p86-101

ENDNOTES

1 A set of legal, urban planning, environmental, and social measures aimed at regularizing informal settlements and granting titles to their occupants (Brasil, 2009).

2 In their research, Ribeiro, Daniel and Abiko (2016) focused on analyzing and correlating the ZEIS maps from the Master Plans of São Paulo city over a span of 12 years (2002 and 2014), aiming to assess changes and establish a theoretical foundation for further studies on the potentials and limitations of this urban planning tool.

3 ZEIS 5 are plots or groups of plots, preferably vacant or underutilized, located in areas with urban services, facilities, and infrastructure, where there is private interest in developing market-rate and social interest housing projects. According to Teixeira (2018) the ZEIS 5 was created due to pressure from the real estate market to develop units aimed at families with incomes above six times the minimum wage during the 2014 revision of the PDE.

4 single-family, horizontal multifamily up to 20 housing units (UH),horizontal multifamily above 20 UH, vertical multifamily up to 5 floors, and vertical multifamily above 5 floors.

Chapter 4
Urban Expansion and Transformation of the Ecosystem Value of the Territory:
The Case of the Northern Metropolitan Border of Bogotá

Juan Eduardo Chica-Mejía
https://orcid.org/0000-0003-3666-9470
Universidad de Bogotá Jorge Tadeo Lozano, Colombia

Laura Amezquita Garcia
Universidad de Bogotá Jorge Tadeo Lozano, Colombia

Andrés Felipe Rueda Tellez
Universidad de Bogotá Jorge Tadeo Lozano, Colombia

ABSTRACT

The northern metropolitan area of Bogotá is characterized by a dispersed urban growth, caused primarily by processes of decentralization of the population and economic activities relocated from the metropolitan center. This chapter reviews the case of the Chicú River basin — in the north of the city —in accordance with the hypothesis that the processes of anthropization of the non-urbanized metropolitan territory — caused by patterns of dispersed urban growth and changes in land use into productive economic activities — are transforming the ecosystem services provided by the area and putting the environmental sustainability of the region at risk. Using GIS tools, satellite images, and census data from 2005 and 2018, changes in

DOI: 10.4018/979-8-3693-6089-7.ch004

land use cover were analyzed. The results allowed us to generate scenarios informed by public policy decision-making that are useful to harmonize territorial growth processes and to mitigate negative externalities, in order to safeguard the existing ecosystem services.

1. INTRODUCTION

1.1. Territorial transformations and their impacts on ecosystem services in the northern border of the Metropolitan Region of Bogotá.

Since the end of the 20th century, the metropolitan areas of large cities have undergone significant changes: central areas have been deindustrialized and pressure on peri-urban and rural land has increased due to the relocation of labor markets and economic activities (Harris, 2001). Peri-urban areas have become the focus of urban employment decentralization, because transportation systems have improved and workers do not require frequent face-to-face contact (Marmolejo-Duarte et al., 2012). Digital tools have become an effective mean of collaborative work — by replicating proximity relationships of economic stakeholders within companies and organizations — that allow routine activities to developed remotely (Martin, et al., 2018) and, thus, contribute to the acceleration of economic decentralization processes.

According to Serrano (2019), under the logic of real estate speculation, the rural and suburban areas of northern Bogotá — where the municipality case studies of this research are located — have been occupied with multiple economic activities, which include, mainly, services and low-density housing. The dynamics of the Bogotá metropolitan region show growth patterns that are similar to other global areas — such as those described by Lang and Knox (2009) and Soja (2008) — which are characterized by an increase in urbanized land, specifically in exurban areas along highways or in interstitial sectors between urban settlements. The study on the growth of the urban footprint in the Bogotá region, conducted by the consulting firm IDOM and Findeter (the state Territorial Development Bank), revealed that the growth of urbanization in metropolitan municipalities other than Bogotá is fundamentally dispersed, especially in the northern border. This area represents about 45% of the total urban footprint, since it is 1.3 times larger than the compact urban footprint of the region (IDOM, 2018).

In addition, logistics and industrial economic activities have experienced significant development, especially along the exit routes in the northern and western urban border of the metropolitan region. The municipalities located in that zone have strong functional relations with Bogotá and are the closest to it. In fact, the area of built-up land dedicated to these economic activities in the metropolitan municipalities of the northern zone is greater than that of Bogotá. While in the municipalities this area represents 23% of residential land, in Bogotá it only represents about 14% (IDOM, 2018).

The economic importance of the metropolitan urban border of Bogotá is, as we have already stated, significant. These municipalities concentrate more than 85% of the economic activity of the department of Cundinamarca — which borders Bogotá — and contain approximately 55% of its population. In contrast, the municipalities of the metropolitan ultra-periphery, or rural border, represent about 6% of the economic activity and 3% of the population of the department. Despite this disparity, rural municipalities are crucial for the region as they provide environmental services and meet the food needs of their population (Secretaría Distrital de Planeación, 2015b p.85). According to the same source, "the greatest anthropization per municipality is observed in the first ring of the metropolitan area (…) which decreases towards the southeast and southwest of the region, in terms of distance and road connectivity" (p.56).

This study was conducted with three municipalities: Cota, located in the first ring of Bogotá Metropolitan Region— which is a continuous border — and Tabio and Tenjo, located in the second ring. Figure 1 shows the municipalities studied and highlights their geographic relation with the northern border of Bogotá.

Figure 1. Location of the three municipalities studied (Tenjo, Tabio and Cota) on the Chicú River basin, on the northern border of the metropolitan area of Bogotá

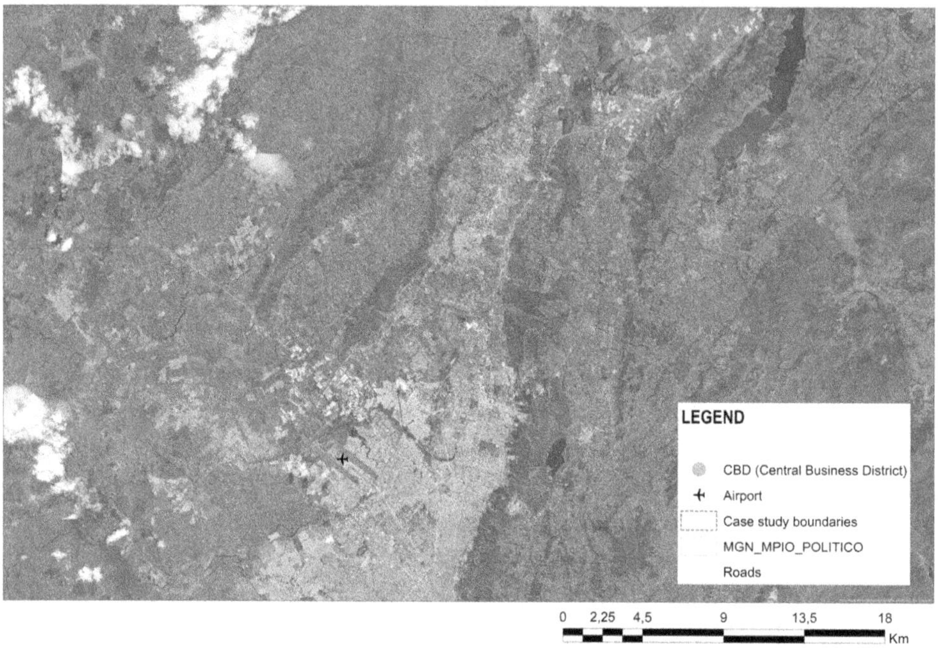

Note: The map shows the defined administrative boundaries of the three municipalities studied. Prepared by the authors using Google Earth.

The concept used by Bogota's policy makers to manage and intervene the border territory of the metropolitan region of Bogotá has evolved over time. The Mayor's Office of Bogota had to define it as part of a broader regional planning system, in which they announced that "progressive territorial areas were outlined to address the various problems resulting from the interaction of the Capital District with the region" (Secretaría Distrital de Planeación, 2015a, p. 132). This approach recognizes the diversity of these relationships, which encompass urban, rural, economic and environmental aspects, and incorporates them into a broader regional planning framework.

In short, the urban border of the metropolitan region of Bogotá has evolved: it went from being a geographical demarcation to become a key element in the management of the complex relationships between the capital and its surrounding municipalities. In this context, the idea that this border is as a transition area between the urban and rural sectors, characterized by its high social and environmental complexity, emerges. It is in this border where the balance of territorial development with the value of ecosystem services — key to effectively addressing the climate crisis — existing in these territories is strategically debated.

1.2. Ecosystem services and green infrastructure in the context of metropolitan growth

Cities are particularly vulnerable to climate change, due to their large and growing population. Achieving climate adaptation in urban areas is therefore essential for their sustainable development (Rosenzweig et al., 2010). Cities affect the natural systems that surround them and are also affected by them beyond their physical boundaries. That is why the interdependence between urban systems and their natural environment has begun to surface as a critical element within urban agendas (Alberti, 1996).

Climate adaptation must address different multi-scale urban planning practices, at municipal and metropolitan levels (Measham et al., 2011; Feria & Ramos, 2017). On the one hand, at the metropolitan level, urban planning strategies must be aimed at conserving natural assets to reduce air pollution and mitigate the effects of climate change in urban centers. Manes et al. (2014) analyzed this type of adaptation for the city of Rome. On the other hand, at the municipal level, these strategies must be aimed at mitigating the urban heat island, as examined by Arellano & Roca (2016) for the case of Barcelona.

According to Füssel (2007), cited by Geneletti & Zardo (2016), adaptation to climate change has historically received less attention than mitigation. However, the interest in adaptation interventions has recently increased, particularly regarding greenhouse gas emissions. Ecosystem-based adaptation is defined as the use of ecosystem services to help people adapt to the adverse effects of climate change. This concept was first introduced by the United Nations Framework Convention on Climate Change in 2008 (Geneletti & Zardo, 2016).

Urban growth, as well as climate change, can exacerbate heat in cities (Mohan et al., 2020). Managing the development and the structure of cities is important to mitigate heat and its adverse impacts (Xu et al., 2019 cited by Schwaab, 2022). In this sense, urban areas distributed in a dispersed way have proven to be more effective in reducing urban heat than compact cities (Sxhwarz & Manceur, 2015; Debage & Shepherd, 2015; Marando et al., 2022) because they intersperse green areas that can counterbalance neighboring urban areas. However, Schwaab (2022) studied small urban patches in Europe and found that they can be warmer than large urban patches, depending on the type of land cover they contain. For example, agricultural areas do not favor the cooling of intermediate zones; this situation shows that urban dispersion is not always favorable to mitigate the urban heat island.

In this sense, the concept of green infrastructure — referring to the green cover existing in regions and cities — has occupied a prominent place in urban planning since the end of the 20th century (Aguilera et al, 2018). According to Rouse et al. (2013), cited by Giannotti et al. (2021), the concept of green infrastructure has been used in the United States since the 1990s to refer specifically to the sustainable management of stormwater. In Europe, the term began to be used more recently to indicate particularly ecological connectivity focused on preserving biodiversity and the provision of ecosystem services, both in urban and rural territories. According to the public policy of the European Union (EU), green infrastructure should comprise a network of natural and semi-natural areas and other environmental elements, which must be strategically planned, designed, and managed to provide a wide range of ecosystem services (EC., 2013).

From the perspective of land use planning, connectivity and multifunctionality of green infrastructure are two key aspects that must be considered in public policies (Feria & Ramos, 2017). On the one hand, the concept of connectivity highlights the value of green infrastructure networks for urban growth. On the other hand, the concept of multifunctionality underlines the central role that green infrastructure plays in land use planning as strategic infrastructures for the sustainability of urbanized areas (Ramos & Hurtado, 2021). Therefore, from a land use planning perspective, green infrastructure planning should compensate for urban development while seeking to enhance connectivity with metropolitan border natural systems.

It is worth mentioning that urban planning is the way to address climate change adaptation strategies (Rueda, 2017) since it can promote comprehensive solutions to mitigate and adapt to its effects, as long as the criteria for ecologically sustainable urban development are met (Hidalgo García, 2017; Gifreu, 2018). Therefore, as Geneletti & Zordo (2016) mention, it is necessary to strengthen the interaction between climate adaptation plans and other local planning instruments. Strong coordination of urban planning with other actions and policies is therefore required to ensure the success of climate change adaptation measures, considering that these measures must be applied in harmony with the enhancement of ecosystem services.

Bogotá's Territorial Planning Plan (POT in Spanish), adopted by Decree 555 of 2021, continues to emphasize on the articulation of territorial planning instruments, land uses, mobility, public services and the conservation of the main ecological structure and the value it provides for the territory. On the one hand, the document proposes — among other commitments — that the main ecological structure be protected, and that harmonious and sustainable relationships be generated between the city and its rural environment. It also proposes, on the other hand, that the resilience capacity of the territory be increased in the face of the occurrence of disasters derived from variability and climate change, through the construction of ecosystemic connectors that cross the city and connect its green areas (Alcaldía Mayor de Bogotá, 2021).

In this sense, it is important to understand how the growth of the metropolitan border of the city towards the north — widely affected by processes of population decentralization and relocation of economic activities from the metropolitan center — has affected the ecosystem services provided by this territory. As Mayorga (2022) mentions, the transformation of the peri-urban territory of Bogotá has been widely driven by processes of urban expansion, industrialization and consolidation of highway corridors that have generated the loss of agricultural areas and the reduction of the ecological connectivity.

1.3. The metropolitan borders and the growth of urbanization

The concept of urban border has evolved significantly in recent decades, reflecting the complexity of urban-rural dynamics. Suárez-Daza (2021) defines the urban-rural interface as a transition zone between the city and the countryside characterized by hosting tense and conflicting dynamics. Likewise, Gil-Grandet (2019) points out that "The urban border category emerges due to the importance that these areas have when analyzing the city and its region, since multiple processes that involve rural, urban and hybrid dynamics are manifested in them" (p. 10). Thus, the concept of urban-rural border has surfaced to highlight the existence of a transition area between the urban and the rural environment. This border concept refers to a space that meets and mixes different land uses, such as residential, agricultural, industrial and conservation areas. The hybrid nature of these border areas makes them prone to becoming conflict zones, as the stakeholders who inhabit and make use of them have different interests. However, these areas also offer opportunities for sustainable development and integrated land management.

A multitude of concepts have emerged in this research and understanding them is a challenging task. Their meanings have evolved over time; sometimes they appear as synonymous, and other times, contradictory. The denotation of the concept of urban border has significantly transformed. In the 1950s, the idea of "urban cores" arose within theories of center-periphery transferred into the urban context. This literature provided a binary center-periphery vision. In the following decades, particularly in Latin America, the notion of marginalization and segregation materialized and from there came the distinctions between countryside and city, center and periphery, urban and suburban, concentrated or extended model, and compact and dispersed model. Theoretical discussions about these binary categories have, in many cases, marginalized the concern for eco-sustainability and environmental services, elements that are key within the discussion about the sustainable development of territories in the current climate change scenarios.

The contemporary discussion on urban borders also includes two unavoidable fronts: the multifunctionality and multiscalarity of the border concept (Gil-Grandet, 2019; Zasada, Fertner; Gallent, Bianconi & Andersson, 2006). Zasada et al. (2011) developed the vision of "multifunctionality" in peri-urban agriculture areas in England, suggesting that these do not only produce food, but also provide ecosystem services, recreation, and other benefits to the urban population. This approach highlights the adaptability of peri-urban areas in the face of urban expansion pressures. Regarding multiscalarity, we understand that territories are heterogeneous and have productive needs, both in terms of resource demand and supra-urban, supra-regional, and even supra-national productive circuits (Crevoisier & Rime, 2021; Theurillat, Rérat & Crevoisier, 2015). The interstices between different urban settlements are spaces that may well be used to offer environmental services or for real estate expansion, depending on the type of planning conducted and the regulatory capacity of local and higher-level governments. For example, the process of conurbation of large central cities with small satellite municipalities around them generally leads to territorial conflicts. Thus, intervention in the territory involves developing a governance process that comprises local or national authorities, real estate agencies, activities from other productive industries, and the population.

In Hispanic literature, the concept of the urban border has acquired greater complexity. López Medina (2015) presents the concept of "*Des-Borde Urbano*" [urban De-Border] as a "dynamic and complex concept, since it introduces the time factor, as well as the ideas of growth and control" (p. 14). This perspective emphasizes power relations and change as fundamental elements in understanding urban borders.

The concept of urban border has been fundamental in the integration of Bogotá and its metropolitan region The District Planning Secretariat (SDP in Spanish) has outlined this concept, recognizing the importance of the relations between the capital and the surrounding municipalities in the following way: "the relationship of the city of Bogotá with its immediate surroundings is established in the MEPOT [Exceptional Modification to the Bogota's Territorial Planning Plan], among other aspects, with the aim of harmonizing matters associated with land use planning instruments, land use, mobility and the main ecological structure, related to phenomena such as conurbation and the pressure it exerts on the neighboring municipalities" (Secretaria Distrital de Planeación, 2015a, p. 48).

This definition recognizes the complexity of the interactions between Bogotá and its neighboring municipalities, covering aspects such as territorial planning, land use, mobility and ecological structure.

Over the past ten years, the collaborative governance of urban borders in Bogotá — centered on the participation of multiple stakeholders in decision-making processes — has received growing attention. This collaborative governance carries with it a certain degree of political tension. Urban expansion in border areas has put pressure on the Regional Ecological Structure (RES), making it necessary to implement ecological restoration strategies and establish green corridors that do not go beyond the first ring. The Land Use Model marginally addresses ecosystem services, although it does speak of the integration of Bogotá with its region and states that it "seeks to protect and articulate the Main Ecological Structure (MES) on an urban scale with the RES, generating ecosystem and water system connectivity. In addition, it incorporates comprehensive risk management in the city and seeks to consolidate the Bogotá River not only as an articulating axis with the region, but as a pivot that integrates a network of parks that citizens can enjoy" (Secretaria Distrital de Planeación, 2015a, p. 87).

In this context, this study seeks to identify how the dynamics of urban growth in the northern metropolitan border of Bogotá — in terms of the increase of its population and its economic activities — are generating important externalities in the ecosystem services of the metropolitan territory. Within the climate change scenarios to which the region is exposed, the growth of the urban heat island is the aspect of greatest concern, because it not only subjects the population to a state of vulnerability, but also calls into question the efficiency of development and land management instruments.

2. MATERIALS AND METHODS

Different methods have been applied in this study, which has a quantitative and spatial character. The methods used account for the qualitative, social and productive variables of the entire Chicú River basin, which is where the municipalities studies are located. The results were consolidated in three stages, which must be read in accordance with the scope and limitations of the existing information, under the strict care of data processing. First, the census data on population and housing for the years 2005 and 2018 — published and reviewed by the National Administrative Department of Statistics (DANE in Spanish) — were reviewed. Secondly, land cover in 2006 and 2019 was analyzed using GIS data from Corporación Autónoma Regional (CAR) of Cundinamarca, which is the environmental authority of the region. Finally, a methodological synthesis was conducted to harmonize the terms and criteria for data exploration.

2.1. Census data

This study is an analysis of the information provided by the National Population and Housing Census (CNPVIN Spanish) of 2005 and 2018 (DANE, 2005; 2018). The specific information analyzed was that of the dispersed rural areas of the three municipalities studied, which are located on the Chicú River basin. The census information focuses on the living conditions of people, dwellings and households as units of analysis, as Table 1 shows.

Table 1. Units for the analysis of population and housing censuses in Colombia

Analysis unit	Type of variables collected	Scope and Limitations
People	Demographic and social information on residents.	Allows analyzing the detailed structure of the population. The data is sensitive to the temporality of the census.
Dwellings	Typology, available services and construction materials.	Allows assessing access to basic services. Does not capture rapid changes in infrastructure.
Households	Characteristics and living conditions.	Allows analyzing patterns of cohabitation and overcrowding. Definition of household may vary (nuclear, extended, composite) in different cultures and contexts, which may make accurate comparisons difficult.

Note: Prepared by the authors based on DANE, 2018.

The open data published by DANE were integrated and analyzed using the National Geostatistical Framework (NGF)[1], which offers a unified coding and a hierarchical structure that facilitates the georeferencing of statistical units. Thus, the categories presented in Table 2 are used almost interchangeably.

Table 2. Spatial categories used by DANE.

Urban Section	**Generally, covers the most densely populated areas within municipalities, including municipal capitals and population centers.**	**Average of 20 to 22 contiguous blocks in urban areas. Generally delimited by main streets and avenues.**
Rural Section	Includes areas with lower population density, mainly covering dispersed rural areas.	Geographic extensions averaging 20 square kilometers (2000 hectares), delimited by political-administrative boundaries and natural elements of the landscape.
County Seat	Main urban area of a municipality.	It is the geographical area defined within an urban perimeter. Its boundaries are established by agreements of the Municipal Council. It corresponds to the place where the administrative headquarters of a municipality is located.
Population Center	Concentrations of housing in rural areas with urban characteristics.	Concentration of at least twenty (20) contiguous, neighboring or attached dwellings, located in the rural area of a municipality or a departmental district.
Dispersed Rural Area	Rural areas with dispersed housing.	They cover an average area of 20 square kilometers and are delimited by political-administrative boundaries and natural and cultural elements of the landscape.

Note: Prepared by the authors based on DANE (2018).

The administrative seat of the municipality (i.e., the mayor's office) is in the county seat category. Since the population center may or may not have an institutional presence, its main categories are hamlet, police inspection and departmental district (areas that do not belong to any municipality and are under the direct administration of the department), which only exist in some departments of Colombia.

DANE classifies geographic areas in its censuses primarily into urban sections and rural sections. However, this classification can be limited as it does not adequately recognize the intermediate characteristics of "population centers." Urban sections and rural sections are cartographic divisions created by DANE for statistical purposes.

2.2. Land use coverages

The analysis of land cover, which accounts for the ecosystem services of the Chicú River basin in this study, was conducted using information from the years 2006 and 2019, which are closer and more comparable with the information found in the population and housing censuses analyzed. In order to process the data thoroughly and to consider the limitations in accessing geographic data with the categories developed by DANE, the databases published by the Corporación Autonoma Regional (CAR) — the entity that executes and manages environmental issues for the department of Cundinamarca — were used. This information is an important guideline for all stakeholders who have a presence in the territory, given that the CAR acts as an environmental authority. CAR has the capacity to intervene in the regulation of land uses and destinations and environmental and it also has conservation responsibility.

Law 99 of 1993 granted the CAR the authority to prepare Hydrographic Basin Management and Planning Plans (POMCA in Spanish). For this study, the POMCA of the Chicú River basin were consulted, specifically, the environmental zoning compiled by the CAR in these documents. The primary source of information is a series of satellite images collected through Landsat systems. The limitations of this series of images forced us to perform data processing. The images retain the spirit and rigor necessary for the study of ecosystem services.

Figure 2 shows the four-stage methodological route that was drawn up for this research, which started with compiling the information and finished with obtaining comparative results at the two points in time studied, 2006 and 2019.

Figure 2. Methodological route for the analysis of Landsat satellite image cover

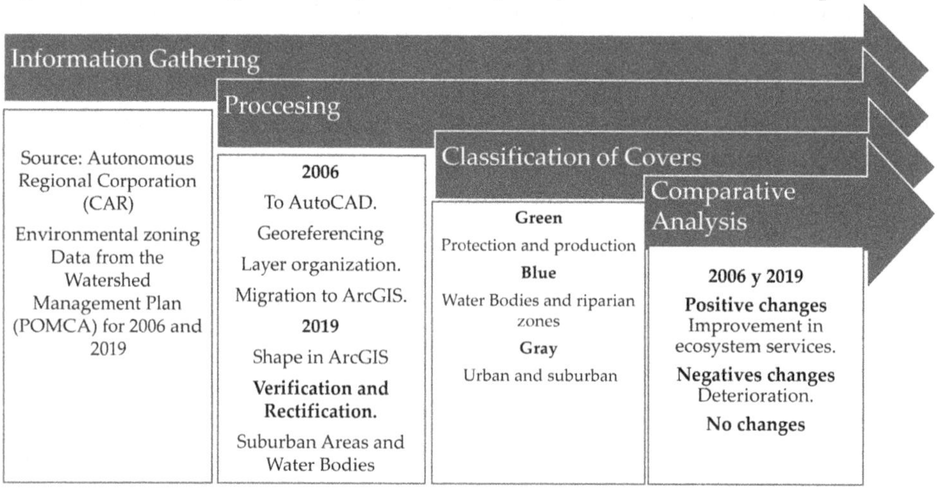

Source: Prepared by the authors

2.3 Harmonization of information sources and methods

The contrast method used in this study seeks to make comparable the two main sources of information: DANE census data (2005 and 2018) and satellite images from the CAR (2006 and 2019). This approach allows a comprehensive understanding of the changes in the Chicú River basin, both in terms of population and housing, as well as land use and cover.

This effort to determine the spatial order and distribution allowed us to analyze the evolution of the spatial structure of the territory, and then to examine in contrast the two moments in time. Identifying the grey or built infrastructure shows the urban dynamics, particularly housing, although it does not ignore the existence of rural housing that occasionally appears in populated centers and, obviously, in dispersed rural areas. Our aim is to correlate the settlement of the population with its demands and eventual offers of ecosystem services. Although census data do not provide direct information on the elements of green infrastructure (forest cover and agricultural areas) and blue infrastructure (water bodies), satellite images allowed us to identify and quantify elements (natural and otherwise) of the landscape. This served to contribute to the understanding of the dynamics of these services. A summary is presented below in Table 3.

Table 3. Summary of the methodological phases

Analytical exercise	Criterion	Census data	Satellite images
Determining spatial order and distribution	Urban /core	County seat Urban Section	Urban zones Changes in density
	Peri-urban	Settlements	Urban-rural/Suburban transition areas
	Sprawl	Dispersed Rural	Does not apply
Analysis of change analysis	Grey infrastructure (Dwellings)	Households censused in 2005 and 2018	Environmental zones 2006 and 2019
	Characteristics of the population	Comparison of density, shape and distribution	Classification of artificial cover, Verification and rectification of soil cover
	Grey infrastructures	Not applicable	Water bodies, rivers, wetlands

Note: The table shows the harmonization of the data used from the main sources consulted. Prepared by the authors.

3. RESULTS

3.1. Characteristics of the northern urban border of Bogotá: ecosystem services vs. urbanization processes.

The Chicú River basin is part of the upper Bogotá River basin. This basin plays a crucial role in maintaining the water and ecological balance of the area. On the one hand, it helps regulate the local hydrological cycle and contributes to recharging aquifers and maintaining ecological flows. On the other hand, it helps conserve biodiversity in the territory, since the ecosystems associated with this basin are home to a significant diversity of flora and fauna (Corporación Regional Autónoma, 2006; Andrade et al., 2013).

Regarding climate regulation, there is evidence that supports the fact that the vegetation cover and the water bodies from the Chicú River basin are a vital source of ecosystem services, contribute to regulate the local microclimate and mitigate the effects of the urban heat island (Suarez-Daza, 2021). However, it has been subject to a considerable process of anthropization that has transformed its ecological dynamics and reduced its capacity to provide such services. Agricultural activity, urbanization, and infrastructure works have altered the natural historical course of the river and modified its ecological structure, as well as its capacity for self-purification (Universidad Nacional de Colombia, 2024).

In this regard, the analysis for 2019 shows that the land cover dedicated to productive activities and dispersed urban growth in the lower part of the basin is extensive and significant. On the contrary, the green cover — or protection areas — that provide ecosystem services for the region — which are in the upper parts of the basin and in the setback areas of the Chicú River and its tributaries — represented about 38% of the total. In that year, the areas dedicated to production activities represented 43% of the total land, while the suburban areas were about 17%. It is worth noting, as Figure 3 shows, that a large part of the suburban land is located towards the southern and southwestern border of the city, on roads of hierarchical value for the region, such as the Calle 80 highway — the exit route to Medellín — and the Chía-Cota-Funza road — which runs through the region on its western edge. On the former, the land is used mainly for industrial and logistic purposes, while on the latter, the land is mainly for residential use. Additionally, in areas close to the compact urban areas — which only represent 2.5% of the total land — peri-urban land dispersed along rural roads and under isolated parceling processes can be found.

Figure 3. Urban, peri-urban and rural land cover in the Chicú River basin in 2019

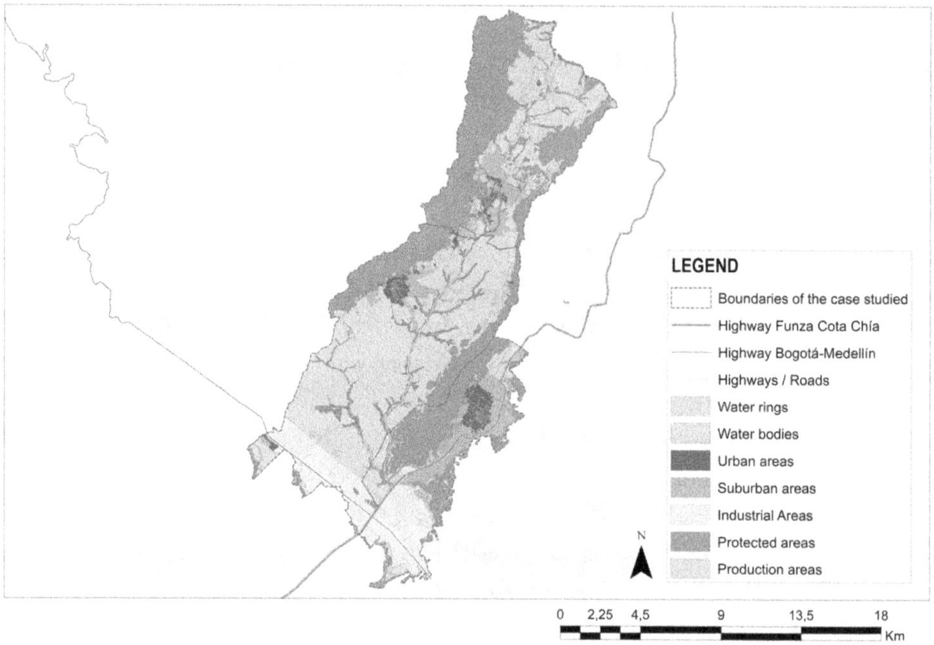

Note: The figure shows where the land covers are located, grouped into three types: protection areas and production areas (green infrastructures), water bodies (blue infrastructures), and urban and suburban/peri-urban areas (grey infrastructures) in 2019. Prepared by the authors based on the land cover information provided by the CAR.

3.2. Intercensal changes and effects on the territory

Peri-urban growth in the Chicú River basin is a process that has accelerated in the present century, in response to decentralization processes from the metropolitan center. Figure 4 shows that in the period 2006-2019 the growth of suburban or peri-urban areas doubled, going from 8.8% to 16.7% of the total land of the basin. In that same period, the municipalities council seats, the compact urban areas, also grew rapidly: they went from 0.6% to 2.5%. It is worth noting that during this period the protected area dedicated to green cover also grew significantly by about 14 percentage points.

Figure 4. Changes in urban, peri-urban and rural land cover in the Chicú River basin

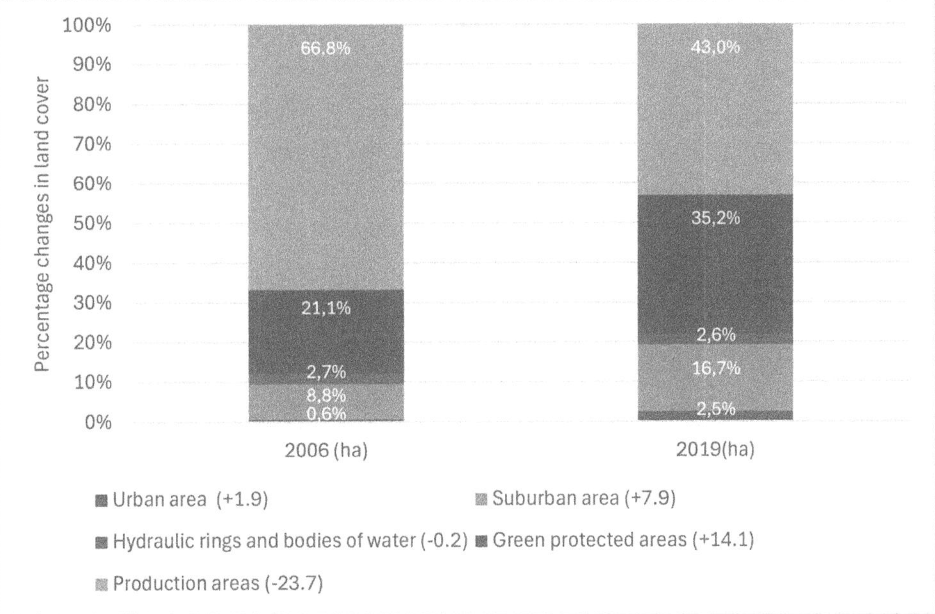

Note: The figure contains information on the percentage value of each of the land cover categories in 2006 and 2019, as well as the change in percentage points during this period. Prepared by the authors based on the land cover information provided by CAR.

The growth of the green cover, as Figure 4 shows, was mostly due to the conversion of production areas used for agricultural activities. This growth was mainly concentrated in the northern part of the basin, which is less affected by urbanization processes, as well as in relict areas in the lower part of the basin. Likewise, the analysis of the cover changes shows an increase of the extensive peri-urban area dedicated to economic and logistical activities around the Calle 80 highway, on the Chía-Cota-Funza road and in the areas that are close to the municipal council seats during the period analyzed. This growth has occurred under patterns of dispersed urbanization, especially in the municipality of Tabio in the northern part of the basin (Figures 5 and 6). Quantification of data for the period 2006-2019 shows that in Tabio, peri-urban growth was almost 10 times what it was at the beginning of the period, while in Tenjo and Cota it was slightly more moderate: 2.4 times and 1.4 times, respectively.

Figure 5. Urban, peri-urban, and rural land cover in the Chicú River basin: changes in protected green areas

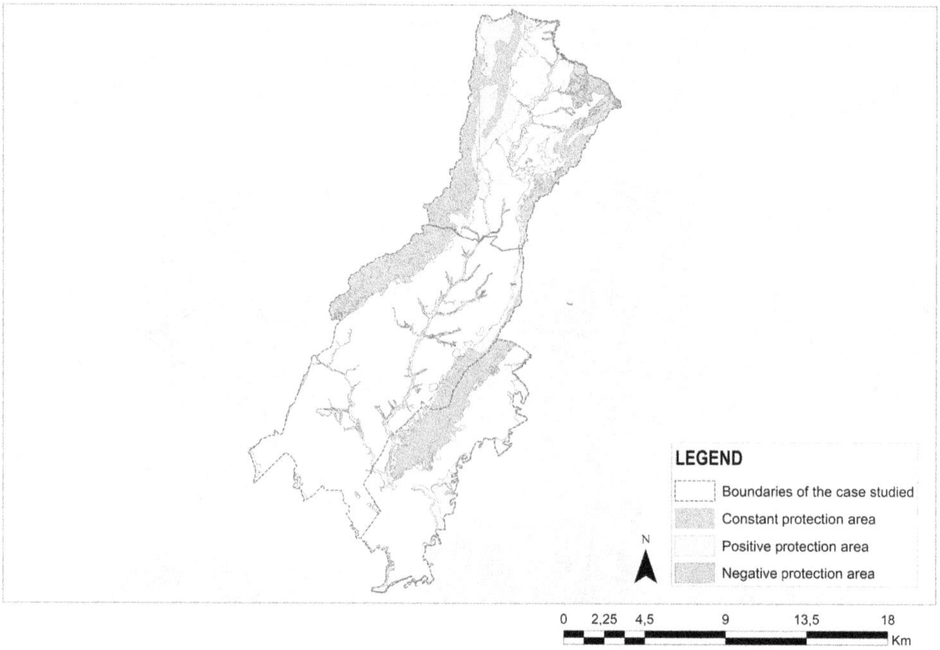

Note: The figure shows changes in the cover of protected green areas. Positive growth, pre-existing areas that remain, and negative growth are shown in green, grey and red, respectively. Prepared by the authors based on the land cover information provided by the Cundinamarca Regional Autonomous Corporation.

Figure 6. Figure 6. Urban, peri-urban, and rural land cover in the Chicú River basin: changes in urbanized areas

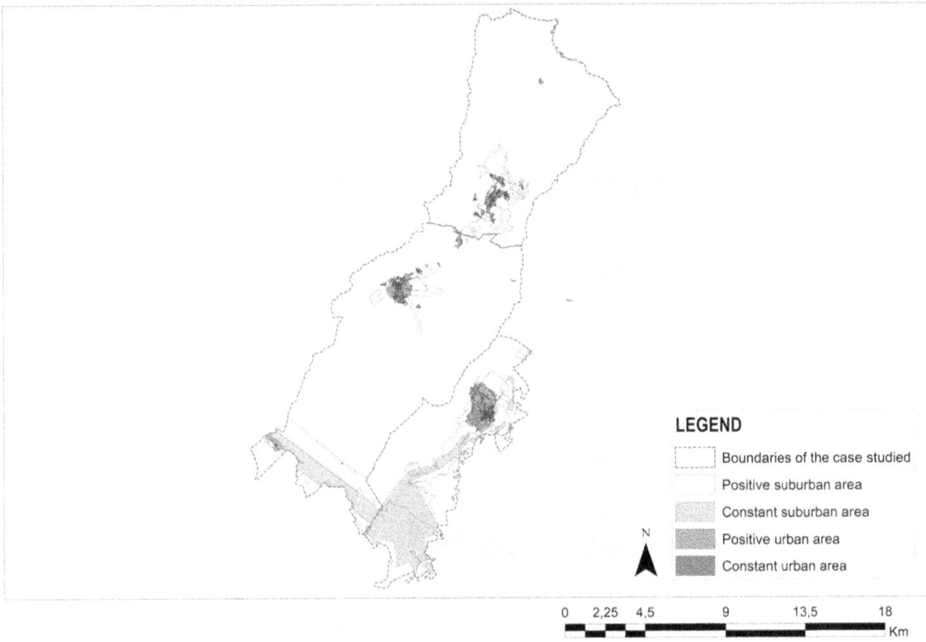

Note: The figure shows changes in the coverage of urbanization. Positive growth, pre-existing areas that remain, and negative growth are shown in green, grey, and red, respectively. Prepared by the authors based on land cover information provided by the Cundinamarca Regional Autonomous Corporation.

The analysis of the behavior of the population — conducted using census data — reinforces what has been observed in the existence and changes in land cover. The data from the Population and Housing Census (DANE, 2005) show that approximately 40% of the population lived in urban areas, 55% in rural areas, and only 5% were in the transitional or peri-urban areas (Figure 7). Specifically, in the rural dispersed area there were 10,300 housing units and 900 mixed units, while in the population centers the differences between one use and another remain. However, the magnitude in the population centers is noticeably smaller with a ratio of 2,300 residential units versus 100 mixed-use units. In summary, what we observe is that the rural dispersed area has a residential population comparable to that of the municipality council seat. This information indicates that there is a strong presence of inhabitants in rural areas, who, it is suggested, exert a potential pressure on the ecosystem services existing in these areas.

Figure 7. Distribution of the population in the study area: urban centers, population centers, and dispersed rural areas.

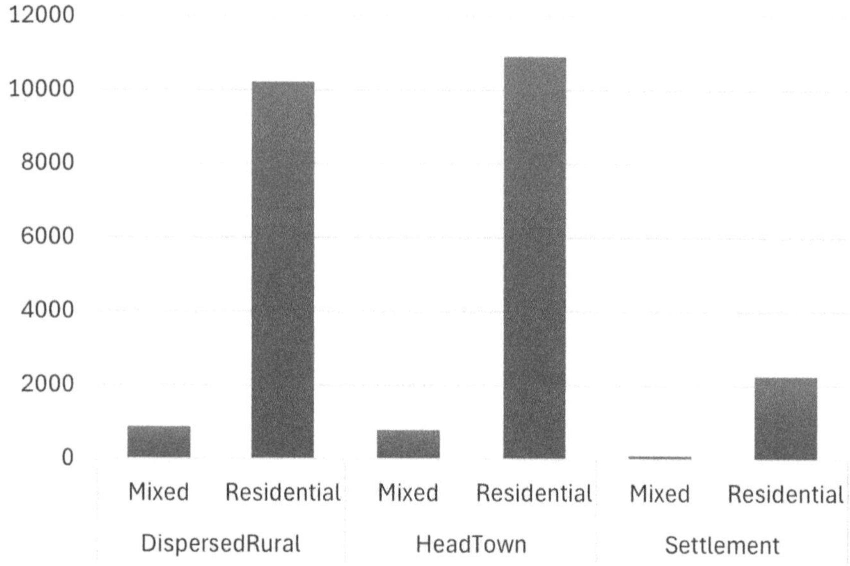

Note: Prepared by the authors based on Census data (DANE, 2005).

Most of the housing units registered in rural areas are houses, followed by apartments. This information suggests that urbanization is growing, but still dispersed, and that the inhabitants prefer horizontal housing.

Likewise, the intercensal population growth analysis (2005-2018) shows that the urban population grew by 18%, the peri-urban population grew by 6% and the population in sprawl areas grew by 1%. However, the housing growth analysis shows that there was a 43% growth in housing units in urban areas, 13% in peri-urban areas and 12% in sprawl areas. This means that the growth in the number of housing units exceeds population growth in all categories, reinforcing what has already been observed in the analysis of land cover in the face of the significant growth of peri-urban and dispersed rural land (Figures 8 and 9).

Figure 8. Changes in population distribution (2005-2018)

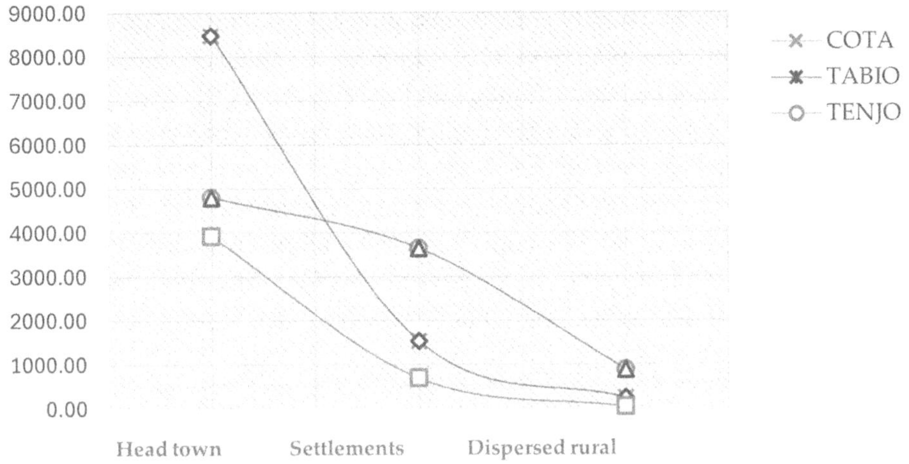

Note: Prepared by the authors based on Census data (DANE, 2005, and DANE, 2018).

Figure 9. Changes in housing distribution (2005-2018)

Note: Prepared by the authors based on Census data (DANE, 2005, and DANE, 2018).

Intercensal data indicate that the increase in housing generation between 2005 and 2018 was 63% in urban areas, 18% in populated centers, and 19% in dispersed rural areas. It is noteworthy that the construction of new homes was concentrated in Tabio, where there are almost twice as many dwellings as in the other two municipalities (6,825 in Tabio, compared to 3,626 in Cota and 1,384 in Tenjo). Although this information does not counteract the importance of Cota as an urban center, it does indicate a housing supply and demand pattern that does not privilege proximity to the central area of Bogotá. Cota has fewer dwellings in the municipality council seat than Tabio but has a higher number of dwellings in the dispersed rural areas. This may indicate a higher level of rural development or a tendency towards dispersed rural living.

Overall, the construction of houses predominates in all areas, representing 75.5% of the total, compared to 30.8% of apartments. We might think that an intercensal population increase such as the one observed would be reflected in an increase in the construction of denser dwellings, but this is not what occurs in the study area.

4. DISCUSSION

The urban growth observed in the peri-urban and dispersed areas of the northern metropolitan border of Bogotá poses significant challenges in terms of managing ecosystem services and environmental sustainability. This growth is linked not only to the physical expansion of urban and peri-urban areas, but also to a transformation of land uses and population growth that has increased the pressure on natural resources. These changes, motivated in part by the deindustrialization of the central areas of Bogotá, have led to a relocation of economic activities to the periphery, exacerbating the impacts on ecosystem services (CEPAL, 2023; Departamento Nacional de Planeación, 2004; Secretaría Distrital de Planeación, 2015b).

The multifunctionality of urban-rural space brings with it the urgent need to harmonize environmental conservation. This harmonization must consider the multiplicity of functions that these areas can fulfill, from providing ecosystem services to providing opportunities for recreation, agricultural and industrial production and, consequently, housing (Andrade, Remolina & Wiesner, 2013). This territorial reality requires the recognition of the complexity and multifunctionality of these border areas, as mentioned in the theoretical approach of this document.

Evaluating the growth and densification patterns experienced by the Chicú River basin allowed us to observe a trend towards densification of the urban council seat and a more dispersed development in peri-urban and rural areas. This situation reflects an imbalance in territorial development that could be optimized through planning oriented toward sustainability, specifically, of this urban-rural interface. What is happening today is an accelerated transformation of the landscape that may compromise the ecological integrity of the area.

In addition, the notable difference between intercensal population growth and housing production growth may be revealing land speculation. Such speculation has contributed to the housing stock not growing proportionally to the increase in population. This phenomenon not only alters the dynamics of local housing markets, but also intensifies the pressure on ecosystem services by encouraging dispersed and less efficient development.

Conflicts between different land uses in these peri-urban areas comes mainly from the tension between economic development and conservation. The evidence we found in this study coincides with the findings of other authors, who defend the idea that the land market preempts all planning and that, despite the existence of territorial policy instruments, their use and understanding remain very limited (Araque, Cantor & Moreno, 2022; Ruiz, 2015; Alfonso-Roa & Amézquita, 2017).

Therefore, policy- and decision-makers need to design strategies to maintain and improve ecosystem services in transition zones, including ecological corridors, and promoting green infrastructure. The implementation of this new planning paradigm would require close collaboration between municipal authorities, the CAR of Cundinamarca, and other relevant stakeholders. Furthermore, local and regional authorities must put in place mechanisms to continuously monitor, evaluate and guarantee the effectiveness of the measures implemented to protect ecosystem services. From this perspective, the question of the ideal balance between dispersed and compact development is complex and does not have a single answer, as it depends on multiple factors related to the geography, demographics, economy and politics of each region. In the case of the Chicú River basin, this question not only remains unanswered, but it is still an issue that needs to be addressed.

Not only from the methodological point of view of this research, but from the analysis of the effectiveness of the intervention in the territory, we discovered that the rural-urban dichotomy limits the understanding of the characteristics of these areas and does not facilitate the outline of clear guidelines for their sustainable development[2]. Understanding the specific characteristics of each of these border areas would help design more equitable policies that address their specific needs and facilitate the management of the challenges that arise at the urban-rural interface. The peri-urban areas studied in this document require a specialized approach that recognizes their unique role in connecting the urban and rural fabric, and their potential to serve as buffer zones that balance development and conservation.

Considering the border area as an interface entity in itself allowed us to observe differentiated growth patterns. For example, while in Cota growth was more balanced between urban and dispersed rural areas, in Tabio and Tenjo we see significant growth in peri-urban areas. This suggests that these transition zones are developing their own dynamics that cannot be adequately captured or managed under the traditional rural-urban paradigm.

The reality of Bogotá's northern border demands a development model that considers the urban-rural interface as a dynamic and multifunctional continuum, capable of adapting to the changing needs of an expanding metropolis.

5. CONCLUSIONS

This research analyzed the transformation processes — in terms of land cover changes and population growth — of the Chicú River basin on the northern metropolitan border of Bogotá in the period 2006 and 2019, which roughly coincides with the intercensal period. This work sought to shed light on the transformation of this urban border and on the possible negative impacts that increasing urbanization, decentralization of people and economic activities — relocated from the metropolitan center especially to the peri-urban or dispersed rural areas — have on the ecosystem services provided from by territory. Our analyses have proved that such processes are indeed real and have revealed that, in addition, there are potential speculative practices in the occupation of the territory. Such speculation is evidenced by the fact that the number of housing units grew more than the population in the period analyzed. This growth has occurred mainly under dispersed patterns, in areas not continuous with the municipal council seat, in the low parts of the basin. Such areas have an ecosystemic importance for the territory due to their value for agriculture or because they are linked to the main ecological structure of the region.

It is therefore necessary to design public policies — supported by land use planning instruments — that enable strategies to generate an orderly and non-speculative growth of the territory, to promote the conservation of the ecosystem services provided for the region, including plans to preserve ecological corridors and existing green covers. The fact that the metropolitan region of Bogotá was recently formed[3] means that there are no comprehensive territorial planning instruments. At the moment, each municipality has the power to plan its own development and they do so through their respective Territorial Planning Plans. In this context, it is important to generate regional agreements that articulate actions that allow a better understanding of the situation of border areas and support decision-making regarding urban functionality and expansion, within a harmonious relationship with the conservation of existing ecosystem services. These agreements should generate actions that contain peri-urban growth under dispersed patterns and that seek to strengthen the areas of urban expansion around existing municipal council seats and population centers.

While this research gathers evidence from the metropolitan region of Bogotá — from recent urban growth processes due to the decentralization of housing and economic activities from the metropolitan center, in accordance with what has been observed in other metropolitan territories — further studies are required to examine the possible recent effects that the COVID-19 pandemic has had on these processes. In this way, not only will the effects be evident in quantitative terms, due to the increase in urbanization, but also in the types of activities other than housing. These types of activities follow new patterns of decentralization and reveal the multi-scalar effect of conflicts related to the conservation of existing ecosystem services.

REFERENCES

Aguilera, B., Rodríguez, E., & Gómez, D. (2018). Definició d'infraestructures verdes: Una proposta metodològica integrada a través d'una anàlisi espacial. *Documents d'Analisi Geografica, 66*(2), 313–337. DOI: 10.5565/rev/dag.419

Alberti, M. (1996). Measuring urban sustainability. *Environmental Impact Assessment Review, 16*(4-6), 381–424. DOI: 10.1016/S0195-9255(96)00083-2

Alcaldía Mayor de Bogotá. (2021). Plan de Ordenamiento Territorial Bogotá Reverdece 2022- 2035. Recuperado de https://bogota.gov.co/bog/pot-2022-2035/

Alfonso-Roa, Ó., & Amézquita, L. (2017). La Segmentación del mercado residencial formal en la zona metropolitana de Bogotá en la última década. In *Ó. Alfonso-Roa, Bogotá en la Encrucijada del Desorden. Estructuras sociespaciales y gobernabilidad me-tropolitana (págs* (pp. 83–120). Universidad Externado de Colombia. DOI: 10.4000/books.uec.1875

Andrade, G., Remolina, F., & Wiesner, D. (2013). Assembling the pieces: A framework for the integration of multi-functional ecological main structure in the emerging urban region of Bogotá, Colombia. *Urban Ecosystems, 16*(4), 723–739. DOI: 10.1007/s11252-013-0292-5

Araque, A., Cantor, L., & Moreno, P. (2022). Norma y precio del suelo urbano en la ciudad de Bogotá. *EURE* 48(143), 1-22. https://dx.doi.org/.DOI: 10.7764/EURE.48.143.13

Arellano, R., & Roca, C. J. (2016). Identifying urban heat island: the Barcelona case. In Back to the Sense of the City: International Monograph Book. En *Back to the Sense of the City: International Monograph Book* (págs. 798-812). Centre de Política de Sòl i Valoracions. DOI: 10.5821/ctv.8130

CEPAL. (2023). Las ciudades y la vivienda brindan una oportunidad para transformar el modelo de desarrollo de América Latina y el Caribe hacia uno más inclusivo, igualitario y sostenible. Obtenido de https://www.cepal.org/es/noticias/ciudades-la-vivienda-brindan-oportunidad-transformar-modelo-desarrollo-america-latina

Corporación Regional Autónoma. (2006). Elaboración del Diagnóstico, Prospectiva y Formulación de la Cuenca Hidrográfica del Río Bogotá - Subcuenca Río Chicú. Obtenido de Subcuenca Rio Chicú: https://www.car.gov.co/vercontenido/55

Crevoisier, O., & Rime, D. (2021). Anchoring Urban Development: Globalisation, Attractiveness and Complexity. *Urban Studies (Edinburgh, Scotland), 58*(1), 36–52. DOI: 10.1177/0042098019889310

Departamento Administrativo Nacional de Estadísitca- DANE. (2018). Censo de Población y Vivienda. Recuperado el 19 de 09 de 2019, de http://systema59.dane.gov.co/bincol/RpWebEngine.exe/Portal?BASE=CNPVBASE4V2&lang=esp

Departamento Administrativo Nacional de Estadística (DANE). (2005). Censo general 2005. Recuperado de https://www.dane.gov.co/index.php/estadisticas-por-tema/demografia-y-poblacion/censo-general-2005-1

Feria, T. J., & Ramos, J. S. (2017). Naturaleza y ciudad. Perspectivas para la ordenación de la infraestructura verde en los planes territoriales metropolitanos en España. *Boletín de la Asociación de Geógrafos Españoles*, *74*(74), 117–141. DOI: 10.21138/bage.2447

Füssel, H. M. (2007). Adaptation planning for climate change: Concepts, assessment approaches, and key lessons. *Sustainability Science*, *2*(2), 2. DOI: 10.1007/s11625-007-0032-y

Geneletti, D., & Zardo, L. (2016). Ecosystem-based adaptation in cities: An analysis of European urban climate adaptation plans. *Land Use Policy*, *50*, 38–47. DOI: 10.1016/j.landusepol.2015.09.003

Giannotti, E., Vásquez, A., Galdámez, E., Velásquez, P., & Devoto, C. (2021). Planificación de infraestructura verde para la emergencia climática: Aprendizajes desde el proyecto" Stgo+", Santiago de Chile. *Cuadernos de Geografía*, *30*(2), 359–375. DOI: 10.15446/rcdg.v30n2.88749

Gifreu, F. J. (2018). Ciudades adaptativas y resilientes ante el cambio climático. Estrategias locales para contribuir a la sostenibilidad urbana. *Revista Aragonesa de Administración Pública*, *52*(52), 102–158. DOI: 10.71296/raap.129

Gil-Grandet, N. (2019). El borde urbano un concepto dinámico e integral para el estudio de los espacios urbano regionales. *Revista Latinoamericana de Estudiantes de Geografía*, 6. Obtenido de https://releg.org/pdf/releg2019n6_pp10-20.pdf

Harris, R. (2001). The Knowledge-based Economy: Intellectual Origins and New Economic Perspectives. *International Journal of Management Reviews*, *3*(1), 21–40. DOI: 10.1111/1468-2370.00052

Hidalgo, G. M. (2017). Las ciudades como objetivo de desarrollo sostenible. *Boletín IEEE*, *5*, 22–32.

IDOM. (2018). *Estudio del crecimiento y evolución de la huella urbana para Bogotá Región.*

Lang, R., & Knox, P. (2009). The New Metropolis: Rethinking Megalopolis. *Regional Studies*, *43*(6), 789–802. DOI: 10.1080/00343400701654251

López, M. J. (2015). Des-Bordes urbanos: Un concepto en construcción. *Revista Hábitat y Sociedad*, (8), 15–41. DOI: 10.12795/HabitatySociedad.2015.i8.02

Manes, F., Silli, V., Salvatori, E., Incerti, G., Galante, G., Fusaro, L., & Perrino, C. (2014). Urban ecosystem services: Tree diversity and stability of PM10 removal in the metropolitan area of Rome. *Annali di Botanica*, 4, 19-26., 4, 19-26.

Marando, F., Heris, M. P., Zulian, G., Udías, A., Mentaschi, L., Chrysoulakis, N., Parastatidis, D., & Maes, J. (2022). Urban heat island mitigation by green infrastructure in European Functional Urban Areas. *Sustainable Cities and Society*, *77*(103564), 103564. DOI: 10.1016/j.scs.2021.103564

Marmolejo, C., Chica, J. E., & Masip, J. (2012). ¿Hacia un sistema de metrópolis españolas policéntricas?: Evolución de la influencia de los subcentros en la distribución de la población. *ACE: Arquitectura. Ciudad y Entorno*, *18*(18), 163–190. DOI: 10.5821/ace.v6i18.2548

Martin, R., Aslesen, H. W., Grillitsch, M., & Herstad, S. J. (2018). Regional innovation systems and global flows of knowledge. In *New avenues for regional innovation systems-theoretical advances, empirical cases and policy lessons*,127-147 DOI: 10.1007/978-3-319-71661-9_7

Mayorga Guzmán, J. M. (2022). Análisis multitemporal de la transformación del paisaje en áreas periurbanas del norte de Bogotá D.C. para el periodo 1956 – 2021. (tesis de maestría). Universidad Distrital Francisco José de Caldas, Recuperado de: http://hdl.handle.net/11349/30659

Measham, T. G., Preston, B. L., Smith, T. F., Brooke, C., Gorddard, R., Withycombe, G., & Morrison, C. (2011). Adapting to climate change through local municipal planning: Barriers and challenges. *Mitigation and Adaptation Strategies for Global Change*, *16*(8), 889–909. DOI: 10.1007/s11027-011-9301-2

Mohan, M., Sati, A. P., & Bhati, S. (2020). Urban sprawl during five decadal period over National Capital Region of India: Impact on urban heat island and thermal comfort. *Urban Climate*, *33*, 100647. DOI: 10.1016/j.uclim.2020.100647

Ramos, J. S., & Hurtado, R. C. (2021). Análisis de servicios ecosistémicos para la configuración de una infraestructura verde en el área metropolitana de Sevilla. ACE: *Arquitectura. Ciudad y Entorno*, *16*(46), 9884. DOI: 10.5821/ace.16.46.9884

Rosenzweig, C., Solecki, W., Hammer, S. A., & Mehrotra, S. (2010). Cities lead the way in climate-change action. *Nature*, *467*(7318), 909–911. DOI: 10.1038/467909a PMID: 20962822

Rueda, S. (2017). La lucha por la mitigación del cambio climático se ganará o se perderá en las ciudades. *Revista Democracia y Gobierno Local*, (37), 10–19.

Schwaab, J. (2022). Sprawl or compactness? How urban form influences urban surface temperatures in Europe. *City and Environment Interactions*, *16*, 100091. DOI: 10.1016/j.cacint.2022.100091

Secretaría Distrital de Planeación. (2015a). Construyendo una visión regional común entre Bogotá y sus territorios circunvecinos. Colección Integración Regional (Vol. 12). Bogotá D.C.: UNCRD, Secretaria Distrital de Planeación. Obtenido de https://www.sdp.gov.co/gestion-socioeconomica/integracion-regional-y-nacional/publicaciones/construyendo-vision-regional-comun-entre-bogota-y-sus-territorios-circunvecinos

Secretaría Distrital de Planeación. (2015b). Región metropolitana de Bogotá: Una Visión de la Ocupación del Suelo. Bogotá: Alcaldía Mayor de Bogotá. Obtenido de https://www.sdp.gov.co/sites/default/files/region_metropolitana_de_bogota_una_vision_de_la_ocupacion_del_suelo.pdf

Serrano Romero, R. O. (2019). *Movilidad urbana y espacio público: reflexiones, métodos y contextos*. Universidad Piloto de Colombia.

Soja Edward. 2008. Post metrópolis. Estudios críticos sobre las ciudades y las regiones. Madrid. Traficantes de sueños.

Suarez-Daza, F. (2021). Percepciones eco políticas del borde norte de Bogotá, Colombia. (U. d. Andes., Ed.) Obtenido de Universidad de los Andes: http://hdl.handle.net/1992/54023

Theurillat, T., Rérat, P., & Crevoisier, O. (2015). The real estate markets: Players, institutions and territories. *Urban Studies (Edinburgh, Scotland)*, *52*(8), 1414–1433. DOI: 10.1177/0042098014536238

Universidad Nacional de Colombia. (18 de abril de 2024). Estructura Ecológica Principal de la Sabana de Bogotá. Instituto de Estudios Urbanos. Obtenido de https://periodico.unal.edu.co/articulos/los-rios-urbanos-son-vitales-en-tiempos-de-escasez-de-agua-por-eso-urge-recuperarlos

Zasada, I., Fertner, C., Piorr, A., & Nielsen, T. A. (2011). Peri-urbanisation and multifunctional adaptation of agriculture around Copenhagen. *Geografisk Tidsskrift-Danish Journal of Geography,* 111(1), 59-72, 111(1), 59-72.

ENDNOTES

1 The methodology of this research is based on the use of the National Geostatistical Framework (NGF) as a spatial reference framework, in accordance with the guidelines of the National Administrative Department of Statistics (DANE). The NGF is an essential tool to improve the quality, interoperability and accessibility of statistical data in Colombia. It provides a precise geographic structure that is useful for the analysis and dissemination of information. The NGF is the mandatory spatial framework for the development of the statistical process for the members of the National Statistical System (SEN).

2 For example, the traditional classification of urban and rural sections, as well as council seats, population centers and dispersed rural areas used by DANE do not capture the reality of peri-urban areas, which function as important transition areas (DANE, 2018).

3 The metropolitan region of Bogotá is an associative model enshrined in Article 325 of the Colombian Political Constitution, developed by Organic Law 2199 of 2022.

Chapter 5
Popular Urbanization in Bogotá:
An Intersectional Reading in Search of Wellbeing and Sustainability – Case Study of Alto Fucha Ecoterritory

Milena Rincon-Castellanos
http://orcid.org/0000-0002-2517-3464
Department of Architecture, Pontificia Universidad Javeriana, Bogotá, Colombia

Jaime Hernández-García
http://orcid.org/0000-0001-6456-1673
Department of Aesthetics, Pontificia Universidad Javeriana, Bogotá, Colombia

ABSTRACT

Women's political and community action, particularly in informal urban-rural border territories sustained from processes of social reproduction, offer other dimensions from intersectional feminisms to rethink wellbeing and sustainability. Intersectionality accounts for the intertwined action between capitalism, patriarchy and colonialism in the construction of an extractivist relationship with the land and women's bodies, feminized and racialized, reproducing impoverishment, subordination and naturalization of violence. Other dimensions of welfare and sustainability are related both to the extractivist logics of the land and bodies, as well as to the agenciamientos (agency) motivated by the personal, political and community desire to defend the territory-body-land. In this context, this chapter discusses the processes of social reproduction in informal or popular urbanization and the search for wellbeing and sustainability from intersectionality, taking as a case study the Alto Fucha

DOI: 10.4018/979-8-3693-6089-7.ch005

1. INTRODUCTION

Wellbeing and sustainability, together with categories that demand a dignified life, such as the right to the city, the right to housing, social equality, and others, constitute an adequate and just political horizon to be pursued. However, in their essential content, there are conceptualizations that not only respond to differentiated positions, but also reflect epistemic constructions crossed by capitalist, patriarchal and colonial thinking. An example of these biases is the silencing of the multiple violence suffered by bodies and the land in order to think of both wellbeing and sustainability. Intersectionality allows to highlight these conceptual silences in order to delegitimize the apparent scientific neutrality; at the same time, it calls for the construction of epistemic-ethical-political reflections (Leyva & Icaza, 2019) that invite to reconfigure the hegemonic social frameworks from which reality is understood and inhabited. From this place of enunciation and from which it is intended to have a larger approach, the purpose of this chapter is to delve into the processes of social reproduction in one of the peri-urban areas of the city of Bogotá, in order to reflect on welfare and sustainability.

There is a vast literature on popular urbanization in cities and in Latin America, from which it is possible to point out the tension between these settlements and a marked need to bring welfare and sustainability to them. There is a consensus that points out that these settlements of informal origin are based on being neighborhoods built by the inhabitants themselves as a common reality of these territories, generally located on the periphery of cities, and in particular are built outside urban regulations. Different epistemological approaches to their understanding, such as the theory of Marginality, which situates the housing problem of popular urbanization in itself. However, in contrast, the Dependency Theory, denounces that the barriers faced by excluded groups are not inertial or temporary, but are the result of the inequitable actions of the traditional dominant groups (Jaramillo, 2012). Theoretical approaches specific to Latin America have proposed alternative views to understand this socio-spatial reality, which Priscilla Connolly (2014) has called "the Latin American paradigm of popular habitat" recognizing the role of communities in its production.

The changes that the world experienced in the 1980s, particularly with the fall of the Soviet bloc and the multilateral development financing agencies, promoted the Washington Consensus, which gave rise to neoliberal policies that conceived or reinforced the conception of housing as a commodity and emphasized the right to property (Ortiz Flores, 2016). This right is inspired in the proposals of Hernando

De Soto (1989, 2000) as a 'strategy to reduce poverty', who states that the implementation of adequate property information and legalization policies would allow activating the "dead capital" that families, located in the informal city possess with their housing (Connolly, 2014).

Recent literature, from poststructuralist and postcolonial perspectives, points to the intertwining of capitalism and colonialism as structural systems that influence the configuration of informal or popular settlements. In this sense, Fadaei (2018) specifies the underlying challenge of reading informality and understanding it from experience and everyday life in the face of removing the veil of poverty. This view aims to build a new framework of recognition that makes visible the agency of the population living in informal settlements, which has been overshadowed by the same precarious conditions that can be the result of both global capitalist forces and the actions that governments take in these territories at the local level.

The literature in Latin America focuses, on the one hand, on the critique of capitalism and imperialism, highlighting the resistance of oppressed groups, and on the other hand, poses the post- structuralist challenge of the persistent division between the formal and the informal, where the identification of popular urbanization as an expression of creativity, community and sustainability does not yet subvert the dichotomous order. Faced with the dynamics and magnitude of popular urbanization, theories have inspired intervention actions that have ranged from eradication, replacement by modern housing, incorporation into urban perimeters and neighborhood improvement (Jaramillo, 2012).

Now, focusing on a global framework, in the Sustainable Development Goals (Naciones Unidas, 2018) sustainability is woven into a web of dimensions of life, where the essential content of wellbeing is associated with a health issue, suggesting to think of wellbeing as the absence of disease (Goal 3). This approach has been controversial from the political stance of "good living" (*Buen Vivir*), a term used by native communities in Latin America, which particularly countries such as Ecuador and Bolivia have integrated into their political constitutions.

Buen Vivir is derived from the Quechua concept of Sumak Kawsay, which generally means living in harmony, in balance and in community; questioning the Western concept of development and wellbeing of comfort and individuality (Gudynas, 2011). *Buen Vivir* can be defined as the practice and ideology of living with respect and abundance in balance with the earth, the community and the surrounding world. *Buen Vivir* promotes public "well- being" in terms of the individual in the social context of his or her community and in harmony with nature (Shebell & Moser, 2019); and does not conceptually distinguish between human beings, nature and society, as all forms of life are seen as parts of a symbiotic whole (Calisto Friant & Langmore, 2015). *Buen Vivir* advocates a way of life that is harmonious with natural cycles, favoring economies based on non-degrading activities, through which nature and society can flourish (Acosta, 2010). In this sense, it opposes neoliberal and capitalist models of production, accumulation and consumption; promoting "ecological criteria, human dignity and social justice" (Escobar, 2015, p. 455).

Despite of the above discussions, most theories on popular urbanization still understand wellbeing as an issue of poverty reduction, and sustainability since the environmental impact caused by these settlements. Similarly, these theoretical positions reproduce a silence and positioning of the subjects in peri-urbanization from an "otherness", constituting a great challenge in the persistence of discourses of identity construction (Varley, 2013). These approaches leave aside the centrality of the economic structure and the consequent conquest of central and peri-central areas by real estate capital triggers pressure for expulsion, understood through gentrification, displacement and dispossession (Janoschka, 2016). In this regard, Rolnik (2017) points out that housing and urban policies renounced the function of distributing wealth, a common good that society agrees to divide or provide to those who have fewer resources, to become a mechanism for income extraction, financial gain and accumulation of wealth, a strategy of colonization of urban land and housing.

In the face of the capitalist domination of wellbeing as the absence of disease, decolonial positions such as Buen Vivir, as mentioned earlier, focus on a broader view that connects land and communities. In this approach, however, there remains a silence in the face of the multiple violence experienced by certain bodies. In other words, the silencing of pa-triarchy as an axis of oppression persists and is the point of greatest challenge. Therefore, indigenous feminisms demand a good life as a right and not only as a path of opposition to capitalism (Leyva & Icaza, 2019).

In regard with the urgent need to build a social framework that invokes the subversion of the capitalist, patriarchal and colonial system to a broader understanding of popular urbanization, this chapter delves into the processes of social reproduction in the Alto Fucha Ecoterritory in order to reflect on wellbeing and sustainability from the perspective of intersectionality. The Alto Fucha Ecoterritory is an informal origin area located in the urban-rural edge of the city of Bogotá, with an international, national and local reference for its community and popular feminist organization. Its self-designation as an Ecoterritory stems from the research of its women inhabitants to question the urban regulation and resist eviction pressures. Alto Fucha is a territory of ancestral origin of the Muisca people (Chibcha and Muisca are two terms used interchangeably to refer to the original inhabitants of the eastern Andes, in the central departments of Colombia: Cundinamarca and Boyacá (Langebaek, 2019)), spun by the Fucha River, the eastern hills and its community. The actions of women from practices of inhabiting intimately linked to social reproduction braid the defense of the territory in a broader struggle, in the defense of the territory- body and territory-land; and with it, a look at the welfare and sustainability in terms of territorial sovereignty.

Within this framework and through the lens of intersectionality, this chapter discusses the processes of social reproduction in popular urbanization in search of wellbeing and sustainability, using the Alto Fucha ecoterritory in Bogotá as a case study. To this end, it first presents the theoretical discussion on intersectionality in dialogue with popular feminism in terms of wellbeing and sustainability. Second, the methodology and the case study are presented, followed by the third section on the discussion of the results, explaining how social reproduction evolves and the implications for wellbeing and sustainability. The fourth section presents the main arguments on how women's housing practices and their defense of life help to understand the challenges of popular urbanization and contribute to thinking about wellbeing and sustainability in these areas. The chapter concludes with some final remarks.

2. THEORETICAL FRAMEWORK: INTERSECTIONALITY IN A DIALOGUE WITH POPULAR FEMINISM. DIMENSIONS FOR THE PURSUIT OF WELLBEING AND ITS CONTRIBUTION TO SUSTAINABILITY

Intersectionality, according to Viveros Vigoya (2016), as a theoretical and methodological perspective, seeks to explain the intertwining of power relations maintained through identity categories of race, class, gender, among others, that simultaneously cross and construct bodies. Intersectionality as a term was coined by Kim-berle Crenshaw in 1989 to point to the invisibility and legal fragmentation that denies the oppressions that can simultaneously cross corporealities, in this case being female and black (Ahmed, 2018; Platero, 2014; Suárez Bonilla, 2014; Viveros Vigoya, 2016, Crenshaw 1989, 1991). Crenshaw's (1991) arguments are based on the different ways in which race and gender intersect and affect the lives of black women, whose forms of discrimination are not delimited in either race or gender studies.

An important point made by Crenshaw (1991) is that he places the multiple violence that has been legitimized behind these forms of discrimination at the center of intersectionality. Thus, a fundamental question is how these identity differences end up creating categories of social stratification and thus political domination (Migliario et al., 2020). Intersectionality poses the challenge of understanding how there is a mutual constitution between identity categories, beyond a summation and establishment of hierarchies between them (Rodó de Zarate, 2019). It is about a matrix of domination in which some identity categories, such as white, male, represent a privilege and others, such as black, female, represent a condition of oppression; and, above all, to highlight that in the intersection of these axes, more complex inequalities are constituted, beyond a simple summation (Collins, 1990).

Intersectionality invokes to look at the logics of appropriation of land and women's bodies, particularly those sustained by the capitalist, patriarchal and colonial triad. Federici (2010) is a theoretical reference that provides a starting point to connect this triad of domination with the processes of social reproduction. In her text "Caliban and the Witch, Women, Body and Accumulation", she offers a historical overview of the intimate link between capitalism and violence as the main objective of this accumulation system. She points out slavery and land dispossession as forms of capital accumulation, specifying how the exploitation of women's bodies is part of the primitive accumulation of capital: "Capitalism was the first system to provide for the regulation and mechanization of the body as a key condition for the accumulation of wealth" (Federici, 2022, p. 174). That is to say, the silencing of the practices of social reproduction, of the reproduction of the labor force to go to the factory, is what has offered all the conditions for sustaining the system. Social reproduction is a non-commodified zone of capital, but whose unpaid work is essential and indispensable for the sustenance of capitalism referred to the forms of material provisioning, and the care and interaction of the construction of social ties to produce human beings, identified as care or affective labor (Fraser, 2014).

In this sense, from a feminist approach to economics since the seventies, they have argued how these gender relations structure the patriarchal, capitalist and colonial order (Cielo et al, 2016). Patriarchy, in particular, organizes society around the sexual division of labor, whose distribution based on a dichotomous and biological structure between men and women naturalizing women to the activities of the house, the home (Brito, 2008). Capitalism and the sexual division of labor have reproduced this place as a territory of subordination through the silencing and undervaluation of social reproduction of work (domestic and care tasks) performed mainly by women, giving primacy to economic productivity. This set of social reproduction practices is organized politically, economically and spatially through the public-private difference, taking place both in the actual space and in women's bodies; thus, embodying a form of oppression that explains the impoverishment and historical subordination of women, feminized and racialized. In this chapter, these legitimized and normalized violence are associated with coloniality.

The temporal context that gives rise to the recognition of social reproduction begins in the 1970s. At that time, there was a considerable increase in theoretical and empirical work, on a par with the initiatives of women's movements around the world, aimed at implementing reform programs that guarantee gender equality in the spheres of justice, politics and social rights (Molyneux, 2010). According to research by Ripio-Rodriguez and others (2019), feminist demands emerged within the context of what is known as "the new social movements", which represented new approaches vis-à-vis the labor movement of the nineteenth century. However, in the 1980s and 1990s, they encountered the triumph of the neoliberal political project and the consequent impoverishment of the countries of the South. Thus, in a context where class analysis loses centrality, Marxist feminists retake the idea of exploitation to characterize the situation of women in the contemporary world. In this way they analyze, on the one hand, the relationship between capitalism and patriarchy, highlighting synergies between these two systems, and at the same time, rejecting universalist views that dissociate economic exploitation and sexual domination. On the other hand, Marxist feminists raise the critique of Marxist categories in the absence of the category of gender. In this line, feminist researchers such as Cristina Vega (2020), based on feminist Marxist research, reiterate how the capitalist system determines the quality of existence in its constant dynamics of accumulation, configured by the dispossession of bodies and territories.

This social, political and economic order is clearly reflected in space, the public-private division has been the legitimizing mechanism of the imbrication of patriarchy, capitalism and colonialism. In line with this, feminist approaches from geography (McDowell, 1999; Massey, 1994; García-Ramon, 2019) and architecture (Colectiu-Punt 6, 2019; Muxi, 2018,) have pointed out the non-neutrality of space arguing how power structures are projected in space influencing the ways of inhabiting. In this way, the domestic space understood as the interior of the dwelling in a form of capture of thought denying the possibility of understanding this space from other logics and other configurations.

In line with the above, studies on the expanded conception of capitalism, which relates to the broader circuits that assemble the territory, community care work is part of the processes of social reproduction (Cielo, 2023). In this sense, Cielo (2023) situates community dynamics and the logics of self-organization as aspects that are also part of the reproduction of life. Community care is also essential in sustaining life, materialized through the care of people, animals and common goods. Collective interest and leaderships configured in different forms of organization consolidate bonds of cooperation and responsibility (Caffentzis & Federici, 2013). From this frame of reference, Cielo (2023) connects with the readings that deconstruct the traditional concept of vulnerability to situate itself from the sense proposed by Butler (2010). That is, to stop situating vulnerability in bodies, based on bodily attributes, to understand it as a human condition that places all human beings in the same place of precariousness. That is, we are precarious because we require other social, political and affective ties to sustain life. In this sense, the expanded reproduction of life is situated in which the community is based on interdependent beings that require infrastructure, territory, physical and emotional care.

From the studies of the expanded view of capital, which are not disconnected from the intersectional stance, Nancy Fraser (2014) discusses three hidden processes in which the triad of domination operates or as she calls them "Marx's hidden dwellings": 1) social reproduction, 2) nature as a resource and 3) public power and private power. Through these processes she seeks to account for the existence of non-commodified social relations that provide the conditions of existence of capitalism.

Now, popular feminisms, initially only applied in their own territories, have begun to consolidate with intersectionality in dialogue with indigenous feminisms and eco-feminisms to think their own practices of counter-hegemonic struggle in defense of land and life (Diaz & Torno, 2021). Thus, colonial and precolonial domination is embedded in political action to denounce territorial wounds, of the land and of women's bodies in particular. In this line of action, from indigenous feminisms, Adriana Guzmán (2019), a Bolivian indigenous feminist, together with other Aymara women (*Mujeres Creando Comunidad* group) proposes the category "community feminism", as a result of a process of resistance, transgression and epistemic construction from their feelings and reconceptualization of the hegemonic understanding of "community". Similarly, Lorena Cabnal (2015), Community Feminist and Mayan-Xinka indigenous, from Guatemala, co-founder of the community-territorial feminist movement, proposes the *acuerpamiento* as a counter-hegemonic political practice and restoration with the land. "Acuerpar or acuerpamiento" as an embodied practice of political action is defined as follows:

"The personal and collective action of our bodies outraged by the injustices experienced by other bodies. That are self-convened to provide themselves with political energy to resist and act against the multiple patriarchal, colonialist, racist and capitalist oppressions. The *acuerpamiento* generates affective and spiritual energies and breaks borders and imposed time. It provides us with closeness, collective indignation but also revitalization and new strength, to recover joy without losing indignation." (Cabnal, 2015).

In this way, the relationship between territory and bodies is the thread that weaves together the theoretical and methodological perspectives of intersectionality and popular feminisms in Latin America. These principles are embodied in an ontological relationship between territory and body (Zaragocin & Caretta, 2021). From this political position, they demand and reject the extractivist logic of land, the exploitation of women's bodies, and the normalized and silenced violence perpetuated under the systems of domination of patriarchy, capitalism, and colonialism (Cabnal, 2010; Guzmán, 2019, Migliario González, et al., 2020). The link between intersectionality and popular feminisms is relevant because while the former observes the situated reality configured in a matrix of oppressions and privileges, "popular feminisms" explore political horizons of transformation, as observed in the ecoterritory of Alto Fucha.

From this approach, indigenous women defend *Buen Vivir* as a right, in which they put their bodies and thinking of themselves taking away from the imposed identity given by the patriarchal, capitalist and colonial triad and sustain an ancestral struggle against extractivist policies and violence (Gutiérrez, 2019 in Leiva, 2019). In this regard, indigenous women defend counter-hegemonic forms of self-recognition by calling themselves as women-people. In this self-recognition, they do not only demand that the personal is political, but also make visible that they are an organic part of family and community struggles and of native women's movements. In this way, they propose a break with the individualized reading of the body, by connecting the personal-collective of their being and their doing (Leyva, 2019).

Thus, the reading of wellbeing and sustainability has to go through two dimensions. First, to recognize the operating logics of the patriarchal, capitalist and colonial triad that defines wellbeing in a way that it accommodates to the status quo in order to guarantee the sustainability of extractivist practices, both of the land and of women's bodies; and at the same time, it presents land and women's issues as different matters. In this regard, it is not possible to speak of wellbeing if the normalized violence behind the processes of reproduction continues to be sustained, nor is it possible to speak of sustainability if the logics of land appropriation continue to be normalized. Second, to agree on resistance practices that invite to incorporate ways of living from interdependence and eco-dependence in order to defend life and liberate the earth, as proposed by ecofeminism (Herrero, 2011).

Finally, in the processes of social reproduction understood in terms of the intertwined relationship between patriarchy, capitalism and coloniality, as intersectionality allows us to see, wellbeing and sustainability have to do with subverting the logics of land appropriation and violence against women. The former, which have normalized the conception of land as an extractable and infinite resource, and the recognition of the hidden processes of capital, such as social reproduction; and the latter, whose silencing ends up normalizing violence and places of subordination against women and racialized bodies. Thus, the approach of intersectionality and the dialogue with indigenous feminisms is a way of embodying the defense of life that is situated before the peremptory epistemic-ethical-political rupture. Wellbeing and sustainability can abandon the anthropocentric gaze traversed by patriarchal, capitalist and colonial attitudes in order to inhabit the web of life and liberate territories (Cabnal, 2010).

3. METHODOLOGY AND CASE STUDY

The reading of popular urbanization in Bogotá, is a qualitative study that focuses on observing women's life practices in the Alto Fucha ecoterritory in order to delve into the challenges of wellbeing and sustainability previously identified in theory. Their community and political organization is structured around a critical dialogue against urban regulations, at the same time delving into proposals for living in the former rural frontier.

This study is located within critical research, by investigating a central theme that involves the problematization of knowledge, which does not only try to explain reality, but rather to understand it as a social phenomenon based on intersubjectivities that include the researcher, therefore it requires a self-reflective or reflexive component (Carspecken, 2008). This research is also situated within the feminist paradigm by considering the study of problems involving relations of inequality, delving into issues of how gender intersects with other forms of women's oppression, based primarily on the categories of class and gender. The feminist character of the research calls the researcher to a continuous examination of the role of power and authority, granted by the system itself, in the understanding of the research process in general. In this way, it constantly reminds the researcher of the risk and responsibility of not reproducing dichotomous views or extractivist actions with the research participants (Hesse-Biber, 2008). Finally, the case study approach is constructivist in that it does not assume a single reality, understanding that empirical reality and concepts are mutually constructed, again recalling that the researcher does not occupy a neutral position (Blatter, 2008; Sauto, 2005).

The research design started from the main methodological guideline of intersectionality: interdimensionality, which establishes a connection between macro- and micro-social dimensions. This methodological approach, in the words of Sara Ahmed (2019), means bringing the theory closer to the skin in order to recognize the incidence of power structures in the ways of living. The data collection techniques used in the research were in-depth interviews, field observations, and commented tours. The techniques used sought to investigate their community organization in relation to the dynamics of their housing self-production processes and their lived experience. In this way, to explore the processes of social reproduction by observing their social itineraries, trajectories of struggle, personal experiences and their historical and contextual links in the territory (Elizalde, 2008). The data collection was characterized by the attempt to use the comprehensive narrative (Grau Biosca, 2014), which included a conscious exercise of listening not only to the words, but also to the silences and their corporealities during the dialogue, from the recognition of the differences in the hierarchical position among them as residents and from the role as researchers.

The selection of the case study and research participants was developed in two stages. First, general exploration to delve into the organization of women based on popular feminism initiated in January 2021, at a time when the Covid-19 pandemic was still in progress, hence the conversations were conducted virtually. This first inquiry showed the popular feminine force in defense of their territories and their persistent participation in the processes of public policy formulation, as was the case of the formulation of the Land Management Plan (2021). It also allowed the identification in Alto Fucha of a social and political organization based on research and popular education as strategies for living. The second moment was developed directly in Alto Fucha and worked both with older women, called *mayoras*[1] and participants of the same who had a lower level of participation. The fieldwork consisted of 17 in- depth interviews, 4 field observations of the political activities organized by the different community organizations led by men and women, and 9 commented tours guided by three *mayoras*. This allowed us to identify that there are different discourses and positions within the same organizations in the territory, and that are in tension. On the one hand, there are male leaders whose defense of the territory points exclusively to the dispossession of land, and on the other hand, religious positions that are opposed to the defense and demands based on popular feminisms and the lived experience of the *mayoras*. This research delved into the community and personal action of those who were closer to popular feminisms, without ignoring that there is also tension among those who identify with and support this political position.

3.1. Case Study: Alto Fucha Ecoterritory

Alto Fucha is an ecoterritory that, through its narratives and political actions, problematizes the urban concepts imposed "from above" on the popular habitat. At the same time, it explores practices of resistance through popular education, art and models of sustainability, such as urban gardens, the promotion of knowledge, collective creation and defense of the territory. The ecoterritory arises from a process of self-recognition by the community, and in particular from the work of its women, in defense to remain and not be expelled from it in the face of real estate dynamics. It is an urban-rural border area, southeast of Bogotá, located at the foothills of the Eastern Hills, interwoven by the Delirio Reserve, the Fucha River and the popular urbanization. The Ecoterritory is made up of seven neighborhoods of informal origin: Montecarlo, San Cristóbal Alto, Manila, Gran Colombia, Laureles, La Cecilia and Aguas Claras. Figure 1 shows the location of the case study.

Figure 1. Alto Fucha Ecoterritory Location

Source: Own elaboration based on IDECA (2021).

These lands in the Alto Fucha, which were originally farms, began to be subdivided and sold as payment for the care work (guarding and cultivating the land) and in the midst of fraud, both in the sale of the land and in the processing of the deed, according to the residents. According to aerial photographs (IGAC, 1977), the settlement began in the late 1970s, but government recognition (legalization) occurred between 2000 and 2015, when part of the area was approved for sand mining purposes. The mercantilist strategy to extract minerals from the Reserve operates through this strip issued by the Ministry of Environment, Housing and Territorial Development that defined as a space for consolidation of the urban structure and buffer zone and definitive containment of the urbanization processes of the Eastern Hills. However, this strip represented the extraction of 973 hectares of the Reserve, which in practice meant possibilities for urban development. A popular action provisionally suspended the permission for mining, when the Council of State established the reinstatement of the buffer strip on the eastern edge of the city, allowing the legalization of the informal neighborhoods settled there (Aguas Claras, La Cecilia and Laureles), but also the continuity of high-rise housing projects that had acquired construction rights.

Alto Fucha Ecoterritory is classified as socio-economic stratum 1 (to improve clarity, please write this way: used for tax purpose, being stratum 1 the lowest) and its population is 7,327 inhabitants, of which 51.2% are women (DANE, 2018). Figure 2 presents the socio-economic stratification of Bogotá and the location of Alto Fucha Ecoterritory.

Figure 2. Socioeconomic stratification of Bogotá and location of the Alto Fucha Ecoterritory

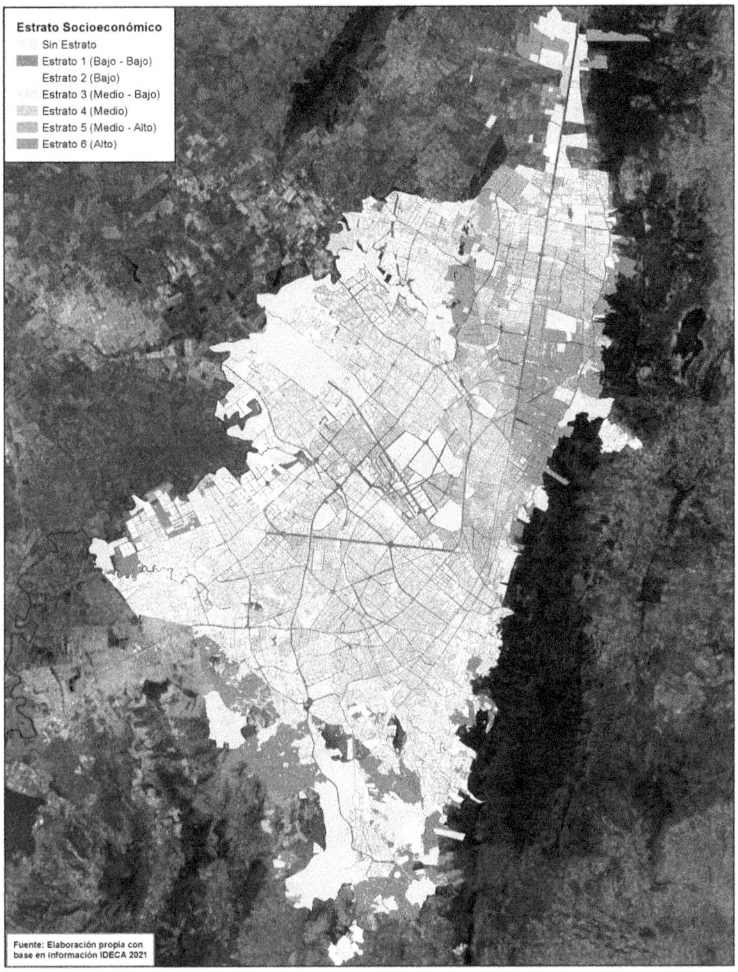

Source: Own elaboration based on IDECA basic cartography (2021).

The meaning of "Ecoterritory" is a proposal to live on the urban-rural border articulated through agro-ecological, social and political processes materialized in a network of family and community gardens as a result of the appropriation of the abandoned plots after the resettlement process that has been accomplished by the municipality. The network of gardens offers the conditions for the possibility of reinterpreting the neighborhood units, understanding them as a single fabric, as micro-territories. The strengthening of the orchard network constitutes a condition of possibility to also reject the eco-neighborhoods proposal promoted from above:

from the government and academia. Figure 3 shows the most recognized micro-territories in Alto Fucha.

Figure 3. Alto Fucha Micro-territories

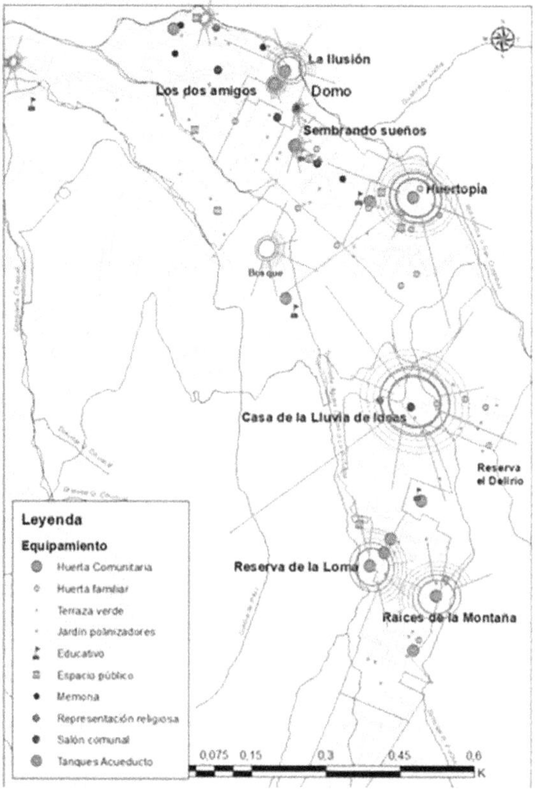

Source: Rincón-Castellanos, 2024

4. RESULTS: SOCIAL REPRODUCTION IN POPULAR URBANIZATION, A CHALLENGE FOR WELLBEING AND SUSTAINABILITY

The entrance to the Alto Fucha Ecoterritory projects a first urban image framed by the Fucha River and houses on its water's edge, colonial buildings, high-rise housing projects and informal urbanization. This landscape reveals the tension experienced by the residents of the popular urbanization in the face of the possibility of being displaced from the territory. The presence of informal housing along the banks of the Fucha River, which has been the object of resettlement, captures the attention of the housing problem, leaving aside the affectation that the logics of land organization represent for this population group and, of course, for women.

The location of Alto Fucha Ecoterritory within the strip that was projected as a buffer zone with the Forest Reserve, and that, in the midst of the massification of high-rise housing projects, a trend towards urbanization is unleashed. This scenario represents for the inhabitants economic and land speculation interests and silent mechanisms of expulsion or "green gentrification" (López, 2022). Figure 4 shows the urban image that interweaves economic and speculative land interests.

Figure 4. Urban image of Alto Fucha Ecoterritory

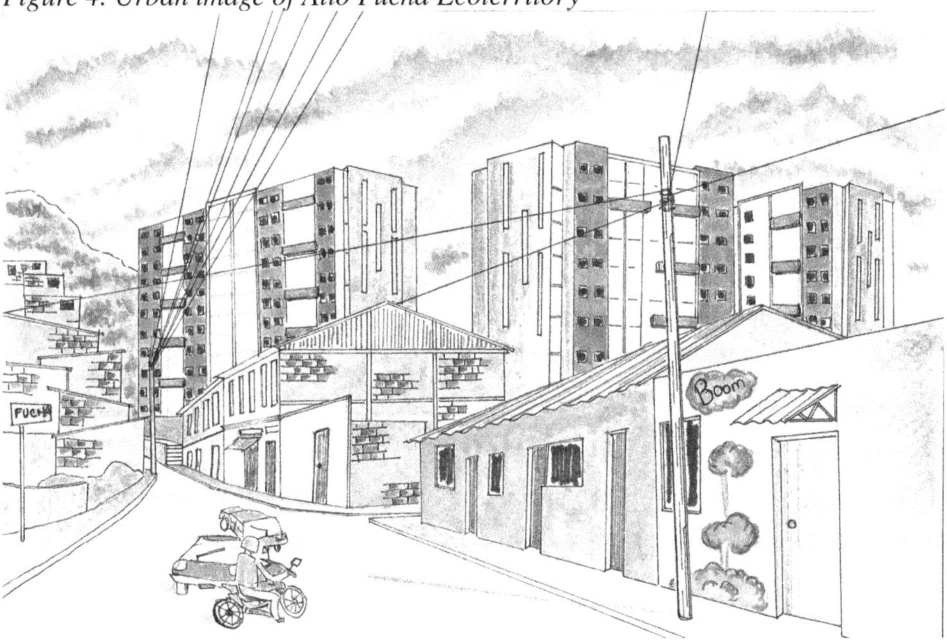

Source: Rincón-Castellanos, 2024.

Previous research carried out in the territory has identified a problem of expulsion in the resettlement process (López, 2022; Sánchez, 2019). This process began in 1998, and by 2020, the municipality administration had already resettled 215 plots (Datos abiertos Bogotá, 2020). Research has indicated that the Policy for the Management of Protected Land in the city (Decree 462 of 2008) has promoted this pressure for expulsion to the extent that the plots after resettlement become part of the Protected Land, but in practice these are not intervened (López, 2022). This lack of intervention has led to the reappearance of illegal occupations on the edge of the Fucha River and in areas classified as unmitigable risk, especially in the Laureles neighborhood. In addition, the occupation of the vestiges of the plots by crime and drug consumption groups has reappeared (Sanchez, 2019).

In the context of this problem, a process of resistance emerges that is oriented towards processes of renaturalization and resignification in order to avoid being expelled from the territory. In this way, communal spaces have been built in the territory that represent territorial references of resistance. An emblematic example of this is the “Casa de la lluvia de ideas” (house of ideas), located in the La Cecilia neighborhood. This project is a self-governing initiative of several collectives of the territory, under the leadership of the collective *Arquitectura Expandida*. This cultural and community self- management house began with first conversations in 2012 and finally in 2019 it was actually built. The initial idea was a community hall to a multiple space where a community library and multiple artistic, cultural, pedagogical activities, as well as citizen participation meetings are currently operating. It is described by its collaborators as a process of physical and social self-construction where the participatory design turns out to be rather an exploration of forms of collective organization where the roles respond to the knowledge of each human being, which in practice these boundaries given by the roles are blurred. *Guadua* (a type of bamboo known as “vegetable steel” because of its excellent tolerance to bending and is widely used in the construction of earthquake-resistant housing (Velazco 2002) was the material chosen in response to the search for articulation with the natural potential of the territory. The transparent material that covers the bamboo structure symbolically represents the relationship between the inside and the outside. This building has been at risk of being dismantled to be replaced with a conventional community hall, after the legalization processes in 2015. This risk constitutes a form of silencing the territorial governance that has been consolidating in Alto Fucha Ecoterritory (Arquitectura Expandida, 2015). Figure 5 presents the house of Brainstorming.

Figure 5. Brainstorming House

Source: Rincón-Castellanos, 2024

After legalization in 2015, the neighborhood began a process of improvement. By 2019, road improvements and façade interventions were being carried out. By 2021, the municipality administration intervened Manila, Laureles and La Cecilia neighborhoods, within the framework of the "Housing and Decent Environments in Urban and Rural Territory" program. The investment project "Integral Improvement of Neighborhoods with Citizen Participation Bogotá" improved 44 road segments in the neighborhoods and 3 areas of public space in the neighborhoods La Cecilia, Laureles, Gran Colombia and Manila. The road interventions consisted of paving roads and improving sidewalks. In the initial exploratory tours, the women referred to these interventions as silent forms of expulsion of the original communities. They also described them as forms of hardening of the popular urbanization and of the Eastern Hills. With the word "hardening" they refer to the use of cement in the improvement without a proposal of articulation with the natural potential of the territory. This term is also used to denounce new constructions on the Forest Reserve. This hardening is felt by the women as a form of deepening of territorial wounds due to the mistreatment and destruction of the natural environment.

Other researchers direct their criticism to the territorial homogenization represented by the neighborhood interventions of paving and green railings everywhere. Figure 6 shows a part of the intervention where the characteristics of the intervention can be observed through paving and green railings in a sector with the presence of ranch type housing.

Figure 6. Neighborhood intervention. Paving and green railings

Source: Rincón-Castellanos, 2024

They also point out the disarticulation with the local environmental conditions. For example, it is possible to name the disarticulation with the plots that were subject to resettlement and with protection areas and risk zones. Figure 7 represents the relationship between the neighborhood intervention (road segment) and the Fucha River, where the configuration of a border that reaffirms the dichotomy between the natural and the artificial can be observed.

Figure 7. Neighborhood improvement along the river bank

Source: Rincón-Castellanos, 2024

Other examples of neighborhood interventions are the adjustment of sidewalks in response to the unevenness of the terrain and also with the way in which the urban border is configured. Figure 8 shows the intervention of the improvement of roads and sidewalks in areas close to the urban-rural border where the presence of balconies can be observed as a response to the unevenness of the terrain made by both the municipality administration and the community. Likewise, the road can be seen as an urban-rural border.

Figure 8. Neighborhood intervention on the urban-rural border

Source: Rincón-Castellanos, 2024

Interventions in more consolidated areas of the Ecoterritory, with housing between 2 and 3 floors, can be seen in form of the tendency to homogenize (Pava & Escallón, 2020). Interviews with experts expressed the criticism of homogenization in regard that equality is not about everything looking the same. In this sense, the issue of homogenization of popular urbanization through neighborhood intervention has to do with the non-recognition of social and economic diversity, as well as physical and environmental conditions. In the midst of this intervention process, the Commission in Defense of the Alto Fucha Territory (La Comisión) was consolidated, a group articulated in the network of micro-territories, born in defense of remaining in the territory, acting under the slogan "no decision about us, without us". Figure 9 shows a neighborhood intervention in a consolidated area that certainly projects an image of improved physical conditions.

Figure 9. Neighborhood intervention in a consolidated area

Source: Rincón-Castellanos, 2024

5. DISCUSSION: WOMEN'S DWELLING PRACTICES AND THE DEFENSE OF LIFE IN POPULAR URBANIZATION, BETWEEN WELLBEING AND SUSTAINABILITY

The defense of life is the slogan that mobilizes the political action of women in the ecoterritory of Alto Fucha, making connections between territorial wounds and the exploration of forms of re-existence in the territory. These territorial wounds are related to the forms of dispossession of the physical territory as well as of one's own body, which are articulated with forms of recognition that reproduce and maintain identity constructions of an otherness that is sustained by appropriation logics and patriarchal, capitalist and colonial extractivist practices. Re-existence is linked to the exploration of memories, meanings and feelings in an intimate connection with the territory. In this way, living from the defense of life and territory implies, on the one hand, understanding the relations of power and oppression maintained by the same normative and institutional devices. And on the other hand, the political bets of re-existence that direct the gaze to the political horizons of transformation in relation to the ways of recognition and distribution.

Recalling that women's political action is based on popular feminisms, they propose territorial sovereignty as a political horizon, one in which the land is defended by denouncing the extractivist logics of the land and the violence suffered by women and racializing bodies in order to inhabit from the agreement. Quoting again Cabnal (2015), a practice that allows to cultivate the capacity to feel political indignation in face of territorial injustices and wounds of other corporealities to truly act from a collectivity.

The political horizon based on the defense of the territory and the settlement is permanently constructed and reconstructed from the practices of inhabiting in everyday life. Thus, the process of reproduction of women's life in the popular urbanization is intimately linked to the defense of life. The process of social reproduction is presented from the practices of inhabiting conceived through the four spheres of everyday life: personal, political, productive and reproductive (Colectiu-Punt 6, 2019). In this way, the practices of healing, defense of the territory and sustaining life are highlighted as the practices of social reproduction in the peri-urban areas of the city that represent a dissident social and political framework for a reading of wellbeing and sustainability.

5.1. Personal sphere and healing

The practice of healing that is built and embodied around the sense of "body-territory" seeks to re-exist through the reconstruction of this connection. This practice of inhabiting seeks to repair territorial wounds in order to re-exist from an intimate connection with the territory. This practice goes through a process of self-recognition, sowing and gathering that summons existence from the nature and ancestral spirit of the territory.

In this sense, the Fucha River and the flow of its waters, as memory and vestiges of the Muisca indigenous people, have inspired the process of self-recognition of women. Fucha means woman in the Muisca language (Muysccubun, 2009). Thus, they recognize themselves as *Las Fuchas*, the "guardians of the territory" and as *mayoras*, among others that include men, such as *hijuefuchas*. Self-recognition is based on knowing the territory because it is not possible to defend and love what one does not know, and this is how they express it in the different meetings. This self-recognition speaks of healing as a process of individual, collective and political transformation in the territory, going through the understanding of the lived experience in order to situate it, position it and orient it towards the resignification of its existence from the territory. The reconstruction of the body-territory link as a principle of the practice of healing is thus expressed in their stories:

"Healing with the land, from the dialogue around the paths we travel, from the closeness to the flow of the river, returning to the riverbed, returning to the river to heal" (Laurel/E- 20-7-2021).

Cultivating the land has materialized the social struggle for the defense of the territory, configuring a network of community and family gardens as a political response to the abandonment of the plots remaining after the intervention of the "resettlement" program. The network of gardens as resistance has its roots in the political action of the group "Huertopía", the result of the research work of one of its members as already mentioned (Sánchez, 2019). This network works as micro-territories that sustain the defense of the territory on a personal scale and with a territorial scope. Cultivating as a practice of healing is an inspiration of the *mayoras,* who inhabit this practice from the word, from resistance, from a political act. The feelings and thoughts of women, elders and popular educators are written through plants. This is how one of the leaders expresses the planting process:

"I am one with nature, it is in each plant, in each tree, it is that connection to heal, I am embraced by the same territory, it is the practice of planting, it is the feeling of the call of the earth, The orchard is my writing" (Arrayán, E-2-2021).

Cultivating as a healing practice, represents the care of life. Through this practice, links are built with the territory and with other corporealities in order to understand and build from differences. In their words, they refer to this practice as lulling life. This means looking for strategies to care for and sustain life. This is how it sounds in the words of the *mayoras*:

"To cultivate is to lull life" (Arrayán, E-2-2021). "We began to cultivate with affection because a plant is a living being and that is how it should be treated" (Chinchimaní, E-1-2023).

The *Juntanza* (getting together) is the thread that weaves the body-territory link and resistance on this personal scale. Women's circles are also a reflection of the practice of *juntanza.* Dialogues are built in the midst of ancestral rituals, sometimes guided by women of Muisca origin. Between water, fire and incense, they recover ancestral memory. The women's circles, and in essence the circularity represents a horizontal gathering, there is no hierarchy. In the middle of the dialogues, a process of recognition of the other takes place through the sharing of words and experience. Figure 10 represents the healing circle on the banks of the Fucha River ritualizing life between water, earth, air and fire.

Figure 10. Felícita Campos Women's Circle, 2023

Source: Rincón-Castellanos, 2024.

5.2. Political sphere and territorial defense

Territorial reconfiguration is the practice that places territorial sovereignty as the horizon of political action. In this sense, the concept of "ecoterritory" germinates from the research of Jhody Sanchez (2019), inhabitant of the territory, as a way to confront the silent processes of displacement through the resettlement process and the legal limbo when they were part of the Forest Reserve.

The second version of "Ecoterritory" by Laura Navas (2022) expands its boundaries, including the El Delirio Trail, an ancestral path, as a determinant of a new threshold of the territory. This proposal, based on an ecofeminist perspective, includes the protection and care of the commons as a new aspect in the defense of the territory. Figure 11 presents the second proposal for territorial reconfiguration elabo-rated by Navas (2022), highlighting as common goods the informal settlement and the environmental reserve and its ecological and landscape value, together with the community that lives there.

Figure 11. Second proposal for the territorial reconfiguration of the Alto Fucha Ecoterritory.

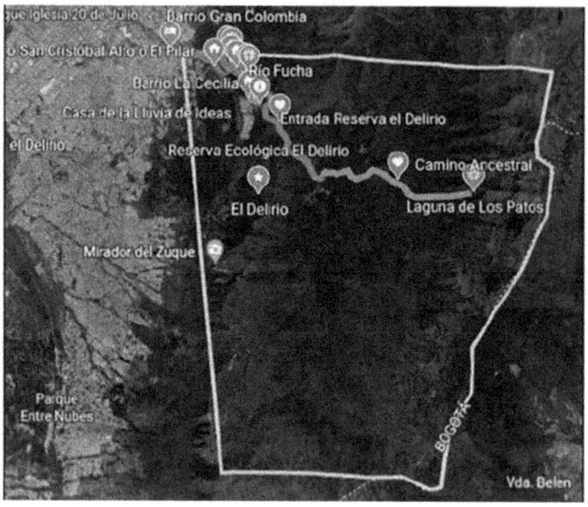

Source: Navas (2022)

The defense of the commons is harmonized with community management, and this is explained in the intimate and public spheres:

"This project seeks to contribute to the community management of the Alto Fucha Ecoterritory, through the collective systematization of women's contributions in a scenario of political dispute over the use of common goods for community purposes" (Navas, 2022, p.2).

5.3. Social reproduction and productivity spheres and life support

Unlike the previous spheres, this section presents the spheres of social reproduction and productivity together, recalling the existing intertwining between them from feminist economics (Gago, 2019; Fraser, 2014; Pérez Orozco, 2006). This is not to say that there is no connection between the two previous spheres, but to highlight the overlap that occurs between them, insofar as the sphere of social reproduction generates the conditions of possibility for the sphere of productivity. Self-built refers to spatial configurations woven from the satisfaction of basic needs (bedroom, bathroom, kitchen), but also from women's desire to configure their own space. Two moments of the self-production process are taken into account in this research: 1) the access to the land and 2) the construction or organization of the dwelling.

Regarding access to plots, in Alto Fucha and in general in the territories of informal origin in Colombia, the possibilities of access are related to: payment for being farm caretakers, inheritance, usufruct, purchase to legal or illegal developers or invasion (Hernández-Garcia, 2016), these las two not common in Alto Fucha. In this phase of the process of self-production of housing, there is a tendency to silence women paid (productive) and unpaid work (social reproduction). In the stories, this tendency is visible in some of the women who acknowledge both the economic contribution and the work related to the construction process of the men. In the stories, the contribution of both the productive and reproductive aspects that women also make in the management of access to the lot is highlighted, as is heard in their voices:

"My parents took care of the farm and my grandmother, then we lived in a little ranch, here on the farm in Manila, here we farmed. Between all of us men, women and children we sowed and harvested, others helped to cook and the men went out to sell to the stores or in the market places" (Arrayán, E-2-2021).

Observing in a different story related to the purchase of the plot, the overlapping again between the productive and reproductive sphere arises between the financial contribution of women (productive) in obtaining the plot and the care work that happens in between (reproductive). Additionally, there is a process of indebtedness that, as Verónica Gago (2019) explains, constitutes a mechanism for extracting capital value from areas from which it is apparently not possible to extract more capital. In this way, it is interesting to highlight the contribution of women in the access to the plot through their financial contribution derived from remunerated activities. Thus, the financial contribution such as indebtedness, which can fall on the household depending on the form of internal distribution of income, is heard in their accounts as follows:

"My husband, well, at that time he was earning well. So we bought the plot with that. And then, with my severance pay, about 20 days later, we started to buy the bricks, the cement, the beams and all that was what consumed the most money. We paid a cousin and between the two of them, they built the house. Through Codensa [Bogotá energy company] they lent me 5 million and we bought the plaster and the house was finished, he practically did everything" (Bromelia, E-3-2021).

On the housing scale, the stories show the continuity of the intertwining between social reproduction and productivity identified through savings for the acquisition and storage of materials and the hiring of a master builder for the construction of the house. In their accounts, the savings represented in material for the house as a task of social reproduction that comes from an economic activity becomes visible. The housing construction process is narrated as follows:

"My mom, as she got money, she was buying. We lived in the *ranchito* and so we kept the materials there in the *ranchito*. And when she had more or less enough to build the walls, she paid a master builder who was a neighbor here and helped her build the walls" (Arrayán, E- 2-2021).

Regarding the construction and organization of the dwelling, configurations emerge that in some cases maintain a link with the kitchen, others seek a detachment from this place, and others are configured from other spatialities within the dwelling. The following are seven types of configurations observed in the dwellings through the women's accounts: a) ranch-dwelling, b) kitchen-garden, c) kitchen-workshop, d) kitchen-dwelling, e) attic, f) study room, and g) room (in the case of different sexual preferences). As a whole, it is possible to mention that these spatial configurations, which are a form of response to the search for a space of their own, are also constituted as micro- territories of defense in the Alto Fucha. The figure presents the micro-territory that is configured between the dwelling, the space for the community pot and a fountain "Nuestra Madre Agua" as a symbolic representation of struggle, resistance and connection with the territory. This territory is also configured by a garden. Figure 12 presents the construction of micro-territories and their symbolic and material multiplicity through social reproduction.

Figure 12. Micro-territories and Social Reproduction

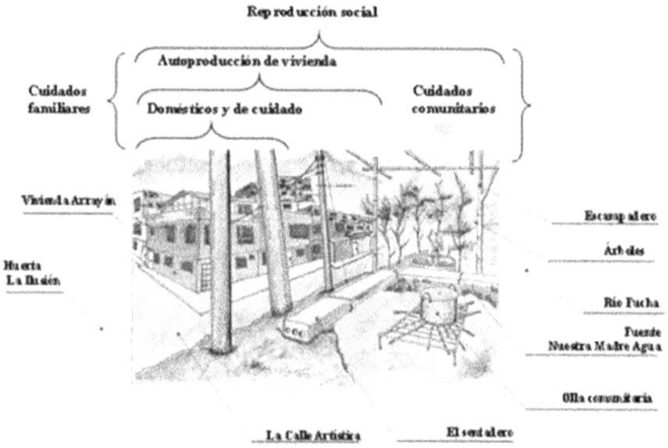

Source: Rincón-Castellanos, 2024

The micro-territories, as a materialization of the search for one's own space through the garden, the house itself, the attics and the study rooms, are germinated from the link that is built with nature and the ancestral spirit of the place. These micro-territories constitute a practice of inhabitation that suggests thinking of these places as communal shelters of resistance in the ecoterritory of Alto Fucha.

The defense of life that women in Alto Fucha argue and inhabit, that also takes place in other popular territories, is being built with popular feminist theoretical foundations, where intersectionality as a starting point for the reading of inequalities, the proposals from indigenous and ecofeminist feminisms, are put into dialogue in the territory. Thus, the underlying sense of wellbeing and sustainability is aligned with the defense of the territory- land, the body-territory, and the *acuerpamiento*. From this political positioning, the sovereignty of the territory (body-land) is the political horizon that guides their practices of inhabiting. Sovereignty seeks a social construction that allows abandoning the individualistic and extractivist sense of the logics of land appropriation, to rethink the ancestral and spiritual bond with the land and the corporealities, to take care of and protect it as a common good. Such bond is the common good that materializes through community webs that sustain the defense of life (Gutiérrez, 2017). Such a link is only possible to be defendable by situating from a counter-hegemonic social framework that allows dismantling the egalitarian and individualistic approach to the value of life; in which it is recognized that all lives are important and that all lives require social, political, affective and environmental links to exist (Butler, 2010). In this way, it is suggested to think about wellbeing and sustainability in the popular urbanization from a social political framework, whose political horizon operates from interdependence and eco-dependence, while denouncing the multiple territorial violences and wounds.

6. CONCLUSIONS

Wellbeing and sustainability from intersectionality and its dialogue with Indigenous popular feminisms call for the construction of a social epistemic-ethical-political framework that denounces the extractivist logics of land and bodies sustained by the patriarchal, capitalist and colonial triad. The theoretical approaches presented since intersectionality discuss the centrality of capitalism, which implies leaving aside other axes of inequality, such as patriarchy; deriving in the silencing of other forms of inequalities and the complex web that sustains and reproduces them. Thus, the more traditional theoretical views on popular settlements suggest thinking of capitalism as the dominant and only axis in the structure of inequality, and even recent views from the defense of land and communal action, as mentioned with the *Buen Vivir* (Gudynas, 2011), which defend an anti-capitalist and anti-colonial social and political stance.

In the urgent need for the construction of an epistemic-ethico-political framework on wellbeing and sustainability from an intersectional perspective and its dialogues with other feminisms; it calls, on the one hand, for the denunciation of the multiple violence that feminized and racialized women's bodies and the land itself are subjected to; and on the other hand, for the recognition of the social and political community agencies that women sustain through the different practices of inhabitation in the process of social reproduction (healing, defense of the territory, and sustaining life) in popular urbanization.

Violence in popular urbanization has to do with the oppression experienced, especially by women, in terms of class, the extractivist and mercantilist logic of the land, and in terms of the silencing of the practices of care given through self-construction around which family and community care revolves, and thus the legitimization of them (land and bodies). In other words, resistance in defense of land and women's bodies are inseparable struggles. The *agenciamiento* (agency), from the intersectional perspective in its dialogue proposed in this chapter with ecofeminism, invokes an inhabiting of interdependence and eco-dependence (Herrero, 2011). From the point of view of indigenous feminisms, inhabiting as acuerpamiento is configured from the defense of territory and life, as observed in women's inhabiting practices in the Alto Fucha ecoterritory. This political action calls for the dismantling of the individualistic idea of subjects as inhabitants in popular urbanization, in order to conceive them in a social, political and communitarian network, in an intimate relationship with the land and other corporealities.

In line with the construction of an epistemic-ethical-political framework to understand popular urbanization, the defense of territory and life is the political horizon of territorial sovereignty, which implies an opposition to the naturalized appropriation of territories. Territorial sovereignty moves from a self-recognition in an intimate bond with the land and the recovery of ancestral memory, cultivating the capacity to feel political indignation in the face of violence and injustices suffered (land and bodies) (Cabnal, 2010). In this sense, the defense of territories suggests thinking about abandoning the idea of material wealth as a central indicator of wellbeing and sustainability. Consequently, wellbeing and sustainability as rights linked to the liberation of land, and not as a human right.

Acknowledgments: This chapter is related to the research project IN-HABIT (INclusive Health And wellBeing in a small and medium size ciTies), funded by the European Union's Horizon 2020 Research and Innovation Program under Grant Agreement No. 869227. Also with the doctoral thesis of Milena Rincon-Castellanos, funded by the Pontificia Universidad Javeriana of Colombia, the Pontificia Universidad Católica of Chile and the COES (Center for Social Conflict and Cohesion Studies) of Chile, id: ANID/FONDAP n°15130009. Special recognition to the women of the Alto Fucha Ecoterritory for their wisdom and shared interpellations between river and mountain.

Conflicts of Interest: The authors declare no conflicts of interest. The funders had no role in the design of the study; in the collection, analyses, or interpretation of data; in the writing of the manuscript; or in the decision to publish the results.

REFERENCES

Ahmed, S. (2018). *Vivir una vida feminista.* Ediciones Bellaterra.

Alcaldía Mayor de Bogotá (2021*). Decreto 555 por medio del cual se adopta la revisión general del Plan de Ordenamiento Territorial de Bogotá DC.*

Blatter, J. (2008). Case study. In L. Given (Ed.). *The SAGE Encyclopedia of qualitative research methods.* V.1 y 2. Estados Unidos: SAGE Publications, Inc.

Brito, M. (2008). *Más allá de la dicotomía: la distinción entre lo público, lo privado y lo doméstico. Tesis de Maestría. Universidad Autónoma Metropolitana.* Unidad Iztapalapa.

Butler, J. (2010). *Marcos de guerra. Las vidas lloradas.* Paidós.

Cabnal, L. (2010). *Feminismos diversos: el feminismo comunitario.* ACSUR-Las Segovias.

Cabnal, L. (2015). *Lorena Cabnal. Feminista comunitaria.* https://suds.cat/experiencies/857-2/

Caffentzis, G., & Federici, S. (2013). Comunes contra y más allá del capitalismo. In Menendez, M., & Conze, C. (Eds.), *La Vida en el centro. Feminismo, reproducción y tramas comunitarias.* Bajo Tierra Ediciones.

Calisto Friant, M., & Langmore, J. (2015). The Buen Vivir: A policy to survive the Anthropocene? *Global Policy*, *6*(1), 64–71. DOI: 10.1111/1758-5899.12187

Carspecken, P. F. (2008). Critical research. In L. Given (Ed.). *The SAGE Encyclopedia of qualitative research methods.* V.1 y 2. Estados Unidos: SAGE Publications, Inc.

Cielo, C. (2023). Reproducción ampliada de la vida. economía feminista y ecología política. [Clase No. 2]. *Diplomado en Economía popular y feminista.* Buenos Aires: Clacso.

Cielo, C., (2016). Aportes de la economía feminista para el análisis del capitalismo contemporáneo. *Revista Acadêmica (Pontifícia Universidade Católica do Paraná)*, •••, 157–175.

Colectiu-Punt 6. (2019). *Urbanismo feminista. Por una transformación radical de los espacios de vida.* Barcelona: Virus Editorial.

Connolly, P. (2014). La ciudad y el hábitat popular: Paradigma latinoamericano. In B, Ramírez & E. Pradilla (Eds.). *Teorías sobre la ciudad en América Latina*, (397-441). Ciudad de México, México: Universidad Autónoma Metropolitana.

Crenshaw, K. (1989). Race, Reform and Retrenchment: Transformation and Legitimation in Anti-Discrimination Law, *Harvard Law Review*,101, pp. 1.331-1.387.

Diaz, J., & Torno, C. (2021). *Debates picantes de los feminismos populares. Estado y Autonomía*. Madre Selva.

Elizalde, S. (2008). Debates sobre la experiencia. Un recorrido por la teoría y la praxis feminista. *Oficios terrestres*, (23), 18 – 30.

Escobar, A. (2015). Development, critiques of. In G. D'Alisa, F., Demaria, G. & Kallis, G. (eds), *Degrowth. A vocabulary for a new era*, (pp. 29–32), Abingdon & New York, NY: Routledge.

Fadaei, A. (2018). Formal-informal nexus in academic debates: A literature review. *Territorio*, (84), 167–174. DOI: 10.3280/TR2018-084023

Federici, S. (2010). *Calibán y la bruja. Mujeres, cuerpo y acumulación originaria.* Madrid: traficantes de sueños.

Federici, S. (2022). *Ir más alla de la piel repensar, rehacer y reinvidicar el cuerpo en el capitalismo contemporaneo*. Madrid: Traficantes de sueños.

Fraser, N. (2014). Tras la morada oculta de Marx. Por una concepción ampliada del capitalismo. *New Left Review*, (86), 57–86.

Gago, V. (2019). *La potencia feminista o el deseo de cambiarlo todo*. Madrid: traficantes de sueños.

García-Ramón, M. (2019). La Geografía del género. In Monk, J., Prats, M., & Veleda, S. (Eds.), *María Dolors García-Ramon. Geografía y género, disidencia e innovación*. Icaria Editorial.

Grau Biosca, E. (2014). Saber que alguien lo escucha. El método de la narrativa en la investigación La verdad de las mujeres. Víctimas del conflicto armado en Colombia. In Mendia Azkue, I., Luxán, M., Legarreta, M., Guzmán, G., Zirion, I., & Azpiazu Carballo, J. (Eds.), *Otras formas de (re)conocer. Reflexiones, herramientas y aplicaciones desde la investigación feminista* (pp. 147–160). Hegoa.

Gudynas, E. (2011). Buen vivir: Germinando alternativas al desarrollo. *América Latina en Movimiento – ALAI-*, 462, 1-20.

Gutiérrez, R. (2017). *Horizontes comunitario-populares. Producción de lo común más allá de las políticas estado-céntricas*. Madrid: Traficantes de sueños.

Guzmán, A. (2019). *Descolonizar la memoria. Descolonizar los feminismos*. Tarpuna Muya.

Hernández-Garcia, J. (2016). Hábitat popular, un modo alternativo de producción de espacio para América Latina? In Hernández, I. (Ed.), *Estética de los mundos posibles: inmersión en la vida artificial, las artes y las practicas urbanas* (pp. 245–258). Pontificia Universidad Javeriana.

Herrero, Y. (2011). *Cambiar las gafas para mirar el mundo. Una nueva cultura de la sostenibilidad.* Madrid: libros en acción.

Hesse-Biber, S. N. (2008) Feminist research. In L. Given (Ed.). *The SAGE Encyclopedia of qualitative research methods*. V.1 y 2. Estados Unidos: SAGE Publications, Inc.

IDECA -Infraestructura de Datos Espaciales de Catastro Distrital-. (2021). *Cartografía básica*. https://www.ideca.gov.co/

IGAC -Instituto Geográfico Agustín Codazzi-. (1977). *Fotografía aérea 1977*

Janoschka, M. (2016). Gentrificación, desplazamiento, desposesión: Procesos urbanos claves en América Latina. *Revista INVI, 31*(88), 27–71. DOI: 10.4067/S0718-83582016000300002

Jaramillo, S. (2012). Urbanización informal: Diagnósticos y políticas. Una revisión al debate latinoamericano para pensar líneas de acción actuales. In Salazar, C. (Ed.), *Irregular: Suelo y mercado en América Latina* (pp. 33–83). El Colegio de México.

Langebaek, C. H. (2019). *Los muiscas. La historia milenaria de un pueblo chibcha*. Penguin Random House.

Leiva, X., & Icaza, R. (2019). *En tiempos de muerte: cuerpos, rebeldías y resistencias*. Cooperativa Editorial Retos.

López, A. (2022). Agentes, procesos y activismos ciudadanos en la urbanización de áreas de valor medioambiental en Bogotá. *Tesis Doctoral*. Escuela Internacional de Doctorado.

Massey, D. (1994). *Space, place and gender*. University of Minnesota Press.

McDowell, L. (1999). *Género, identidad y lugar: un estudio de las geografías feministas*. Ediciones Cátedra.

Migliario González, A., Mazariegos García, D., Rodríguez Lezica, L., & Díaz Lozano, J. (2020). Interseccionalidades en el cuerpo-territorio. In *Cruz Hernández & M. Bayón Jiménez (Coords.). Cuerpos, Territorios y feminismos. Compilación latinoaméricana de teorías, metodología y prácticas políticas* (pp. 63–82). Clacso.

Molyneux, M. (2010). *Justicia de género, ciudadanía y diferencia en América Latina*. Ediciones Universidad de Salamanca.

Muxi, Z. (2018). *Mujeres, Casas y Ciudades. Más allá del umbral.* DPR.

Navas Florián, L. N. (2022). *Sistematización de la experiencia ecofeminista de concertación de una operación comunitaria para la Reserva Natural del Delirio en Bogotá. Trabajo de grado.* Universidad Nacional de Colombia.

Ortiz Flores, E. (2016). De Vancouver 1976 a Vancouver 2006. In Internacional del Hábitat, C. (Ed.), *Hábitat I (1976), Hábitat II (1996) & Hábitat III (2016).* Habitat Internacional Coalition.

Ripio Rodriguez, V. Ferrer Valero, S.; Palomo Cermeño, E. & Duarte Hidalgo, C. (2019). *Feminismo. La historia.* Madrid: Ediciones Akal. S.A

Rodó de Zarate, M. (2019). Intersectionality. In Orum, A. (Ed.), *The Wiley Blackwell Encyclopedia of Urban and Regional Studies.* John Wiley & Sons Ltd. DOI: 10.1002/9781118568446.eurs0164

Rolnik, R. (2017). *La guerra de los lugares. La colonización de la tierra y la vivienda en la era de las finanzas.* Ediciones.

Sánchez. (2019). *Aportes desde la agroecología para habitar el Alto Fucha desde la noción de Ecoterritorio: una apuesta de Huertopía para la permanencia en los cerros orientales de Bogotá. Tesis de pregrado.* Universidad Pedagógica Nacional.

Shebell, E & Moser, S (2019). Planning for the Buen Vivir: socialism, decentralisation and urbanisation in rural Ecuador. *IDPR*, 41(4).

Unidas, N. (2018). *La agenda 2030 y los Objetivos de Desarrollo Sostenible. Una oportunidad para América Latina y el Caribe.* https://repositorio.cepal.org/server/api/core/bitstreams/cb30a4de-7d87-4e79-8e7a-ad5279038718/content

Varley, A. (2013). Postcolonialising informality? *Environment and Planning. D, Society & Space*, *31*(1), 4–22. DOI: 10.1068/d14410

Vega, C. (2020). Rutas de la reproducción y el cuidadopor América Latina. Apropiación, valorización coelctiva y política. In Menendez, M., & Conze, C. (Eds.), *La vida en el centro. Feminismo, reproducción y tramas comunitarias* (pp. 81–144). Bajo Tierra Ediciones, Minerva Ediciones y Escuela de Formación Feminista.

Viveros Vigoya, M. (2016). La interseccionalidad: Una aproximación situada a la dominación. *Debate Feminista*, *52*, 1–17. DOI: 10.1016/j.df.2016.09.005

Zaragocin, S., & Caretta, M. A. (2021). Cuerpo-Territorio: A Decolonial Feminist Geographical Method for the Study of Embodiment. *Annals of the Association of American Geographers*, *111*(5), 1503–1518.

Chapter 6
Impact of Transportation Infrastructure on Socio-Spatial Fragmentation in Bogotá's Peri-Urban Area: A Case Study of Suba Locality

Mónica Marcela Suárez Pradilla
https://orcid.org/0000-0001-5864-4771
Universidad Escuela Colombiana de Ingeniería Julio Garavito, Colombia

Roger Smith Cardozo Pinilla
https://orcid.org/0009-0003-7783-576X
Universidad Escuela Colombiana de Ingeniería Julio Garavito, Colombia

Vasco Barbosa Brandão
https://orcid.org/0000-0002-0657-3171
University of Johannesburg, South Africa

ABSTRACT

The phenomena of peri-urbanization in the cities of the Global South are closely linked to the implementation of transport infrastructures, which facilitate urban expansion beyond the limits of consolidated areas. This study aims to assess how the dynamics of transport infrastructures contribute to socio-spatial fragmentation, generating exclusion and inequality in peripheral areas. For this purpose, the locality of Suba has been selected, one of the largest peripheral areas of Bogota, where approximately 1.2 million people live and where different economic strata coexist, with an unequal supply of infrastructure and transportation. The 2023 mobility survey conducted by the District Mobility Secretariat of Bogota was used to eval-

DOI: 10.4018/979-8-3693-6089-7.ch006

uate economic, time, accessibility and transportation mode indicators, as well as the characteristics of the transportation infrastructure. A composite indicator was obtained by applying an entropy model. The results reveal that economic inequality is the main cause of spatial fragmentation in the Suba locality.

1. INTRODUCTION

More than 56% of the world's population is currently urban, according to the Word Cities Report 2022 (United Nations Human Settlements Programme (UN-Habitat), 2022). However, in developing countries, this percentage is close to 81%, and most of these urbanization processes are taking place in the peripheries of large cities, where urban planning processes are not yet consolidated. In these areas, developed sectors coexist with marginal areas, which poses great challenges to urban managers and administrators (Ahani & Dadashpoor, 2021; Varkey, 2019).

This process results in physical and social segregation of different population groups within the urban space. The expansion of linear transport infrastructures acts as physical barriers that limit access to services and opportunities, thus intensifying socio-spatial fragmentation (Shaw et al., 2020).

Thus, the dynamics of exclusion and inequality that develop in peripheral areas due to the construction of transport infrastructures and the implementation of public transport systems, make it necessary to study the socio-spatial fragmentation, this is fundamental to design more inclusive and sustainable urban policies, which promote the integration and well-being of all affected communities as mentioned by Khanani (2019).

Causes and Consequences of Socio-Spatial Fragmentation Due to Transportation Infrastructures

The lack of comprehensive and coordinated urban planning can result in an uneven distribution of transportation infrastructure in urban and peripheral areas (Yu et al., 2023). This favors certain areas over others, limiting access to essential services such as health, education, commerce and job opportunities in some sectors (Engels, 2016). In addition, transportation infrastructures act as physical barriers that decrease accessibility and connectivity, generating gentrification processes that lead to the displacement of vulnerable communities and the creation of socially segregated suburbs (Lima, 2001).

Peri-urban areas are particularly affected at the environmental level by the construction and operation of transportation infrastructure. Air and noise pollution negatively impact these communities (Bolay et al., 2005), making certain areas less attractive to live in and reinforcing spatial segregation (Hidayati et al., 2019). The implementation of public transport systems without proper integration and coordination with other urban infrastructure and services generates high costs for users and excludes low-income communities (Rokem & Vaughan, 2018).

The lack of affordable fares creates additional barriers to mobility, exacerbating socio-spatial fragmentation. Moreover, when infrastructure is inadequate for public transport-such as well-planned stations, stops, and routes-its effectiveness and reach are limited (Lee et al., 2020). Areas without adequate access to public transport become isolated and marginalized, accentuating inequality problems in different communities (Taşan-Kok & Stead, 2013). In this sense, transport infrastructures are intrinsically related to social inequality, highlighting the difficulties in implementing inclusive urban policies aimed at improving the quality of life of inhabitants.

Spatial fragmentation varies according to the level of urban planning, in Europe, one of the most important effects has to do with mobility; in many peripheral areas, the lack of efficient public transport increases car dependency, limiting mobility for those without access to a vehicle, this is also reflected in real estate development, where more accessible communities increase land values, displacing low-income residents (Cassiers & Kesteloot, 2012; Gil-Alonso Fernando and López-Villanueva, 2023). Infrastructure expansion transforms natural habitats, affecting biodiversity and local ecosystems (Petrisor, 2017), for example, in Paris, the network of highways and the peripheral ring road separate the city center from suburban areas, creating significant spatial and social inequalities (Demazière, 2018). In Barcelona, transport infrastructures, such as ring roads and new metro lines, have improved connectivity, but have also contributed to spatial segregation and the creation of exclusive neighborhoods (Zambon et al., 2017).

In large Asian cities, transport infrastructure tends to favor more developed and economically prosperous areas, while low-income areas and informal settlements are marginalized and suffer extensive environmental impacts (Prasad et al., 2022). In Latin American cities, there is a great disparity between urban and peri-urban areas. Peripheral areas, generally densely populated by low-income communities, have limited access to essential services, such as inadequate and poor-quality transportation (Cass et al., 2003). In many Latin American cities, the lack of urban and transportation planning and regulation has created marginal sectors that represent a challenge for sustainable urban development (Marchant Santiago et al., 2022). In Mexico, highways and expressways divide neighborhoods and create physical barriers that increase segregation; peripheral areas have limited access to public transport, increasing car dependency (Morales, 2024). In São Paulo, transportation infrastructure divides communities, creating inequalities in access to services (Rodriguez et al., 2012).

In Colombia, large cities have extensive peripheral settlements Mosquera Becerra (2014). In Bogotá, specifically in the locality of Suba, there is one of the largest and most populated peripheries, with a great diversity both in socioeconomic and geographic terms. The peripheral areas of Suba have characteristics that distinguish them from the rest of the locality and the city in general. In these areas it is common to find informal settlements that have grown in a disorderly manner and without adequate urban planning, often lacking basic services such as drinking water, sewerage, electricity and effective transportation (Guzmán et al., 2017).

There are also sectors where new real estate projects have been developed, both social housing and higher income housing, which has generated a heterogeneous mix of communities, all with limited access to efficient public transportation. Although the TransMilenio system reaches certain areas, many zones lack adequate coverage, forcing residents to rely on traditional buses and informal transportation, access roads to these areas are often in poor condition and may be insufficient for the demand, especially at peak hours, generating high travel times (Bucheli Guevara, 2019).

This study area was chosen because of its great socioeconomic disparity. The population, for the most part, belongs to strata 1 and 2 (socioeconomic stratification in Colombia is the classification of residential properties, according to Law 142 of 1994, to apply differential rates to public services: households with higher incomes pay more, while households with lower incomes receive subsidies, according to the National Administrative Department of Statistics (DANE); there is a high percentage of people working in the informal economy, reflecting the lack of formal and stable employment opportunities. Finally, some of these areas are located in risk areas, prone to landslides and flooding due to lack of planning and geographical characteristics (Bocarejo et al., 2016).

The main objective of this research is to analyze how transportation infrastructures contribute to socio-spatial fragmentation in the urban periphery of the Suba locality in the city of Bogotá, Colombia. In order to identify the mechanisms through which these infrastructures affect social cohesion and to evaluate possible mitigation strategies, a series of transportation indicators were evaluated using the mobility survey of the District Secretariat of Mobility of the year 2023 for the city of Bogota.

Structure of the Document

This paper is structured in six main sections, in section 2, a review of the literature on socio-spatial fragmentation and its relationship with transportation infrastructure is presented. Then, section 3 describes the case study, section 4 presents the data and methodology used. The fifth section presents the results obtained, followed by an analysis and discussion of the results. Finally, section 6 presents the conclusions and then the references.

2. LITERATURE REVIEW

The literature on the relationship between socio-spatial fragmentation and transport infrastructure in peripheral areas is approached from a variety of approaches, related to the configuration of cities. From urban geography, which examines segregation patterns, to contemporary research using advanced spatial analysis techniques, the literature review reveals both significant advances and areas where knowledge is still limited. First, studies that identify the main factors contributing to socio-spatial fragmentation will be explored. Then, gaps in the current literature will be identified, highlighting the need for new research that addresses these gaps and proposes effective solutions for more inclusive and equitable urban planning.

Impact of Transportation Infrastructures on Socio-Spatial Fragmentation in Peripheral Areas.

The development of transport infrastructures is fundamental in the expansion and transformation of cities (Yasin et al., 2020). However, in peripheral areas, these infrastructures often have a contradictory effect, by improving connectivity they intensify socio-spatial fragmentation. Road and rail connections or the implementation of mass transit systems, in addition to modifying the accessibility of certain sectors, influence the segregation of communities and the distribution of social and economic opportunities (Binder & Matern, 2020). In this section, we analyze how transport infrastructures increase the socio-spatial fragmentation of peripheral areas by increasing inequalities and the dynamics of urban exclusion. Next, we identify the main approaches of studies that have attempted to explain this phenomenon, in order to identify the challenges faced by the phenomenon of peri-urbanization.

Transportation infrastructures in peripheral areas if they are not the product of the articulation of urban planning, transportation policies and socioeconomic dynamics can intensify or mitigate phenomena such as segregation as they enhance socioeconomic separation (Carrilho & Trindade, 2022) and gentrification (Adugbila et al..., 2023), because they can improve economic and social opportunities for residents of the peripheries (Yoo et al., 2024), which ends up displacing the original populations (Khanani et al., 2021). In addition, these projects transform socio-spatial landscapes and promote economic development, but also increase inequality and land values, displacing vulnerable communities (Ostrensky et al., 2022).

Transportation infrastructures, such as roads, railroads, and highways, can have counterproductive effects by creating physical barriers (Salas-Olmedo et al., 2015), which limit the mobility of residents and their ability to access services, jobs, educational opportunities and other essential services. Particularly, geometric and functional features can limit accessibility and reinforce social fragmentation

(Sdoukopoulos et al., 2023). Another important aspect is the type of infrastructure, if they are oriented to motorized traffic, they hinder pedestrian mobility (Matos & Lobo, 2023) and exacerbate socio-spatial segregation in the peripheries (Gottero et al., 2023).

The economic impact of transportation infrastructure in peripheral areas manifests itself in several dimensions (Rosik & Wójcik, 2022). Improved connectivity stimulates economic growth because it facilitates access to markets and resources, promoting investment and commercial development (Chen et al., 2016), this stimulates the real estate market and produces a reconfiguration of residential areas, affecting affordability and socioeconomic diversity (Haoran et al., 2022). In addition, property values are affected due to the proximity to road projects (Hidayati et al., 2019).

Some negative effects are presented by pollution and noise (Casais & Grau Valldosera, 2023), in addition, the fragmentation of the natural landscape affects ecological connectivity, modifying the functioning of ecosystems and reducing their capacity to provide essential ecosystem services, such as climate regulation and water purification (Doyle & Havlick, 2009; Jaeger et al., 2007). Particularly, road infrastructures cause ecological fragmentation, affecting biodiversity and local microclimates (La Rosa et al. 2018). Another important aspect in this approach is the need to anticipate PM 10 emissions in road construction projects to mitigate adverse effects on human health and the environment (Dede et al., 2022).

Connectivity is essential to improve accessibility and decrease spatial segregation (Brovarone, 2021), and with-it opportunities for employment, education and services are distributed more equitably, otherwise barriers are created between communities and social cohesion is limited (Cervero, 2014; Mortoja et al., 2020). Improved accessibility boosts regional competitiveness, but also leads to increased spatial mobility and affects quality of life, with mixed effects on social cohesion as shown in the work of Bocarejo et al. (2016), who evaluate how a mass public transport system in Bogotá has contributed to improve interaction between peripheral areas and the urban center, partially mitigating socio-spatial fragmentation.

Public policies and urban planning strategies play a crucial role in determining how resources are distributed and to what extent they contribute to cohesion (Bourne & Simmons, 2003); also, it is important to identify the effects on social segregation and on the quality of life of inhabitants in order to achieve a balanced development of cities (Nogués & Salas-Olmedo, 2009). Kanai & Schindler (2022) analyze how connectivity policies designed to improve economic opportunities in segregated regions can generate new urban spaces and housing projects that often exacerbate social fragmentation (Iqbal et al., 2022).

The literature review shows that the studies that have been developed have an interdisciplinary character, however, there is a need to integrate more studies from transportation engineering, economics and to explore how culture in its various forms can give a broader understanding of how transportation infrastructure influences sociospatial fragmentation. There is a significant gap in research on sociospatial fragmentation in rural areas or in less developed regions, where transportation infrastructure can have very different effects. There is a lack of studies analyzing the long-term effects of transport infrastructure on sociospatial fragmentation; most research tends to focus on short-term impacts, which limits the understanding of temporal dynamics and progressive changes in fragmentation. The literature often focuses on certain transport infrastructures such as roads and railroads, neglecting other forms of infrastructure (e.g., maritime or air transport networks) that can also contribute to sociospatial fragmentation.

Although there are studies that address sociospatial fragmentation in specific contexts, there is a lack of comparative analysis at the global level. Cultural, economic and political differences between regions may influence how fragmentation manifests itself, but this has been insufficiently explored in the comparative literature. Studies on sociospatial fragmentation and transportation often do not sufficiently incorporate the perspectives of affected local communities. Lack of citizen participation in transport infrastructure planning and evaluation can lead to incomplete or biased conclusions.

With the emergence of new technologies and the digitization of transportation, there is a gap in understanding how these innovations are reshaping sociospatial fragmentation. Research on how digital transportation platforms (such as Uber or bike sharing) affect the socio-spatial structure is still emerging. While the importance of public policy in socio-spatial fragmentation is recognized, there is a gap in the analysis of different forms of governance and how these can mitigate or exacerbate fragmentation. The relationship between transportation policies and other sectors, such as housing and the economy, also needs further exploration.

3. CASE STUDY LOCALITY OF SUBA, CITY OF BOGOTÁ.

Suba is a locality that was formerly an independent municipality before being annexed to Bogotá in 1954. It is located between the hills of La Conejera and Suba, which physically separates it from the rest of the city (Figure 1). Some of Bogotá's most important ecosystems are found in this area, including the wetlands of La Conejera, Juan Amarillo, Córdoba and Guaymaral (Secretaría Distrital de Planeación, 2009).

With an area representing 15.2% of Bogotá's total urban area, Suba is characterized mainly by its residential use. It also has two important commercial areas: Suba Pueblo and Prado Veraniego, which have been established as centralities through the Land Management Plan (Castillo Mejía, 2013).

Suba can be divided into three main sectors; the high socioeconomic strata are located near the Autopista Norte, where land use for educational and recreational purposes predominates, with the presence of schools, universities, recreational centers and sports clubs. The middle strata are concentrated in the Suba Centro area, while the low strata are located mainly in the Rincón area, with a predominance of strata 2 and 3.

Figure 1. Location and distribution of the transportation system within the locality of Suba in the city of Bogotá D.C.

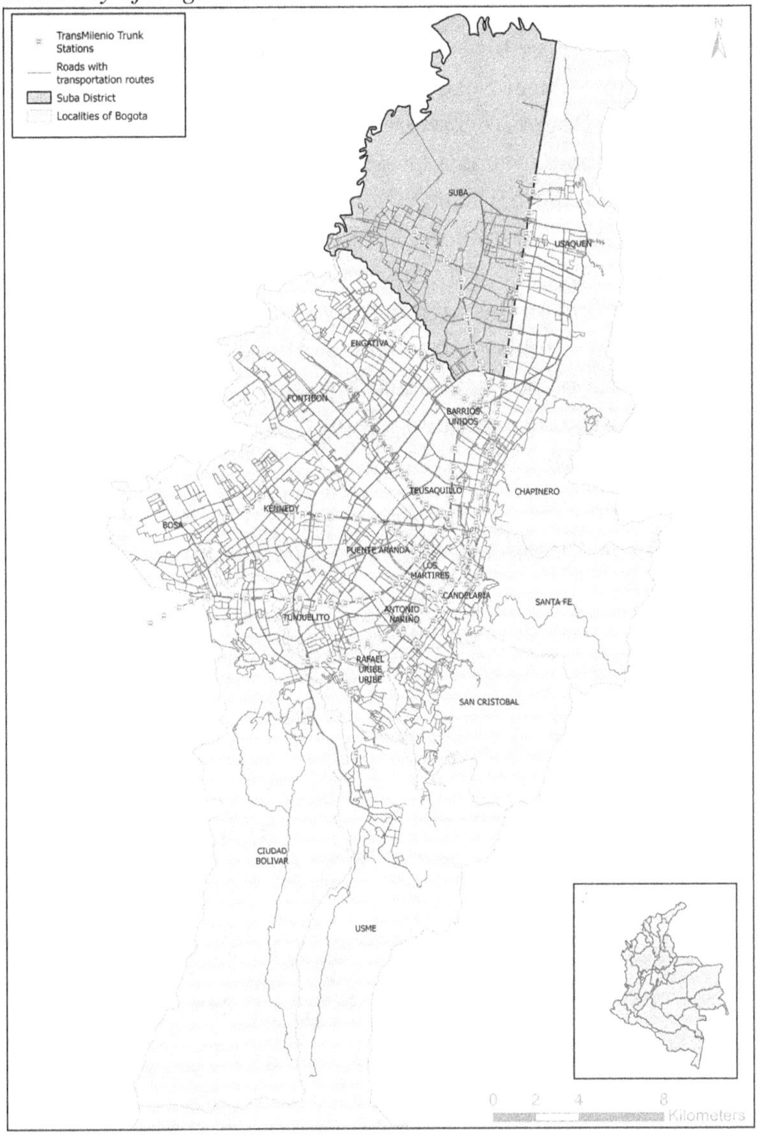

Source: Prepared by the author

Suba is urban land covers a total of 6,271 hectares (ha), of which 559 ha are protected. Within this urban land are located 5,251 blocks, occupying a total of 7,363 ha. The locality is divided into twelve Zoning Planning Units (UPZ), which facilitate land management. These UPZs are classified into three categories: consolidated residential, qualified residential, development, and incomplete urbanization. The main UPZs are Tibabuyes, Suba and Rincón (Moreno Barón, 2021).

The distribution of land uses in Suba is not equitable, it has 12 facilities per 10,000 inhabitants, a number lower than the city average, which is 19 facilities per 10,000 inhabitants, this places Suba as the second locality with the second lowest number of facilities in Bogota (Secretaría de Planeación, 2020).

Currently, Suba's population is approximately 1,260,000 people, with 397,049 households according to the 2018 DANE census. The active population, comprised between 14 and 59 years old, represents 68.3%. Suba is one of the most densely populated areas of Bogota, reaching in some areas more than 500 inhabitants per square kilometer (hab/km²). This high density is largely due to high rates of overcrowding in horizontal neighborhoods such as Rincón de Suba or Lisboa. Figure 2 illustrates the growth of population and households in Suba (Figure 3), mainly driven by the high birth rate and immigration processes (Dirección de Análisis y Diseño Estratégico, 2022).

Figure 2. Mortality and migration rate of the Suba locality (per 1000 inhabitants)

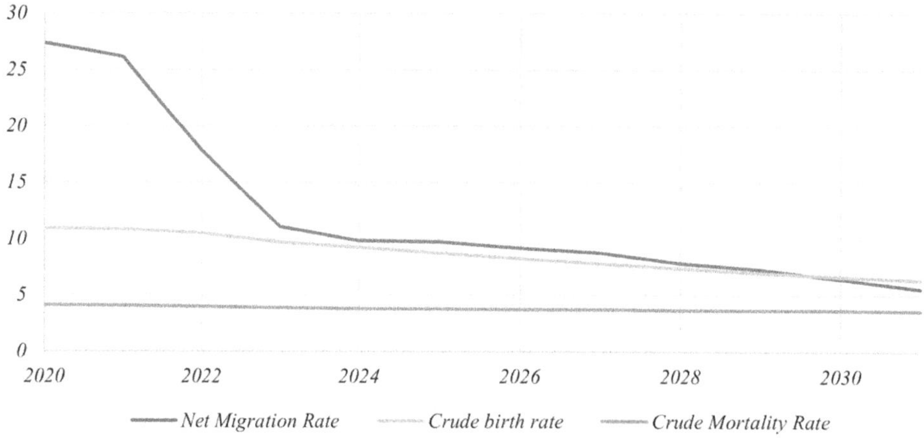

Source: Prepared by the author

figure 3. Number of households and persons per household in Suba

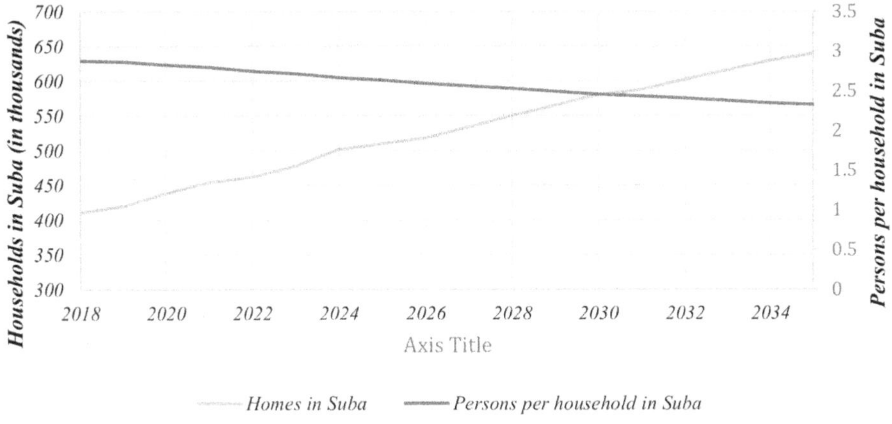

Source: Prepared by the author

Currently, the most densely populated areas of Suba are located in the peripheral neighborhoods of the locality, where multidimensional poverty reaches 3.7%. In these sectors, the lack of adequate urban planning is reflected in the lack of facilities, green areas and mobility services (Andean Parliament, 2022).

Suba has experienced recent transformations driven by both public and private investments, which are changing its social profiles and generating new forms of interaction. These transformations are related to the production of social housing, a process that intensified in Bogotá starting in the 1970s. At that time, the growth of the city began in the center and progressively expanded, promoting socio-spatial segregation, accentuated by the change in land use and the proliferation of gated communities (García Galindo & Carrero Barón, 2017).

Currently, Suba is the scene of significant real estate interventions, especially in high-rise developments, which is generating areas of high population density far away and with insufficient public services.

Urban development in Bogotá has not been synchronized with the evolution of transportation infrastructure. In the 1990s, only two intermediate roads connected Suba to the rest of the city, and the supply of public transportation has historically been deficient, with minimal coverage. In addition, most neighborhoods in Suba lack adequate road infrastructure, except for areas located near major highways (Secretaría Distrital de Movilidad, 2020).

4. DATA AND METHODOLOGY

Data

This section presents and describes the data collected to estimate the socio-spatial segregation index based on transportation indicators. For this purpose, information from the Origin-Destination Trips section of the Mobility Survey 2023 conducted in Bogotá D.C. is used. The analysis includes all types of functional trips (work and study) and non-functional trips (other trips), and the modes of transportation evaluated by the survey, which include motorized, non-motorized, public transportation, among others. The choice of the Mobility Survey 2023 is based on its character as the most recent and comprehensive source of data on the mobility of the inhabitants of the capital (Mobility Observatory, 2023).

Several datasets were used to construct the transportation variables, including: total travel time, first mile times, waiting times, main mode of transportation used, monthly income, monthly cost of transportation, number of vehicles per household, and population density. In addition, through the use of Geographic Information Systems (GIS) tools, average access distances to Integrated Public Transportation System (SITP) stops and TransMilenio trunk stations were determined.

From the information collected, key indicators were calculated to evaluate the different aspects of transportation and its impact on socio-spatial fragmentation. These indicators are described below and their importance within the analysis is highlighted.

Calculation of Indicators

Performing economic inequality index analysis as a first approach is basic when considering socioeconomic disparities in peripheral mobility patterns, which helps to understand inequalities and transportation access constraints within the dynamics of these urban areas. Research indicates that economic inequality significantly influences mobility, as people in lower income groups often face barriers that restrict their movement and access to opportunities (Brea-Martínez & Dribe, 2024). Lucchini et al. (2023) show that regions with higher inequality indices exhibit lower rates of upward mobility, reinforcing the idea that economic disparities directly affect mobility.

The Pietra index was chosen to evaluate the economic inequality conditions of the inhabitants because it allows visualizing how economic inequalities affect the distribution and access to transportation infrastructure (Cao et al., 2019). This index measures the concentration of different socioeconomic groups in specific areas and compares this distribution with that expected in an equity scenario. By focusing on income, the Pietra index shows the contrasts in transportation access faced by low-income populations, helping to identify the most disadvantaged and vulnerable areas in terms of access. Combining this index with other indicators can effectively measure social inequality due to the transport sector, particularly in peripheral areas.

Equation (1) presents how Prieta's index was calculated based on the income reported by individuals in the mobility survey.

$$P = \frac{1}{2}\sum_{i=1}^{n}\left|\frac{y_i}{\mu} - \frac{1}{n}\right| \quad (1)$$

Where:

y_i is the individual's income,

μ is the average income of the study area and

n is the total number of individuals.

The range of this indicator is between 0 and 1; values close to 0 indicate low segregation (suggesting an equitable distribution of socioeconomic groups in the areas analyzed), while values close to 1 reflect high segregation (meaning that socioeconomic groups are unevenly distributed compared to the expected distribution).

In addition to the Pietra indicator, the percentage of income spent on transportation, calculated as the proportion of monthly income that an individual spends on transportation over total monthly income, is evaluated. This indicator helps to reflect how the economic burden of transportation varies in relation to an individual's income, providing insight into the affordability and financial impact of transportation as a function of income level.

Another factor that has a great impact on the socio-spatial segregation of transportation is travel times, idle times and first-mile times; time plays a segregating role in peripheral areas due to the impact on accessibility that it generates (Tomasiello et al., 2022). Long travel times, which are generated when peripheral areas are far from centers of opportunity attraction, significantly limit people's access to jobs, health services and education, perpetuating socioeconomic inequalities (Brandes & Emary, 2016). Moreover, first-mile times, which includes the time required to get from home to a transportation station or stop, are often longer in peripheral areas due to poor or non-existent infrastructure (Iyer, Menezes, et al., 2023). This situation creates an additional barrier that limits mobility accessibility and reinforces exclusion. Likewise, long waiting times to access transportation services, especially in less favored areas with lower frequency of services and mobility options, increase frustration and discourage the use of public transportation, favoring dependence on private means for those who can afford it (Méndez et al., 2023). Together, these factors generate a cycle of disadvantage that perpetuates segregation, exacerbating inequality in access to transportation opportunities.

For the analysis of the time variable within the document, three indicators were used: i) travel time, calculated as the total average travel time from the point of origin to the destination, ii) time spent in the first mile, which represents the proportion of the total travel time spent accessing the first means of transportation, and iii) waiting and connection time, calculated as the proportion of the total travel time spent waiting for public transportation or making intermodal connections. These three indicators allow an understanding of how time impacts accessibility and equity in transportation, particularly for inhabitants of peripheral areas.

To evaluate accessibility to public transport, the indicator of proportionality of access to public transport was used, which measures the proximity of residents to transport stations, both for mass systems - TransMilenio, and for collective systems - SITP. This indicator is calculated as the closest distance to a station, divided by the maximum distance a person is willing to travel to access these systems: 500 meters for SITP and 1 kilometer for TransMilenio (taking into account different forms of access, e.g., feeder service) (Hasselwander et al., 2023). This ratio considers the realistic willingness of people in terms of distance to access public transport, based on studies and urban practices that suggest that these distances are common thresholds for acceptable accessibility. The values assumed reflect a balance of accessibility with user comfort, ensuring an accurate assessment of the coverage of the transport system and its impact on urban mobility (Gutiérrez, 2009).

Finally, indicators are calculated that break down the modes of access to mobility, classifying them into i) active mobility, ii) motorized systems and iii) public transportation. This breakdown facilitates a comprehensive view of the transportation options used and how these options affect their accessibility and mobility. Active mobility, which includes walking and bicycles, is often more available and less expensive, but its viability may be limited in areas with poor infrastructure. Motorized systems, such as private cars or motorcycles, may reflect people's economic capacity and access to resources, while public transport directly affects connectivity and accessibility in peripheral areas (Biljecki et al., 2013; Iyer, Menezes, et al., 2023).

The distribution of these modes of transportation reveals how socio-spatial segregation manifests itself in mobility practices. A high percentage of active mobility in peripheral areas may indicate a lack of adequate infrastructure for motorized and public transport, while a high reliance on motorized systems and public transport in central areas may reflect better integration and accessibility (Biljecki et al., 2013).

Entropy Model

In the previous description, the economic, time, accessibility and transportation mode indicators were addressed individually, highlighting their usefulness in understanding socio-spatial segregation in transportation. However, this paper aims to integrate these models to provide a more complete view of the phenomenon. To achieve this, composite indicator methods are employed, which allow the calculation of overall values that more accurately reflect vulnerability in transportation access. This integrated approach provides a deeper understanding of how various factors interact to influence socio-spatial segregation. This model is especially useful for allowing a consistent integration of data into a single indicator, obtaining a quantitative approximation of socio-spatial segregation that considers variability in access to transportation and differences in mobility.

To calculate the socio-spatial segregation index, we will use the entropy model, a method widely recognized for its ability to measure inequality in the distribution of characteristics between different areas (Iyer, Nandini, et al., 2023). The entropy model, based on information theory, evaluates the distribution of a variable (in this case, access to transportation) relative to its expected distribution in an ideally equal society. Calculated as shown in Equation (2) and where p_i is the proportion of a variable of a given area.

$$H = -\sum_i p_i \log(p_i) \qquad (2)$$

This model is used because of its sensitivity to variations in distribution and its ability to capture both the intensity and extent of segregation, important factors sought in the model (Yekimov et al., 2023). Unlike other models that may focus only on specific aspects of the distribution or assume homogeneous distributions, therefore, the entropy model provides a more dynamic and adjustable measure that more accurately reflects complex socio-spatial realities.

Methodology

This section details the methodology used to analyze the socio-spatial fragmentation due to transportation infrastructure in peripheral areas based on economic inequality indices and various indicators related to access to transportation. The methodology includes analysis of the Pietra index, assessment of travel times, and analysis of accessibility and transportation modes (Figure 4). The importance and level of relationship between the indicators is evaluated using an entropy model.

Figure 4. Methodological diagram

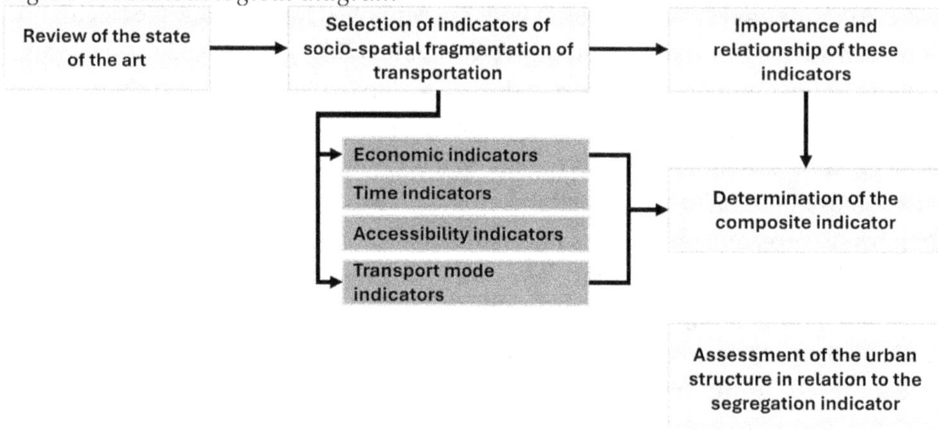

Source: Prepared by the author. While this study is based on quantitative data from the 2023 Mobility Survey, future research could benefit from incorporating qualitative perspectives from residents. Focus groups or in-depth interviews with community members could reveal the emotional and experiential dimensions of inequality and segregation in transportation. As Bucheli Guevara (2019) points out, residents of segregated areas of Bogotá often express feelings of disconnection and marginalization that are not fully reflected in quantitative indicators.

5. DISCUSSION OF RESULTS

This section presents the results of the model's cluster analysis. The methodology allowed us to obtain a distribution of weights that reinforce the theory that income, time, mobility and accessibility are factors that exacerbate the socio-spatial segregation of peripheral territories, as is the case of the Suba district.

Table 1 shows the results obtained from the entropy model, applied to the variables described above, with which the following analyses can be carried out. The highest weights assigned to variables such as the Pietra index (0.180746) follow a high contribution to the segregation index, indicating that inequality in income distribution is a peremptory factor in transportation-related social exclusion, implying that there is considerable inequality in how different socioeconomic groups in the locality access the transportation system given their economic income. Therefore, a high value of the Pietra index suggests that certain sectors of the locality face significant barriers to accessing transportation given the weight assigned within the composite segregation index (see figure 5).

Table 1. Results of the Entropy model for the variables considered for the calculation of the segregation index.

Indicator	*Mean*	*Deviation*	*Cuartil 75%*	*Composite Index Weight*
Pietra Index	*0,305*	*0,399*	*0,319*	*0,181*
Revenues earmarked for transportation	*0,144*	*0,088*	*0,204*	*0,061*
Travel Times	*51,991*	*15,266*	*60,337*	*0,013*
Time allocated to the first mile	*0,101*	*0,057*	*0,126*	*0,047*
Standby and connection time	*0,089*	*0,122*	*0,090*	*0,142*
Accessibility to TransMilenio	*0,255*	*0,229*	*0,462*	*0,175*
Accessibility to SITP	*0,252*	*0,111*	*0,292*	*0,038*
Active mobility	*0,292*	*0,220*	*0,428*	*0,076*
Motorized systems	*0,533*	*0,258*	*0,734*	*0,044*
Public transportation	*0,141*	*0,138*	*0,213*	*0,163*

Source: Prepared by the author

On the other hand, accessibility to the TransMilenio system (0.174996) also reflects a great importance within the composite segregation index, suggesting that in contexts where mass transportation infrastructure is limited or distant, people face greater barriers to access opportunities (labor, education and services), which increases their social exclusion. Given that the TransMilenio system is one of the main modes of transportation in Bogota and mainly in the Suba district (40% of trips are made on the TransMilenio system in the district), proximity to its stations is a key factor for social integration. In peripheral areas such as Suba, where TransMilenio stations are considerably far away, the difficulty in accessing the system translates into inequalities, limiting people's mobility and restricting access to the opportunities offered by the city, which reinforces socio-spatial segregation (see figure 6).

Mobility by public transport (0.163303) also carries considerable weight, reflecting the importance of efficient access to public transport in reducing exclusion, given that access to public transport can contribute significantly to socio-spatial segregation. If these peripheral and low-income areas have limited or less efficient access to public transport, this can intensify social exclusion and limit mobility opportunities for these locality groups (see figure 7).

Another factor with greater weight is the waiting and connection times index (0.142427, see figure 8), which suggests that long waiting times and delays in intermodal connections are significantly affecting the user experience, so if schedules are infrequent and access to transportation options is limited, residents of these areas may face long waiting times, which limits their mobility and quality of life, intensifying social exclusion and limiting equitable access to opportunities.

We have just analyzed how Pietra's indexes of accessibility to the TransMilenio system, public transport mobility, and waiting and connection times play a high influence within the composite indicator of segregation. However, the interconnectedness of these indicators reflects the potential for inequality in access to transportation as described below.

A high value of the Pietra index points to significant inequalities in the distribution of transport access between different areas, highlighting that certain areas, particularly peripheral or less socioeconomically advantaged areas, are disadvantaged in terms of transport availability and quality. This inequality is accentuated by the index of accessibility to the TransMilenio system, which evaluates the proximity to the stations of the mass transit system.

Areas with low accessibility to TransMilenio tend to coincide with areas of lower socioeconomic status, limiting their residents' access to fast and efficient transportation, and exacerbating segregation. Mobility by public transport, which measures the proportion of trips made using mass transit, indicates the significant reliance of residents on public transport for their daily commute. However, in areas with high dependence on public transport, deficiencies in accessibility and service efficiency translate into additional barriers, such as long waiting times and inadequate coverage. This is reflected in the waiting and connection time index, which calculates the proportion of total travel time spent waiting and making intermodal connections. A high wait and connection time index suggests that residents face long waits and inefficient coordination between different modes of transportation, which not only affects travel efficiency but also user satisfaction. These idle times can discourage the use of public transport, causing residents of less socioeconomically advantaged areas to face greater difficulties and barriers in their commutes. The combination of these indicators reveals how transport infrastructure deficiencies and operational problems amplify inequality and social exclusion.

Another consideration to take into account are the indicators with relatively low weights, the travel time index, time spent in the first mile, income spent on transportation, number of vehicles per household, population density, accessibility to the SITP, active mobility and motorized systems within the composite index reflect how the entropy method weights the factors according to their relative contribution to inequality in access to transportation. Therefore, indicators with lower weights tend to show relatively low variability or less impact on socio-spatial segregation compared to other factors, indicating that their contribution to the composite index is less significant in the specific case study of Suba.

This low weight in the contribution of the index is reflected in the fact that the indicators, although relevant, may not fully capture the intensity of inequality compared to the other factors described above. These indicators may show less extreme variations or have a more limited impact on segregation when integrated into the composite index. Thus, the entropy method reveals that, despite their importance, these factors contribute in a more limited way to the explanation of the socio-spatial segregation of the locality, where accessibility and efficiency of public transportation play a more prominent role in shaping mobility inequalities. Although the indicators analyzed offer a robust understanding of the structural causes of segregation, the inclusion of community voices could further illuminate how these patterns are experienced on the ground. Understanding perceptions of mobility, insecurity, or service quality from residents themselves could help refine both academic interpretations and public policy interventions.

Figure 5. Pietra index and transportation segre9ation index within the Locality.

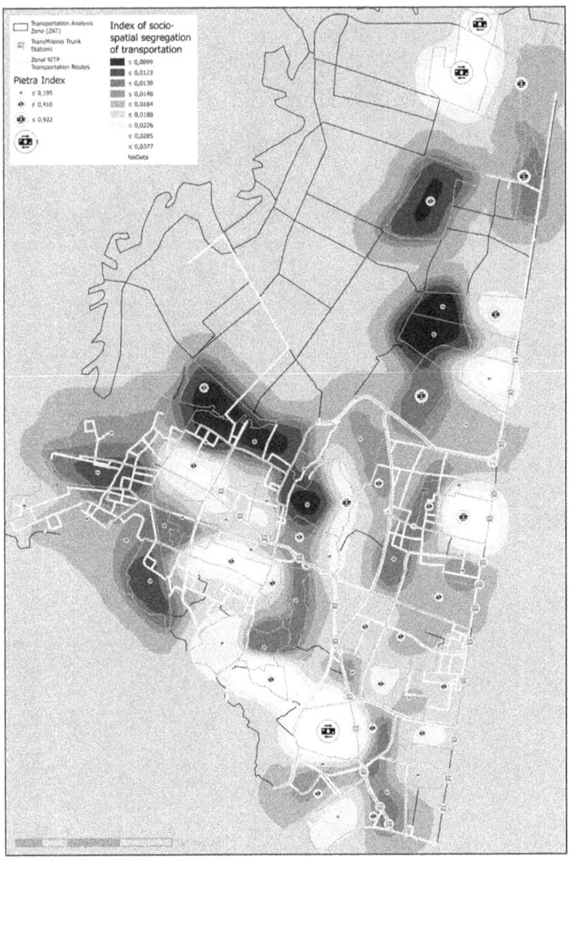

Figure 6. TransMilenio accessibility rate and transport segregation index within the locality

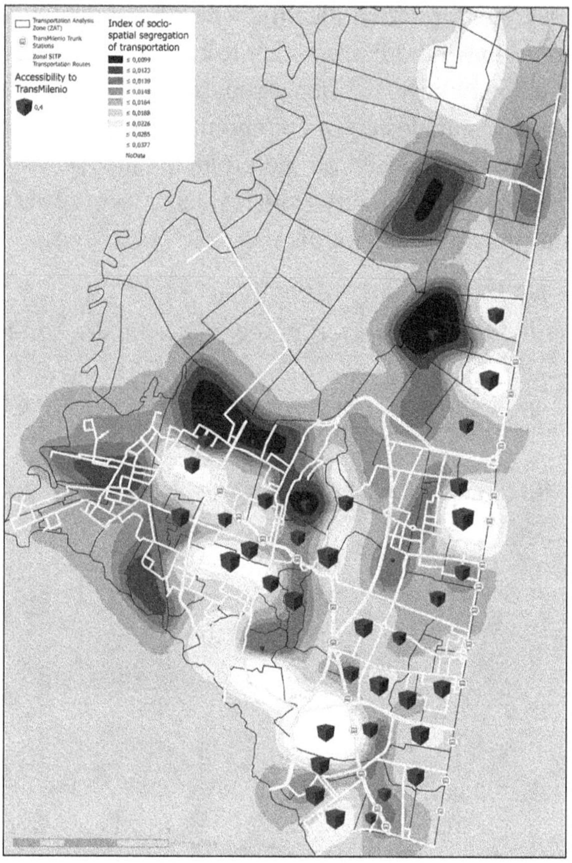

Figure 7. Distribution by modes of transport and transport segregation index within the locality

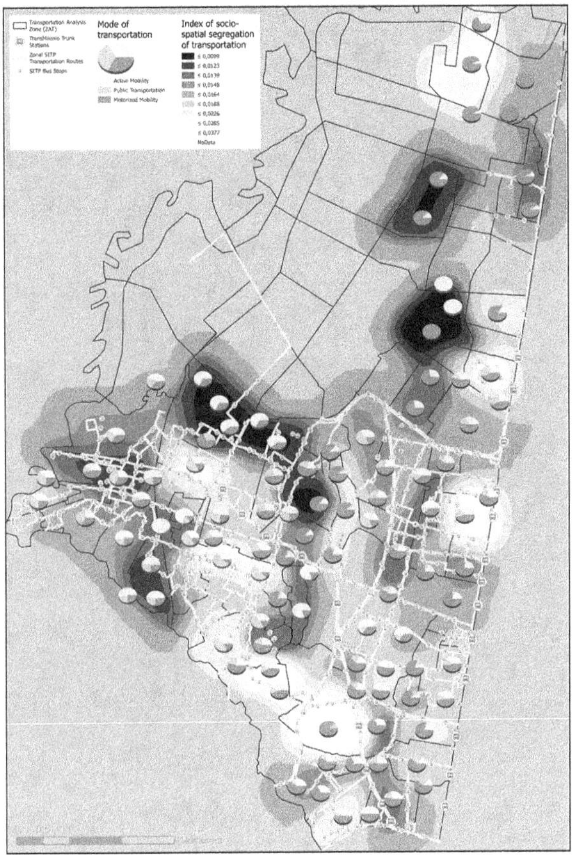

Figure 8. Travel time, waiting time, access and transportation segregation index within the locality.

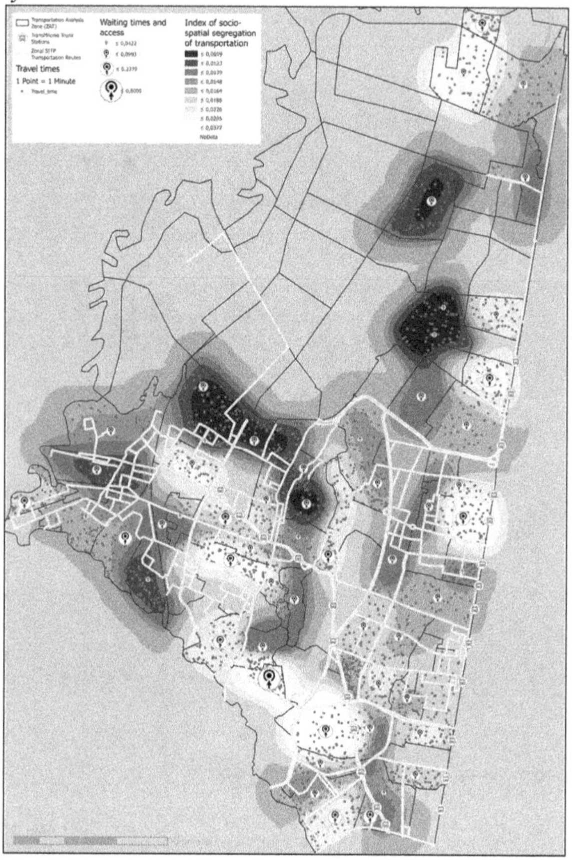

Source: Prepared by the author

Considering that Suba is one of the largest and most diverse localities in Bogotá, it presents considerable socioeconomic inequality where about 29% of the population lives in poverty, while approximately 12% is in extreme poverty, this socioeconomic disparity is manifested in spatial segregation, where higher income areas tend to be better equipped in terms of infrastructure and services, in contrast to low-income areas. In addition, it can be said that socioeconomic stratum 1 (12%), stratum 2 (17%) and stratum 3 (25) tend to face the greatest economic difficulties and have limited access to basic services and positive conditions in terms of transportation. While strata 3 (25%) and strata 4 (23%) tend to have more adequate access to services and greater economic stability to access various modes of transportation, thus improving access to decisions in terms of transportation and mobility. On the other hand, strata 5 (15%) and strata 6 (8%) enjoy a high standard of living, with access to high quality services and a greater economic capacity allowing them to access more comfortable modes of transportation, strategic locations in terms of mobility and conditions of opportunities (work, study and services) that fit their workplaces.

This distribution shows the socioeconomic diversity in Suba and highlights the significant disparities in terms of access and services between the different strata. The data indicate that, although Suba has a mix of economic strata, a considerable part of its population lives in conditions of poverty or lower middle class and faces difficulties in terms of mobility and accessibility, so it is important to highlight that the indicators that obtained a low weight within the model do not denote a low significance within the segregation indicator, but on the contrary indicate that there is a low variability indicating that in general most areas are affected by the situations represented by the indicators.

To better understand the socio-spatial segregation model, perform the decision tree in Figure 9, which analyzes how some of the factors influence the probability of obtaining a higher segregation index. The model showed an accuracy of 0.7778, indicating an outstanding ability to correctly classify the zones taking into account the indicators. For class 0 (low probability of segregation) the model shows an accuracy of 73% and a recall of 89%, indicating that it correctly identifies most of the low segregation cases and has a high capacity to detect true negatives. While for class 1 (high probability of segregation), the model shows an accuracy of 86% and a recall of 67%, reflecting an ability to predict high segregation, although with a smaller margin in detecting all relevant cases.

Figure 9. Decision model with representative variables for defining transportation segregation.

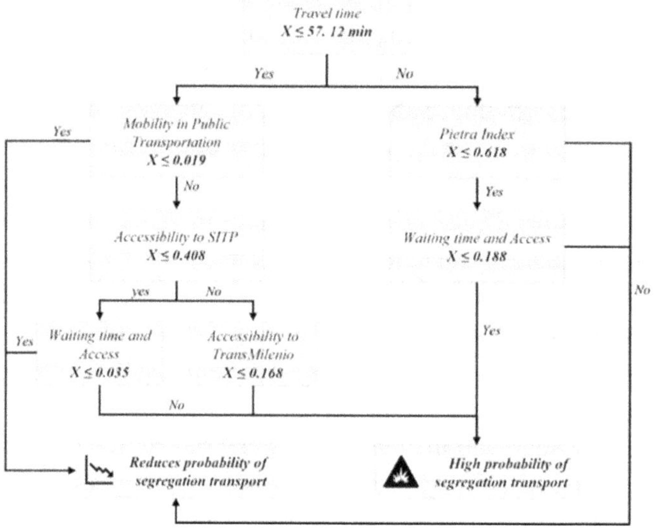

Source: Prepared by the author

6. CONCLUSIONS

The research performs a comprehensive evaluation of the socio-spatial segregation index through the analysis of transportation data from the Mobility Survey 2023 in Bogotá D.C. The inclusion of variables such as total trip length, first mile times, waiting times, main mode of transportation, monthly income, transportation costs, number of vehicles per household and population density have allowed finding a relationship between transportation and socio-spatial segregation.

Evaluation of the Pietra index, together with the percentage of income spent on transportation, provides insight into how economic inequalities limit access and increase the financial burden of transportation for low-income groups. In addition, travel, first mile and wait times show how barriers in transportation infrastructure in outlying areas perpetuate inequality and restrict access to opportunities. Measuring the proportionality of access to public transportation confirms differences in coverage and accessibility in peripheral areas, while the breakdown of transportation modes reveals mobility patterns that reflect disparities in infrastructure and resources.

The conglomerate analysis of the model, the results highlight how various factors influence the socio-spatial segregation of transportation in the Suba district, with emphasis on the integration of economic indicators, time, accessibility and modes of transportation. The Pietra index, with a significant weight of 0.181, highlights the importance of economic inequality in transportation-related social exclusion. This index indicates that inequality in income distribution significantly affects access to transportation for different socioeconomic groups in Suba. Accessibility to the TransMilenio system (0.175) and public transport mobility (0.163) also play crucial roles, reflecting how limitations in infrastructure and mass transit coverage intensify social exclusion by hindering access to employment and educational opportunities.

The waiting times and connection index (0.142) shows that long waiting times and poor coordination between transport modes aggravate socio-spatial segregation, affecting the quality of life and mobility of residents in peripheral areas. Although indicators such as travel times, time spent in the first mile and others have lower weights, their contribution to the composite index is relevant but secondary compared to the previously mentioned factors. These results underscore the need to improve transportation infrastructure and its efficiency to mitigate inequalities in access and reduce socio-spatial segregation in Suba.

7. REFERENCES

Adugbila, E. J., Martinez, J. A., & Pfeffer, K. (2023). Road infrastructure expansion and socio-spatial fragmentation in the peri-urban zone in Accra, Ghana. *Cities (London, England)*, *133*, 104154. DOI: 10.1016/j.cities.2022.104154

Ahani, S., & Dadashpoor, H. (2021). A review of domains, approaches, methods and indicators in peri-urbanization literature. *Habitat International*, *114*, 102387. DOI: 10.1016/j.habitatint.2021.102387

Biljecki, F., Ledoux, H., & Oosterom, P. V. (2013). Transportation mode-based segmentation and classification of movement trajectories. *International Journal of Geographical Information Science*, *27*(2), 385–407. Advance online publication. DOI: 10.1080/13658816.2012.692791

Binder, J., & Matern, A. (2020). Mobility and social exclusion in peripheral regions. *European Planning Studies*, *28*(6), 1049–1067. Advance online publication. DOI: 10.1080/09654313.2019.1689926

Bocarejo, J. P., Portilla, I., & Meléndez, D. (2016). Social fragmentation as a consequence of implementing a Bus Rapid Transit system in the city of Bogotá. *Urban Studies (Edinburgh, Scotland)*, *53*(8), 1617–1634. DOI: 10.1177/0042098015588739

Bolay, J.-C., Pedrazzini, Y., Rabinovich, A., Catenazzi, A., & García Pleyán, C. (2005). Urban environment, spatial fragmentation and social segration in Latin America: Where does innovation lie? *Habitat International*, *29*(4), 627–645. DOI: 10.1016/j.habitatint.2004.05.003

Bourne, L. S., & Simmons, J. (2003). NEW FAULT LINES? RECENT TRENDS IN THE CANADIAN URBAN SYSTEM AND THEIR IMPLICATIONS FOR PLANNING AND PUBLIC POLICY. *Canadian Journal of Urban Research*, *12*(1), 22–47. https://www.jstor.org/stable/44387635

Brandes, T., & Emary, C. (2016). Feedback control of waiting times. *Physical Review. E*, *93*(4), 042103. Advance online publication. DOI: 10.1103/PhysRevE.93.042103 PMID: 27176250

Brea-Martínez, G., & Dribe, M. (2024). Economic Inequality and Social Mobility. Oxford University Press EBooks. DOI: 10.1093/oso/9780197761090.003.0003

Brovarone, E. V. (2021). Accessibility and mobility in peripheral areas: A national place-based policy. *European Planning Studies*. Advance online publication. DOI: 10.1080/09654313.2021.1894098

Bucheli Guevara, J. F. (2019). Living Together: A Capability Approach to Spatially Segregated Areas of Bogota [Doctoral dissertation]. University of Cambridge.

Cao, M., Zhang, Y., Zhang, Y., Li, S., & Hickman, R. (2019). *Using different approaches to evaluate individual social equity in transport. A Companion to Transport.* Space and Equity., DOI: 10.4337/9781788119825.00024

Carrilho, J., & Trindade, J. (2022). Sustainability in Peri-Urban Informal Settlements: A Review. *Sustainability (Basel), 14*(13), 7591. DOI: 10.3390/su14137591

Casais, N., & Grau Valldosera, F. (2023). Infrastructural peripheries in the city-region: Airport spatial influences. In Richards, S., Schmidt, R.III, Sanliturk, C., & Palaiologou, F. (Eds.), *Region* (pp. 271–294). Routledge., https://www.lboro.ac.uk/departments/abce/ahra2021-region/

Cass, N., Shove, E., & Urry, J. (2003). *Changing infrastructures, measuring socio-spatial inclusion/exclusion: final report to the Department for Transport.* Lancaster University.

Cassiers, T., & Kesteloot, C. (2012). Socio-spatial Inequalities and Social Cohesion in European Cities. *Urban Studies (Edinburgh, Scotland), 49*(9), 1909–1924. DOI: 10.1177/0042098012444888

Castillo Mejía, A. M. (2013). Dinámica de las construcciones por usos de la localidad de Suba en los años 2002 y 2012. https://www.catastrobogota.gov.co/sites/default/files/archivos/suba.pdf

Cervero, R. (2014). Transport Infrastructure and the Environment in the Global South: Sustainable Mobility and Urbanism. *Jurnal Perencanaan Wilayah Dan Kota, 25*(3), 174–191. DOI: 10.5614/jpwk.2015.25.3.1

Chen, Y., Salike, N., Luan, F., & He, M. (2016). Heterogeneous effects of inter- and intra-city transportation infrastructure on economic growth: Evidence from Chinese cities. *Cambridge Journal of Regions, Economy and Society*, rsw019. Advance online publication. DOI: 10.1093/cjres/rsw019

Dede, M., Asdak, C., & Setiawan, I. (2022). Spatial-ecological approach in cirebon's peri-urban regionalization. *IOP Conference Series. Earth and Environmental Science, 1089*(1), 012080. DOI: 10.1088/1755-1315/1089/1/012080

Demazière, C. (2018). Strategic Spatial Planning in a Situation of Fragmented Local Government: The Case of France. DisP - The Planning Review, 54(2), 58–76. DOI: 10.1080/02513625.2018.1487645

Dirección de Análisis y Diseño Estratégico. (2022). Diagnostico Local de Suba. https://www.integracionsocial.gov.co/images/_docs/entidad/11_Diagnostico_Local_Suba_2021_VF_.pdf

Doyle, M. W., & Havlick, D. G. (2009). Infrastructure and the Environment. *Annual Review of Environment and Resources*, *34*(1), 349–373. Advance online publication. DOI: 10.1146/annurev.environ.022108.180216

Engels, J. I. (2016). Infrastructure and Fragmentation: The Limits of the Integration Paradigm. In Schiefelbusch, M. (Ed.), *In Linking Networks: The Formation of Common Standards and Visions for Infrastructure Development* (1st ed., pp. 19–34). Routledge., DOI: 10.4324/9781315592497

García Galindo, W., & Carrero Barón, D. F. (2017). Dinámica Inmobiliaria Bogotá - Región. https://www.catastrobogota.gov.co/sites/default/files/Dinamica%20Inmobiliaria%20Bogota%20Region%202017%20-%202020_20210331_VersionDiseno_v1_20210520.pdf

Gil-Alonso, F., & López-Villanueva, C. (2023). Metropolitan Spatial Reconfiguration and the Mobility Transition: Sustainability Challenges in the Fragmented City. In *Urban Dynamics in the Post-pandemic Period: Tourist Spaces and Urban Centres* (pp. 305–324). Springer International Publishing.

Gottero, E., Larcher, F., & Cassatella, C. (2023). Defining and Regulating Peri-Urban Areas through a Landscape Planning Approach: The Case Study of Turin Metropolitan Area (Italy). *Land (Basel)*, *12*(1), 217. DOI: 10.3390/land12010217

Gutiérrez, J. (2009). Transport and Accessibility. DOI: 10.1016/B978-008044910-4.01030-0

Guzman, L. A., Oviedo, D., & Bocarejo, J. P. (2017). City profile: The Bogotá Metropolitan Area that never was. *Cities (London, England)*, *60*, 202–215. DOI: 10.1016/j.cities.2016.09.004

Haoran, Y., Cong, W., & Youyang, Y. (2022). The Spatial Structure Evolution of China's High-Speed Rail Network and Its Impacts on Real Estate Investment. *Applied Spatial Analysis and Policy*, *15*(1), 49–69. Advance online publication. DOI: 10.1007/s12061-021-09390-7

Hasselwander, M., Nieland, S., Dematera-Contreras, K., & Goletz, M. (2023). MaaS for the masses: Potential transit accessibility gains and required policies under Mobility-as-a-Service. DOI: 10.1016/j.multra.2023.100086

Hidayati, I., Yamu, C., & Tan, W. (2019). The Emergence of Mobility Inequality in Greater Jakarta, Indonesia: A Socio-Spatial Analysis of Path Dependencies in Transport–Land Use Policies. *Sustainability (Basel), 11*(18), 5115. DOI: 10.3390/su11185115

Iqbal, A., Nazir, H., & Memon, R. M. (2022). Shopping centers versus traditional open street bazaars: A comparative study of user's preference in the city of Karachi, Pakistan. *Frontiers in Built Environment*, *8*, 1066093. Advance online publication. DOI: 10.3389/fbuil.2022.1066093

Iyer, N., & Menezes, R. Barbosa, & Hugo. (2023). Mobility and Transit Segregation in Urban Spaces. DOI: 10.48550/ARXIV.2304.07086

Iyer, N. G., Menezes, R., & Barbosa, H. (2023). Transport and Mobility Segregation in Urban Spaces. *International Journal of Population Data Science*, *8*(3). Advance online publication. DOI: 10.23889/ijpds.v8i3.2268

Jaeger, J. A. G., Raumer, H. S., Esswein, H., Müller, M., & Schmidt-Lüttmann, M. (2007). *Time series of landscape fragmentation caused by transportation infrastructure and urban development: a case study from Baden-Württemberg*., DOI: 10.5751/ES-01983-120122

Kanai, J. M., & Schindler, S. (2022). Infrastructure-led development and the peri-urban question: Furthering crossover comparisons. *Urban Studies (Edinburgh, Scotland)*, *59*(8), 1597–1617. DOI: 10.1177/00420980211064158

Khanani, R. S. (2019). *The Impact of a road Infrastructure project on Socio-Spatial Interaction and Quality of Life of Planned and Unplanned Fragments in Kisumu City* [Essay (Master)]. University of Twente.

Khanani, R. S., Adugbila, E. J., Martinez, J. A., & Pfeffer, K. (2021). The Impact of Road Infrastructure Development Projects on Local Communities in Peri-Urban Areas: The Case of Kisumu, Kenya and Accra, Ghana. *International Journal of Community Well-being*, *4*(1), 33–53. DOI: 10.1007/s42413-020-00077-4

Lee, J., Arts, J., Vanclay, F., & Ward, J. (2020). Examining the Social Outcomes from Urban Transport Infrastructure: Long-Term Consequences of Spatial Changes and Varied Interests at Multiple Levels. *Sustainability (Basel), 12*(15), 5907. DOI: 10.3390/su12155907

Lima, J. J. (2001). Socio-spatial segregation and urban form: Belém at the end of the 1990s. *Geoforum*, *32*(4), 493–507. DOI: 10.1016/S0016-7185(01)00019-7

Lucchini, L., Langle-Chimal, O., Candeago, L., Melito, L., Chunet, A., Montfort, A., Lepri, B., Lozano-Gracia, N., & Fraiberger, S. (2023). Socioeconomic disparities in mobility behavior during the COVID-19 pandemic in developing countries. ArXiv. Org. DOI: 10.48550/ARXIV.2305.06888

Marchant Santiago, C., Sánchez Acuña, R., & Monje-Hernández, Y. (2022). Long-Term Features of Cities in Latin America and the Caribbean: Socio-Residential Segregation, Territorial Inequality, and Spatial Fragmentation. In González Pérez, J. M., Irazábal, C., & Lois González, R. C. (Eds.), *The Routledge Handbook of Urban Studies in Latin America and the Caribbean* (Vol. 1, pp. 177–201). Routledge., DOI: 10.4324/9781003132622-10

Matos, B., & Lobo, C. (2023). The Barrier Effect and Pedestrian Mobility/Accessibility on Urban Highways: An Analysis Based on the Belo Horizonte/Minas Gerais/Brazil Ring Road. *Sustainability (Basel)*, *15*(4), 3408. Advance online publication. DOI: 10.3390/su15043408

Méndez, J. G., García-Moreno, L. M., Murillo-Hoyos, J., & Molina, C. J. (2023). Social Inequality in Popular Neighborhoods: A Pre- and Post-Pandemic Perspective from Joint Accessibility. *Sustainability (Basel)*, *15*(13), 10587. Advance online publication. DOI: 10.3390/su151310587

Morales, E. R. (2024). Planned Socio-Spatial Fragmentation: The Normalisation of Gated Communities in Two Mexican Metropolises. *Urban Planning*, *9*, 6879. Advance online publication. DOI: 10.17645/up.6879

Moreno Barón, J. A. (2021). Documento Técnico de Base Plan de Desarrollo Local 2021-2024. http://www.suba.gov.co/sites/suba.gov.co/files/documentos/tabla_archivos/documento_tecnico_de_base_final.pdf

Mortoja, M., Yigitcanlar, T., & Mayere, S. (2020). What is the most suitable methodological approach to demarcate peri-urban areas? A systematic review of the literature. *Land Use Policy*, *95*, 104601. DOI: 10.1016/j.landusepol.2020.104601

Mosquera Becerra, M. J. (2014). Socio-spatial Transformation and Contested Space at the Street Level in Latin America: The Case of Cali, Colombia. DOI: 10.15760/etd.1952

Nogués, S., & Salas-Olmedo, M. H. (2009). Land Use and Transport Integrated Policies in Peripheral Areas.

Ostrensky, V. P., Porsse, A. A., & Frota, L. M. (2022). Public Transport and gentrification. Evidence from São Paulo Metro new stations. DOI: 10.1111/rsp3.12536

Petrisor, A. (2017). A diversity-based approach to the spatial development of socio-ecological systems. Urbanism. Arhitectură. Construcţii, 143–162. https://api.semanticscholar.org/CorpusID:7105419

Prasad, D., Alizadeh, T., & Dowling, R. (2022). Smart city place-based outcomes in India: Bubble urbanism and socio-spatial fragmentation. *Journal of Urban Design*, *27*(4), 483–503. DOI: 10.1080/13574809.2021.2022978

Rodriguez, C., Lima Sakr, F., Griffiths, S., & Hillier, B. (2012). The relationship of spatial configuration and socio-economic conditions in São Paulo, Brazil. Proceedings: *Eighth International Space Syntax Symposium*, 1–24.

Rokem, J., & Vaughan, L. (2018). Segregation, mobility and encounters in Jerusalem: The role of public transport infrastructure in connecting the 'divided city.'. *Urban Studies (Edinburgh, Scotland)*, *55*(15), 3454–3473. DOI: 10.1177/0042098017691465

Rosik, P., & Wójcik, J. (2022). Transport Infrastructure and Regional Development: A Survey of Literature on Wider Economic and Spatial Impacts. DOI: 10.3390/su15010548

Salas-Olmedo, M. H., García, P., & Gutiérrez, J. (2015). Accessibility and transport infrastructure improvement assessment: The role of borders and multilateral resistance. *Transportation Research Part A, Policy and Practice*, *82*, 110–129. https://doi.org/https://doi.org/10.1016/j.tra.2015.09.009. DOI: 10.1016/j.tra.2015.09.009

Sdoukopoulos, A., Pitsiava-Latinopoulou, M., & Politis, I. (2023). Assessing the fragmentation-barrier effect in urban areas: The case study of Thessaloniki, Greece. *IOP Conference Series. Earth and Environmental Science*, *1196*(1), 012078. DOI: 10.1088/1755-1315/1196/1/012078

Secretaría de Planeación. (2020). Proceso de Revisión del Plan de Ordenamiento Territorial de Bogotá D. C. https://www.sdp.gov.co/sites/default/files/11_suba_-_diagnostico_pot_2020.pdf

Secretaría Distrital de Movilidad. (2020). Informe Preliminar de Rendición de Cuentas Locales: Localidad de Suba. https://www.movilidadbogota.gov.co/web/sites/default/files/Paginas/04-10-2021/informe_preliminar_rdc_gestion_2020_localidad_suba.pdf.pdf

Secretaría Distrital de Planeación. (2009). Conociendo la Localidad de Suba: Diagnóstico de los aspectos físicos, demográficos y socioeconómicos. https://oab.ambientebogota.gov.co/?post_type=dlm_download&p=4145

Shaw, B. J., van Vliet, J., & Verburg, P. H. (2020). The peri-urbanization of Europe: A systematic review of a multifaceted process. *Landscape and Urban Planning, 196*, 103733. DOI: 10.1016/j.landurbplan.2019.103733

Taşan-Kok, T., & Stead, D. (2013). Analysing the Socio-Spatial Vulnerability to Drivers of Globalisation in Lisbon, Oporto, Istanbul, Stockholm and Rotterdam. In Resilience Thinking in Urban Planning (1st ed., pp. 71–91). Springer Dordrecht. DOI: 10.1007/978-94-007-5476-8_5

Tomasiello, D. B., Santos, D. H. M., Oliveira, J. P., Braga, C. G., Pereira, R., Tomasiello, D. B., Santos, D. H. M., Oliveira, J. P., Braga, C. G., & Pereira, R. (2022). A time interval metric for cumulative opportunity accessibility. https://doi.org/DOI: 10.31235/OSF.IO/UX5AH

United Nations Human Settlements Programme (UN-Habitat). (2022). World Cities Report 2022. https://unhabitat.org/sites/default/files/2022/06/wcr_2022.pdf

Varkey, A. (2019). A Review of Peri-Urban Definitions. *Land Use Changes and Challenges to Development., 39*(I), 111.

Yasin, M. Y., Yusoff, M. M., Abdullah, J., & Noor, N. (2020, November 29). Hj. Mohd. (2020). Is urban sprawl a threat to sustainable development? A review of characteristics and consequences. *Geografia : Malaysian Journal of Society and Space, 16*(4). Advance online publication. DOI: 10.17576/geo-2020-1604-05

Yekimov, S., Kluger, V., Sobirov, B., & Ahrorov, F. (2023). Dynamic entropy model of transport flows. DOI: 10.1051/e3sconf/202338905035

Yoo, S., Kumagai, J., Sho, K., & Managi, S. (2024). Impact of high-speed railway on gentrification and regional inequality in Japan. *Transportation Research Part D, Transport and Environment, 134*, 104346. DOI: 10.1016/j.trd.2024.104346

Yu, P., Yung, E. H. K., Chan, E. H. W., Wong, M. S., Wang, S., & Chen, Y. (2023). An integrated approach for examining urban fragmentation in metropolitan areas: Implications for sustainable urban planning. *Journal of Cleaner Production, 419*, 138151. DOI: 10.1016/j.jclepro.2023.138151

Zambon, I., Serra, P., Sauri, D., Carlucci, M., & Salvati, L. (2017). Beyond the 'Mediterranean city': Socioeconomic disparities and urban sprawl in three Southern European cities. *Geografiska Annaler. Series B, Human Geography, 99*(3), 319–337. DOI: 10.1080/04353684.2017.1294857

Chapter 7
Evaluating Walkability in Peri-Urban Areas for Enhanced Urban Sustainability:
A Case Study of Milan's Southern Margin

Deniz Çam
https://orcid.org/0009-0006-0787-6250
Politecnico di Milano, Italy

Çağlanur Kösel
https://orcid.org/0009-0005-3428-5045
Politecnico di Milano, Italy

ABSTRACT

The act of walking is becoming not just a means of transportation but a crucial to creation of sustainable cities. This transformation is significant in cities that are more vulnerable to impacts of climate change. The study focuses on pedestrian mobility in peri-urban areas so, increasing pedestrian mobility in these areas is an important role as climate change impacts will gradually increase in cities. Also, it focuses on importance of pedestrian mobility to develop sustainable urban areas. This micro-scale model, which can use the proposed quantitative and qualitative urban design factors to measure walkability, offers a different approach to sustainability for the peri-urbans. Furthermore, it provides an opportunity for spatial evaluation to increase the sustainability of peri-urban areas. As a case study, it focuses on the urban margin: Gratosoglio which is located south of Milan, a major Italian city. The

DOI: 10.4018/979-8-3693-6089-7.ch007

main conclusion illustrate how walkability is affected by urban design elements and the importance of walkability in developing sustainable and climate-sensitive areas.

1. INTRODUCTION

This study examines the walkability performance of urban peri-urban areas based on the qualitative and quantitative factors of urban design. In this context, it presents a model that is anticipated to contribute to urban environmental studies and to urban environments becoming more sustainable and livable areas in the future. Based on contemporary literature on pedestrian mobility and walkability from a critical perspective, it focuses on the role and importance of walkability in creating sustainable peri-urban areas.

In recent years, climate change, which is a global problem, has been affecting cities more and more due to industrial and anthropogenic activities, rapid urbanization and improper land use. Increasing urban development and growth create new environments in temporal and spatial contexts, and the habitats within these environments undergo maladaptive changes or rapidly develop adaptive conditions against this change (Lambert and Brans et al, 2021; Miles and Carlen, 2021). Cities are increasingly affected by the effects of climate change, and since these effects are increasing, peri-urban areas are gaining importance in the context of creating sustainable urban peripheries. There is no clear standard definition of peri-urban areas, but they can generally be defined as areas located on the edges of integrated urban centers (Malano and Maheswari, et al. 2014). Cities with dynamic urbanization processes that exceed traditional boundaries and reach surrounding settlements/regions, along with population growth and especially migration from cities, have become the focus of researchers. These dynamic processes have led to the rethinking of peri-urbanisation these days (Dupont, 2005; Geneletti et al., 2017; Barbossa et al., 2022).Therefore, they share many characteristics of urban and rural landscapes. Generally speaking, they consist of a combination of residential, industrial and agricultural land uses. They can also host important natural resources and contain biodiversity. Above all, they are often characterized by a rapid transition from rural to urban landscapes. In many of the world's megacities, peri-urban areas also have poorer urban infrastructure and lower demographic density. Urban peripheries can also show very different characteristics depending on whether they are located in developing or industrialized countries (Malano and Maheswari, et al. 2014).

With increasing urbanization and the consequences of climate change having a greater impact on cities, urban peripheries are also changing, and this change is seen in some areas. for example; changes in land use, changing forms of household composition and increasing pressure on common natural resources so, more than half of the world's 6.6 billion people live in urban areas, which account for 3% of the world's land area. The proportion of the world's population living in urban areas increased from less than 5 percent in 1800 to 47 percent in 2000 and is expected to reach 65 percent by 2030. But more than 90 percent of future population growth will be concentrated in cities. in developing countries and a large percentage of this population will be poor (Arha and Audichya et al. 2014). Even from this perspective, when considered it in the context of creating sustainable urban areas, urban peripheries will play a much more key role in urban planning and urban design in the future. The peri-urban area refers to a transition or interaction zone where urban and rural activities come together and landscape features are subject to rapid changes triggered by human activities, and the trend towards gradually increasing urbanization is a result of the increasing population and this urbanization is responsible for the growth in the peri-urban area (Arha and Audichya et al., 2014). Therefore, these interaction zones will need to be considered more carefully in the context of sustainability.

Walking is becoming more than just a means of transport, but a fundamental building block in the creation of sustainable cities (Moura et al., 2017). The importance of walking is increasing as urban environments become increasingly vulnerable to the impacts of climate change. Walking also provides many environmental benefits (Ercan and Belge, 2020) and plays a critical role in the development of compact cities (Forsyth, 2015). Therefore, walking should be considered not just as a means of navigation, but as a tool that yields positive results for both individuals and the environment. Walking reverses the logic of city people, even their most common conditioning (Frederic Gros, 2008, p: 34). From the perspective of individuals, the easiest and fairest way for everyone to socialize and interact with other city residents is walking (Gehl, 2010). Walkability, a form of "green mobility" with minimal environmental impact, offers an important opportunity to make cities more resilient to climate change, especially air pollution (Forthsyth and Southworth, 2008). It also serves to limit urban sprawl by allowing the creation of walkable environments within polycentric urban structures (Ercan and Belge, 2020).

Most megacities face threats of urban sprawl due to the increasing population in urban areas and the resulting concentration of urban peripheries In today's urban landscapes, the role of urban peripheries is undergoing a significant transformation, especially in the face of climate change (Aşıcı, 2023). These areas are gaining importance as they will form the growth axes of the cities of the future. In this context, a sustainable and resilient urban design perspective should directly address urban peripheral areas, and pedestrian walkability has a unique potential in shaping the future of these areas. This study investigates the importance of pedestrian-oriented urban design in the development of sustainable and climate-resilient cities. Such designs can significantly increase a city's ability to adapt and thrive in the face of environmental challenges. In this context, the research investigates the characteristics that define walkability and proposes a methodology for micro-scale walkability assessment. This model combines both quantitative and qualitative indicators. This research addresses both quantitative and qualitative factors of urban design, as analyzing only physical features provides incomplete conclusions about what the experience of walking on a particular street is like. 9 Perceptual features can influence the walking environment (Forsyth, 2015). This approach allows assessment of walkability levels in specific urban areas, highlighting the importance of pedestrian movement. Additionally, the study underlines the central importance of green mobility, such as walking, within sustainable urban transport systems, ultimately contributing to the development of climate-resilient cities.

As a case study, the research examines the urban margins located in the south of Milan, a major Italian metropolitan city. The analysis focuses on a specific unit: Gratosoglio. These areas lie within and beyond the municipal boundaries, presenting a unique context where diverse urban elements coexist. The study analyzes the role of pedestrian mobility in achieving urban sustainability and resilience within this heterogeneous landscape. Additionally, investigates the walkability levels within the urban margins of southern Milan, focusing on the question of walkability in these areas. This study proposes a micro-scale walkability evaluation method that integrates qualitative and quantitative urban design factors. The method identifies walkability indicators specific to urban areas and utilizes these indicators to establish an evaluation framework. Subsequently, the framework is employed to measures the walkability level of the southern margins of Milan. These measurements provide a foundation for spatial evaluation, enabling the development of sustainable urban margins. Following the description of the research methodology, a final summary of the findings is provided. The findings of this research elucidate the impact of pedestrian mobility and accessibility qualities on peri-urban areas, underlining the crucial role of walkability in fostering climate-sensitive and sustainable design principles. The findings illuminate potential contributions to contemporary urban design practices.

Finally, the research explores urban design and planning strategies that can raise the levels of sustainability, climate neutrality and pedestrian walkability of this urban-rural transition zone in the south of Milan. It highlights the contributions of this micro-scale research model based on a pedestrian-oriented, inclusive, sustainable, climate-sensitive and people-centered approach.

This research examines the features that define walkability in peri-urban areas and both quantitative and qualitative indicators of urban design in 5 sections. In the first part of the study, basic concepts are defined, information is given about the case of study, and at the same time, the position of the study in the general context of contemporary literature, expected results and the purpose of the study are defined.

The second part focuses on the methodology of the research, the third part focuses on the examination of Milan's southern margin (i.e. Gratosoglio). In the last two section includes the experimental results that can be drawn from the research, their interpretation, and also discusses the findings of the research.

2. MATERIAL AND METHOD

This study proposes a micro-scale model that evaluates the role and importance of walkability in urban peripheries in the context of achieving and creating sustainable and livable urban areas. It uses some principles of urban design to evaluate walkability. It also defines the quantitative and qualitative nature and factors of these principles. It creates a more meaningful series of indicators by including physical properties in the measurement. Then, it determines the sub-indicators defined for each indicator, and the model creates a meaningful whole by defining the method to be used (Table 1). Urban design qualities and principles are different from qualities such as sense of comfort, actual safety and level of attractiveness, which reflect how the individual reacts to a place and how people weighs, that is, evaluates the conditions there when considering his own attitudes and preferences (Ewing, 2009). Accordingly, this study defines indicators in urban design qualities and physical features. By prioritizing the relationship between urban design and walkability, the study defines the building blocks that are important for creating sustainable areas. Additionally, no matter how walkability is defined, it is important to consider the possibility that there may be much more than just physical components that come together to create a walkable place; many different factors need to be taken into account (Forsyth, 2015). At this point, the study argues that more can be done in urban design. Some of the quantitative and qualitative principles of urban design are; Accessibility, Attractiveness and Comfort, Safety and Public Open Spaces and Recreational Facilities define these concepts and include them in the methodology as indicators (Table 1).

Table 1. Indicators of walkability, references from the literature on these indicators, research tools for data collection and spatial analysis

Indicators	Sub-indicators	References	Methods
Accessibility	1. Sidewalk width & condition; 2. Existence of Sidewalk; 3. Continuity of Sidewalks; 4. Presence & location of pedestrian path; 5. Access to public transports / stops; 6. Car & bicycle parking spaces; 7. Availability of crossing; 8. Accessibility to public services (schools, administrative buildings and health and religions) area within walking distance; 9. Availability of bike lines.	Ercan & Belge (2020),Krambeck & Shah (2006), Speck (2013), Cervero et. al., (2009), Wibowo, Tanan and Tinumbia (2015), Handy (2020), Hansen (1959), Handy (2018), Jacobs (1993), Lotfi & Koohsari (2009).	• Mapping of street network. • Continuity of sidewalks (obstacles and disconnections). • Mapping of pedestrian network and alternative mode. • Mapping of public transportation networks and stops). • Parking facilities for cars and bike. • Isochrone analysis.
Attractiveness and Comfort	1. Existence of landmarks; 2. Diversity of land use; 3. Obstacles of sidewalks(vehicle parking on sidewalks); 4. Presences of trees, shelters, benches, lighting elements and water fountains; 5. Natural landscape; 6. Maintenance and cleanliness of sidewalks; 7. Existence of facilities for disabled persons; 8. Human scale design; 9. Visual attractive structures (heritage and historical buildings, monuments, sculptures).	Krambeck & Shah (2006), Ercan & Belge (2020), Belge (2012), Moura, Cambra & Gonçalves (2017), Belge & Akkar (2017), Spoon (2005), Gehl (2010), Jacobs (1995), Carmona(2021), Lotfi & Koohsari (2009), Asadi-Shekari et al, (2013).	• Land use Map • Spatial analysis of amenities • Mapping of obstacles on sidewalks • Mapping urban landscape • Analyzing maintenance of sidewalks • Analysing height and span(clearance) ratio • Mapping historical and registered building, monuments and sculptures.
Public Open Spaces and Recreational Facilities	1. Availability of natural spaces and parks; 2. Presence of gathering places and squares; 3. Availability of facilities(indoor and outdoor sports facilities, playgrounds.	Barcelona (2013-2018), Moura, Cambra & Gonçalves (2017),Lee and Talen(2014), Ercan & Belge (2020), Moura et al. (2017)	• Mapping of open space system and recreational facilities. • Land-use analysis.
Safety	1. Barriers; 2. Traffic Calming; 3. Disabilities platforms and ramps; 4. Lightening on the streets; 5. Length of crossline; 6. Sidewalk condition; 7. Frequency of street use (GPS marks); 8. Land-use (mixed use places) (to more eyes on the street).	Jacobs (1961), Ercan & Belge (2020),Belge (2012), Gehl (2010), Ewing and Handy(2009), Gündoğdu & Dinçer(2020), Rahaman, Lourenço & Viegas (2012), Kelly et al., (2011), Evans (2009), Forsyth (2015), Koh & Wong (2013).	• Mapping of lightening on the streets • Land use analysis • Frequency mapping of streets based on GPS marks • Mapping Traffic Calming • Analyzing of pedestrian crossing and sidewalks

[1] These tools are used for assessment of walkability and prepared by authors.

2.1. Accessibility

Accessibility in urban planning is defined as the ability of individuals to access desired places in the city. Walking is the most basic mode of transport in terms of accessibility and an important criterion for livable cities with easy walking infrastructure (Wibowo et al., 2015). It expresses the degree of ease of reaching destinations and participating in desired activities. Accessibility and its degree are present here because it should be noted that when accessibility is only defined, it remains alone in terms of meaning and its background cannot be explained. Accessibility can be described as the potential of interaction possibilities (Handy, 2020) and this definition differs from the traditional definition in that it is a measure of the intensity of the possibility of interaction rather than a measure of convenience (Hansen, 1959). The concept of accessibility simply means how well connected an area or place or even a city on a large scale is and how well its residents have access to basic services, education, healthcare and recreational facilities, etc. It is a measure of how easily you can access areas and even places. In short, accessibility is a way of characterising the options available (Handy, 2018). Moreover, as it is usually defined, the level of accessibility from a particular place includes the distribution of destinations around it, the access to these places, areas, parks, streets, public buildings, green areas, etc. It reflects the convenience of access by various means and the amount and character of the activity found there (Handy, 2018). The most basic conclusion that can be made is this: What matters to people is how easy it is to get where they need to be. It is how convenient it is to reach the services they need or want, and this is the criterion of the concept of accessibility.

This research examines the first indicator, accessibility sub-indicators, as seen in its analysis of the concept of accessibility (table 1). In the review, references from many articles and theses are given, and the connection of the study's criteria with the literature and their position in the literature are detailed. Observations were made by strengthening accessibility sub-indicators with intensive field surveys and field visits in different periods, and finally, the studies specified in the methods, that is, mapping, were carried out. When the area is evaluated from the pedestrian perspective in terms of accessibility, it is stated that the most important element is the pavement (Jacobs 1993). Sidewalks are free and belong to the public, therefore their access cannot be restricted, and they are public spaces (Ercan & Belge, 2020). It is a legitimacy that makes these streets public and puts them at the service of pedestrians. These streets are public and accessible to everyone. The condition and standards of public streets were included in the analysis and found their place among the sub-indicators. The maintenance and implementation of pedestrian infrastructure is as important as its existence; unmaintained pavements can become unusable. A clean pedestrian environment increases pedestrian mobility and urban mobility (Krambeck & Shah, 2006). Another important concept that should be mentioned is the concept of continuity. Pavement continuity has a very important place in pedestrian choices. It is worth noting that mapping the pavement network is important in this respect. In the evaluation of this sub-indicator that will contribute to the accessibility indicator, whether continuity is broken and the presence of obstacles that will prevent continuity are measured. Access to different modes of transportation is another important criterion in walkability. The effect of using public transportation, which is one of the important means of transportation, on walkability cannot be underestimated, and therefore, in cities that develop with a focus on public transportation, users who do not use public transportation also find the opportunity to walk more, thanks to the uses and built environment shaped around public transportation (Speck, 2013). While contemporary concepts attach importance to pedestrian mobility, they include approaches that strengthen pedestrian connections with different modes of transportation, and they encourage city residents to engage in pedestrian mobility by providing opportunities for walkability. In order for the accessibility indicator to become a more meaningful criterion, this study included the presence of bicycle and vehicle parking spaces, whether bicycle transportation is provided, and whether public spaces are accessible within walking distance, which are the most important elements. accessibility to public service areas pedestrians within 10 to 20 minutes walking distance - e.g. It includes access to areas with a maximum of 800 meters (Lotfi & Koohsari, 2009). Unobstructed pedestrian movement and orientation to such service areas and public areas is another important element and enables pedestrians to be aware of the public space network they are in, which increases their opportunity to move more easily and spend time in the area by keeping them away from the fear of getting lost (Jacobs, 1995). In accessibility assessment, there are factors that affect travel demand such as land use intensity and diversity (Cervero et al., 2009). However, this study analysed these factors under the attractiveness indicator. As seen in the research (Table 1), all of these create the 'accessibility' indicator, which contributes both quantitatively and qualitatively.

2.2. Attractiveness and Comfort

Pedestrian accessibility indicators are now discussed quite comprehensively in the literature, and this is done based on many sub-segments and environmental factors (Asadi-Shekari and et al, 2013). Beyond pedestrian accessibility factors, attractiveness and comfort really play a key and very important role. As stated by Krambeck and Shah (2006), according to the global walkability index, attractiveness and comfort are one of the most important walkability indicators, and it is also an important indicator that makes urban public spaces (i.e. one of them is streets) walkable from a pedestrian perspective. Pedestrian environment, venues, streets, squares, etc. Making areas attractive is as important as making them accessible and has a vital impact (Moura et al, 2017). According to Belge (2012), the quality of the street network and the presence of public facilities are important in terms of attractiveness and this should be taken into consideration in designs. Therefore, in the study, in addition to the accessibility indicator, the attractiveness indicator was also included in the model. It would be misleading to measure whether the pedestrian space is truly walkable without measuring the attractiveness evaluation and comfort indicator. It also enriches the evaluation process.

However, when it comes to walkability criteria or evaluation, attractiveness and comfort, suitability of the street network and its condition (maintenance and cleanliness), pedestrian facilities and facilities offered, land use diversity in the built environment, suitability of walking paths for disabled people, planting, interesting urban landscaping and in particular, visual diversity and diversity of activities should be considered as sub-indicators (Belge & Ercan, 2022). Accordingly, as seen in (table 1), the sub-indicators of the 'attractiveness and comfort' indicator were enriched and took the necessary place in the model. Human scale, a sub-indicator not mentioned above, is a criterion that should be emphasized. As Gehl (1987; 2010) emphasizes, human-scale design greatly affects pedestrian mobility, and the need for city planners and architects to support and design an integrated pedestrianization that can develop more lively, safe, sustainable and healthy cities will be more important than it is now in the cities of the future. In fact, considering the urban space as a meeting place will provide a very strong theoretical background for human-scale design. Similarly, comfort also has physical and environmental aspects that greatly influence pedestrian behavior and choices. Street furniture is the physical component of comfort, including the landscape elements on the street and their human-scale design, the condition and design of the sidewalk, as well as the features and location of sidewalk lighting (Belge & Ercan, 2022). Numerous factors, including continuous pavements and smooth, uneven roads, distinct walking zones on pavements, and the quality of raised or textured pavement for the comfort of pedestrians of various ages and physical abilities, all influence pavement width (Akkar & Belge, 2020).

In this research, as can be seen for the 'attractiveness and comfort' indicator (table 1), maps were produced with the help of GIS, such as analysis of the built environment, mapping on the presence of amenities, landscape elements and the location of green areas. In addition, analyzing height and span (clearance) ratio was made for human scale, which is an element of urban design. This can actually be called 5 km/h architecture, as Gehl (2010) emphasizes. He emphasizes that the contact between the street and the building can be with the bottom 5 floors, and as you go higher than the 5th floor, the contact with the city is lost. He also adds that the 3rd floor of a building is a threshold (Figure 1) and as an important threshold it indicates a height of 6.5 m, which is equal to a 4-storey building, but as the end point threshold, that is, the maximum threshold is 13.5 m (a 5-storey building). corresponds to the building).

Figure 1. Gehl, J. (2010). Cities for people. Island press.

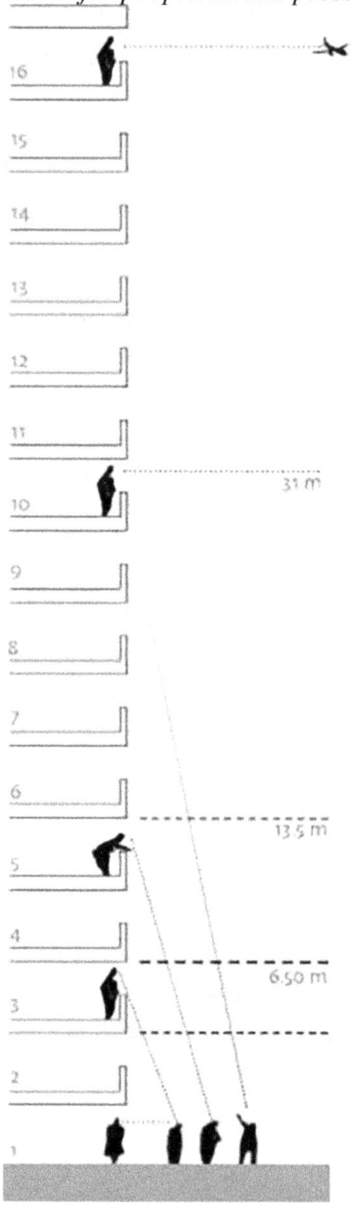

Figure 2. Vestir Bem e Barato Só Aqui, Porto (Authors archive, 2024)

Having a horizontal field of view means that people's attention and concentration will be directed only to the ground floors when moving along the building facades (Figure 2). Ground floors are known to be attractive if they are rich in variety. This greatly increases the likelihood that that street or pedestrian path will be chosen (Jacob, 1995). It is also worth noting that mixed land uses (i.e. the diversity it creates) and the degree of access to these destinations are significantly related to the walkability assessment. It is also worth noting that there is a positive relationship between the number of destinations and the number of walks (Spoon, 2005). Visually pleasing structures or sculptures or even historical architectural structures can increase the use of that area in terms of attractiveness. Therefore, 'Visual attractive structures (heritage and historical buildings, monuments, sculptures)' as a sub-indicator that will contribute to this indicator has been added.

2.3. Public Open Spaces and Recreational Facilities

Pedestrians walk either for a goal or for a stroll. Depending on this purpose, pedestrian behavior may vary. The speed of the springs is one of those quantitative things that varies in particular. While a goal-oriented person walks at a higher speed, people who walk for sightseeing walk slower and experience more of the surroundings. For both of these, open public spaces are important urban elements.

The presence of a public space within the walking route, as a welcoming place or even as an ending point, can make that route more walkable. Open green spaces, natural areas, meeting areas and squares are important for the accessibility of pedestrians and disadvantaged groups, and they must be connected to each other through a good quality pedestrian path or a path (i.e., if it passes through natural areas, this could be called a path) (Ercan & Belge, 2020). Measuring how built environment and land use features contribute to walking is an important factor in walkability, and the purpose of the walk may be for exercise, recreation or access to a service, or it may be to travel to a job. For this reason, the walking route and the presence of public open spaces around it and the existence of recreation areas and even facilities are indicators that affect the walking (Moura et al., 2017) Public open spaces are different from each other and often unique. Reaching these areas and meeting places (i.e. these can be parks) by walking contributes to social life, and this contributes to the creation of livable and walkable areas. It would be useful to give the Barcelona urban mobility plan as an example under this indicator. This mobility plan sees the reproduction of public open spaces within urban congestion as important. In other words, the presence of a public open space or recreation area on or in the immediate vicinity of the walking routes provides the background for the Barcelona super block model, as it is foreseen that it makes walking more attractive and provides comfort. While the super block model was being modified, one of the main issues was to design public open spaces and recreation areas that could be easily accessed by pedestrians and to recreate them in urban areas. For example, redesigning some of the vehicle parking areas within the super blocks or the streets used by the vehicles as completely green areas and pedestrian areas supported this idea (UMP Barcelona, 2013). The strong connection of pedestrian paths and sidewalks to the open public space system allows people to reach more places by walking in their daily lives, and this also contributes to another quality: comfort. While it is important for people not only to walk from one place to another but also to spend time there, it allows for increased social participation and socialization (Gehl, 2010). GIS-based mapping and analysis of land use features has taken its place in the literature in walkability assessment (Lee & Talen, 2014).

This research considers public open spaces and recreation facilities as sub-indicators important in measuring walkability;

I. Availability of natural spaces and parks;
II. Presence of gathering places and squares;
III. Availability of facilities (indoor and outdoor sports facilities, playgrounds).

These were seen as important in terms of the contribution of open space systems to walkability and were mapped, while a more meaningful synthesis was produced with land use analysis.

2.4.Safety

Pedestrians are the most fragile and vulnerable street and road users, so the risk of traffic accidents is one of the most important concerns for these users (Koh & Wong, 2013). Vehicle density, traffic volume and perceived car dominance along the street are the main problems for pedestrians. The emotions that pedestrians feel during their walk affect whether they will choose this route or not and their perception of safety, so the pedestrian should not have a feeling of inferiority. At the same time, the same situation occurs when pedestrians feel that they cannot decide for themselves, that is, they are dependent on traffic, and their use of the street and road gradually decreases (Kelly et al., 2011). Pedestrians prefer to reach or access more places by walking on their daily routes, but beyond that, safety, which is an important issue, can change many things. Pedestrians generally want to avoid crimes and accidents, so they prefer clearly visible and readable routes, and they think that a safer environment is provided here only when they can see the entire street or road. Well-lit streets and paths encourage pedestrians to walk here. In this way, they think that the risk of being a victim of crime is less, which is the exact opposite of walking on a run-down and dark street. One of the most important walkability criteria is safety. Safety is examined in two dimensions;

I. Actual,
II. Perceived.

This study only addressed the actual dimension of the safety factor. For this purpose, the sub-indicators shown in (table 1) were used. The actual safety dimension measures the physical safety of the pedestrian. Designs that increase the safety of pedestrians and disadvantaged groups can be achieved thanks to the physical factors of the urban area, including street widths, street environment designs, and other management measures that can be used in addition to reducing traffic congestion and traffic flow rate, reducing noise and crime (Ercan & Belge 2020; Forsyth, 2015). Separation of pedestrian and vehicle traffic is one of the most striking and one of the methods that reduce the above-mentioned negativities. In addition, reducing vehicle speed is another important element that increases pedestrian safety. In terms of design, measures such as narrow streets, traffic slowing street designs, and safe pedestrian crossings increase actual pedestrian safety. Many more measures can be added to these, but as emphasized by Gehl (2010), the basis of all of them is the concepts of designing cities for pedestrians and the city as a meeting place, and the human scale design approach lies in the background of all of them. Urban areas with high crime rates are often described as unsafe by pedestrians, which is actually one of the main problems of the case study. Located in the southern urban margins, this area has been mentioned many times with its low crime rates. Pedestrians find areas with high traffic congestion and noise unsafe, so they conclude that these areas are not walkable (Evans, 2009; Gehl, 2010). This study identified 9 different sub-indicators for the safety indicator, added them to the measurement model and completed the evaluation method. these;

I. Barriers;
II. Traffic Calming;
III. Disabilities platforms and ramps;
IV. Lightening on the streets;
V. Length of crossline;
VI. Sidewalk condition;
VII. Frequency of street use (GPS marks);
VIII. Land-use (mixed use places) (to more eyes on the street).

It should be noted here that increasing actual safety can also contribute to perceived safety. Jacobs (1961) defined perceived safety and stated its qualities. At this point, it is important for research. As he emphasized, the concept of 'eyes on the street' naturally provides surveillance, so interventions or design approaches such as more common areas and opening buildings to the street make a unique contribution to safety. . For this indicator, the research evaluated the diversity of land use and the intensity of use of the route with GPS-based tracks.

This case study analyses the pedestrian walkability of Via Costantino Baroni, a secondary road in the residential area of Gratosoglio, south of Milan. By examining the case area and the spatial development and change of the regions where this area first established its relationship with the city from past to present, it reveals the change or transformation of the urban periphery, its problems and the potentials in terms of walkability at both the neighborhood and city scale. These potentials will play an important and key role in creating sustainable and livable urban areas for these urban peripheries, which will become even more important in the future when the effects of climate change are taken into consideration.

Secondary and primary data were used in the research. The primary ones include direct field studies, observations and even interviews. When talking about secondary data, it includes information and data obtained from literature research, as well as archive data and datasets. This literature research; book, article, journal article, etc. consists of studies. Within the scope of field studies, comprehensive studies were carried out to determine the situation and spatial conditions and characteristics of the case study. During this process, the conditions and dynamics of the area were examined by intensive research in the field, and thus, direct observation and mapping were made and different tools were used. Spatial analyzes were mapped in order to reveal the factors affecting the walkability level along with the maps. Photographs were taken from the field in order to provide evidence for direct observations made in the study area and to make the field more understandable to the reader. Image elements were examined to describe the different features and spatial character of the area. As Lynch (1964) emphasizes, in order to define the spatial characteristics of the area, the main image elements (landmarks, nodes, borders and traces) must be examined. While the perception of an area, the perception of a part of the city, or the perception of a building or even a bridge may vary from person to person, stating that living in a city is actually living in an image completes the idea behind why the spatial characteristics of the area are important (Lynch, 1964). City image is actually the representation of the city in the human mind, formed by the environmental components of the city and the meanings given to those components by people. This image stored in the person's memory affects the environment in the relationship between humans and the environment.

It has a really critical role in perceiving and recognizing and accordingly in changing, differentiating and shaping physical and psychological behaviors (Eraydın, 2016). In this way, image elements will show the characteristic features of the area. Interviews were conducted to understand the users of the area (i.e. pedestrians) from their perspective. During these interviews, open-ended questions were asked to understand their perception of the area and their perceived sense of safety and comfort in the area. Perception and felt concepts of safety and attractiveness deeply affect the use of public spaces in the city. It is impossible to create living cities and sustainable cities without focusing on these concepts. Being able to safely use streets, parks and squares, which are the basic building blocks of cities and their indivisible parts, is a factor that cannot be ignored in order to create attractive, living cities for people (Belge & Ercan, 2022). The fact that places are lively and attractive allows people to feel a sense of safety in that place, which significantly affects the perceived safety of pedestrians. As Jane Jacbo (1961), lively and busy places contain more people, which means more observation and surveillance. In this way, people feel safer in crowded and lively places. As Gehl (2010) emphasizes, one of the factors that most affects the step taken out of the house, which is the first step of people leaving the house, that is, joining the city on foot, is the liveliness in the street and in the place, which confirms the saying 'people attract people', as is a saying that many societies have.

I. Southern Margin of Milan: Gratosoglio

Milan is located in the Lombardy region, in the north of Italy. It is the second largest commune and metropolitan city in Italy by population. Traditionally considered the Italian capital of the economy (Dalmasso et al., 1972), Milan has experienced many urban transformations since the beginning of the 21st century. Milan, once primarily an industrial city, has evolved into the central hub of a larger metropolitan area with a population exceeding seven million people (OECD, 2006). As Milan's economic and social attractiveness increases and it becomes connected to surrounding regions, it attracts both population and sectors. This causes the city to expand and create a larger urban attraction area (Balducci et al., 2017). Identify three elements of path-dependency shaping regional urbanization processes in and around Milan (De Vidovich & Scolari, 2022). These elements have determined that Milan has historically had a polycentric structure, with connections to surrounding cities thanks to this structure. Additionally, it has been noted that Milan's radial growth model has led to unclear distinctions between urban and suburban areas. (De Vidovich & Scolari, 2022). As in many other European cities, the suburban neighborhoods built between the 1950s and the 1970s in Milan will continue to exist in the future and will redefine this part of the city (Figure 3).

Figure 3. Milan Urban Area and Surround (Prepared by Authors from QGIS, 2024)

Figure 4. The Case Study Area: Gratosoglio (Prepared by Google Earth, 2024)

The Case area, Gratosoglio, is also located in the suburban area known as 'Milano Sud', to the south of Milan (Figure 4). It is situated on via dei Missaglia street, which runs towards the outskirts of the city. Generally, the region contains public housing built in the 20th century, public services such as parks, schools, sports fields, social cooperatives, cultural facilities, and large pedestrian areas. It is also equipped with various public services, such as an Oratory, the House of Associations, two meeting centers for the elderly, a multifunctional center for the disabled, the Baroni primary school (which is included in the Arcadia comprehensive institute), and the Kandinsky Professional Institute of Business Services (Regione Lombardia, n.d.). Transportation from the central area to Gratosoglio is provided by public transportation (metro line / Piazzale Abbiategrasso; tram nr. 3, 15 / Duomo-Rozzano; Duomo/Gratosoglio). The neighborhood was established in the early sixties following the demand to provide large housing for workers who came to work in industries (Regione Lombardia, n.d.). These mass housing units generally consisted of high-rise buildings (9-10 stories), and later, 8 towers with 16 floors, called "Torri Bianche,"(i.e. White tower) were built. (Figure 5 and 6) . The neighborhood generally had a vibrant social structure in the 70s due to community initiatives, the church in the center, and cultural events, but later, after the economic crisis in the mid-70s, the social fabric in the neighborhood weakened. Today, according to the "Piano di Governo del Territorio: Schede dei Nuclei di Identità Locale" document prepared by Comune di Milano in 2023, Gratosoglio, located in NIL 41, has a population of approximately ten thousand according to the 'Census tract' data determined by the Milano municipality (Comune di Milano, 2023). When the land use is examined, public spaces, educational areas, street markets, and social and religious services are concentrated. In the mapping of the area specified in this document prepared for the year 2030, the creation of large pedestrian areas is also envisaged in the Gratosoglio" regeneration and transformation" section (Comune di Milano, 2023).

Figure 5. Construction of 'Torri Bianche and Social Housing (Retrieved from: Link 1, Access date: 2024)

Figure 6. Plan and Model of the Gratosoglio District, BBPR study (Retrieved from: Link 2, Access date: 2024)

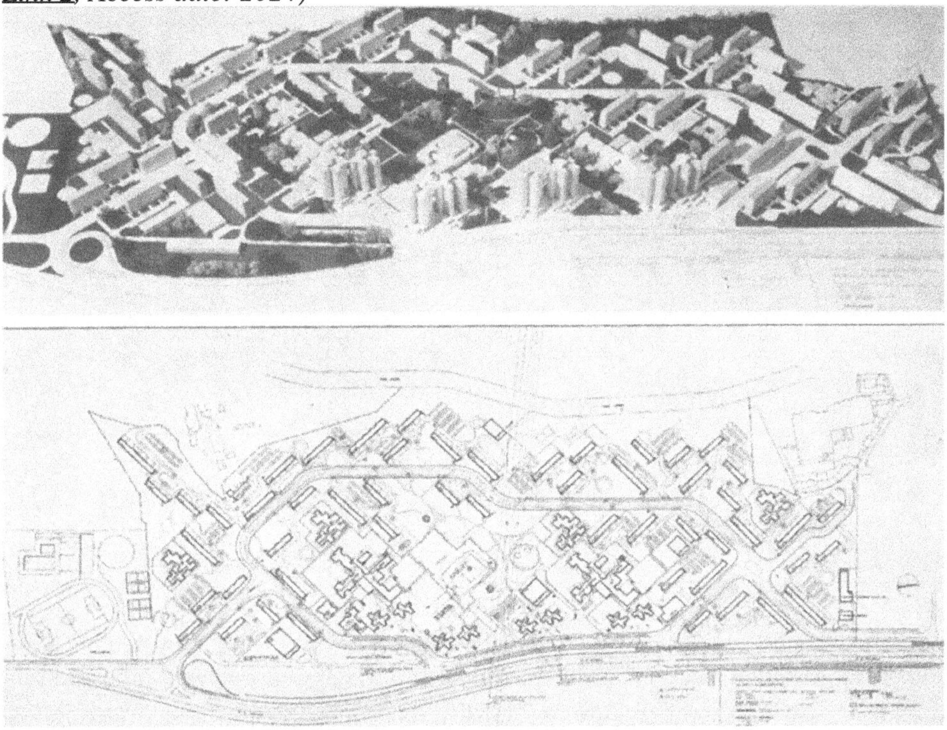

When Gratosoglio is examined socio-demographically, the living population has aged over time, and it is also stated as a "naturally occurring retirement community" (NORC), which indicates a neighborhood where the majority of elderly people concentrate and develop (Marchesi, 2023). For this reason, there are uses in the area that appeal mostly to the elderly population. However, based on observations made by the inhabitants of Gratosoglio in other sources examined, there are also problems such as the aging of the local population, problematic migration, lack of attractiveness of common areas, lack of meeting places, vandalism problems, and the problem of empty housing (Il Sud Milano, 2024). However, the vibrant social fabric of the neighborhood, various associations, communities, and Municipio 5 come together and create important initiatives, interventions, and projects together with the local people to solve these problems. These include a fund known as 'Pnrr and Pinqua' (Innovative Program for the Quality of Living) designated for Gratosoglio, which provides for the redevelopment of open spaces, the reuse of abandoned areas, the provision of lighting and safety, and the development of pedestrian paths (Il Sud Milano, 2024).

Figure 7. Via Costantino Baroni (Authors, 2024)

Via Costantino Baroni, which will be discussed within the study area, is an important road that establishes the main connection with via dei Missaglia and surrounds the use in the area (Figure 7). The different uses mentioned for Gratosoglio's land use, which provide a vibrant social fabric, include housing, open spaces, and public services, which are connected and accessed via this internal road. Therefore, this main connection via Costantino Baroni was chosen in the study area for the walkability study. Considering all the positive and negative features mentioned for Gratosoglio, walkability via Costantino Baroni was evaluated. With this walkability study, the aim is to create more reliable, diverse, attractive, and walkable areas focused on solutions to public problems in the short term. In the long term, it aims to contribute to sustainability in a peri-urban area.

II. RESULTS AND DISCUSSION

2.1. Accessibility

When the accessibility assessment in Via Costantino Baroni is made, considering the sub-indicator of accessibility to public services, access opportunities within walking distance are in good condition. Access to schools is possible with a 5-minute walk along the street. In line with this isochrone analysis, the 5-minute walk axis and 10-minute walk axis of the case study via Costantino Baroni were produced and mapped by including public services and public transportation stops (a).

(a) **(b)**

Figure 8. **Isochrone analysis (a), Quality of sidewalks and pedestrian path analysis (b)** *(***a***); In this image, pedestrian accessibility to public services is visualized and the 5-minute walking distance is mapped with Isochrone analysis. (***b***); The case area was closely examined and a map was prepared showing the pavement width, continuity, quality and condition and visualizing the surrounding uses.*

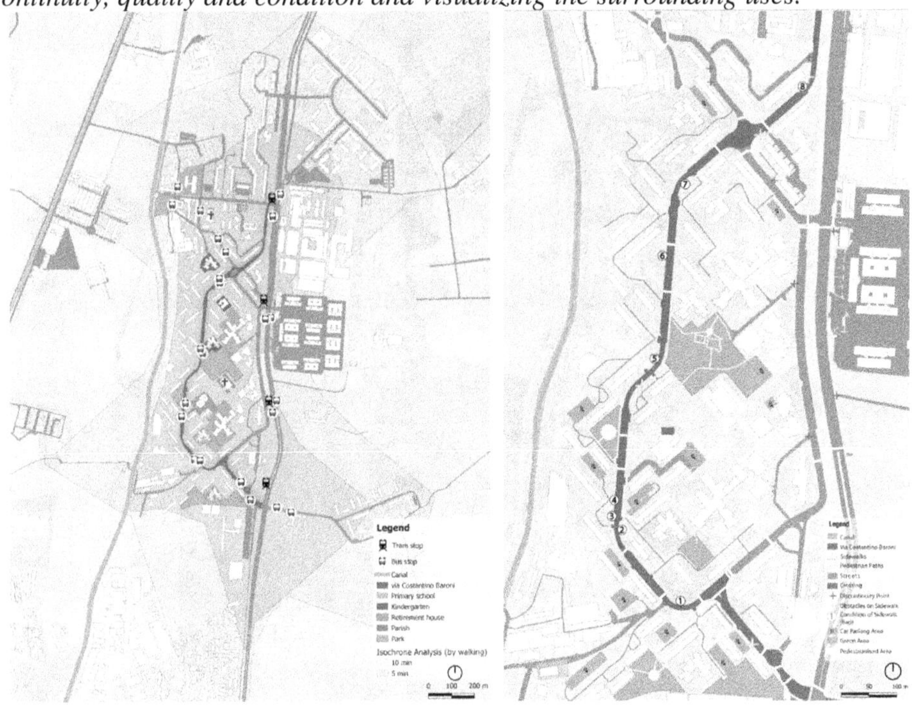

Another result from this map is that the accessibility of the public transportation system in this case study is quite good. Only a tram and bus stop in the south can be seen for pedestrians, at an average distance of 400-500 meters, that is, a 5-minute walking distance. This means that the accessibility of the public transport stops there is not very good. The fact that the bus, one of the public transportation vehicles, has a route on the street, which is the case study, is a very effective situation in terms of 'access to public transportation vehicles', which is one of the accessibility sub-indicators. It has also been observed that the canal in the west of the case study and the main road in the east are thresholds. Having good access to trams, one of the sustainable means of transportation, contributes to the sustainability of the urban perimeter. When viewed from the perspective of sustainable urban perimeters of the future, its design and existence have been evaluated as both a strong aspect and an opportunity. The study obtained these results from isochrone analysis. In another map produced in the evaluation of the accessibility indicator, condition of sidewalks, continuity of sidewalks, existence of pedestrian path, existence of obstacles and discontinuity problems and crossing lines were analyzed and mapped (b).

Figure 9. Authors archive, 2024

Figure 10. Authors archive, 2024

Figure 11. Authors archive, 2024

The analysis revealed that there was parking on pavements in the case area, which impeded the mobility of pedestrians and disadvantaged groups. Another conclusion is that since pavements are not maintained adequately, they create situations that cause breaks at certain curve points and decreases in walking levels. The above-mentioned pavement quality problems and obstacles (Figure 9) cause the walkability level to decrease on this 1.640 km street. The accessibility indicator not only measures access to one or several destinations, but also evaluates the quality of the pavement and situations that may hinder pedestrians. When the continuity of the pavements was examined, no problems were encountered, especially regarding the connection with other streets. Pavement continuity is in good condition in the area and in the streets connecting to the area around it. While no problems were encountered at the pedestrian crossings (Figure 11), it was noticed that the pedestrian crossings were renewed by the municipality, and the existence of the crossings was evaluated as positive in terms of both safety and accessibility. However, it should be noted that the lack of a dedicated bicycle path for cyclists forces them to cycle on sidewalks or in the middle of vehicle traffic (Figure 10). Overall, the accessibility indicator is in good condition, but minor administrative interventions (maintenance and repairs) would enhance pedestrian mobility and planning integrity.

2.2. Attractivennes and Comfort

In the Attractiveness and Comfort indicator, one of the important elements is the land use and its relationship with the street selected for the case study (Via Costantino Baroni), which is important in this study. When the attractiveness indicator is considered specifically, it should be emphasized that the diversity in land use increases the walkability performance and capacity of the area (Krambeck & Shah, 2006; Ercan & Belge, 2020; Moura et al., 2017). The diversity in land use and the relationship of these different uses with the street, which is a pedestrian space, have many effects. The fact that pedestrians spend more time in the area, pedestrians prefer that route and help them spend their walks better and establish a relationship with the area. As a result, as you can see in (a), the diversity in the land use analysis is low. The limited ground level uses and the lack of different uses that will attract pedestrians' attention other than housing and their low numbers do not create a good result in terms of attractiveness in the case study. The presence of open public spaces can contribute in terms of comfort, but the presence of nature landscape areas that are directly accessible from via Costantino Baroni is also limited.

(**a**) (**b**)

Figure 12. Land-use analysis (a), Mapping of, facilities for disabled persons, landscape elements on the sidewalk, amenities, and obstacles (b).

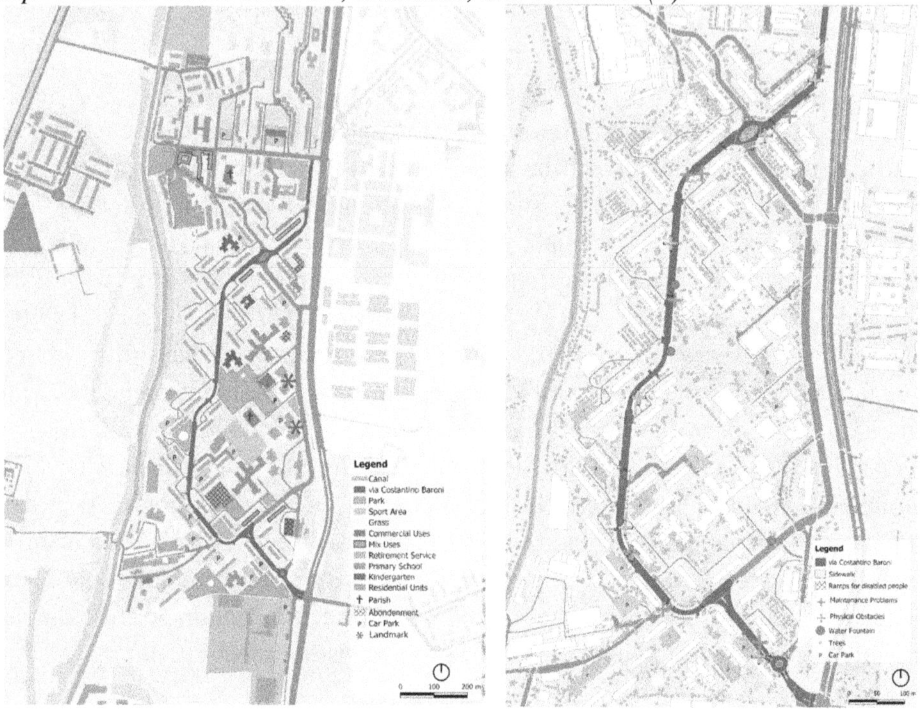

(**a**); This figure includes a map showing land use. The map shows which land uses are present in the case study area and their locations. (**b**); Here, the disabilities found in the field, maintenance and cleaning problems, places with disability ramps along the pavement and other shelters that can provide shade with trees are shown.

The land use assessment revealed that due to the predominantly residential nature of the area, outdoor activities are restricted within or close to the case study area, affecting the potential for sustainable and livable urban environment development. As Gehl (2010) emphasizes, when a person sees that other people are on the street or in public areas, they want to be there comfortably and find a reason to get out of their homes. When considered from this perspective, the deficiencies of the area in terms of attractiveness indicator have a negative effect on walkability. From another point of view, namely comfort, it is an important criterion that pedestrians are adequately protected from the negative effects of the climate (Krambeck & Shah, 2006). From this point of view, the discontinuity of the trees (b) found throughout the case study and their absence at many points do not sufficiently protect pedestrians from the effects of the climate. Only the rows of trees located in the north of the area can be a positive example of this (Figure 15). The fact that the pavement is much wider at some points and that there is no design suitable for this does not sufficiently protect pedestrian spaces from the negative effects of the sun on summer days (Figure 13). There are many problems in the presence of amenities (b), which are one of the sub-indicators of comfort. These are; the lack of sufficient resting points along the street, which is a much more important element especially in this area where the elderly live more. Therefore, they prefer to go to many places by car because they are determined that the street is uncomfortable. There are no benches where they can rest or wait when they stop, but there are in some parks connected to this case study, but this causes pedestrians to stray from the route.

Figure 13. Authors archive, 2024

Figure 14. Authors archive, 2024

Figure 15. Authors archive, 2024

During the observations, people were observed sitting and resting at bus stops even though they were not waiting for public transportation vehicles. Amenities are a sub-indicator that affects walkability in the context of comfort and cannot be ignored (Ercan & Belge, 2020; Lotfi & Koohsari, 2009). As a result, it is necessary to draw attention to another sub-indicator, which is obstacles, maintenance and cleanliness. When the area was examined under this indicator, not many positive points were found, but when examined in terms of these sub-indicators, it was concluded that the situation was not good at all. Cleaning and maintenance problems are evident on the pavements (Figure 14). The sidewalks are covered with rubbish in many places, causing pedestrians to cross and descend from the road, which has negative health consequences. It also has many negative impacts in terms of livability and sustainability. It has been observed that vehicles park on the sidewalk at many points (Figure 13). This creates major problems for the walkability of disadvantaged groups in particular. As observed in the area, the presence of ramps and different facilities for disabled individuals has attracted attention. This is the only sub-indicator that can be evaluated positively under this indicator. In conclusion, when viewed in terms of the attractiveness and cleanliness of the area, there are effects that will seriously reduce the walkability capacity.

2.3. Open Public Spaces and Recreational Facilities

Open public spaces are important urban elements that the presence of these elements within the walking route or even being an inviting place or a starting point can make that route more walkable. Thus, for pedestrians and underprivileged groups to be accessible, open green spaces, natural areas, meeting places, and squares are crucial. These areas also need to be connected to one another by a high-quality pedestrian path or footpath (i.e., if it passes through natural areas, this could be called it a path) (Ercan & Belge, 2020). Walking speed may vary depending on the purpose of the walk, therefore, if the purpose of the walk is exercise or just a stroll, open green areas have more importance in this direction. If the purpose of the walk is to access a service in particular, the walk may become faster, at which point the presence of public open spaces provides easier movement. The presence of recreation and public areas or their facilities (i.e. outdoor or indoor recreation facilities) are indicators that affect walking capacity (Moura et al., 2017).

Figure 16. **Green system and natural elements analysis.** *In this figure, all categories of green areas, natural areas, public gathering areas, those with permeable surfaces and those with hard ground, trees and parks in the case study area are mapped.*

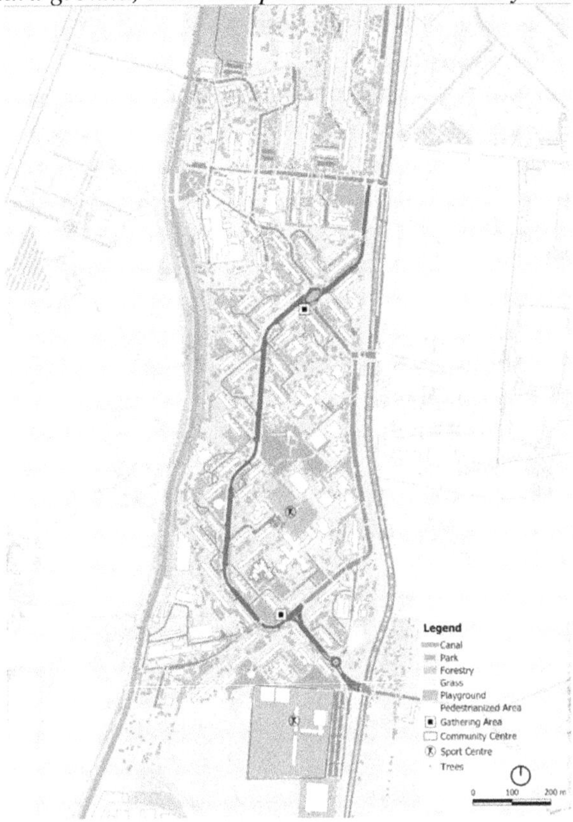

While examining this indicator, public open spaces and recreational facilities/areas were considered as important sub-indicators in measuring walkability. These are;

I. Presence of natural areas and parks;
II. Presence of gathering places and squares;
III. Presence of facilities (indoor and outdoor sports facilities, playgrounds).

Since open space systems are important in terms of their contribution to walkability, they were examined by mapping and evaluated by physical examination on the land, and evaluations were made after a process that would contribute more to the results by producing a more meaningful synthesis with land use analysis. As a result, the presence of natural green areas in the case area and the access to them provided by paths can actually take its place among the positive findings together with the wide-open space usage opportunities provided by being a peri-urban area. Especially the presence of the canal in an accessible location offers opportunities that can contribute to walkability together with these natural green areas, however, there are no opportunities for access to these areas and there is no legible and perceptible design. The inclusion of the canal and its surroundings in this case study area is important in terms of walkability and creating a sustainable area.

Figure 17. Authors archive, 2024

Figure 18. Authors archive, 2024

Figure 19. Authors archive, 2024

There are 4 parks in the case study area, their accessibility and interconnection due to their locations were evaluated positively. However, according to the findings, the lack of sufficient maintenance and repair work and even cleaning work in these areas reduces the level of use of these areas. Accordingly, due to the decrease in the use of these areas, they are in the area as green areas that people do not prefer during their walks. Moreover, pedestrians who want to use these areas or residents who want to do sports prefer the facilities outside the area. In addition, the lack of sufficient uses in these areas (i.e. sports equipment or different recreational uses, etc.) causes people to use their cars or public transportation directly to go to sports facilities, parks and recreation areas outside the area. When the evaluation is made on the basis of gathering places and squares, it is evaluated positively that 1 of them is a community center and there are 2 additional gathering places (Figure 17). In this way, the existence of these areas, which have effects on increasing the level of walkability, draws attention.

To sum up, there are many opportunities, but long-term neglect (Figure 18) and abandonment have reduced the frequency of use of these public open spaces and green areas examined under this indicator. Therefore, these areas that are not preferred decrease the level of walkability, however, the presence of these areas in the case study area (Figure 18) and their sufficient connection (Figure 19) with each other can increase the level of walkability. When considered in terms of the existence or non-existence of these areas, it increases the walkability capacity of the area, excluding recreational facilities and their diversity

2.4. Safety

When considering street and road users in cities, it should be known that the most fragile and defenseless users are pedestrians, therefore attention should be paid to factors such as traffic speed because the risk of traffic accidents is one of the most important concerns for pedestrians (Koh & Wong, 2013). It is very important that pedestrians do not have a sense of inferiority because this determines whether pedestrians will choose to walk that route or not. The presence of mixed land uses is important for 'eyes on the street' and is a key to street safety (Jacobs, 1961).

(**a**) (**b**)

Figure 20. Traffic calming analysis (a), Actual safety analysis path analysis (b)

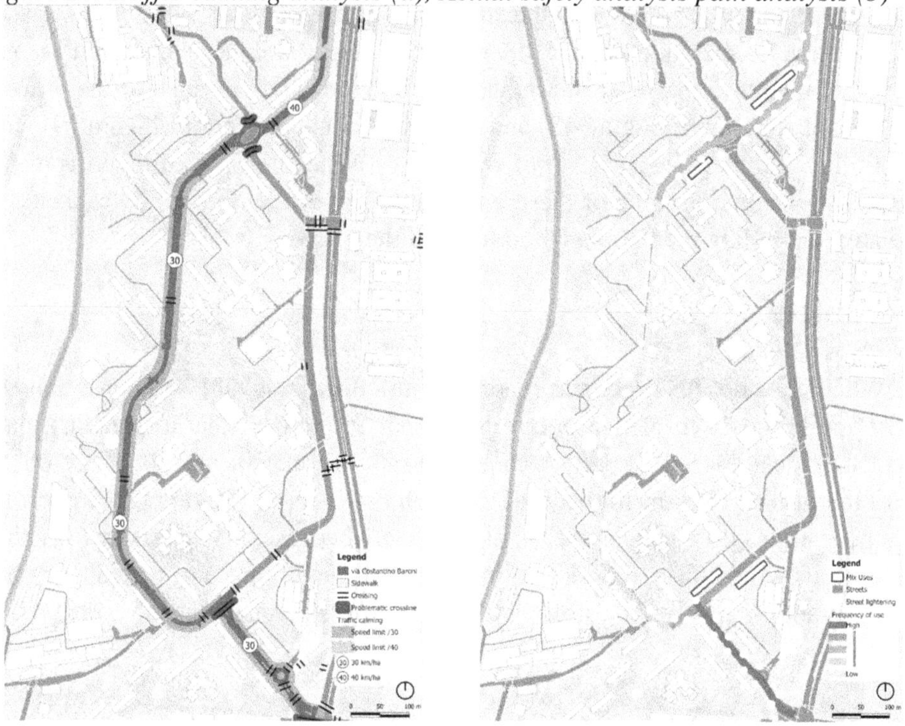

(**a**); In this figure, vehicle speed limits are mapped and pedestrian crossings are mapped. (**b**); In this figure, the locations of street lighting elements, GPS tracks (from Open Street Map) in the area, and mixed uses in land use are mapped

In the case study, the determined vehicle speed limit on the street for pedestrian safety was examined (a) and it was observed whether this was complied with during the field observations. As a result, vehicle speed was limited to 30 km/h in the majority of the case study area. This is a very positive finding in terms of pedestrian safety and accident risk and contributes to the increase in walkability. Limiting vehicle speed is an important element in crossings and the safety of children walking to school and is a useful arrangement.

Figure 21. Authors archive, 2024

Figure 22. Authors archive, 2024

Figure 23. Authors archive, 2024

The fact that the crossing lines in the street design are designed inward, i.e. towards the vehicle lanes, causes vehicles to reduce their speed when approaching the crossing lines (Figure 21). Another remarkable finding is that the crossings, especially in the school surroundings, have been renewed and made more visible (Figure 21). Crossings are important points for pedestrians because pedestrians must feel safe during these crossings, otherwise they may push the pedestrian away from their route and force them to produce another option, which has negative effects on walkability. At this point, 3 crossings were found to be problematic. The reason for this is that the crossings are in one piece and very long. There is no raised floor or barrier designed for pedestrians to wait at the crossing and to control the safety of the road again, so pedestrians are faced with a long crossing. It has been observed that they do not use these crossings most of the time and draw their own shortcuts (Figure 22). It should not be forgotten that the intersection design may also have an effect on this. Nevertheless, it has been concluded that vehicle speed regulation, i.e. traffic calming application, has positive effects on walkability. When evaluating actual safety, it is important for pedestrians that the streets and pedestrian areas are bright and clearly visible. In this context, when the case study area is examined, the lack of sufficient quality street lighting creates a safety problem (Figure 23). Street lighting should be done not only for vehicles but also for pedestrians. It is known that a human-scale design approach can help and contribute to this.

Figure 24. Authors archive, 2024

Figure 25. Authors archive, 2024

The fact that the ground floor uses in the area are very few and designed only at the beginning and end points of the area has prevented the liveliness of the area and different uses that can draw people to the street. This causes fewer people to spend time in the area and not be able to experience it, thus causing fewer people on the street (Figure 25). This is one of the factors that reduce safety as it creates deserted streets. The density of residential uses supports the eyes on the street approach as emphasized by Jacobs (1961). In fact, a perception of safety is created since especially the residences on the first 3 floors can observe the area better, but the fact that the buildings are placed sideways to the street in terms of design also affects the view (Figure 24). When GPS traces were analyzed (b), more traces were seen in areas with mixed uses in the area. This is a result that supports the approach that mixed uses allow people to spend more time on the street or in pedestrian areas. Since the traces were concentrated in only a few small areas of the area, it was concluded that pedestrian activity was not concentrated in the area. This is a finding that was also noticed during field observations (Figure 25). Therefore, GPS traces also support field observations (b). In summary, the actual safety of the area was found to be low according to the findings. Although the studies for safety were positively received technically (vehicle speed limits and designs for crossing at many points), when urban design quality was considered, the actual safety level was evaluated as low according to the sub-indicators examined. This situation also causes the level of walkability to be low, causing people (i.e. pedestrians) not to feel safe on the street.

5. CONCLUSION

In conclusion, this study emphasizes the role and importance of pedestrian mobility in urban planning and design processes in creating sustainable, climate-sensitive and livable spaces in peri-urban areas. While emphasizing this, it presents a model that evaluates the importance of this process in peri-urban areas and addresses it in detail. In this context, it has been determined that key indicators such as accessibility, attractiveness & comfort, open public spaces & recreational facilities and safety play a critical role in the creation of walkable areas. Evaluations made on the peri-urban area model underline that designs that encourage pedestrian mobility contribute to the creation of urban areas that are resilient to climate change and sustainable. In the analyses made on Via Costantino Baroni in the Gratosoglio area, factors such as low land use diversity and inadequacy of public spaces and deficiencies in the cleaning and maintenance of the area, which negatively affect pedestrian mobility, have been determined and it has been determined that pedestrians do not prefer these areas. In this context, the study provides important clues on how peri-urban areas can be transformed through pedestrian mobility and how to create more comfortable and attractive spaces for pedestrians, and points out that more inclusive, climate-sensitive and human-centered approaches should be adopted in urban design and planning processes. As a result, encouraging pedestrian-oriented areas will not only increase the livability of urban areas, but will also contribute to the creation of more resilient and sustainable urban environments against future climate change effects. In this context, the results of the research provide important findings from both theoretical and practical perspectives, providing a new perspective on studies on the creation of pedestrian-oriented urban areas.

REFERENCES

. Arha, A., Audichya, R., & Pant, D. C. (2014). Challenges in the urban and peri-urban transition zones and strategies for sustainable cities: experiences from selected cities. The safety of water, food, energy and liveability of cities: Challenges and opportunities for peri-urban futures, 71-85.

Asadi-Shekari, Z., Moeinaddini, M., & Shah, M. Z. (2013). Non-motorised level ofservice: Addressing challenges in pedestrian and bicycle level of service. *Transport Reviews*, *33*(2), 166–194. DOI: 10.1080/01441647.2013.775613

Aşıcı, G. (2023). Kır-kent çeperinin iklim değişikliği perspektifinden incelenmesi: Denizli örneği (Master's thesis).

Belge, Z. S. (2012). Increasing walkability capacity of historic city centers: The case of Mersin (Master's thesis, Middle East Technical University).

Belge, Z. S., & Akkar Ercan, Z. M. (2017). Daha Yaşanabilir Kentler İçin Mikro Ölçek Bir Yürünebilirlik Modeli.

Belge, Z. S., & Ercan, M. A. (2022). Mobility and the Role of Pedestrian in the Making of Public Space: The Case Study of Mersin. *Transportation Research Procedia*, *60*, 386–393. DOI: 10.1016/j.trpro.2021.12.050

Carmona, M. (2021). *Public places urban spaces: The dimensions of urban design*. Routledge., DOI: 10.4324/9781315158457

Cervero, R., Sarmiento, O. L., Jacoby, E., Gomez, L. F., & Neiman, A. (2009). Influences of built environments on walking and cycling: Lessons from bogotá. *International Journal of Sustainable Transportation*, *3*(4), 203–226. DOI: 10.1080/15568310802178314

Comune di Milano. (2023). *Piano dei Servizi: Schede dei Nuclei di Identità Locale - Dal NIL 1 al NIL 15*. Comune di Milano.

De Vidovich, L., & Scolari, G. (2022). Seeking polycentric post-suburbanization: A view from the urban region of Milan. *Urban Geography*, *43*(1), 123–133. DOI: 10.1080/02723638.2020.1858587

Dupont, V. (Ed.). (2005). *Peri-urban dynamics: population, habitat and environment on the peripheries of large Indian metropolises: a review of concepts and general issues*. New Delhi: Centre de sciences humaines.

Eraydın, Z. (2016). Kentsel Markalaşma Stratejilerinin Kent Belleği ve Kent İmgesi Üzerine Etkileri: Ankara Örneği. İdealkent, 7(20), 830-855.

Ercan, M. A., & Belge, Z. S. (2020). *Measuring Walkability for More Liveable and Sustainable Cities: The Case of Mersin City Centre*. Urbanism and the New Habitat.

Evans, G. (2009). Accessibility, Urban Design and the Whole Journey Environment. *Built Environment, 35*(3), 365–385.

Ewing, R., & Clemente, O. (2013). *Measuring Urban Design: Metrics for Livable Places*. Island Press. DOI: 10.5822/978-1-61091-209-9

Ewing, R., & Handy, S. (2009). Measuring the unmeasurable: Urban design qualities related to

Forsyth, A. (2012). Defining Suburbs. *Journal of Planning Literature, 27*(3), 270–281. DOI: 10.1177/0885412212448101

Forsyth, A. (2015). What is a walkable place? The walkability debate in urban design. *URBAN DESIGN International, 20*(4), 274–292. DOI: 10.1057/udi.2015.22

Forsyth, A., & Krizek, K. (2010). Promoting Walking and Bicycling: Assessing the Evidence to Assist Planners. *Built Environment, 36*(4), 429–446. DOI: 10.2148/benv.36.4.429

Forsyth, A., & Southworth, M. (2008). *Guest Editorial: Cities Afoot—Pedestrians*. Walkability and.

Forsyth, A., & Southworth, M. (2008). Cities afoot—Pedestrians, walkability, and urban design. *Journal of Urban Design, 13*(1), 1–3. DOI: 10.1080/13574800701816896

Geneletti, D., La Rosa, D., Spyra, M., & Cortinovis, C. (2017). A review of approaches and challenges for sustainable planning in urban peripheries. *Landscape and Urban Planning, 165*, 231–243. DOI: 10.1016/j.landurbplan.2017.01.013

. Gündoğdu, H. M., & Dinçer, E. (2020). Tekirdağ Kent Merkezinin" Yürünebilirlik" Açısından Değerlendirilmesinde Bir Yöntem Araştırması. Planlama, 30(3).

Handy, S. (2020). Is accessibility an idea whose time has finally come? *Transportation Research Part D, Transport and Environment, 83*, 102319. DOI: 10.1016/j.trd.2020.102319

Hansen, W. G. (1959). How accessibility shapes land use. *Journal of the American Institute of Planners, 25*(2), 73–76. DOI: 10.1080/01944365908978307

Kelly, C. E., Tight, M. R., Hodgson, F. C., & Page, M. W. (2011). A comparison of three methods for assessing the walkability of the pedestrian environment. *Journal of Transport Geography, 19*(6), 1500–1508. DOI: 10.1016/j.jtrangeo.2010.08.001

Koh, P. P., & Wong, Y. D. (2013). Comparing pedestrians' needs and behaviors indifferent land use environments. *Journal of Transport Geography*, *26*, 43–50. DOI: 10.1016/j.jtrangeo.2012.08.012

Krambeck, H., & Shah, J. J. (2006). The global walkability index. Cambridge, USA: Massachusetts Institute of Technology (MIT).

Lambert, M. R., Brans, K. I., Des Roches, S., Donihue, C. M., & Diamond, S. E. (2021). Adaptive evolution in cities: Progress and misconceptions. *Trends in Ecology & Evolution*, *36*(3), 239–257. DOI: 10.1016/j.tree.2020.11.002 PMID: 33342595

Lee, S., & Talen, E. (2014). Measuring walkability: A note on auditing methods. *Journal of Urban Design*, *19*(3), 368–388. DOI: 10.1080/13574809.2014.890040

Lotfi, S., & Koohsari, M. J. (2009). Analyzing accessibility dimension of urban quality of life: Where urban designers face duality between subjective and objective reading of place. *Social Indicators Research*, *94*(3), 417–435. DOI: 10.1007/s11205-009-9438-5 PMID: 20390026

Malano, H., Maheshwari, B., Singh, V. P., Purohit, R., & Amerasinghe, P. (2014). Challenges and opportunities for peri-urban futures. The Safety of Water, Food, Energy and Livability of Cities: Challenges and Opportunities for Peri-Urban Futures, 3-10.

. Marchesi, I. (2023). Quartieri che invecchiano: Spazi, servizi e relazioni. Gratosoglio, Milano (tesi di Master). Politecnico di Milano, Scuola di Architettura Urbanistica e Ingegneria delle Costruzioni.

Miles, L. S., Carlen, E. J., Winchell, K. M., & Johnson, M. T. (2021). Urban evolution comes into its own: Emerging themes and future directions of a burgeoning field. *Evolutionary Applications*, *14*(1), 3–11. DOI: 10.1111/eva.13165 PMID: 33519952

Moura, F., Cambra, P., & Gonçalves, A. B. (2017). Measuring walkability for distinct pedestrian groups with a participatory assessment method: A case study in Lisbon. *Landscape and Urban Planning*, *157*, 282–296. DOI: 10.1016/j.landurbplan.2016.07.002

Rahaman, K. R., Lourenço, J. M., & Viegas, J. M. (2012). Perceptions of pedestrians and shopkeepers in European medium-sized cities: Study of Guimarães, Portugal. *Journal of Urban Planning and Development*, *138*(1), 26–34. DOI: 10.1061/(ASCE)UP.1943-5444.0000094

Schmeidler, K. (2010). Walking as a sustainable transport mode in cities.

Speck, J. (2013). *Walkable city: How downtown can save America, one step at a time*. Macmillan.

Spoon, S. (2005). What Defines Walkability: Walking Behavior Correlates. DOI: 10.17615/ddw2-sr16

Wibowo, S. S., Tanan, N., & Tinumbia, N. (2015). Walkability measures for city area in Indonesia (case study of Bandung). *Journal of the Eastern Asia Society for Transportation Studies*, *11*, 1507–1521.

Zhang, Q., Yung, E. H. K., & Chan, E. H. W. (2018). Towards Sustainable Neighborhoods: Challenges and Opportunities for Neighborhood Planning in Transitional Urban China. *Sustainability (Basel)*, *10*(2), 406. DOI: 10.3390/su10020406

ADDITIONAL READING

Gehl, J. (1987). Life between buildings.

Gehl, J. (2010). *Cities for people*. Island press.

Gros, F. (2008). *A philosophy of walking*. Verso Books.

Il Sud Milano. (2024, February 14). Gratosoglio merita di più: smentiamo la triste idea che si può vivere male o solo peggiorare. https://www.ilsudmilano.it/2024/02/14/gratosoglio-merita-di-piu-smentiamo-la-triste-idea-che-si-puo-vivere-male-o-solo-peggiorare/

Jacobs, A. B. (1995). *Great Streets*. MIT Press.

. Jacobs, J. (1961). The death and life of great American cities.

Lynch, K. (1964). *The image of the city*. MIT press.

Chapter 8
Development of a Methodology to Identify Urban Ecosystem Services by Applying Tools for Intervening and Planning Lake Landscapes:
The San José de Uzuña Dam of the Arequipa Region

Jazmin R. Uracahua-Irco
Universidad Nacional de San Agustin, Peru

Johrdy V. Quispe-Choquehuanca
Universidad Nacional de San Agustin, Peru

Cinthya L. Butron-Revilla
https://orcid.org/0000-0002-5485-9772
Universidad Nacional de San Agustin, Peru

Edith G. Manchego-Huaquipaco
Universidad Nacional de San Agustin, Peru

ABSTRACT

Interpreting the benefits derived from urban ecosystem services is crucial for managing lake landscapes, enabling the simultaneous achievement of multiple objectives in

DOI: 10.4018/979-8-3693-6089-7.ch008

urban landscape conservation. This study focuses on the assessment of the capacity of the ecological infrastructure of the San José de Uzuña dam in Arequipa, Peru. This assessment uses the zoning criteria proposed by the ECOTERR environmental tool, complemented by semi-structured interviews with users of the dam. The methodological-logical framework developed constitutes a valuable resource in the urban discourse on eco-system services and the management of urban landscapes. Consequently, this research provides significant data that can be used for specific interventions to improve ecosystem services in similar contexts.

INTRODUCTION

The significance of recognizing the benefits derived from urban ecosystem services (UES) in a city is essential for the effective management of lakescapes, enabling the simultaneous achievement of multiple urban landscape conservation goals. Water resources have garnered researcher's attention due to their relevance in the analysis and conservation of lakescapes. The study of urban lake ecosystems (Fisher et al., 2001), as well as rivers and watersheds (Water & Corporation, 1980), has experienced significant progress when approached from a landscape perspective. This perspective demonstrates that rivers are natural forces that actively shape our geography.

On the other hand, the domestication and channeling of water into large irrigation and hydroelectric production systems involve a profound territorial transformation, which must be considered and analyzed through the lens of landscape architecture (Paisajeo.org, n.d.). Consequently, the relationship between hydraulic engineering and the natural territory leads us to question the relevance of urban and architectural design in the implementation of water systems. Therefore, it is essential to consider that large-scale hydraulic systems, such as dams, are true geographic modelers with the capacity to transform the landscape (Sherry & Soranno, 2006). Thus, these should not be conceived solely as pieces of infrastructure, but also as an integral part of the ecosystem and its habitability.

In this context, various research studies (Wen et al., 2014a; Haeger, 2010, Castillo Haeger, C. A. 2010) recognize the relevance of studying lakescapes to contribute to landscape conservation. The lakescape is a social space that develops within a delimited ecosystem, a unique, fragile, and transcendent territory. Furthermore, it integrates a unique, dynamic, and temporal totality: lake, shore, and watershed; water, land, and air; different uses and human activities; a natural and cultural landscape with a specific social dimension and an administrative reality that should be reflected in a new vision of planning (Haeger, 2010). In other words, a comprehensive and contextual planning of the lakescape within the territory.

One of the most studied topics regarding the waterscape is related to climate change. In this context, the waterscape (lakes, rivers, etc.) is altered by the pollution that is currently occurring. This landscape, often untouched yet vulnerable, needs a new vision of this resource, as changes are accelerated and its availability is vital for life. According to the IPCC (Intergovernmental Panel on Climate Change, 2001), it is very likely that many parts of the world will experience changes in the amount, frequency, and distribution of rainfall. This will lead to changes in water availability that will imply greater competition for water resources, even more so in the hydrological cycle. Water scarcity, changes in precipitation intensity, rising air temperatures, and changes in precipitation have increased competition for freshwater, in some cases generating a greater flow of pollutants and sediments into lakes and rivers, whose contamination harms species.

Situated in a general context, it is important to consider that to analyze the landscape at a territorial level, it is essential to understand its dimensions, which are: (i) Anthropological: Refers to the social construction of the lakescape. This dimension relates elements such as culture and history, recognizes a particular social imprint with acquired rights and a unique way of occupying a specific urban-rural territory. (ii) Economic: The economic polyfunctionality of a lakescape can be appreciated in its agricultural, forestry, or hydrological function, production, and the development of tertiary activities such as leisure and sports. The communities surrounding a lake depend on it for supply, food, and other livelihoods. (iii) Governance: This dimension intervenes in different development and management plans and instruments. The organization has developed by intervening in land planning, with existing protection tools for parks or reserves. The governance of a lakescape is constituted through the participation of institutions and government with agreements and accords, instruments, and laws. (iv) Ecological: The ecological dimension, considered one of the most important for the study of the lakescape, is developed through a biophysical matrix of the territory. These dimensions are also considered in analyses of waterscapes, whether in a particular or general way.

While the waterscape has been frequently analyzed from a perspective related to the increase in climate change, this makes urgent the need for new management and a new vision of these water resources, where not only regulations are generated but also projects that contribute to environmental education and promote the care of these resources (Hernández Aja, 2009). It is expected that excess nutrients will become an increasing threat to rivers, coastal areas, and coral reefs (Izquierdo et al., 2005). However, by establishing environmental awareness in society and raising awareness of these water resources and their disappearance, a better future and resource conservation for new generations is envisioned.

The new functionality of rural areas (domestic tourism, revitalization of crafts and local agricultural products) can contribute to harmonizing agricultural interests and environmental protection, as the conservation of these landscapes is an indispensable condition for preserving the attractiveness of rural areas. However, the regulations that value and protect landscape preservation are deficient, especially those that only satisfy the desires of populations to enjoy a quality landscape (Hernández Aja, 2009). For this, it is necessary to adopt activities aimed at fostering society's awareness of the landscape, teaching, and training specialists in this field.

Currently, state policies are striving to achieve territorial planning that is integrated and articulated on an information base. Within this, the 2014 National Agreement aims to establish opportunities for the use of natural resources, including tourism. It is understood then that the lakescape, located in a fragile and important ecosystem, must be taken into account in territorial planning. Zubelzu Mínguez and Allende Álvarez (2014) characterize the landscape and consider the following principles: (i) management must start from the premise that all territory is landscape and requires management. (ii) the need should not be equated with the mere protection of landscapes a priori. (iii) The potentially receptive population must be an active part of landscape management, granting the value that each type of landscape possesses.

Among the objectives of the European Landscape Convention, prepared by the Council of Europe (Florence, 20-10-2000), is the protection, management, and planning of landscapes. Protection aims to "maintain the significant or characteristic aspects of a landscape"; management aims to "guide and harmonize induced transformations"; and planning aims to "actions of a nature to improve, restore or create landscapes" (Izquierdo et al., 2005). They also mention the cultural benefit attributed to them as recreational spaces (opportunities for tourism) and educational spaces (formal and non-formal education and training).

In this context, a dam is considered an interpretative environmental resource and an urban ecosystem service. Considering that tourist activity in dams occurs due to the new ecosystem created, such as fauna and flora, which are the components that exert the greatest attraction on visitors, the activities carried out should not be merely recreational but should also achieve environmental awareness in users. This is achieved through good planning and coordination between the community and the authority.

Furthermore, it is important to note that large hydraulic irrigation infrastructures are based on productive agricultural activities and the need for sustainable rural development. However, many of them lack an environmental and social study before and after the construction of the hydraulic infrastructure. Affecting the waterscape (lakes, rivers, etc.), this pollution harms the species inhabiting it and its surroundings. With climate change being a factor that is increasing the vulnerability of water resources and thereby the landscape, the need for projects that contribute to environmental education and promote the care of these resources is evident. (See Figure 1).

Figure 1. Relationships between Hydraulic Infrastructure and the Lakescape

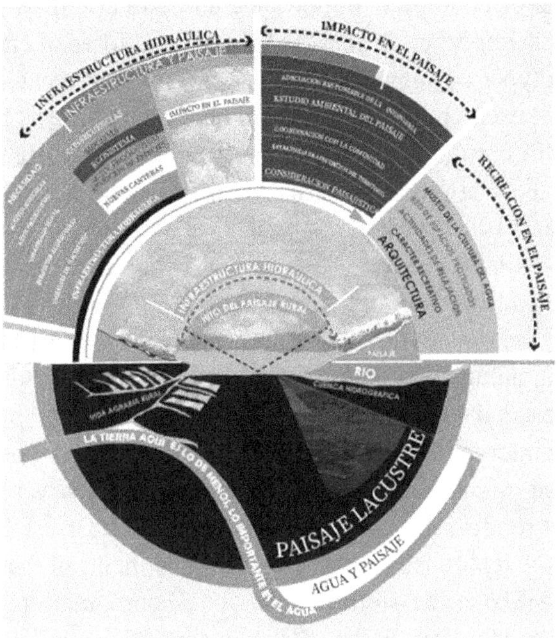

Therefore, it is essential to consider the importance of managing urban ecosystem services and applying environmental tools. The relationship between ecosystems and ecosystem-society and human well-being, through the use of the concept of urban ecosystem services, has been addressed with greater emphasis in recent years, both in the scientific field and in the context of public environmental management and decision-making (Arguedas Marín, M. P. 2022). However, at the level of policies and environmental management instruments, the link between research and the application of knowledge is still a pending issue, especially in developing countries (Rangel Montavo, L. E. 2015, Ascue Cuba, J. C. 2018). Thus, within the framework of theoretical conceptualization from the interpretation of landscape in the territory, the impacts of waterscape conservation on climate change, and finally, understanding the management of urban ecosystem services and the application of environmental tools, the present study concretely applies the ECOTERR tool in the analysis of the territory. The analysis of the territory is based on information about the current use, habitats, flora, and fauna of the territory. After identifying this information, each component is evaluated to generate the territorial sensitivity and ecological risk assessment as a result.

The sensitivity assessment requires an analysis of the properties, characteristics, and functions of each of the environmental components, which is carried out through the results of ecological importance and vulnerability. In the ecological risk assessment, it is important to analyze the potential force of effects, such as use, activities, or other types of intervention that can be observed currently in the study area and that affect each component, determining the degree as high, medium, or low. After having the cartography of the potential intensity of effects, it is combined and analyzed together with the sensitivity map, which will result in the ecological risk. The ecological risk, for each component, is a double-entry matrix: between sensitivity and potential intensity of effects that is qualified in three levels and at the discretion of the researcher.

Finally, having the sensitivity and ecological risk assessment for each environmental component, an analysis and synthesis of all the sensitivity and ecological risk maps will be carried out, to thus obtain which zones are the most sensitive or of greatest risk in the intervention area and be able to take action. The results show the zoning of the green infrastructure, through maps of sensitive areas and ecological risk areas, which is reinforced with interviews with 24 dam users. The second block of results showed the relationships between the components of the lakescape and its capacity to provide urban ecosystem services (UES) of regulation and maintenance. The results show key learnings in the advancement of this methodological research framework that could be useful for adopting specific interventions related to UES. In this sense, the main objective of this research is based on evaluating the capacity of the green infrastructure (GI) of the San José de Uzuña dam in Arequipa, Peru, applying zoning criteria proposed by the ECOTERR environmental tool, complemented by the contextual understanding obtained from interviews.

METHODOLOGY

Lakescapes represent unique urban environments that combine natural and built elements, providing a series of fundamental ecosystem services for human well-being and environmental sustainability. At the intersection of these landscapes, the urgent need arises to develop effective methodologies to identify and assess the services that urban ecosystems provide. This research focuses on the creation of an innovative methodology designed specifically for this purpose, with a particular focus on urban lakescapes.

Case Study

The Arequipa region, located in the central western part of South America and in the southwestern part of Peru, is distinguished by being one of the most arid deserts on the planet. Despite this aridity, rainfall in the high areas of the region, which flows through the rivers and gives rise to fertile valleys, enables the development of agricultural and livestock activities, fundamental pillars of the local economy. The region is made up of eight provinces, among which the province of Arequipa stands out for concentrating 16.5% of the regional territory and housing 75.16% of the total population. The city of Arequipa, with a population exceeding one million inhabitants, functions as the central development core of the southern macro-region, exhibiting a high population density as a result of its socioeconomic dynamism and a monocentric urban structure.

The Arequipa region is characterized by its rich biological diversity, housing 19 life zones of great ecological relevance. Regarding the conservation of its natural heritage, the region has 15 areas under state protection: 4 managed by the National Service of Natural Areas Protected by the State (SERNANP), 3 private conservation areas, and 8 areas considered a priority by the regional government. However, it is important to note that the intervention area of this study, located in the Chili River basin, is not included within these protected zones. According to the ecological zoning of Arequipa, this basin is defined by the presence of a desert zone of thorny scrub, where the San José de Uzuña dam is located in the Polobaya district, the specific place where this research is developed. *(See Illustration 1)*

The Polobaya district is one of the twenty-nine that make up the Province of Arequipa. It spans 441.61 km2 and has a population of 797. This district is outside the management of the Metropolitan Development Plan of the city of Arequipa. Therefore, part of the territorial analysis of the Polobaya district is carried out through the Territorial Conditioning Plan of Arequipa (PAT), a planning instrument that integrates various aspects of the territory, including agricultural areas, communication routes, flora, fauna, water resources, mining activity, the geographical environment surrounding the study area, and the different surrounding towns. This plan establishes guidelines and objectives that must be considered when formulating intervention proposals in the territory, such as specific zoning, road systems, river courses, and areas intended for the protection of flora and fauna.

Specifically, the study area of this research is delimited within the Polobaya district, a rural community belonging to the province of Arequipa. This area, characterized by its natural environment and agricultural activities, is directly impacted by the presence of the San José de Uzuña dam. The study area, which encompasses the entire contour of the dam, covers an approximate area of 405.71 hectares. Therefore, the detailed analysis of this area is essential to understand the current situation of the environment, as it will provide crucial information to establish the criteria and premises that can guide the intervention proposals.

Figure 2. Geographic Location of the Case Study

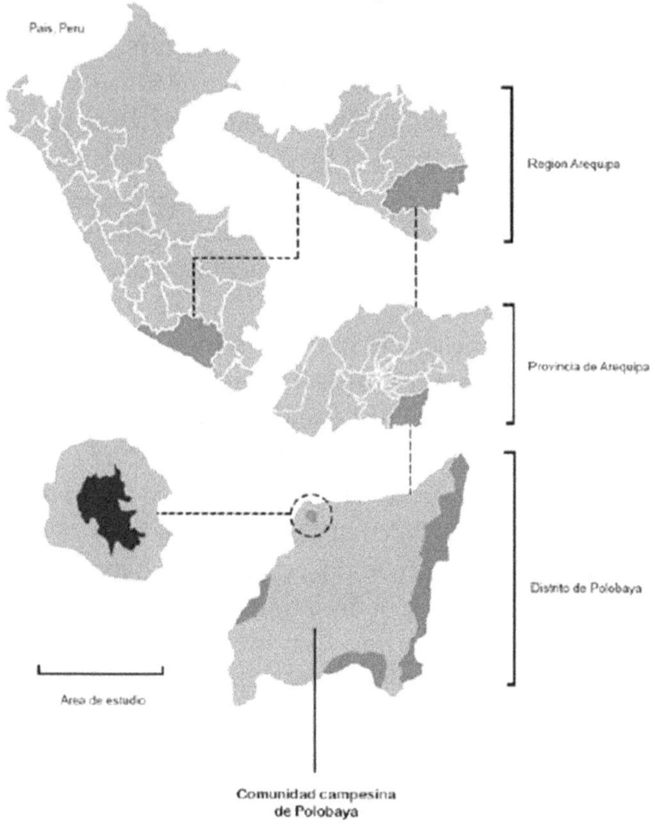

Materials and Resources Used

To create the ECOTERR cartography, various sources of information and methods of mapping the territory were employed. The base source was the Territorial Conditioning Plan of Arequipa (PAT), whose information in shapefile format was provided by the Arequipa Planning Institute (IMPLA). This data was integrated into a Geographic Information System (GIS), generating macro-scale maps that covered the entire reservoir. Subsequently, field visits were carried out, using observation sheets and the place-mapping methodology to map the dam landscape at an intermediate scale. These visits, of a perimeter nature, focused on the components indicated by ECOTERR: soil, water, vegetation, and fauna. The collected information was recorded in field observation sheets, where the areas of interest were drawn and complemented with photographs.

The information obtained from the PAT and the knowledge acquired in the field were used to generate ECOTERR maps, which served as the basis for conducting the sensitivity assessment and the ecological risk assessment of the study area. Additionally, a social component was incorporated through interviews conducted in the field with a sample of 24 individuals. For this assessment, a semi-structured questionnaire was used and completed on-site..

Data Collection

Macro-Scale Data Collection

The macro-scale territorial analysis was based on data from the Territorial Conditioning Plan (PAT), through the mapping of four established zoning elements, road systems, river courses, and protected flora and fauna areas. Therefore, an analysis of said content is carried out, from the understanding of its direct or indirect relationships to the study area, in order to know its current state. *See Figure 3*

Figure 3. Mapping for Territorial Assessment at Macro Scale of the Lakescape from Four Elements

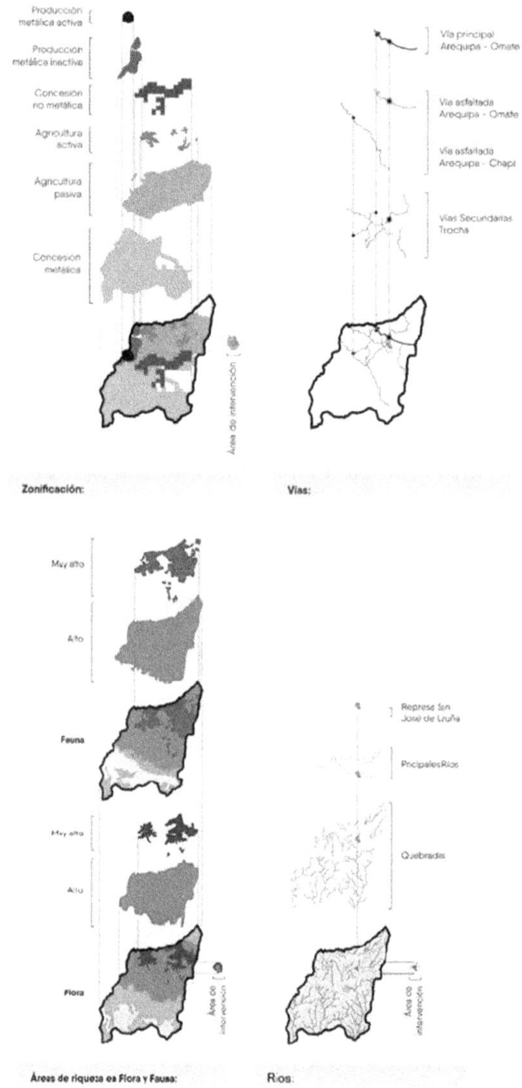

Intermediate-Scale and Transect Data Collection

The territorial analysis at the intermediate scale is carried out through field data collection, utilizing observation sheets and the place-mapping methodology to map at an intermediate scale, considering a specific number of transects for each indicator analyzed. This data collection, of a perimeter nature, focused on the components indicated by ECOTERR: soil, water, flora, and fauna. In the case of the soil component, elements related to relief (altitude, altitudinal floors, slope type, slope percentage) and geomorphology (geomorphology and physiography) were mapped. *See Figure 4.* On the other hand, for the water component, the main rivers, water availability, sub-basins, hydrogeology, flood hazards, and water importance were mapped. *See Figure 5*

Figure 4. Mapping for Territorial Assessment at Intermediate Scale of the Soil Component

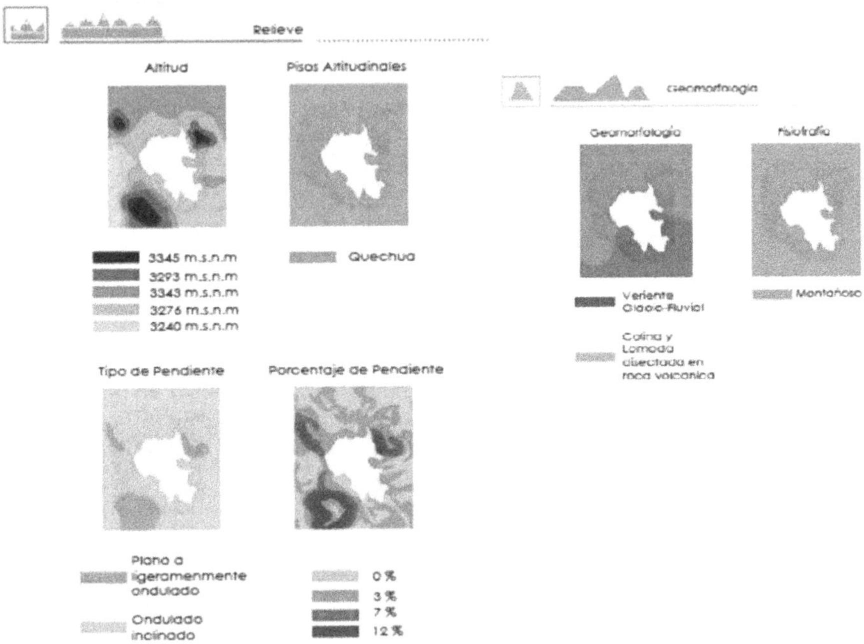

Figure 5. Mapping for Territorial Assessment at Intermediate Scale of the Water Component

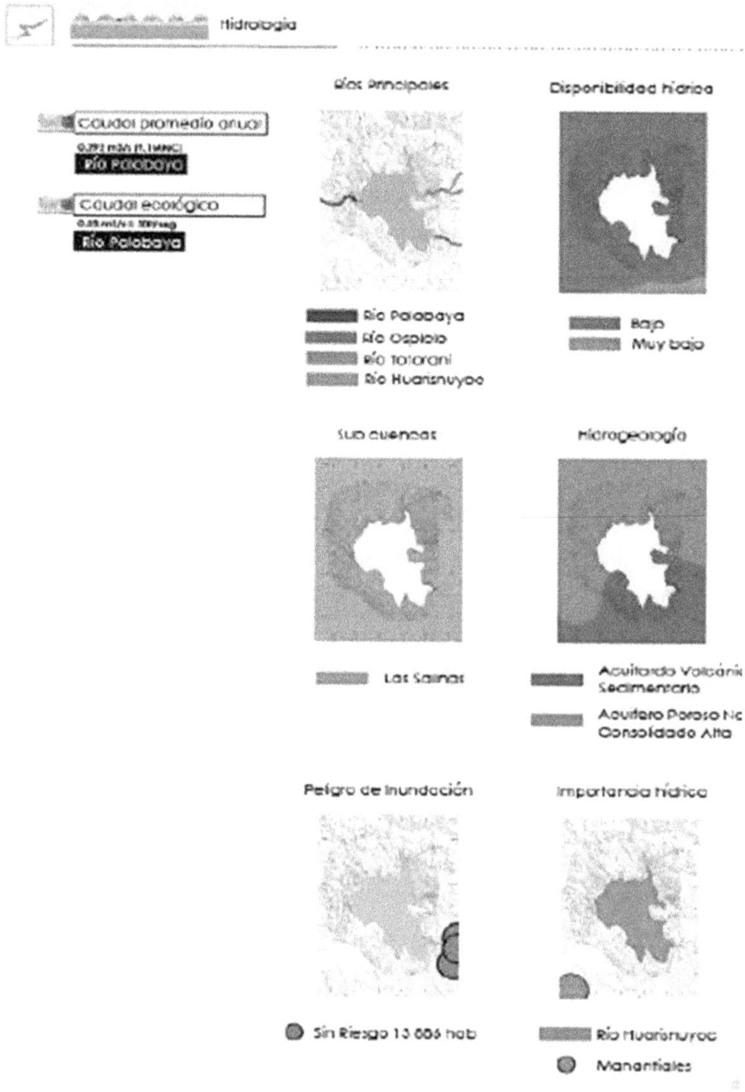

Of the other two components, the one related to vegetation (flora) is mapped. It is mapped from six transects that allowed the identification of five subcomponents: richness of flora, endemic species, agricultural potential, threatened species, and biotechnological value. See Figure 6. Following this, the fauna component is analyzed, in which five subcomponents are also assessed: richness of fauna, threatened fauna, bird fauna, mammal fauna, and amphibian diversity. See Figure 7.

To carry out the flora and fauna assessment, a comprehensive analysis of the species present in the study area was conducted, culminating in the creation of a detailed natural inventory. In order to obtain a more accurate understanding of the distribution and abundance of species, a methodological approach was implemented that combined macro-level data analysis with micro-scale observations.

At the macro level, maps derived from the Territorial Conditioning Plan of the city of Arequipa, specifically adapted to the study area of the San José de Uzuña dam, were used. These maps provided an overview of the distribution of flora and fauna in the territory, including information on threatened and endemic species, classified according to their level of ecological importance.

To complement this information and obtain a greater level of detail, intermediate-scale mapping was carried out in specific sectors of the study area, using transects to record the presence of flora and fauna species. These transects allowed for the identification and documentation of the species found in different microhabitats, such as riparian zones, scrub areas, and cultivation zones. Additionally, photographs were taken of the observed species to facilitate their subsequent identification and analysis.

The result of this meticulous fieldwork was the development of a natural inventory that includes a detailed list of the flora and fauna species present in the study area, as well as information on their relative abundance and spatial distribution. This inventory constitutes a fundamental tool for the assessment of green infrastructure and the sustainable management of natural resources in the area, as it allows for the identification of areas of greatest ecological value and the species that require special attention for their conservation.

The results obtained through this intermediate-scale mapping and the analysis of the transects complement the information provided by the macro-level maps, allowing for a more complete understanding of the biological diversity present in the study area. This detailed information is essential for the assessment of green infrastructure and the formulation of management strategies that promote biodiversity conservation and the sustainable use of natural resources in the San José de Uzuña dam area.

The maps presented below have been elaborated based on the interpretation of the Territorial Conditioning Plan of the city of Arequipa, with a specific focus on the study area of the San José de Uzuña dam. These maps constitute a fundamental visual tool for understanding the spatial distribution of the different landscape components and their relationship with the dam's green infrastructure.

The precise delimitation of the study area, represented in the maps, allows for visualizing the extent and limits of the zone that will be subject to analysis and assessment. This delimitation is essential to guarantee the accuracy and relevance of the data collected during fieldwork and subsequent analysis. The maps presented include information on the location of the transects used for intermediate-scale mapping, as well as the distribution of the main landscape features, such as vegetation, water bodies, and areas of human use. This cartographic information will serve as the basis for the analysis of territorial sensitivity and ecological risk, as well as for the identification of priority areas for the conservation and sustainable management of natural resources in the study area.

Figure 6. Mapping for Territorial Assessment at Intermediate Scale of the Flora Component

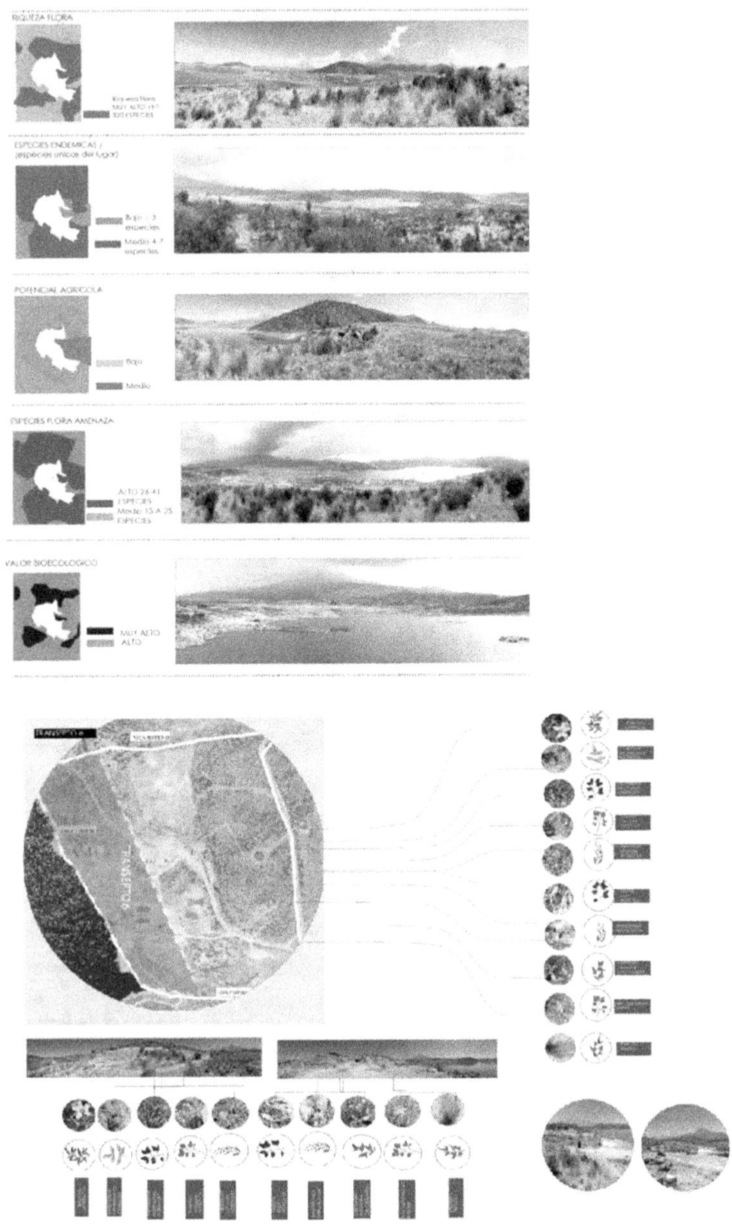

Figure 7. Mapping for Territorial Assessment at Intermediate Scale of the Fauna Component

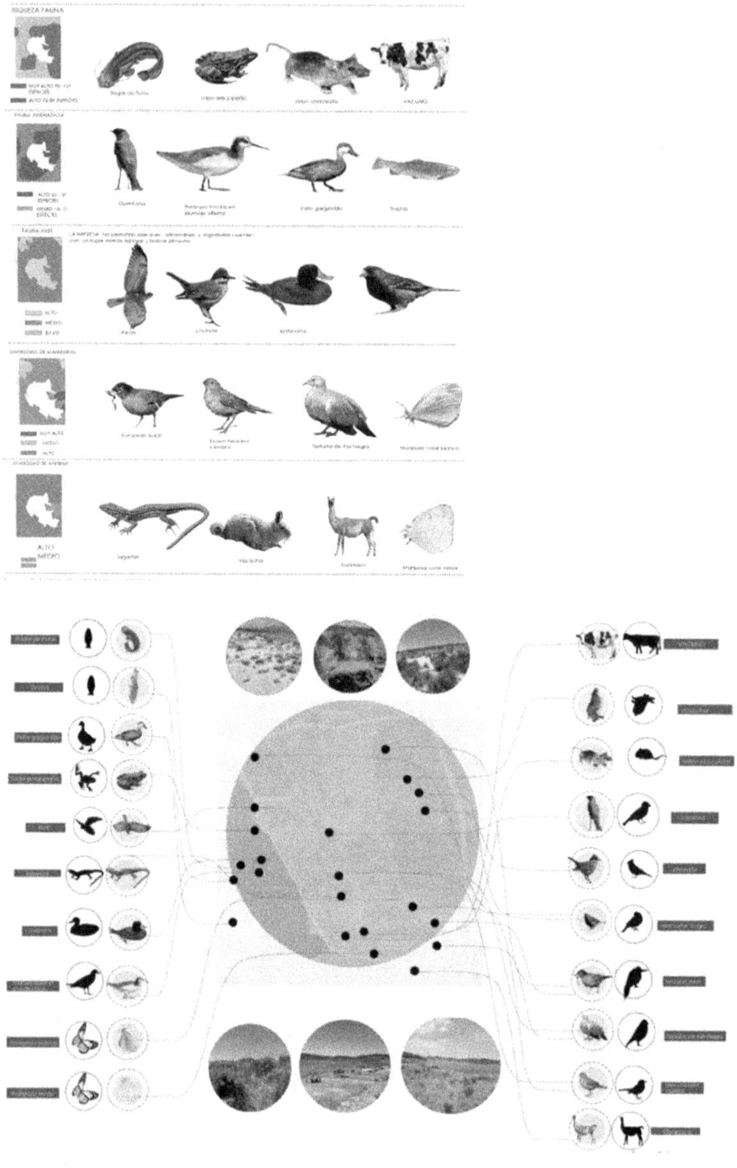

After completing the data collection for mapping the assessment at macro and intermediate scales, the ECOTERR environmental tool is applied again in the study area to generate the Synthesis Map of Sensitivity and Ecological Risk of the intervention area.

For the evaluation of the synthesis map of sensitivity, an analysis of the properties, characteristics, and functions of each of the environmental components is required. This analysis is carried out through graphic overlay, taking into consideration the ecological importance and vulnerability of each component. For the ecological risk assessment, it is important to analyze the potential of effects, such as human use and activities, that affect each environmental component. The degree of intensity of these effects was determined as high, medium, and low. Then, the potential intensity of effects was combined and analyzed with the sensitivity map, resulting in the Ecological Risk map. Finally, having both maps, the Zoned Environmental Objectives (OAZ) could be graphically determined.

Social Component Data Collection

This third type of collection is carried out through semi-structured interviews. The methodology for the interviews consisted, firstly, in the elaboration of a questionnaire with questions based on environmental awareness, recreation, and tourism topics. Questions such as "Why is the dam important?", "What aspects do you consider negative about the dam?", and "What should be improved?" were asked in order to assess the importance of the San José de Uzuña dam for the visiting population. Interviewees were selected based on visitors types observed during fieldwork at the dam, from external visitors and students to community members and producers of Polobaya.

The interviews yielded percentages that highlighted the importance of the dam and, in turn, the visitors' concern about the pollution that is generated and could be generated in the future at the dam, indicating that environmental awareness is important. Additionally, conversations were held with community members, who indicated that the dam has currently been a source of income within their administrative system, allowing for job creation through the rotation of those in charge, as well as the placement of commercial stalls where natural products such as yogurt, cheese, and fruit from the community's own producers are sold.

RESULTS

Environmental Understanding Applying the ECOTERR Environmental Tool

To apply the ECOTERR methodology, information was collected on the current land use, present habitats, flora, and fauna at both macro and intermediate scales. Subsequently, each environmental component (air and climate, surface water, soil, scenic landscape, vegetation, and fauna) was assessed to generate the sensitivity and ecological risk of the project intervention area as a result. The combination of both maps allowed for obtaining the synthesis map of zoned environmental objectives (OAZ).

Sensitivity Assessment

The sensitivity assessment requires a comprehensive analysis of the properties, characteristics, and functions of each environmental component. These are: (i) Ecological importance: The relevance and ecological function of each component in the intervention area were assessed, taking into account its contribution to biodiversity, water regulation, air quality, and other ecosystem services. (ii) Vulnerability: The degree of fragility or susceptibility of each component to natural effects, human activities, land uses, and other factors that may alter its balance and functioning was evaluated.

The first component to be assessed in the analysis of the environmental sensitivity of the study area is air and climate. For this, three key assessment areas were considered: (i) Areas with good climatic conditions: These areas are characterized by favorable conditions for air quality and climate, such as moderate temperatures, low incidence of strong winds, and adequate humidity levels. (ii) Areas relevant for decontamination: These areas play a crucial role in improving air quality, as they act as sinks for carbon and other air pollutants. (iii) Areas with environmental burden due to pollution: These areas have a higher concentration of air pollutants due to various sources, such as industrial emissions, vehicular traffic, or intensive agricultural activities.

The intensity of incidence of each of these areas was measured on a scale of low, medium, and high, using a color gradation to visually represent the magnitude of the impacts. Next, an overlay of the maps of the three assessed areas was performed, which allowed for obtaining two new maps corresponding to: Ecological Importance Map, this map reflects the relevance of each area for the maintenance of air quality and climate, as well as its contribution to related ecosystem services. The areas with the greatest ecological importance are those that present a combination of good climatic conditions and a high decontamination capacity. Vulnerability Map, this map shows the susceptibility of each area to the negative impacts of air pollution and other factors that can alter air quality and climate. The most vulnerable areas are those with a high environmental burden due to pollution and a low decontamination capacity. *(See Figure 8)*

Figure 8. Air and Climate Sensitivity Assessment

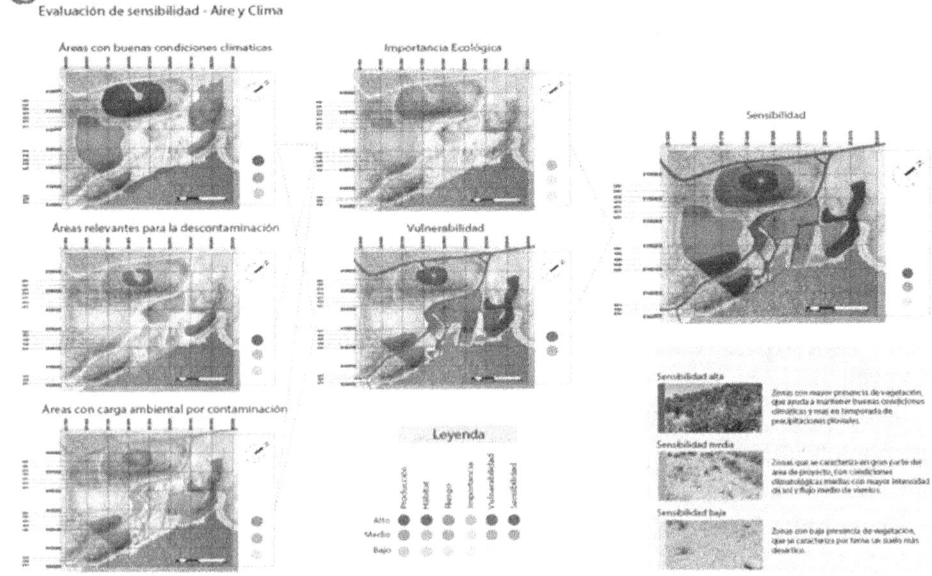

Finally, a joint analysis of the ecological importance and vulnerability maps was conducted, assigning different intensities to each area according to their combined values. The analysis produced a sensitivity map for the air and climate components categorizing areas as having high, medium or low sensitivity.

The air and climate sensitivity assessment reveals that areas with a greater presence of vegetation exhibit high sensitivity, as this vegetation contributes to maintaining good climatic conditions, especially during the rainy season. Areas with average climatic conditions and moderate solar intensity and wind flow exhibit medium sensitivity, while areas with sparse vegetation and desert characteristics exhibit low sensitivity.

The second component to be assessed in the environmental sensitivity analysis is that of surface waters. For this, three key assessment areas were considered: (i) Degree of naturalness: This area refers to the state of conservation of surface water bodies and their surroundings, considering the presence of riparian vegetation, the diversity of aquatic habitats, and the absence of significant alterations caused by human activities. (ii) Quality and use: This area assesses water quality in terms of physicochemical and biological parameters, as well as the uses given to water, such as human supply, agricultural irrigation, or hydroelectric power generation. (iii) Relevant impacts due to compaction, flow regulation, or extraction: This area focuses on the specific impacts that can affect the integrity of aquatic ecosystems, such as soil compaction on riverbanks, alteration of the natural hydrological regime due to the construction of dams, or excessive water extraction for different uses.

Similar to the assessment of the air and climate component, the intensity of incidence of each of these areas was measured on a scale of low, medium, and high, using a color gradation to visually represent the magnitude of the impacts. The overlay of the maps of the three assessed areas resulted in two additional graphs corresponding to: (i) ecological importance: This graph reflects the relevance of each area for maintaining the health and functioning of aquatic ecosystems, as well as its contribution to water-related ecosystem services. (ii) Vulnerability: This graph shows the susceptibility of each area to negative impacts caused by pollution, alteration of the hydrological regime, and other factors that can affect water quality and availability, as well as the integrity of aquatic ecosystems.

The joint analysis of the ecological importance and vulnerability graphs allowed for obtaining the sensitivity map of the surface water component. This map classifies the areas into three sensitivity levels: high, medium, and low.

The results of the surface water sensitivity assessment indicate that high-sensitivity areas are those with abundant vegetation, a high degree of naturalness, and watercourses that cross the study area. These areas are particularly important for biodiversity conservation and the provision of water-related ecosystem services. Medium-sensitivity areas correspond to most watercourses in areas with medium naturalness and without significant alterations, while low-sensitivity areas are those with degraded area morphology, temporary watercourses, and those affected by earthworks. (See Figure 9)

Figure 9. Surface Water Sensitivity Assessment

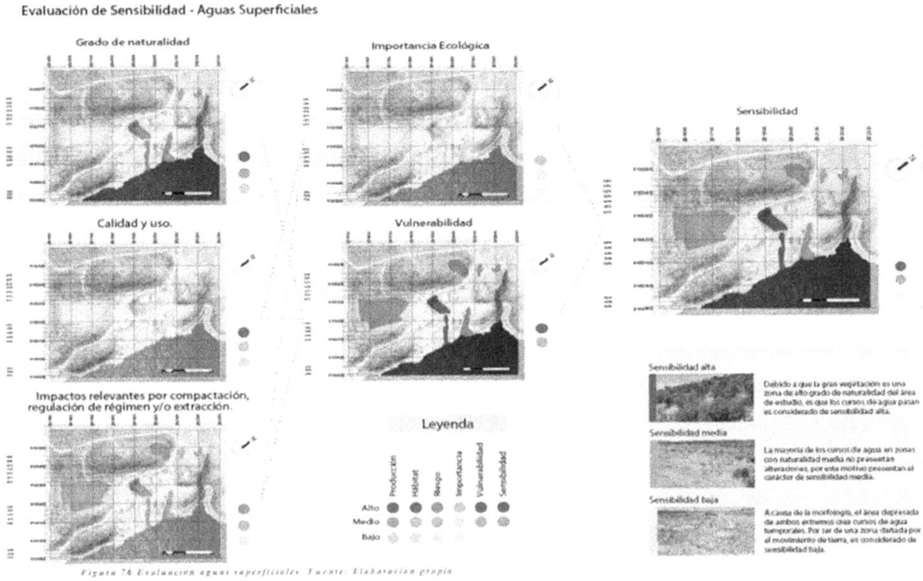

The third component to be assessed in the environmental sensitivity analysis is the soil. For this, three key assessment areas were considered. Firstly, relevant productive function: This area refers to the soil's capacity to support agricultural, livestock, or forestry production. Soil with a high productive function is essential for food security and the economic development of the region. Secondly, notable habitat function: This area assesses the importance of soil as a habitat for a variety of organisms, from microorganisms to plants and animals. Thirdly, risk of impact, contamination, compaction, and erosion: This area focuses on the negative impacts that can affect soil quality and functionality, such as contamination by chemicals or waste, compaction caused by vehicle or heavy machinery traffic, and erosion caused by wind or water. These impacts can degrade the soil structure, reduce its fertility, and affect its ability to support life and provide ecosystem services.

As in the previous assessments, the intensity of incidence of each of these areas was measured on a scale of low, medium, and high, using a color gradation to visually represent the magnitude of the impacts. The analysis of the results of ecological importance and vulnerability allowed for obtaining the sensitivity map of the soil component, which classifies the areas into three sensitivity levels: high, medium, and low.

The results of the soil sensitivity assessment reveal that high-sensitivity areas are the roads within areas of high natural value, as vehicle traffic.and lack of vegetation cover can cause accelerated soil erosion. Areas of vegetation and their surroundings exhibit medium sensitivity, due to their ecological importance and the presence of organic matter and nutrients that contribute to soil fertility. Low-sensitivity areas are those that do not present significant contamination or compaction and have moderate ecological importance. It is important to highlight that the identification of high-sensitivity areas, such as roads in high natural value zones, emphasizes the need to implement mitigation measures to prevent erosion and protect soil quality. These measures may include revegetation of slopes, construction of adequate drainage, and restriction of vehicle access to sensitive areas. (See Figure 10)

Figure 10. Soil Sensitivity Assessment

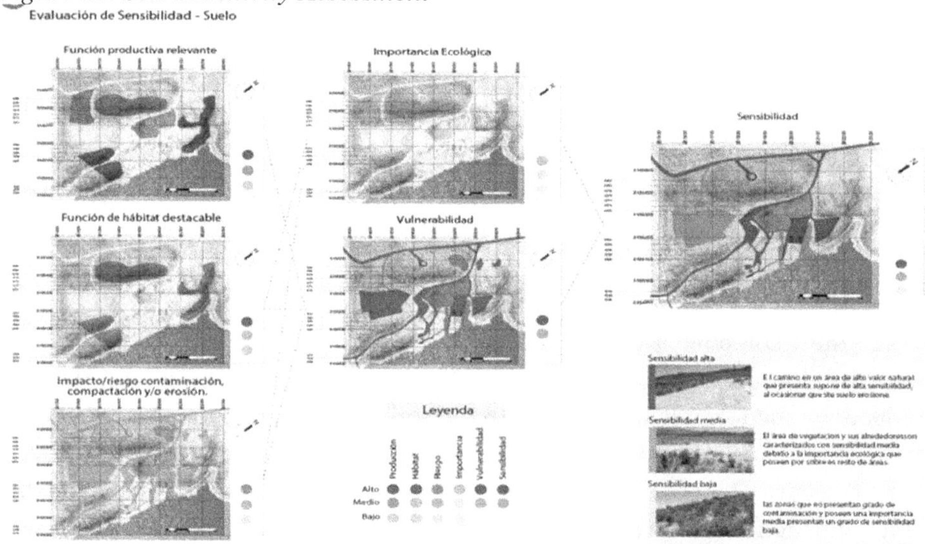

The fourth component to be assessed in the environmental sensitivity analysis is vegetation and fauna. The three key assessment areas correspond to: (i) habitats with relevant species and biocenosis: This area refers to zones that harbor flora and fauna species of special ecological importance, whether due to their rarity, endemism, role in the food chain, or contribution to ecosystem services; (ii) habitats requiring management: This area includes zones that, while not necessarily harboring species of high relevance, require adequate management to ensure their conservation and functioning. This may include degraded areas in the process of restoration, transition zones between different types of vegetation, or areas with invasive species that need to be controlled; (iii) habitats with relevant impacts due to compaction, destruction, and segregation: This area focuses on the negative impacts that can affect the integrity of habitats and the survival of species.

As in the previous assessments, the intensity of incidence of each of these areas was measured on a scale of low, medium, and high, using a color gradation to visually represent the magnitude of the impacts. The analysis of the results of ecological importance and vulnerability allowed for obtaining the sensitivity map of the vegetation and fauna component, which classifies the areas into three sensitivity levels: high, medium, and low.

The results of the vegetation and fauna sensitivity assessment show that high-sensitivity areas are those characterized by their abundant and diverse native vegetation, which harbors a wide variety of animal species. These areas are crucial for biodiversity conservation and the maintenance of essential ecological processes. Medium-sensitivity areas are those with a moderate presence of vegetation and fauna, while low-sensitivity areas are those with a lower presence of vegetation and fauna, where shrub species and lichens predominate, typical of arid and degraded environments. (*See Figure 11*)

Figure 11. Vegetation and Fauna Sensitivity Assessment

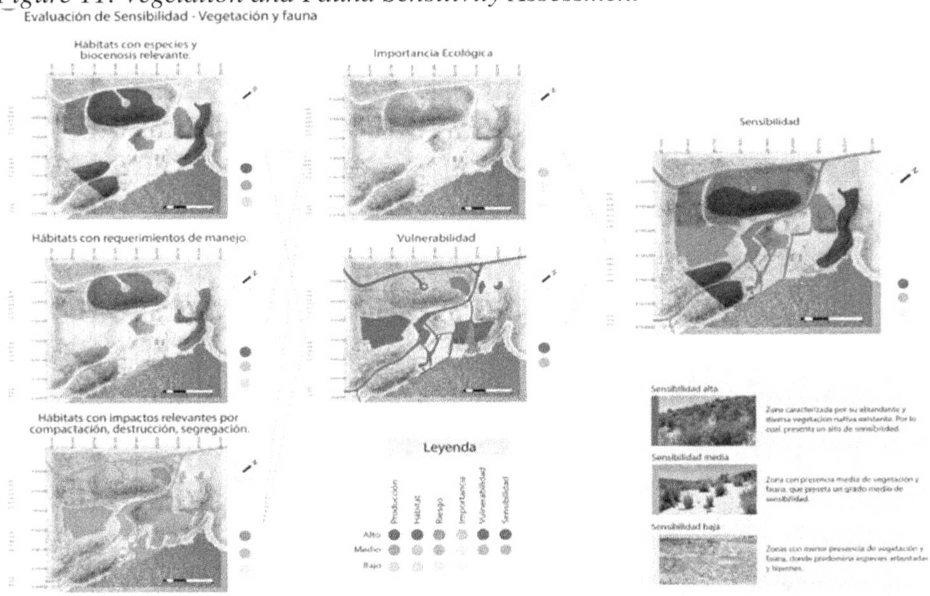

Finally, the fifth component of the sensitivity assessment corresponds to the scenic landscape. For this, the following three key assessment areas were considered: (i) areas of recreational interest: The presence of attractive natural elements, such as water bodies, geological formations, panoramic views, or vegetation diversity, contributes to their scenic value and their ability to generate positive experiences for visitors. These areas are characterized by their natural beauty, unique landscape, and potential for recreational and tourism activities. (ii) Areas with potential aptitude for near-natural recreation: These areas, although not necessarily possessing exceptional scenic value, have natural characteristics that make them suitable for low-impact recreational activities, such as hiking, birdwatching, or environmental interpretation. (iii) Areas that represent relevant burdens due to pollution, destruction, and segregation: These areas present negative impacts that affect their visual quality and their ability to provide satisfactory recreational and tourism experiences.

The analysis of the results of ecological importance and vulnerability allowed for obtaining the sensitivity map of the scenic landscape component, which classifies the areas into three sensitivity levels: high, medium, and low.

The results of the scenic landscape sensitivity assessment indicate that high-sensitivity areas are those that offer panoramic views of the San José de Uzuña dam and the surrounding vegetation, presenting a unique landscape and setting. These areas are especially vulnerable to visual impacts and landscape degradation, thus requiring adequate protection and management measures. Medium-sensitivity areas include hillsides and central areas, which have relevant landscape and natural characteristics but may be less vulnerable to negative impacts. Finally, low-sensitivity areas are those mostly desert and flat, with sparse vegetation, offering a less attractive landscape and being less susceptible to visual impacts and degradation. (See Figure 12)

Figure 12. Scenic Landscape Sensitivity Assessment

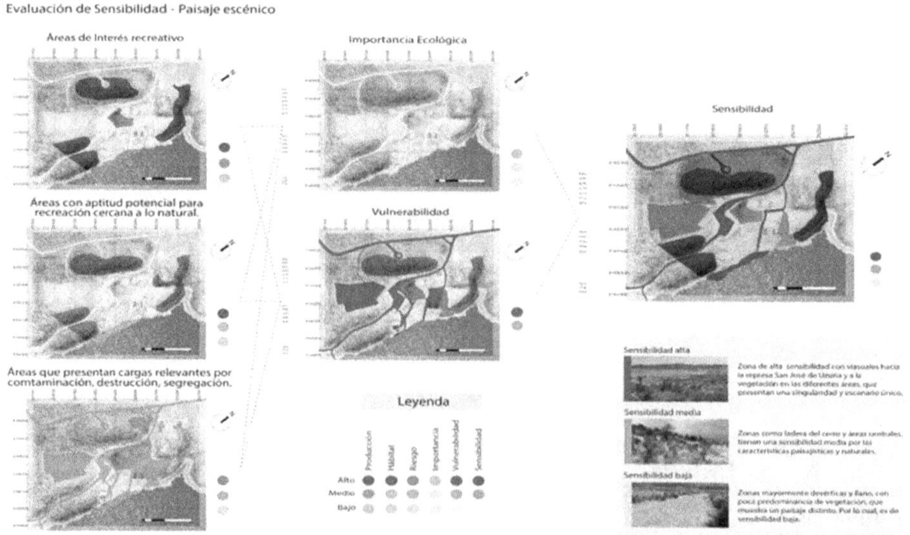

Once the sensitivity of each of the five environmental components (air and climate, surface water, soil, vegetation and fauna, and scenic landscape) was assessed, the results were integrated into a single sensitivity map. This map synthesizes the information from the individual components, presenting a zoning of the study area with different intensities of sensitivity, where stronger tones correspond to the areas most vulnerable to environmental impacts. The overlay of the individual sensitivity maps allowed for the identification of the areas of greatest ecological sensitivity in the study area. The material extraction zones and the areas with the highest concentration of vegetation stood out as the most sensitive. Material extraction generates significant alterations in the soil, topography, and landscape, while dense vegetation plays a crucial role in the regulation of hydrological and biogeochemical cycles, soil protection against erosion, and the provision of habitat for fauna.

The main trails and gullies were also identified as high-sensitivity areas due to their ecological importance and their vulnerability to erosion and pollution. These areas act as ecological corridors that connect different habitats and facilitate the movement of species, in addition to being water recharge zones and regulating water flow. On the other hand, the hill where the viewpoint is located and the edge of the San José de Uzuña dam were classified as low-sensitivity areas. This is because these areas have lower biological diversity and are less susceptible to environmental impacts, as the soil is less fertile and the vegetation is scarcer. Likewise, the areas at the right and left ends of the study area, characterized by their desert landscape and sparse vegetation, were also considered to have low sensitivity. (See Figure 13)

Figure 13. Synthesis Map of Sensitivity

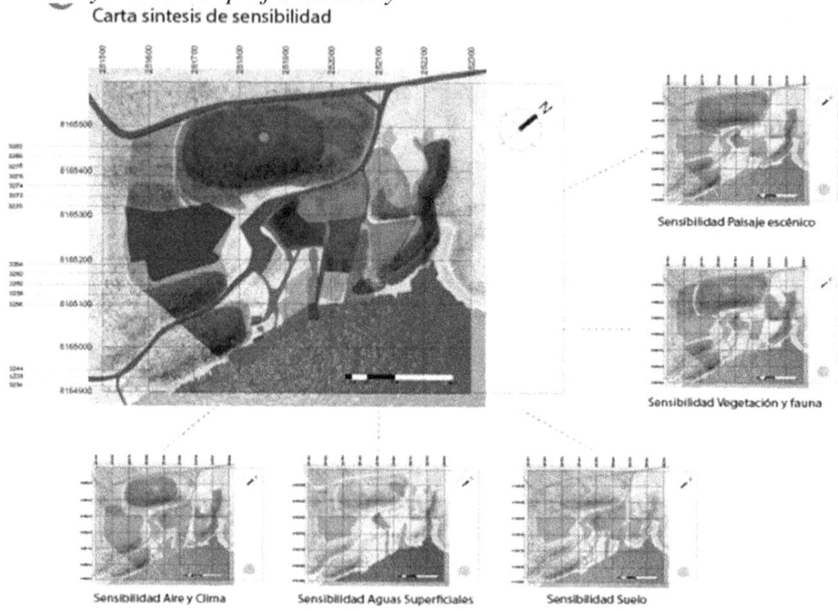

Ecological Risk Assessment

The ecological risk assessment is based on the analysis of the potential force of effects derived from use, human activities, and other interventions currently observed in the study area. These effects can negatively affect each of the previously assessed environmental components (air and climate, surface water, soil, vegetation and fauna, and scenic landscape), and their intensity is classified into three levels: (i) high, corresponding to severe and persistent effects that can cause irreversible or long-term damage to the environmental component; (ii) medium, corresponding to moderate effects that can cause significant alterations in the environmental component, but with the potential for recovery in the medium term; (iii) low, corresponding to mild or temporary effects that do not compromise the integrity of the environmental component in the long term.

To determine the ecological risk of each component, a double-entry matrix was developed that relates the sensitivity of the component to the potential intensity of the effects. Each cell of the matrix represents a specific combination of sensitivity and effect, and it is assigned a risk level (high, medium, or low) according to technical criteria and the expert judgment of the researchers. The cartography of the potential intensity of effects was obtained by identifying and mapping human activities and other factors that can generate negative impacts in the study area. These maps were overlaid with the sensitivity map to generate the ecological risk map of each environmental component.

The first component evaluated is Air and Climate. For this, the assessment area of "Current use or activity" was considered, zoned by colors according to four characteristics: urban use, habitat, road infrastructure, and hydrography. In this way, a cartography of Current Use and Habitat was obtained, from which a new cartography called Potential Intensity of Effects was generated. The latter was analyzed together with the Air and Climate Sensitivity cartography obtained previously. Finally, the Ecological Risk cartography was obtained, represented with colors of different intensity, the strongest being the area of greatest risk in the study area. From the analysis of results, the ecological risk of air and climate resulted in a map with three levels: high ecological risk corresponding to areas of informal non-metallic material movement, which degrade the environment; medium ecological risk corresponding to areas affected by the informal growth of recreational and commercial activities, which do not respect the environment; and finally, low ecological risk corresponding to natural areas of the park and outer zones without threat of negative variability in climatic conditions. (See Figure 14)

Figure 14. Ecological Risk Assessment of Air and Climate

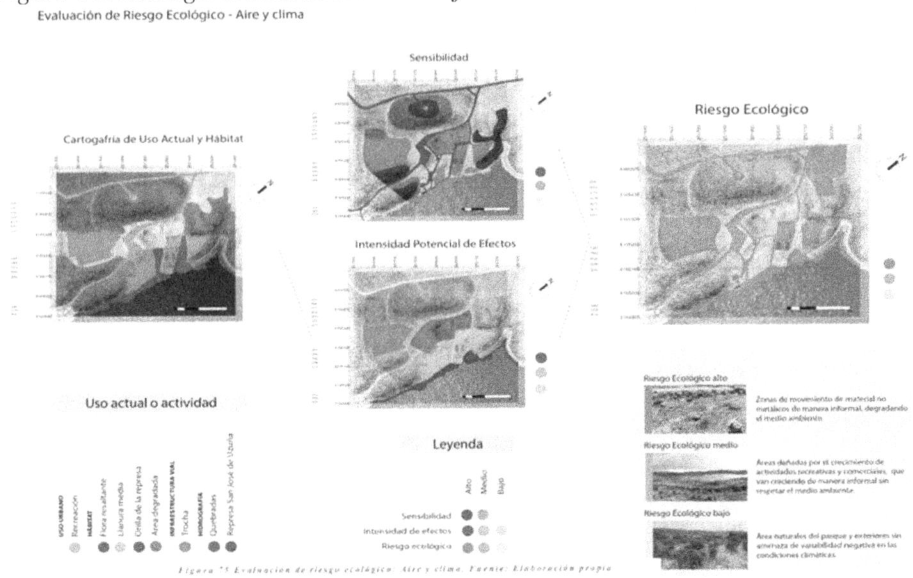

The second component evaluated is Surface Waters. Similar to the previous process, the assessment area of "Current use or activity" was considered, zoned by colors according to four characteristics: urban use, habitat, road infrastructure, and hydrography. From this zoning, a cartography of Current Use and Habitat was derived, from which a new cartography called Potential Intensity of Effects was generated. This Potential Intensity of Effects cartography was combined with the Surface Water Sensitivity map, obtained previously, to finally obtain the Ecological Risk cartography. The ecological risk assessment of surface waters resulted in a map with three risk levels: high, medium, and low, as described below.

High ecological risk contains watercourses in areas of great natural value and habitat for the study area. These watercourses are crucial for maintaining biodiversity and the ecological processes of the area, so any alteration in their quality or quantity can have a significant impact on the ecosystem. Medium ecological risk contains the main watercourse that crosses the study area. Although it does not pass through areas of high natural value, any pollution or alteration in its regime can affect water quality and resource availability for other uses. Low ecological risk contains minor watercourses. Although important for the ecosystem, their smaller size and flow make them less vulnerable to impacts compared to the main watercourses.

It is important to note that, although the main watercourse does not cross areas of high natural value, its classification as medium ecological risk underlines the importance of implementing adequate protection and management measures to ensure its conservation and water quality. The identification of high ecological risk areas, such as watercourses in areas of great natural value, highlights the need to prioritize the conservation of these ecosystems and minimize the impacts of human activities on them. (See Figure 15)

Figure 15. Ecological Risk Assessment of Surface Waters

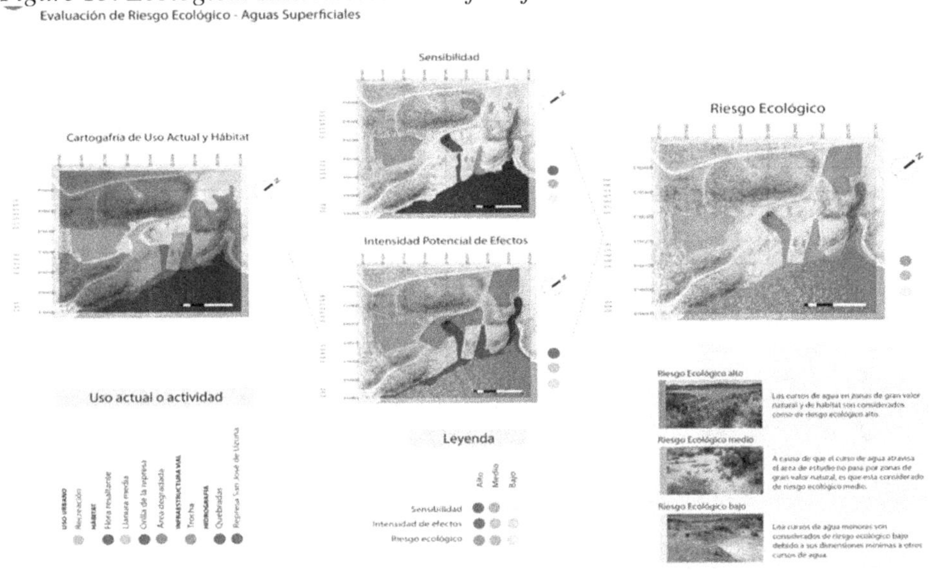

The third component assessed was Soil. To determine its ecological risk, the assessment area of "Current use or activity" was considered, from which a new cartography called Potential Intensity of Effects was generated. This cartography of Potential Intensity of Effects was combined with the Soil Sensitivity map, previously obtained, to finally obtain the Ecological Risk cartography of the soil component.

The ecological risk assessment of the soil resulted in a map with three risk levels: (i) High ecological risk, containing the road near and in the central area, due to it crossing a high sensitivity zone. Vehicle traffic and the possible lack of erosion control measures on these roads can generate a significant impact on soil quality and stability, especially in areas of high natural value. (ii) Medium ecological risk contains the areas on the edges, degraded by earthworks. Although these areas have medium sensitivity, the physical alteration of the soil by human activities increases its vulnerability to erosion and loss of fertility, justifying its classification as medium risk. (iii) Low ecological risk: The perimeter of the analyzed area, categorized as such due to the low pollution observed in the place. These areas, being less exposed to impactful human activities, have a lower risk of soil degradation.

It is important to highlight that the identification of high ecological risk areas, such as the road that crosses sensitive areas, emphasizes the need to implement mitigation and restoration measures to protect the soil and minimize the impacts of human activities. These measures can include revegetation of slopes, construction of adequate drainage, and restriction of vehicle access to sensitive areas. Additionally, it is essential to monitor soil quality in medium and low-risk areas to prevent degradation and ensure the sustainability of terrestrial ecosystems in the study area. (See Figure 16)

Figure 16. Ecological Risk Assessment of Soil

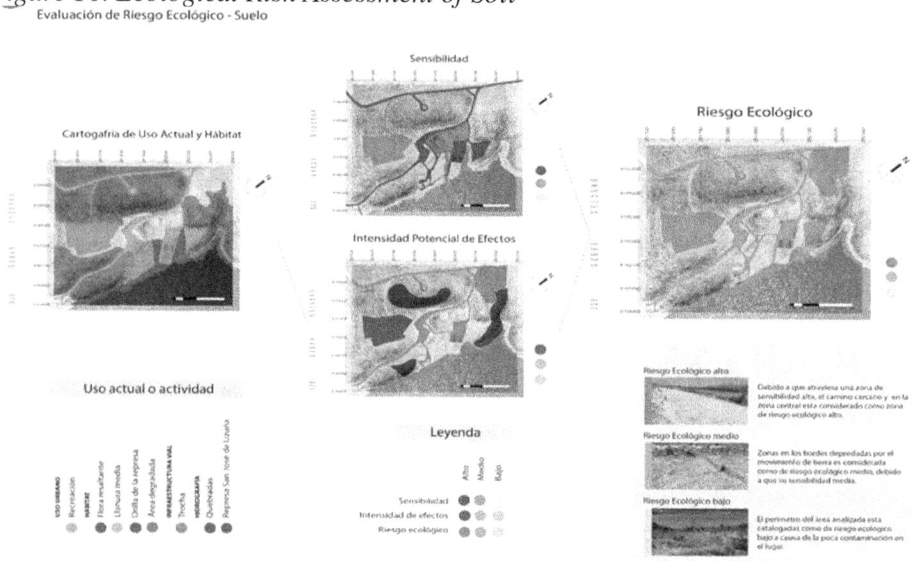

The fourth component assessed is Vegetation and Fauna. To determine its ecological risk, the assessment area of "Current use or activity" was considered, from which a new cartography called Potential Intensity of Effects was generated. This cartography of Potential Intensity of Effects was combined with the Vegetation and Fauna Sensitivity map, previously obtained, to finally obtain the Ecological Risk cartography of this component. The ecological risk assessment of vegetation and fauna resulted in a map with three levels corresponding to high, medium, and low, which are described in the following paragraph.

High ecological risk: Areas with little presence of vegetation and fauna due to the damage caused by degradation, erosion, or high pollution. These areas, having undergone significant alterations, have a low recovery capacity and harbor reduced biodiversity, making them highly vulnerable to future impacts. Medium ecological risk: Areas with a lack of vegetation and fauna due to the growth of commercial land use. The expansion of commercial activities can fragment the habitat, displace species, and reduce the availability of natural resources, affecting the diversity and abundance of flora and fauna. Low ecological risk: Areas that do not present a high risk importance and have remained in their natural state. These areas, by conserving their ecological integrity and biodiversity, are less susceptible to negative impacts and have a greater resilience capacity against disturbances.

It is essential to highlight that the identification of high ecological risk areas, such as those with scarce vegetation and fauna due to degradation or pollution, emphasizes the urgent need to implement restoration and conservation measures to recover biodiversity and associated ecosystem services. It is also important to promote more sustainable land-use practices in medium-risk areas to minimize impacts on vegetation and fauna. The protection of low-risk areas is crucial to ensure the preservation of biodiversity and ecological balance in the study area. (See Figure 17)

Figure 17. Ecological Risk Assessment of Vegetation and Fauna

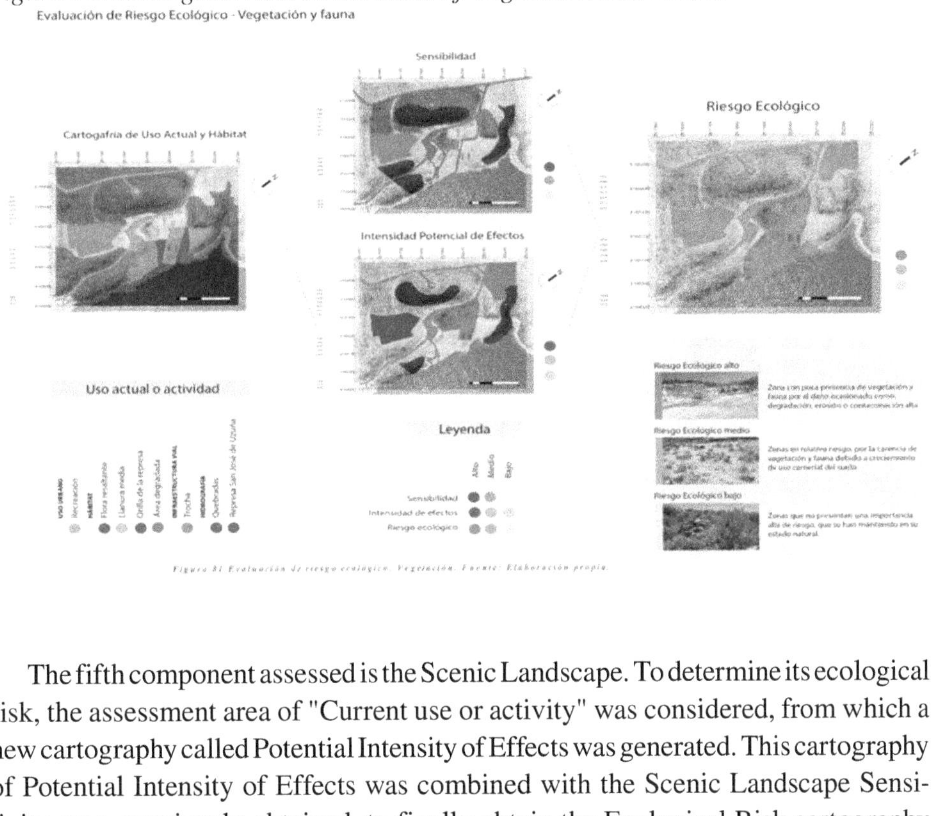

The fifth component assessed is the Scenic Landscape. To determine its ecological risk, the assessment area of "Current use or activity" was considered, from which a new cartography called Potential Intensity of Effects was generated. This cartography of Potential Intensity of Effects was combined with the Scenic Landscape Sensitivity map, previously obtained, to finally obtain the Ecological Risk cartography of this component. The ecological risk assessment of the scenic landscape resulted in a map with three risk levels: (i) high ecological risk: Areas that have undergone severe modifications in the landscape, such as earthworks areas that have generated loss of vegetation cover. These alterations negatively impact the visual quality of the landscape and reduce its aesthetic and recreational value. (ii) medium ecological risk: The hillside area, prone to landscape modifications due to its proximity to vehicle transit routes. The construction of roads, erosion caused by traffic, and the possible deposition of waste can affect the visual integrity of the landscape in this area. (iii) low ecological risk: Areas with small alterations in the landscape, which could lose their particular character in the future. Although they currently have a low level of risk, it is important to monitor these areas and take preventive measures to avoid their degradation and preserve their scenic value.

The identification of high ecological risk areas, such as earthworks zones, emphasizes the importance of implementing landscape restoration measures and controlling activities that can generate negative impacts on the landscape. It is also crucial to promote sustainable development practices in medium and low-risk areas to preserve the visual quality of the landscape and ensure its enjoyment by present and future generations. (See Figure 18)

Figure 18. Ecological Risk Assessment of Scenic Landscape

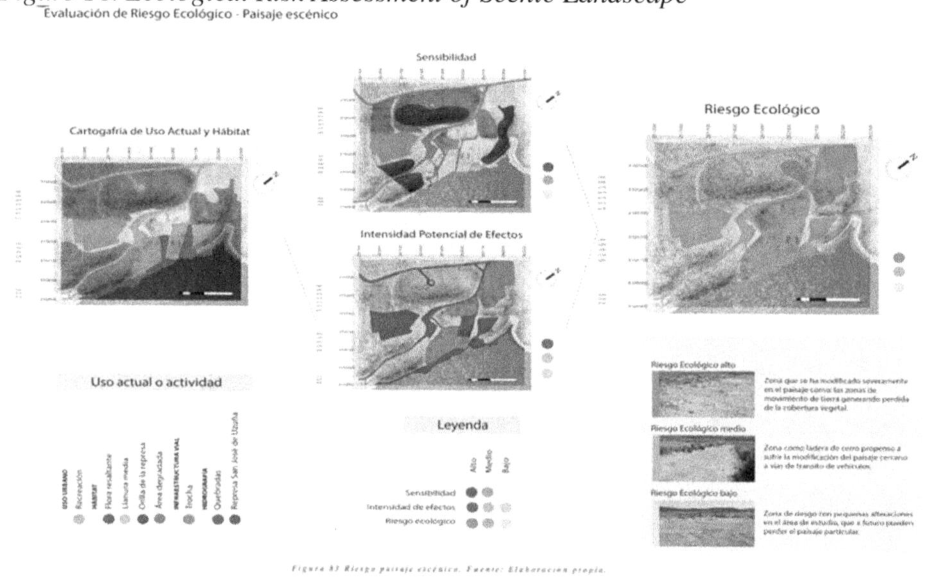

Once the ecological risk of each of the five environmental components (air and climate, surface water, soil, vegetation and fauna, and scenic landscape) was assessed, the results were integrated into a single ecological risk synthesis map. This final map shows a zoning of the study area with different risk intensities, where stronger tones correspond to the areas most vulnerable to environmental impacts. The overlay of the individual ecological risk maps allowed for the identification of the areas of greatest ecological risk in the study area. The material extraction zones and the shore of the San José de Uzuña dam stood out as those with the highest ecological risk. Material extraction generates significant alterations in the soil, topography, landscape, and water quality, while the dam's shore is a sensitive area due to the direct interaction with the water body and its vulnerability to pollution and erosion.

The trails and main roads, as well as the areas of commercial activities, were classified as moderate-risk zones. The transit of people and vehicles on the trails and roads can generate soil compaction and erosion, while commercial activities can produce pollution and landscape alteration. The gullies with temporary water flow during the rainy season also present a moderate risk due to their susceptibility to erosion and changes in the hydrological regime. Finally, the central zone and part of the right edge of the study area were considered to have low ecological risk. These areas, being less exposed to impactful human activities and presenting lower environmental sensitivity, are less vulnerable to negative impacts. (See Figure 19)

Figure 19. Synthesis Map of Ecological Risk

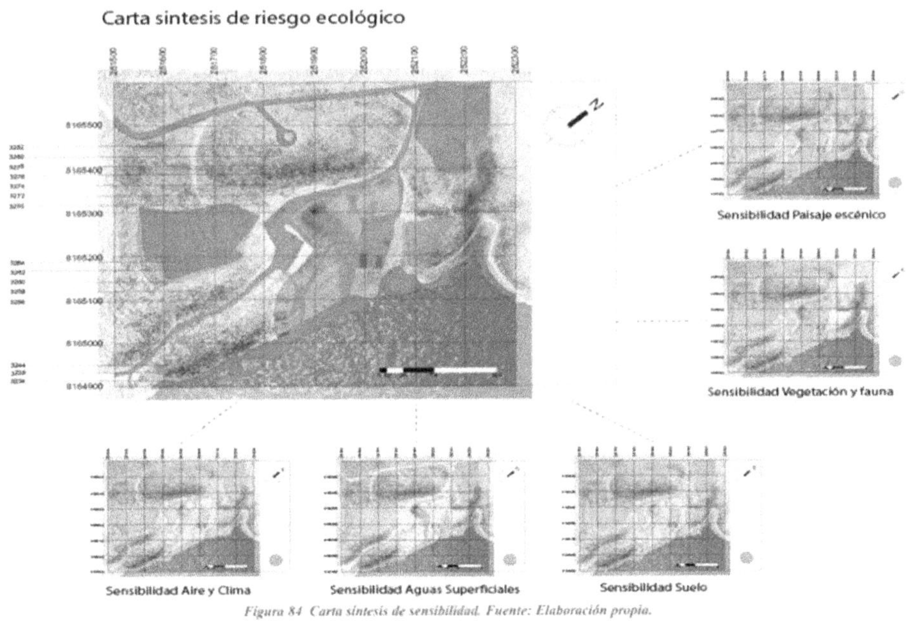

Zoned Environmental Objectives (OAZ)

The analysis and synthesis of the sensitivity and ecological risk maps allowed for the definition of Zoned Environmental Objectives (OAZs) for the study area. These objectives establish intervention priorities and environmental management strategies for each zone, aiming to protect, develop, and restore the environment.

Three clear objectives were defined: The first is protection. This objective applies to areas of high sensitivity and low ecological risk, where the priority is to conserve the integrity of ecosystems and prevent environmental degradation. Management strategies include regulating human activities, promoting sustainable practices, and implementing biodiversity conservation measures. The second is development. This objective applies to areas of low sensitivity and low ecological risk, where it is possible to promote sustainable development that utilizes natural resources responsibly and minimizes environmental impacts. Management strategies include territorial planning, promoting economic activities compatible with environmental conservation, and environmental education.

The third objective is repair, which applies to areas of high sensitivity and high ecological risk, where restoration and rehabilitation measures are necessary to recover environmental quality and degraded ecosystem services. Management strategies include revegetation, erosion control, soil and water decontamination, and promoting biodiversity recovery. The definition of these OAZs provides a strategic framework for environmental management of the study area, guiding actions towards conservation, sustainable development, and ecosystem restoration, based on the specific characteristics and vulnerabilities of each zone. (See Figure 20)

Figure 20. Zoned Environmental Objectives

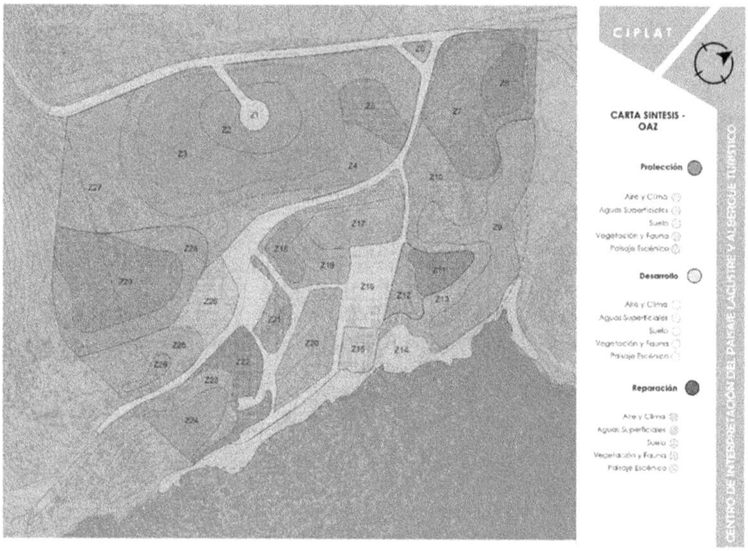

After obtaining the synthesis map of the OAZs, it was simplified to establish the Environmental Zoning Plan. This plan includes specific actions for each of the 20 intervention zones identified in the study area, which have particular characteristics that require differentiated interventions based on the objectives set by the OAZs. From the analysis of results, approximately 75% of the study area has been classified as a protection and restoration zone, due to the presence of favorable habitats and natural environments that have been affected by pollution and human displacement. These zones require conservation, ecological restoration, and impact mitigation actions to ensure their long-term recovery and preservation.

Likewise, vegetation and fauna development zones have been identified, strategically located between the protection zones. These areas play a crucial role in generating a natural environment and preserving the lakescape, so reforestation, biodiversity enrichment, and sustainable management of natural resources will be promoted. Additionally, the study area also has zones with potential for recreation, thanks to its favorable landscape conditions. These zones, mainly located in areas with panoramic views of the dam, the snow-capped mountains, the lake, and the fauna, will be subject to interventions that promote sustainable tourism and environmental education, while ensuring the protection of the natural environment.

Buffer zones have been established on the edge of the San José de Uzuña dam, areas with stable natural conditions that require management actions, such as control activities and passive recreation, to maintain their ecological balance and prevent degradation. Finally, subzones for special treatment have been identified due to their unfavorable conditions, resulting from alterations that have affected their natural state. These zones will require more intensive restoration interventions to recover their ecological and landscape functionality.

Social Understanding of the Context

The interviews conducted with visitors and local residents focused on interpreting the degree of user interest and the importance of the dam. The results indicate that most visitors to the dam are people from outside the community and students, highlighting the tourism potential of the dam. (See Figure 21). It is important to note that, while the dam offers tourism and recreation opportunities, the interviews also revealed the concern of visitors and residents about the existing and potential pollution in the area. (See Figure 22) This underscores the need to implement environmental management measures that ensure the conservation of the landscape.

Figure 21. Typology of Visitors to the Dam

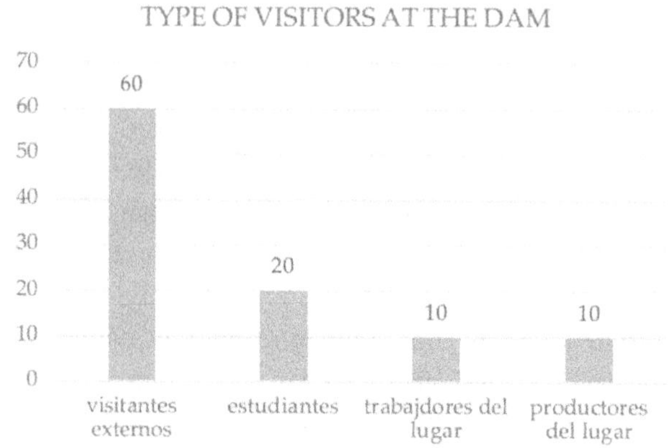

Figure 22. Negative Aspects of the Dam

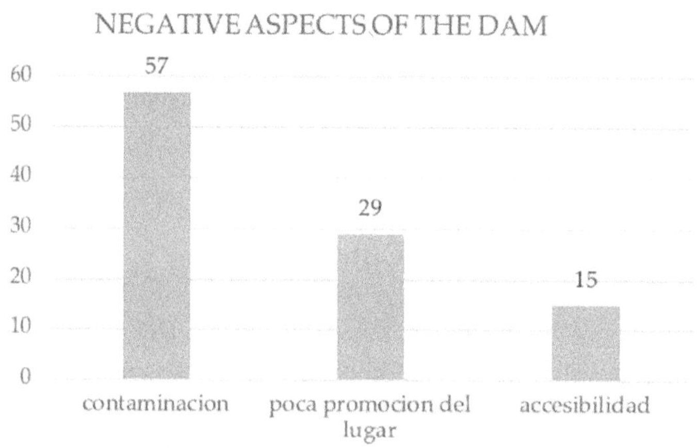

Furthermore, the results indicate that the importance of the dam lies in tourism activity. (See Figure 23). It is evident that the scenic appeal and the range of recreational activities associated with the lakescape generate economic opportunities for the local sector, boosting tourism and creating sources of employment and income for the community. Therefore, the synergies between environmental education and economic development highlight the importance of managing the ecosystem landscape responsibly, ensuring its long-term conservation and maximizing its benefits for society. The promotion of environmentally responsible tourism practices, the implementation of environmental education programs, and the active participation of the community in landscape management are key elements to achieve a balance between environmental conservation and local economic development.

Figure 23. Importance of the Dam

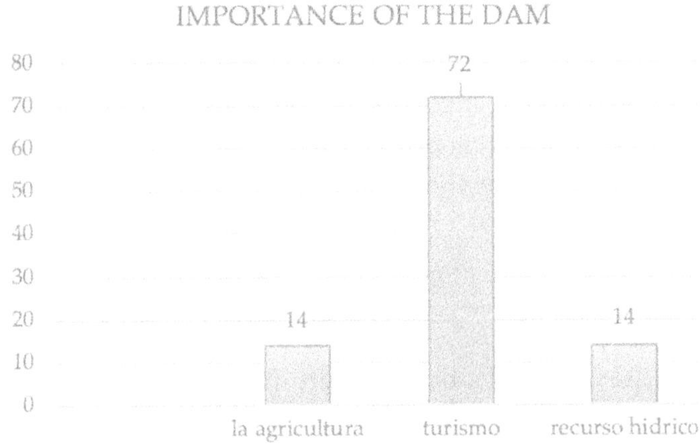

4. DISCUSSION

In recent years, climate change has highlighted the vulnerability of territories, especially those with water resources. The detailed identification and spatialization of landscape vulnerability in these territories allows for recognizing the areas most prone to environmental degradation and water scarcity, providing valuable information for decision-making and the formulation of protection policies and strategies. Additionally, it facilitates land-use planning and the sustainable management of water resources, ensuring their availability for future generations.

This research contributes an innovative methodology for planning territories with water resources, focusing on the specific case of dam-type reservoirs in peri-urban environments. However, its implications transcend this particular context, opening new perspectives for future research. The methodology designed in this research exposes the inherent complexity of territories that harbor water resources, underscoring the need for comprehensive approaches to their management and planning. The Ecosystem Services theory, which seeks to characterize these complex territories, has driven the development of tools, indicators, and methodologies that allow for quantifying and qualifying the various components present in these high-value ecosystems. This quantification and qualification of specific territorial elements and dynamics highlight the need for specialized territorial management instruments, adapted to the particularities of each context.

Ecological planning requires strategies that allow for evaluating sectors, from their importance to their vulnerability to land-use risks or their environmental effects. ECOTERR stands as a valuable tool in this process, providing key information for informed and sustainable decision-making. Historically, the countryside and the city maintained an interactive relationship. Today, the need for a connection with the natural landscape is both economically and socially imperative. The landscape, as a result of the dynamic interaction between natural and human factors, is not static but evolves over time, reflecting the history and transformations of the territory.

5. CONCLUSION

Lakescapes, in particular, have been subject to intense transformation due to pressures such as urbanization, pollution, and climate change. However, these landscapes not only provide aesthetic and recreational value but also offer essential services such as water regulation, air quality improvement, biodiversity, and the provision of natural resources. In this context, urban ecosystem services are defined as the direct and indirect benefits that people obtain from ecosystems within city limits. The effective planning and management of these services require robust tools and methodological approaches that allow for properly identifying, quantifying, and valuing the benefits that ecosystems provide to urban society. In the specific case of lakescapes, the need for a specific methodology intensifies due to their complexity and dynamic interaction with the built environment.

The main objective of this methodology is to establish a structured framework that enables: (i) The identification and classification of the diverse services provided by urban lakescapes. (ii) The assessment of these ecosystem services through both quantitative and qualitative evaluations, employing economic valuation techniques, public perception analyses, and other relevant methods; and the (iii) integration o findings into urban urban planning processes, providing useful and applicable information to support decision-making in the planning and management of urban lakescapes, ensuring their conservation, restoration, and sustainable use.

The landscape, in its dynamic nature, transforms in response to the economic, political, and cultural conditions that surround it. Therefore, its planning and management must consider these dimensions together, seeking techniques that allow for deciphering human intervention in the landscape. In this sense, the ECOTERR methodology and the field surveys conducted have proven their effectiveness in revealing the crucial role of the San José de Uzuña dam for the Polobaya peasant community, as well as in assessing the impact of tourism in the area.

The synthesis map generated by ECOTERR has enabled a comprehensive evaluation of the territory in relation to its ecosystem resources, facilitating environmental protection against the impact of tourism and the identification of protection zones, infrastructure development, and restoration of areas degraded by human action. Furthermore, the ECOTERR methodology is based on territorial mapping, the assessment of sensitivity, vulnerability, and ecological risk of different natural elements such as air, climate, water, soil, vegetation, and landscape. This tool is based on the systematic and rigorous evaluation of these components to guide decision-making in landscape matters.

The development of a methodology to identify and assess ecosystem services in urban lakescapes, as proposed in this research, represents a significant advance in the understanding and management of these critical environments. Its practical application not only facilitates the conservation and restoration of ecosystem services but also promotes an integrated and sustainable approach to urban planning and environmental management.

In the specific case of the San José de Uzuña dam, the ECOTERR tool has allowed for the creation of an environmental zoning plan, especially relevant in the absence of urban planning in the Polobaya sector. This study provides crucial information for the creation of an environmental system that supports decision-making by local authorities, particularly in the stages of inventory and territorial assessment.

In conclusion, this research highlights the importance of integrating the assessment of ecosystem services and the social understanding of the context in the planning and management of territories with water resources. The ECOTERR methodology, together with the surveys conducted, has proven to be an effective tool to address the complexity of these environments and promote sustainable development that benefits both the local community and the environment.

It is suggested that future work explores the application of this methodology in territories with the presence of lakescapes in urban or rural contexts, adapting and refining the proposed tools and approaches to address the particularities of each environment. Likewise, it is encouraged to delve deeper into the management of the territory in these landscapes, adopting an approach based on ecosystem services, which allows for valuing and protecting the multiple benefits that these ecosystems provide to society.

Ultimately, this research contributes to the growing body of knowledge on the sustainable planning and management of territories with water resources, offering a solid and adaptable methodological framework that can be applied in various contexts to promote the conservation of these valuable ecosystems and ensure their responsible use for the benefit of present and future generations.

Supplementary Materials: The following supporting information can be downloaded at:

Acknowledgments: The author(s) disclosed receipt of the following financial support for the research, authorship, and/or pub- location of this article: This research was supported by Red Cyted Lineamientos, planes y Acciones en áreas periurbanas: Ecosistemas en desarrollo equitativo - DPAAPU and by the Universidad Nacional de San Augustin de Arequipa, Peru.

Conflicts of Interest: The author(s) declared no potential conflicts of interest with respect to the research, authorship, and/or publication of this article.

REFERENCES

Arguedas Marín, M. P. (2022). *Propuesta metodológica para identificar sitios prioritarios para restaurar ecosistemas con fines de protección del recurso hídrico: estudio de caso de la microcuenca del Río Cacao*. Atenas.

Ascue Cuba, J. C. (2018). La vulnerabilidad de ecosistemas frágiles en ciudades altoandinas. caso: microcuenca huancaro, Distrito de Santiago–Cusco y el desarrollo sostenido urbano marginal.

Castillo Haeger, C. A. (2010). La organización del espacio lacustre: desde la superación del planeamiento sectorial (Doctoral dissertation, Arquitectura).

Directiva Europea del Paisaje. (2000). *Convenio Europeo del Paisaje*.

Fisher, W. S.. (2001). *Urban lake ecosystems: A multidisciplinary approach to understanding their ecology and management*. Springer Science & Business Media.

González Bernáldez, F. (2014). *Invitación al paisaje: Ensayos sobre el paisaje*. Abada Editores.

Haeger, R. (2010). La planificación del espacio lacustre. Una aproximación conceptual a la elaboración de planes de ordenación de ámbitos lacustres. *Boletín de la Asociación de Geógrafos Españoles*, (53), 127–151.

Hernández Aja, A. (2009). La protección del paisaje en la ordenación territorial y urbanística: instrumentos y técnicas para su aplicación. Revista Catalana de Derecho Ambiental, 1(1).

Izquierdo, R.. (2005). *Cambio climático en los sistemas lacustres de España: impactos, vulnerabilidad y adaptación*. Ministerio de Medio Ambiente.

Mata Olmo, R. (2002). *Manual de paisaje: Guía para la elaboración de estudios del paisaje*. Junta de Andalucía, Consejería de Medio Ambiente.

Paisajeo.org. (s.f.). Paisaje y ecología, una relación indisoluble. Recuperado de https://www.ambientebogota.gov.co/todas-las-investigaciones/-/asset_publisher/pibvwzUnZiNr/content/paisajes-sostenibles-una-estrategia-de-cuidado-ambiental

Sherry, J., & Soranno, P. A. (2006). Landscape influences on water chemistry and primary production in lakes and reservoirs. *Landscape Ecology*, *21*(3), 321–336.

Rangel Montavo, L. E. (2015). Urbanismo y humedales. Caso de estudio: el humedal" La sabana" desarrollo urbano en la zona noroeste de Chetumal, México.

Water & Corporation. (1980). *The urban lake restoration program: Summary report*. U.S. Environmental Protection Agency.

Wen, Y.. (2014a). A framework for assessing urban ecosystem services: Integrating ecological, economic, and social perspectives. *Ecological Indicators*, *45*, 220–231.

Zubelzu Mínguez, M. J., & Allende Álvarez, F. (2014). *Ordenación del territorio: un enfoque integrador*. Ediciones Mundi-Prensa.

Chapter 9

Transforming Peri-Urban Resilience Through Green Infrastructure for Healthier Community:

A Case Study of the Impact of Indoor Air Quality in Hyderabad

Tapanwita Saha
https://orcid.org/0000-0001-5061-9715
Lovely Professional University, India

V. B. Bigith
Lovely Professional University, India

ABSTRACT

Indoor air quality (IAQ) in peri-urban areas of a fast-developing South Indian metropolis, Hyderabad, has deteriorated due to growth in urbanization, industrialization, and emissions from vehicular traffic. This paper examines the effectiveness of green infrastructure (GI) measures on IAQ in Hyderabad, particularly emphasizing urban design strategies and low-VOC paints for reducing indoor pollution. A literature review was conducted on previous IAQ research in Hyderabad, emphasizing urban design and VOC emissions from paints. The chapter also evaluated interventions concerning GI in peri-urban Hyderabad to determine their efficiency in enhancing IAQ. It has been found that poor urban design and the use of high-VOC paints are two primary causes of indoor air pollution in Hyderabad. Some interventions, like urban forests, green roofs, and green walls, have demonstrated the capability of improving IAQ by controlling particulate matter, volatile organic compounds, and

DOI: 10.4018/979-8-3693-6089-7.ch009

carbon dioxide.

1. INTRODUCTION

Hyderabad is a fast-developing city located in the southern region of India; due to this development, many changes in the physical environment and people's way of life have been evident. This has, however, come with increased emissions of air pollution, which have mainly affected peri-urban areas in the process of urbanization (Ghose et al., 2018). These areas are already experiencing the impacts of industrialization, emissions from vehicles, and construction, and the quality of both the ambient and indoor environment has thus become worrisome (Guttikunda & Calori., 2011). This growth, however, has been accompanied by increased emissions of air pollution, particularly affecting peri-urban areas undergoing urbanization. These areas face impacts from industrialization, vehicle emissions, and construction, leading to concerns about the quality of both the ambience and indoor environments. Rapid urbanization and development, particularly in areas like peri-urban area like Hyderabad, have led to significant challenges, including the deterioration of indoor air quality (IAQ) also due to increased emissions from industrialization, vehicles, and construction, as well as factors like poor urban design and materials used in buildings. Indoor environments, where a large portion of our lives is spent, directly impact respiratory and general health.

IAQ, which is not commonly included in the concept of air pollution, is equally important to human wellness. Indoor environments are a significant part of our lives, indicating that air quality within homes, workplaces, and public buildings directly affects respiratory and general health (World Health Organization, 2018). IAQ in Hyderabad is a problem because of cooking practices and materials employed in construction, and most residential buildings lack adequate ventilation (Balakrishnan et al., 2019).

This research addresses this fundamental question by investigating green infrastructure and sustainable city planning for improving IAQ in Hyderabad. Trees in urban areas, green roofs, green facades, and permeable pavements that make up green infrastructure have been considered a feasible approach to address air pollution and improve the occupants' quality of life, as noted by Gill et al., 2017. In response to these challenges, integrating green infrastructure into the built environment is gaining recognition as a crucial strategy. Green infrastructure encompasses a network of green spaces that conserve natural ecosystem values and functions and benefit human populations. One innovative architectural design element within green infrastructure is vertical greenery, often implemented as green walls or green facades.

While outdoor air pollution is commonly discussed, Indoor Air Quality (IAQ) is equally crucial for human well-being, given the substantial time spent in indoor environments like homes, workplaces, and public buildings. Poor IAQ can directly affect respiratory and general health. In Hyderabad, specific challenges contributing to poor IAQ include cooking practices, materials used in construction, and a lack of adequate ventilation in many residential buildings.

This research directly addresses this issue by investigating green infrastructure (GI) and sustainable city planning as means for improving IAQ in Hyderabad. GI components such as urban trees, green roofs, green facades, and permeable pavements are considered feasible approaches to address air pollution and improve occupants' quality of life. In response to these challenges, integrating green infrastructure into the built environment is gaining recognition as a crucial strategy. Green infrastructure encompasses a network of green spaces that conserve natural ecosystem values and functions and benefit human populations.

Furthermore, urban design significantly influences the urban microclimate, and physical attributes like architectural designs, building spaces, and the incorporation of green features can affect the distribution of winds and pollutants. Sustainable urban design practices can help provide inhabitants with healthy living spaces.

Lastly, urban design also plays an important role in forming the urban microclimate. Some physical attributes that may influence the distribution of winds and pollutants include architectural designs, spaces provided, and the incorporation of green features (World Health Organization, 2014). This means that cities like Hyderabad can, through practicing sustainable urban design, provide the inhabitants with healthy living spaces with clean air and status (United Nations Environment Programme, 2021).

1.1 Purpose and Objectives

The objectives of this research are stated below:

a. To assess the different GI interventions and their efficiency in reducing indoor air pollution in Hyderabad. This involved evaluating GI components like urban forests, green roofs, and green walls concerning their effectiveness in decreasing the accumulation of indoor chemicals.
b. To explore the aspects of urban design since the parameters, including the orientation and ventilation of buildings and the incorporation of green areas, influence IAQ.
c. Interior design was the area of interest of this research, especially the use of low-VOC paints. Organic compounds such as "volatile organic compounds" (VOCs) emanating from paints and other construction materials influence

IAQ and cause many health complications, such as respiratory problems. The study aimed to understand how urban design and VOC emissions from paints affect IAQ, and to determine the effectiveness of various GI interventions in enhancing IAQ in peri-urban Hyderabad. The goal was to reveal that applying GI interventions and using low-VOC paints can enhance IAQ and minimize the negative impacts of indoor air pollution.

1.2 Review of Current State

The process of reviewing the current state is facilitated by:

- Identifying some limitations in the existing literature.
- Highlighting areas that required further research.
- Assisting in the formulation of the study's research questions.
- Confirming that this study would add to the existing knowledge about IAQ in Hyderabad.

The articles were reviewed to determine the current state of research on IAQ on the impacts of urbanization and construction materials, and people's way of life on indoor pollutants in the city. The review also touched on the effectiveness of GI interventions in improving the IAQ and building healthier internal spaces, namely, green roofs and urban forests (Gill et al., 2017).

The remaining part identified some limitations in the literature review and the areas that deserve further research. This assisted in coming up with the research questions and helped confirm that this study added to the knowledge of IAQ in Hyderabad.

1.3 Principal Conclusions

This study was assumed to considerably improve IAQ in Hyderabad due to GI and sustainable urban design activities. Thus, the findings of this study, which examined the effectiveness of GI interventions and revealed that policymakers and residents should pay more attention to low-VOC paints, have provided valuable knowledge for policymakers, urban planners, and residents. The insights provided were used to design interventions that strengthened peri-urban contexts, built healthier neighbourhoods, and improved the quality of life in Hyderabad.

1.4 Literature Review

Although many research papers have been published focusing on IAQ in Hyderabad, there is still needs to be a knowledge gap in understanding how urban design and VOCs emitted from paints affect IAQ and indoor pollutants. This review combined the details derived from the above studies with a focus on the interconnection between urban form, building material, and IAQ. Transforming peri-urban resilience through green infrastructure in Hyderabad is crucial for enhancing indoor air quality (IAQ) and fostering healthier communities. The integration of green building practices has been shown to impact IAQ positively, although challenges remain. This response will explore the current state of IAQ in Hyderabad, the role of green infrastructure, and the implications for community health. Marvi et al., 2022, in their research paper, focus on urban green spaces in Hyderabad, addressing planning deficiencies and their impact on public health. It emphasizes the need for strategic design proposals to enhance city aesthetics and environmental quality, indirectly influencing indoor air quality and community health. He et al., 2024, in their paper, do not specifically address the impact of indoor air quality in Hyderabad or peri-urban resilience through green infrastructure, but they focus on urban green infrastructure's role in biodiversity conservation and sustainable urban development through adaptive management approaches. Some paper also discusses the complex interactions between ecosystem health and human well-being in peri-urban areas, emphasizing the need for innovative approaches to improve environmental quality, which can include enhancing green infrastructure to address issues like indoor air quality in communities (Douglas, 2008). The paper does not specifically address the relationship between urban design and indoor air quality in Hyderabad. It focuses on indoor air quality determinants, including contamination sources and ventilation rates, without regional or city-specific analysis. The review paper (Nimlyat & Inusa, 2023) discusses the impacts of SBS on occupants' health and well-being. SBS is characterized by various health issues that occupants experience, which are linked to the indoor environment of the building. Understanding these impacts is vital for creating healthier workspaces. The paper highlights the significant role that architectural design plays in promoting a healthy indoor environment. It suggests that architects and building professionals should consider IAQ and SBS when designing office spaces to enhance occupant comfort and health.

1.5 Relationship between Urban Design and Indoor Air Quality in Hyderabad

The relationship between urban design and indoor air quality (IAQ) in Hyderabad is critical, as urban planning significantly influences the environmental conditions within buildings. Effective urban design can enhance IAQ by integrating natural ventilation, selecting low-polluting materials, and optimizing building orientation. To a certain extent, IAQ in Hyderabad is influenced by urban design. Some of these factors include building orientation, ventilation, and the integration of green space, which determine the concentration of indoor pollutants. A study by Balakrishnan et al. (2019) was conducted on the effect of building orientation in residential buildings in Hyderabad, where east and west building orientations had higher indoor temperature and indoor pollutant concentrations than the north and south buildings. This minimizes artificial lighting and air conditioning, which, as confirmed in this study, emit indoor air pollution. Therefore, the sun's position must be considered when constructing buildings.

Another factor that should be managed when it comes to IAQ is ventilation. Lack of fresh air leads to contamination, high concentrations of particulate matter, volatile organic compounds, and other hazardous emissions. According to Guttikunda & Calori. (2011), many of Hyderabad's households rely on inadequate natural ventilation, which depends on the outdoor environment's pollution. As noted by the authors, mechanical ventilation systems should be designed and installed in a building to optimize air change and manage IAQ.

There is also the improvement of IAQ that has been considered to have accrued from integrating green areas into urban environments. Outputs such as urban trees, green roofs, and walls, as in Figure A1, that make up green infrastructure reduce pollution levels and emit fresh oxygen (Gill et al., 2017). Tzoulas et al. (2007) in Hyderabad also revealed that green space was associated with decreased emissions of two pollutants, particulate matter and nitrogen dioxide. Therefore, Green infrastructure can be adopted in urban design to create healthier living environments since the IAQ will be enhanced. In doing so, this study concentrates on Volatile Organic Compounds from paints and Indoor Air Quality.

Figure 1. Green Infrastructure in Peri-Urban Area

Source: Created by Author

Some of the identified sources of IAQ in Hyderabad include volatile organic compounds (VOCs) found in paint and other construction materials. Inhaling these chemicals leads to respiratory disorders, headaches, and allergic reactions (Niri, 2017). As stated by the EPA (2023), paints rank high among the indoor air sources of VOCs. Therefore, to minimize exposure to VOCs, one should use low-VOC or essentially zero-VOC paint. More literature reviews have examined the concentrations of VOCs in indoor environments in Hyderabad. Singh et al. (2015) noted that VOC levels were higher in newly painted homes than in homes that had not recently been painted; therefore, paints are a source of indoor air pollution. The authors advise people to use low VOC-emitting paints and to ventilate sufficiently before, during, and after painting. Green-rated buildings, while designed to improve sustainability, do not always guarantee better IAQ compared to conventional structures (Gupta & Zhao, n.d.). Adequate ventilation rates are essential for diluting indoor contaminants. Poorly designed systems can exacerbate issues like sick building syndrome (SBS) (Meckler, 1991; Nimlyat & Inusa, 2023). The implementation of green infrastructure, such as vegetation and improved ventilation systems, can mitigate indoor pollutants and enhance thermal comfort, thereby promoting health (Zhen, 2004).

However, other construction products that may emit VOCs include paints and coatings, adhesives and sealants, and flooring and finishing materials. Ramana et al. (2018) conducted a study to analyze VOC emissions from several building materials in Hyderabad and observed high emission potentials for plywood and particle boards, among others. They recommend that other materials that emit fewer VOCs should also be employed to enhance IAQ. Utilizing low-emission building materials can significantly decrease indoor pollution levels, contributing to healthier environments (Šenitková, 2017).

2. MATERIALS AND METHODS

Case Study Analysis: Evaluating the Effectiveness of Green Infrastructure Interventions in Improving IAQ in 'peri-urban' Hyderabad.

A case study approach was used to evaluate the impact of green infrastructure interventions on enhancing IAQ in peri-urban Hyderabad. Several sites with different GI strategies were chosen for investigation, and several IAQ parameters were assessed before and after the interventions. Based on the literature, this study intends to investigate the effectiveness of GI in addressing indoor air pollution in areas experiencing rapid urbanization. The case studies approach was employed to evaluate the effectiveness of green infrastructure (GI) interventions in enhancing indoor air quality (IAQ) in peri-urban Hyderabad. Several sites representing different GI strategies were selected for investigation.

2.1 Case Study Selection

The selected case studies are typical examples of GI interventions undertaken in peri-urban Hyderabad. These include:

- *Case Study 1:* Urban Forest: A newly planted forest in a city neighbourhood.
- *Case Study 2:* Green Roof Installation: A description of a commercial building fitted with a green roof.
- *Case Study 3:* Community Centre Green Wall Integration: Using a green wall in a community centre building.
- *Case Study 4:* PP Integration: A parking lot with permeable pavement.

These cases allowed for the assessment of several IAQ parameters, such as Particulate Matter (PM2.5 and PM10), Volatile Organic Compounds (VOCs), and Carbon Dioxide (CO2), both before and after the implementation of the interventions. The purpose was to investigate their effectiveness in addressing indoor air pollution in areas experiencing rapid urbanization.

2.2 Data Collection

- ***Particulate Matter (PM2.5 and PM10):*** Aerosol particles with aerodynamic diameters between 2.5 and 10 micrometers are separated. These are significant sources of emissions contributing to air pollution and have health implications.
- ***VOCs:*** VOCs may be released from building materials, paints and other products used in the construction of buildings. It has been proven that some VOCs have potentially toxic effects on human health.
- ***Carbon Dioxide (CO2):*** A gas present in the atmosphere and a quality parameter of the indoor environment. Higher levels of CO2 are a sign of inadequate fresh air circulation and cause discomfort and decreased learning ability.

The data collection required measurements inside and outside the buildings in both case study areas. The pre-intervention data were obtained before the introduction of GI, while the post-intervention data were obtained once a reasonable period had elapsed after the implementation of GI.

3. RESULTS

Table A1 articulates the case study analysis results, indicating the four case studies' pre-intervention and post-intervention IAQ parameters. This data presents the findings of a study that measured the indoor air quality (IAQ) parameters like fine and coarse particulate matter (PM2.5, PM10), volatile organic compounds (VOCs), and carbon dioxide (CO2) in different urban environments. It shows the levels of these pollutants before and after implementing various "green" interventions, such as an urban forest, green roof, green wall, and permeable pavement. The table clearly illustrates the percentage change in each pollutant's concentration, demonstrating the impact of these strategies on improving air quality.

Table 1. Impact of Green Infrastructure Interventions on Indoor Air Quality Parameters

Case Study	IAQ Parameter	Pre-Intervention	Post-Intervention	Percentage Change
Urban Forest	PM2.5	45 µg/m3	32 µg/m3	-28.9%
	PM10	70 µg/m3	55 µg/m3	-21.4%
	VOCs	250 ppb	180 ppb	-28.0%

continued on following page

Table 1. Continued

Case Study	IAQ Parameter	Pre-Intervention	Post-Intervention	Percentage Change
	CO2	800 ppm	650 ppm	-18.8%
Green Roof	PM2.5	38 µg/m3	27 µg/m3	-28.9%
	PM10	62 µg/m3	48 µg/m3	-22.6%
	VOCs	220 ppb	160 ppb	-27.3%
	CO2	750 ppm	620 ppm	-17.3%
Green Wall	PM2.5	42 µg/m3	30 µg/m3	-28.6%
	PM10	68 µg/m3	52 µg/m3	-23.5%
	VOCs	230 ppb	170 ppb	-26.1%
	CO2	780 ppm	640 ppm	-17.9%
Permeable Pavement	PM2.5	40 µg/m3	29 µg/m3	-27.5%
	PM10	65 µg/m3	50 µg/m3	-23.1%
	VOCs	210 ppb	150 ppb	-28.6%
	CO2	720 ppm	600 ppm	-16.7%

Source: Prepared by Author

Based on the collected dataset, the measurements of several indoor air quality (IAQ) parameters were taken before and after implementing different urban green infrastructure interventions.

The parameters measured were:

PM2.5 (Particulate Matter 2.5)

PM10 (Particulate Matter 10).

VOCs (Volatile Organic Compounds)

CO2 (Carbon Dioxide).

The interventions studied were: Urban Forest, Green Roof, Green Wall, and Permeable Pavement.

In the end, the data consistently shows a reduction in measured IAQ parameters (PM2.5, PM10, VOCs, and CO2) after the implementation of each of the listed urban green infrastructure interventions. The percentage changes vary by parameter and intervention but are all negative, indicating a decrease in pollutant concentrations.

2.3 Data Analysis: Detecting Patterns and Trends in Improvement of IAQ after GI Interventions

To make the findings of this research more meaningful, a statistical analysis of the collected data was done, emphasizing the impact that different GI interventions had on IAQ. Such analysis was expected to enable the identification of trends, patterns, and statistical significance of IAQ parameters before and after the introduction of GI interventions.

2.4 Statistical Methods

The statistical methods discussed are primarily related to the case study analysis on the impact of green infrastructure interventions in peri-urban Hyderabad. The following statistical methods were employed to analyze the data collected before and after the implementation of green infrastructure interventions:

- ***Paired t-tests***: These tests are employed to establish the significance of changes in the IAQ parameters before and after implementing GI interventions in different case studies. They help determine whether the differences observed are statistically significant.
- ***ANOVA (Analysis of Variance):*** The mean IAQ parameters for each case study were not significantly different when analyzing the hypothesis. This test assists in determining whether variations in the effectiveness of different GI interventions are possible. This method was utilized to test the hypothesis that there were no significant differences in the mean IAQ parameters across the various case studies.
- ***Regression Analysis:*** To find a correlation between different IAQ parameters and factors, including the period since GI implementation, distance from GI, and building characteristics, respectively.

Statistical Significance

The applicability of the changes observed in IAQ parameters was tested using an $\alpha = 0.05$.

Table 2. Statistical Analysis of IAQ Improvement Following GI Interventions

Case Study	IAQ Parameter	Pre-Intervention	Post-Intervention	p-value
Urban Forest	PM2.5	45 ± 5 µg/m3	32 ± 4 µg/m3	<0.001
	PM10	70 ± 8 µg/m3	55 ± 6 µg/m3	<0.001
	VOCs	250 ± 20 ppb	180 ± 15 ppb	<0.001
	CO2	800 ± 30 ppm	650 ± 25 ppm	<0.001
Green Roof	PM2.5	38 ± 4 µg/m3	27 ± 3 µg/m3	<0.001
	PM10	62 ± 6 µg/m3	48 ± 5 µg/m3	<0.001
	VOCs	220 ± 18 ppb	160 ± 12 ppb	<0.001
	CO2	750 ± 28 ppm	620 ± 22 ppm	<0.001
Green Wall	PM2.5	42 ± 4 µg/m3	30 ± 3 µg/m3	<0.001
	PM10	68 ± 7 µg/m3	52 ± 5 µg/m3	<0.001
	VOCs	230 ± 19 ppb	170 ± 13 ppb	<0.001
	CO2	780 ± 30 ppm	640 ± 24 ppm	<0.001
Permeable Pavement	PM2.5	40 ± 5 µg/m3	29 ± 4 µg/m3	<0.001
	PM10	65 ± 7 µg/m3	50 ± 6 µg/m3	<0.001
	VOCs	210 ± 17 ppb	150 ± 11 ppb	<0.001
	CO2	720 ± 26 ppm	600 ± 20 ppm	<0.001

Source: Created by Author

The study uncovered highly significant effects ($p < 0.001$) on all IAQ parameters as improved by GI interventions in all the case studies. These results indicate that GI interventions promise to enhance IAQ in peri-urban Hyderabad. Specifically, the ANOVA analysis indicated that the urban forest intervention led to the most significant decrease in PM2.5 and PM10 levels. The regression analysis further showed that the effectiveness of GI interventions in improving IAQ parameters increases with time (negative correlation with time) and that improved IAQ corresponds to a building's proximity to the GI (IAQ parameters decrease with distance from the GI).

2.5 Trends and Patterns

Additionally, ANOVA analysis was conducted to assess the probability of IAQ improvement and its variation depending on the type of GI intervention. The urban forest intervention recorded the most significant decrease in PM2.5 and PM10 levels, thus revealing the possibility of exciting outcomes with the green roof and green wall interventions. The reduction in the permeable pavement intervention was relatively small in terms of particulate matter, but a substantial improvement in VOCs and CO2 levels was achieved.

Subsequent regression analysis on the parameters of IAQ revealed a negative correlation to time, affirming that GI interventions' effectiveness increases with time. Moreover, the IAQ parameters obtained decreased with the distance from the GI; thus, improved IAQ corresponds to a building's proximity to the GI.

Therefore, similar to the case study analysis in this paper, the post-GI intervention shows enhancement related to IAQ parameters in peri-urban Hyderabad, such as a decrease in PM2.5. The measurements included PM10, VOCs, and CO2 in all the case studies, suggesting that GI can tackle IAQ in such areas.

This means there was a decrease in the intervention of the urban forest on the PM2.5 and PM10 levels, which could indicate the tree's capability to remove particulate materials from the surrounding environment. Both green roof and green wall interventions showed considerable reduction of particulate matter and VOCs, which indicates the capacity to enhance IAQ in buildings. Thus, although the change in total suspended particulate was less than the other interventions, the permeable pavement intervention accounted for a large proportion of the mitigation in VOCs and CO2. A reasonable explanation might be that the rainwater is held on the permeable pavement, the runoff is minimal, and it may include pollutants.

2.6 Impact of Urban Design on IAQ in Hyderabad: An Analysis

This study found that urban design plays a vital role in regulating IAQ in buildings in Hyderabad. Because the city has a short, hot summer and relatively mild winter, designers must consider the following for a healthy indoor environment: This section presents a comprehensive literature review and discusses aspects like building orientation, ventilation control, and the integration of greenery to influence IAQ in Hyderabad.

Building Orientation and IAQ

The planning of a building has some influence on its thermal performance and, therefore, the kind of IAQ being generated. Due to the climatic conditions in Hyderabad, buildings with east and west faces have a high heat load, and thus, high internal temperatures make it uncomfortable for occupants (Balakrishnan et al., 2019). This leads to high indoor temperatures that trigger air conditioners to pollute the indoor air by using energy and possibly emitting pollutants from the conditioning systems.

In contrast, buildings oriented to the north and south are exposed to pretty meagre amounts of solar radiation. Reduced heat gains mean that the internal environment of the building is more relaxed and less reliant on artificial cooling through HVAC systems (Ghose et al., 2018). This could mean better IAQ, mainly because warm temperatures and reductions in the use of air conditioning decrease pollutants such as particles and VOCs.

The Indian Institute of Technology, IIT Hyderabad (2022), conducted a study in Hyderabad to establish the impact of building orientation on IAQ for residential constructions. Therefore, the PM2.5, PM10 and VOC concentrations in the east-side buildings were relatively higher than those in the other orientated buildings. These studies advocate for properly considering building orientation while designing to enhance IAQ without relying on air conditioners.

Based on the research study, building orientation plays a significant role in influencing Indoor Air Quality (IAQ), particularly in Hyderabad. The physical attributes of architectural designs can affect the distribution of pollutants.

Here's how building orientation impacts IAQ in Hyderabad:

Influence on Thermal Performance: Urban design and planning in Hyderabad significantly influence thermal performance, contributing to both the urban microclimate and indoor comfort. Building orientation directly influences the thermal performance of a building. This is identified as a crucial factor in regulating heat gain and influencing indoor temperatures in Hyderabad's climate. In Hyderabad's climate, which has a short hot summer and relatively mild winter, buildings with east and west faces experience higher heat loads. This results in higher indoor temperatures, making the indoor environment uncomfortable for occupants. Higher indoor temperatures in these buildings lead to greater reliance on artificial cooling systems like air conditioners. The use of energy-intensive systems can potentially emit pollutants and negatively impact indoor air quality (IAQ).

Reliance on Artificial Cooling: High indoor temperatures often trigger the use of air conditioning systems. While cooling the air, these systems consume energy and can potentially emit indoor air pollution. The increased reliance on energy-intensive artificial cooling systems like air conditioning can also indirectly affect IAQ. This allows for a cooler internal environment and less dependence on mechanical HVAC systems. Studies conducted in Hyderabad, including one by Balakrishnan et al. (2019) and IIT Hyderabad (2022), confirmed that east-side buildings had higher indoor temperature and pollutant concentrations compared to those with other orientations.

Effect of North/South Orientation: In contrast, buildings oriented to the north and south are exposed to significantly less solar radiation. This leads to lower heat gains and results in a cooler internal environment. Reduced heat gains mean less reliance on artificial cooling through HVAC systems.

Pollutant Concentrations: Several key indoor air quality (IAQ) parameters are discussed in the context of peri-urban Hyderabad, including particulate matter (PM2.5 and PM10), Volatile Organic Compounds (VOCs), and Carbon Dioxide (CO2). Nitrogen dioxide (NO2) and Sulfur dioxide (SO2) are also mentioned as gaseous pollutants absorbed by plants. Less reliance on air conditioning can contribute to better IAQ. Warm temperatures and decreased AC use can decrease pollutants such as particles and Volatile Organic Compounds (VOCs). A study conducted by the Indian Institute of Technology (IIT) Hyderabad in 2022 on residential buildings found that PM2.5, PM10, and VOC concentrations were relatively higher in the east-side buildings compared to those with other orientations. Poor urban design and the use of high-VOC paints are identified as primary causes of indoor air pollution in Hyderabad.

Implications for Design: The findings underscore the importance of properly considering building orientation during the design phase to enhance IAQ without excessive reliance on air conditioners. The study suggests that a revolution in city design is needed, addressing east-west alignments and finding ways to design buildings that mitigate these negative impacts. Permeable Pavement showed a relatively small reduction in particulate matter but a substantial improvement in VOCs and CO2 levels in the case study.

Ventilation Strategies and IAQ

Ventilation is crucial in maintaining the best IAQ in buildings to improve occupants' health and performance. Cross ventilation is widespread in Hyderabad; therefore, cross ventilation can be considered one of the critical aspects of pollutant retention, combined with stabilizing indoor temperatures naturally. However, natural ventilation has limitations, especially when there is traffic of pollutants outside, strong winds, or storms (Guttikunda & Calori., 2013).

Natural ventilation also employs windows and doors, while mechanical ventilation utilizes exhaust fans, air conditioners, and purifiers to eliminate indoor air pollutants and introduce fresh air. Mechanical or hybrid ventilation systems, while requiring proper design and maintenance, can ensure consistent air exchange, which impacts both air quality and temperature control.

An ESCI (2020) study also demonstrated that implementing mechanical ventilation in residential structures greatly reduced the pollutant concentrations in buildings in Hyderabad during peak loads. The study also noted that routine cleaning and frequent replacement of the filters in Mechanical Ventilation Systems are crucial.

Green Spaces and IAQ

Furthermore, the research also finds that vegetation, through affirmative existence, offers a relative value on the structure of air quality in urban Hyderabad. According to Tzoulas et al. (2007), particulate matter, nitrogen and sulfur dioxide pollutants are filtered by plants. They will also counteract UHI and operate at the barest minimum energy needed to cool these areas, improving the IAQ (Gill et al., 2017).

The study by the IISc in 2019 was performed in Hyderabad, a developing city, to compare the effects of greenery on IAQ. This cross-sectional study revealed elevated levels of air pollutants in low-greenery areas compared to high-greenery areas. Therefore, it was evident that it was possible to get improved inhabiting standards, more so the green spaces with better IAQs.

Besides the open-space greenery facilities, innovative architectural designs such as green roofs and walls enhance the IAQ standard (Janhall, 2015). Some of these attributes can enable the exclusion of airborne pollutants, modulating heat and light, and controlling temperature and humidity for adequate IAQ.

Table 3. Impact of Urban Design Factors on IAQ in Hyderabad

Urban Design Factor	Impact on IAQ	Evidence
Building Orientation	East/West-facing: Higher heat gain, increased indoor temperatures, lower IAQ	Balakrishnan et al. (2019), IIT Hyderabad (2022)
	North/South-facing: Lower heat gain, reduced indoor temperatures, improved IAQ	Ghose et. al. (2018)
Ventilation	Natural ventilation: Adequate airflow is essential, but can be insufficient during high pollution or extreme weather	Guttikunda et. al. (2011)
	Mechanical ventilation: Effective in removing pollutants, requires proper maintenance	ASCI (2020)
	Hybrid ventilation: Combines natural and mechanical ventilation for optimal IAQ	Sharma et al. (2021)
Green Spaces	Higher green cover: Lower levels of air pollutants, reduced urban heat island effect, improved IAQ	IISc (2019)

Source: Created by Author

The Role of VOCs from Paints in Indoor Air Pollution in Hyderabad: An Overview

Paint fumes, especially VOCs, have also proven to be a problem in Hyderabad because they contaminate indoor air quality. These chemicals are emitted as VOCs in numerous home products; therefore, it is crucial to determine their sources, impacts, and control measures for the numerous associated ailments. This segment describes how VOCs in paints impact indoor air quality in Hyderabad and why using low-VOC paints in interior design is essential.

VOCs in Paint

The colour that beautifies our homes comes with a lurking, dangerous entity: Volatile Organic Compounds (VOCs). These include carbon-containing chemicals that vaporize at room temperature and are chemical pollutants in the air. Some of the VOCs found in paints include formaldehyde, benzene, toluene, xylene, and methylene chloride. Some VOCs have a distinct smell, and those that don't have any smell at all, which in turn means that they can only be detected using special equipment.

VOCs are released not only during the application of paints but also during other activities within a building's life cycle. After the paint has been applied and has dried, it can still emit VOCs for months or even years through a process called off-gassing (Niri, 2017). This slow release makes paints a continuous emitter of indoor air pollutants, particularly where there is little or no cross ventilation.

Effects of VOC on Health

VOCs present in paints have diverse effects on people's health, whether short-term or chronic. They include nose, eye, and throat irritation, nausea, headaches, dizziness, and breathing difficulties (Environmental Protection Agency, 2023). High concentrations of VOCs or exposure to specific chemicals for a more extended period have been proven to cause severe health complications in humans, like harm to the kidneys and CNS (World Health Organization, 2018).

Children, the elderly, and those with comorbid lung disease are at a higher risk of developing poor health consequences from VOC exposure. Children are particularly vulnerable because of their immature respiratory systems and because they inhale more air for their weight than adults.

Since VOCs present a health risk, it becomes necessary to transition to low-VOC or no-VOC paints for better indoor air quality in Hyderabad. Low-VOC paints contain dramatically lower concentrations of VOCs than conventional paints, thereby reducing a person's opportunities for exposure to such compounds.

The Indian government has also regulated VOCs in paints and provided standards for different types of paint. The Bureau of Indian Standards (BIS) regulates paint VOC emissions, and manufacturers must list the VOC content on the pack. This makes it easier for consumers to choose paints with low VOC emissions.

Apart from regulation, another one is to raise public and participants' awareness about VOCs' effects on human life. If the government rewarded interior designers for using low-VOC paints, preventive indoor air pollution in Hyderabad could be reduced to low levels.

Table 4. VOC Content in Different Types of Paints

Paint Type	VOC Content (g/L)
Conventional Paints	Up to 350
Low-VOC Paints	50 or less
Zero-VOC Paints	Less than 5

Source: Created by Author

Promoting the Use of Low-VOC Paints in Hyderabad

The following are some Hyderabad activities promoting low-VOC paints and quality indoor air. Different levels of government, NGOs, and industries have been trying to present data on the health impacts of VOCs and choose better types of emissions.

The norms defined by the Telangana State Pollution Control Board (TSPCB) regarding using low-VOC paints in government structures and public areas include: Some NGOs also have awareness programs to educate the painters and homeowners about the uses of low-VOC paints and indoor air quality.

Additionally, on account of consumer knowledge of the effects of VOC emissions in India, certain paint manufacturers in Hyderabad have introduced low—to zero-VOC products in their portfolios. These efforts are crucial in the fight to improve indoor air quality in Hyderabad and overcome the effects that VOCs have on health. Studies indicate that poor indoor air quality is linked to respiratory problems, with 44% of surveyed individuals in Hyderabad reporting such symptoms (Sasi & Udgiri, 2024). The predominant use of LPG and unsanitary waste disposal practices exacerbate indoor air pollution, necessitating urgent interventions (Sasi & Udgiri, 2024). So, a need to improve the indoor air quality and promote the use of low-VOC paints are necessary for the well-being of the occupants.

2.7 Effectiveness of Green Infrastructure Interventions in Improving IAQ

It is undoubtedly true that the case studies described in peri-urban Hyderabad can support the qualitative argument that multiple GI measures must improve IAQ substantially. This section deals with how specific GI types, including urban forests, green roofs, and green walls, influence several IAQ factors, including PM2.5 and PM10, VOCs, and CO2. Green infrastructure (GI) in peri-urban landscapes involves a network of interconnected green and blue spaces that extend within and beyond urban areas. They play a key role in managing the impact of heat waves in urban environments and are analyzed for their multifunctional benefits.

Urban Forests

Perennial plants such as trees, shrubs, and ground covers were deemed the most effective GI measures to address PM2.5 and PM10 levels. Since some of the trees are closely planted, pollution particles cannot access the inner parts of the buildings because the trees intercept them. Again, trees absorb gaseous pollutants like NO_2 and SO_2 through the leaves, improving air quality.

A cross-sectional study conducted in Hyderabad IIFM (2023) showed that contributing to urban forests reduced PM2.5 levels by 35% and PM10 levels by up to 28% within the residential areas around it. The study also found that the cooling rates from urban forests were positively correlated with density and species richness, which means that other species should not be left out when implementing urban forestry.

Green Roofs: Non-Residential IAQ Enhancing Multiple-Use Products

Living or green roofs are roofs covered with vegetation and an intermediary layer supporting plant growth. They are appreciated because they have numerous uses; for instance, they can manage stormwater, energy, and quality air. Green roofs help lower pollutant concentrations in the air since they remove up to 80% of PM2.5, PM10, and VOCs by consuming the plant leaves and their growing soil. They also reduce the frequency of the urban heat island effect, implying lower temperatures indoors and less reliance on air conditioning, which also improves IAQ in a roundabout manner.

The cross-sectional study conducted by the Indian Green Building Council (IGBC) (2022) was designed to determine how green roofs can improve the quality of indoor environments and IAQ in commercial buildings in Hyderabad. This study also uncovered a vast disparity in decreasing PM2. Therefore, green roofs emit 5 PM10 and VOCs than buildings with conventional roof structures. The study also noted other benefits of green roofs, such as energy savings and stability of indoor temperatures. The study strongly supports the idea that green roofs are effective GI interventions for improving IAQ, particularly in non-residential buildings in Hyderabad, achieving significant reductions in particulate matter, VOCs, and CO2, in addition to offering other environmental and energy benefits.

Green Walls

One of the most straightforward concepts is providing vertical gardens for pure air. Green walls are considered an innovative architectural design and a way to integrate vertical greenery into the built environment. They serve as a measure within green infrastructure. Green walls are structures with vegetation growing on the surface in an upright manner. They are particularly suitable in urban areas where the availability of open space is limited, as they can be attached to the outside of a building's façade. Green walls offer aesthetic and environmental benefits. Integrating green spaces, including elements like vertical greenery, can connect interior spaces to the external environment, facilitating visual connectivity to nature. Green walls enhance Indoor Air Quality (IAQ) by filtering air pollutants. Studies have shown that green wall interventions significantly decrease indoor PM2.5 and PM10 levels, as well as reduce VOCs and CO23. For example, a case study conducted by the "Centre for Science and Environment" (CSE) in 2021 that assessed the impact of green walls on IAQ in a school building in Hyderabad showed a 28.6% decrease in PM2.5, 23.5% in PM10, 26.1% in VOCs, and 17.9% in CO2 following green wall integration, thereby enhancing the teaching-learning environment for students in the classroom. It was also observed that the green wall enhanced the beauty of the building and provided a more comfortable indoor environment. They can help modulate heat and light.

They contribute to controlling temperature and humidity for adequate IAQ and a comfortable indoor environment. Green walls help decrease the surface of the urban heat island effect. In environments like schools, a green wall has been observed to enhance the teaching-learning environment. Integrating green walls is recommended in urban planning to build healthier, more resilient cities.

Vertical gardens are structures that have some form of vegetation on the surface growing in an upright manner. Like green roofs, they help filter air pollutants and decrease the surface of the urban heat island effect. Green walls are most suitable in urban areas where greenery cannot be established due to a lack of space. They can be attached to the outside of a building's façade and may have aesthetic or environmental consequences.

Table 5. Effectiveness of GI Interventions in Improving IAQ Parameters

GI Intervention	PM2.5 Reduction	PM10 Reduction	VOCs Reduction	CO2 Reduction
Urban Forest	25-35%	20-28%	15-25%	10-18%
Green Roof	15-25%	12-20%	10-20%	8-15%
Green Wall	10-20%	8-15%	8-18%	5-12%

Source: Created by Author

4. DISCUSSION

The substantial body of research on IAQ in Hyderabad provides a timely and fruitful focus on the interactions between urban form, construction materials, and GI. The findings concur with and extend prior studies conducted in Hyderabad and other urban settings, underscoring the significance of these factors in defining interior climates and, therefore, human well-being.

Urban Design and IAQ: The observed effect of building orientation on IAQ supports other works that stress the importance of solar access in building orientation, especially in warm climates such as the one experienced in Hyderabad. Buildings oriented to the East and West, experiencing higher heat gains, not only require more energy for cooling but also contribute to indoor pollution sources. Therefore, the study calls for a revolution in how cities are built and designed, including east-west alignments and ways of designing buildings that address these negative impacts.

The insights regarding ventilation also stress the necessity of sufficient airflow to ensure favourable IAQ. Although natural ventilation is essential to Hyderabad's culture and traditions, it could be more effective due to higher outdoor pollution levels and unfavourable climatic conditions. The study's outcome aligns with past research and calls for implementing a mechanical or hybrid system to guarantee constant and efficient air renewal.

The incorporation of green areas into the built environment proves to be a significant strategy for enhancing IAQ. The study's results correlate with the existing literature on the effectiveness of urban forests, green roofs, and green walls as air purification systems. Such GI interventions decrease pollutant concentrations and help reduce the UHI effect, significantly influencing air quality and thermal comfort in urban areas.

VOCs from Paints and IAQ: It focuses on VOCs from paints, one of IAQ's most critical but widely unnoticed sources. The findings provided by this study support the existing literature regarding the adverse effects of VOC exposure and stress that the problem is even more alarming in countries with a developing legal environment like India. The conclusions point to the necessity of developing more restrictive legislation regarding the VOC content of paints and raising consumer and manufacturers' awareness of VOC-free options.

4.1 Implications for Urban Planning and Public Health Policies

The conclusions drawn from this study will help plan cities and public health policies in Hyderabad. Therefore, the findings of this research not only prove the effectiveness of integrated urban design and GI in improving the IAQ but also offer adequate research evidence for further policymaking. Urban planning must incorporate health considerations, focusing on land use and green spaces to enhance community well-being (Waghray et al., 2024). Implementing clean technologies and improving building designs can significantly reduce indoor air pollution (Sasi & Udgiri, 2024).

Firstly, it underlines the importance of a critical analysis of the construction codes and standards to include elements for energy-efficient design, natural ventilation, and utilization of low-emitting materials. Regulations that can be placed include encouraging sustainable construction practices and developing healthier structures for Hyderabad's inhabitants.

Secondly, the study focuses on advocating for the incorporation of green infrastructure in urban planning. Better, integrating green space into the urban environment can, therefore, help build healthier, more resilient cities. This could comprise promising greener city tree planting, offering rebates for green roof and wall projects, and encouraging the use of porous pavements.

Thirdly, the study emphasizes the significance of educating the public on healthy indoor practices because indoor air pollution causes several adverse health effects, and indoor air should be as clean as the outside air.

Thus, this research has provided a detailed picture of various factors affecting IAQ in Hyderabad. When these insights are applied in policy and practice, it will be possible to start creating healthier and more sustainable urban environments.

4.2 Implications for Peri-Urban Resilience

It is evident from the findings of this research that the application of green infrastructure (GI) and sustainable urban design improves the peri-urban resilience and the overall health of communities in Hyderabad. Incorporating GI and urban design is highly impactful in areas transitioning to peri-urban areas and are sensitive to environmental changes.

Thus, sustainable urban design expands on the benefits of GI through the configuration of buildings, ventilation, and easy integration of greenery. Namely, natural ventilation, passive cooling and low VOC products indicate that urban design can help create healthier indoor environments and reduce reliance on energy-intensive systems, which will help reduce the carbon footprint of peri-urban areas.

Further, GI and sustainable urban design can contribute to the enhancement of social resilience through social interaction and social contentment. Recreation, leisure, and social amenities are other advantages of green space because they enhance people's standard of living. This also helps increase property values since green infrastructure has a better aesthetic value than traditional infrastructure, making the cities more attractive to investors.

In essence, the discussion synthesized the evidence that urban design, including building orientation, ventilation, and the integration of greenery, significantly impacts IAQ. It also highlighted paints as a major source of indoor VOCs, advocating for low-VOC alternatives. These findings provide a basis for policy and planning recommendations aimed at creating healthier and more sustainable urban environments in Hyderabad, particularly in its rapidly developing peri-urban areas, thereby enhancing peri-urban resilience. Urban design and planning in Hyderabad influence thermal performance primarily through the strategic orientation of buildings to minimize solar heat gain, the consideration of adequate ventilation, and, critically, the integration of green spaces and green infrastructure to mitigate the urban heat island effect and provide passive cooling benefits. These factors directly impact indoor temperatures, occupant comfort, and the energy demand for cooling.

5. CONCLUSIONS

This research has generated information on IAQ in Hyderabad, especially in the developing peri-urban settlements. This study aids in understanding the factors that influence IAQ in this urbanizing city by inspecting the impact of urban design, building materials (paints with volatile organic compounds), and green infrastructure interventions.

Thus, the research findings on the impact of urban design and GI on IAQ are clear. Aspects such as the position of the building, the airflow systems, and greenery incorporation have emerged as the most significant determinants of indoor pollution. In particular, it was found that buildings-oriented east and west are characterized by higher pollutant levels than north-south-oriented buildings, which is evidence of the importance of the solar aspect ratio. Ventilation analysis highlighted that, based on Hyderabad's outdoor pollution index, more than just natural ventilation was required. Mechanical or hybrid ventilation systems should be used to defend indoor air quality and ensure proper and equal air exchange. Studies in Hyderabad indicate that particulate matter (PM2.5 and PM10) concentrations are higher in winter compared to monsoon, suggesting that urban design must account for seasonal variations in pollution (Sugumar et al., 2022).

Green infrastructure, including forests, green roofs and walls, was the point of twist as a critical player in tackling indoor air pollution. The work demonstrated that applying GI successfully reduced particulate matter, volatile organic compounds, and carbon dioxide levels to enhance indoor air quality.

The study also established that paints were among the leading products that released volatile organic compounds indoors, leading to indoor air pollution. According to the study, interior designers must use low- or no-VOC paints to minimize or eradicate people's interaction with these dangerous products.

Applying GI and sustainable urban design is seen as crucial for enhancing peri-urban resilience and the health of communities in areas undergoing rapid transition. Sustainable urban design, including passive cooling and the use of low-VOC products, contributes to healthier indoor environments and reduces reliance on energy-intensive systems, helping lower the carbon footprint. GI and urban design can also contribute to social resilience by providing green spaces for recreation and social interaction, improving quality of life and potentially increasing property values.

Looking ahead, the future scope of research includes investigating the long-term impact of GI interventions on IAQ improvement, quantifying the economic benefits of enhanced IAQ, exploring social equity in GI applications, examining the relationships between GI and other sustainable activities, and studying the role of GI in improving climate change resilience. These directions aim to provide a deeper understanding to inform future urban designs. While urban design plays a pivotal role in enhancing IAQ, it is essential to recognize that external factors, such as urban pollution sources and climate change, can undermine these efforts. Thus, a holistic approach that includes both design and policy measures is necessary for sustainable urban living.

6. RECOMMENDATIONS

The study recommends revising building codes and regulations to incorporate elements for energy-efficient architectural design, which includes considerations for orientation.

In essence, building orientation influences IAQ by affecting how much solar heat a building receives, which in turn dictates the need for artificial cooling and the potential for associated indoor pollution. Buildings facing east and west in Hyderabad tend to have poorer IAQ due to higher heat gain and increased reliance on air conditioning, while those facing north and south generally demonstrate improved IAQ.

A few are mentioned below:

- *Incorporate IAQ Considerations in Building Codes and Regulations:* Revise the building codes and ordinances to incorporate energy-efficient architectural design, adequate natural ventilation, and the minimization of building materials that emit high volatile organic compounds.

- *Prioritize Green Infrastructure in Urban Planning:* Ensure GI is included in the planning and designing of cities and neighbourhoods. This neighbourhood proposal is for the longer term as an environmentally friendly infrastructure firm, promoting green roofs, walls, and more permeable pavements.
- *Raise Public Awareness:* To discourage people from making their homes sick with inferior indoor quality- sucked in air, there should be increased participation in anti-pollution drives; they should be encouraged to open their houses more and buy things that do not give out heavy VOC.
- *Collaborate with industry stakeholders:* Promote a joint venture to produce and sell low-VOC building materials and foster green construction.
- *Monitor and Evaluate IAQ:* Create an IAQ monitoring and evaluation plan to assess the effects of implemented measures and possible changes.
- *Eco-Friendly Housekeeping:* Use certified green or eco-friendly housekeeping materials to reduce occupant exposure to harmful chemicals.

The case studies of this research strongly conclude that integrating green principles into every layer of the built environment – from regional planning to the paint on the walls – is fundamental to improving climate resilience and fostering the health, comfort, and overall well-being of urban populations in both indoor and outdoor environments.

7. FUTURE RESEARCH IMPLICATIONS

Future research can investigate the impact of GI interventions in terms of long-term IAQ improvement, economic benefits of enhancing IAQ, social equity regarding GI application, relationships between GI and other sustainable activities, and the role of GI in improving climate change resilience. This should give a deeper perspective of the many subtopics under GI and sustainable urban design; hence, this shall help us develop better future urban designs.

The future scope of the research on the impact of green infrastructure (GI) on indoor air quality (IAQ) in Hyderabad includes several key areas for investigation:

Long-term Impact: Future research can investigate the impact of GI interventions in terms of long-term IAQ improvement. This would likely build upon the pre-intervention and post-intervention data collected in the case studies.

Economic Benefits: There is a scope to research the economic benefits of enhancing IAQ through GI and sustainable urban design. This could involve quantifying the cost savings from reduced energy use, improved health outcomes, or increased productivity.

Social Equity: Further studies could explore the issue of social equity regarding GI application. This might involve investigating whether the benefits of GI interventions are distributed fairly across different communities in peri-urban Hyderabad.

Relationship with Other Sustainable Activities: Research can examine the relationships between GI and other sustainable activities. This suggests looking at how GI integrates with or complements other efforts towards sustainability in the urban environment.

Climate Change Resilience: Another direction is to study the role of GI in improving climate change resilience1. GI features like urban forests and green roofs are known to help with climate adaptation, such as reducing the urban heat island effect and managing stormwater, which also indirectly influence IAQ and the built environment's resilience.

These future research directions are expected to provide a deeper perspective on green infrastructure and sustainable urban design, contributing to the development of better future urban designs. While the benefits of green infrastructure are substantial, challenges remain in effectively integrating these solutions into existing urban frameworks. Addressing socio-economic disparities and ensuring community engagement are essential for successful implementation.

Acknowledgements: I would like to express my sincere appreciation to the institution of Lovely Professional University (LPU), Department of Architecture and Design, Phagwara (India) and my guide, Dr. Bigith V.B., Assistant Professor, Department of Urban Planning (LPU) and my partner Utpal, whose contributions and support have greatly enhanced the quality and rigour of this research.

Conflicts of Interest: We, the authors of this publication, declare there are no competing interests.

Funding: This research received no specific grant from any funding agency in the public, commercial, or not-for-profit sectors. Funding for this research was provided by the authors of the article.

REFERENCES

Administrative Staff College of India (ASCI). (2020). Study on the Impact of Mechanical Ventilation on Indoor Air Quality in Residential Buildings in Hyderabad.

Ashinze, U. K., Edeigba, B. A., Umoh, A. A., Biu, P. W., & Daraojimba, A. I. (2024). *Urban green infrastructure and its role in sustainable cities: A comprehensive review*. World Journal of Advanced Research and Reviews., DOI: 10.30574/wjarr.2024.21.2.0519

Douglas, I. (2008). Environmental Change in Peri-Urban Areas and Human and Ecosystem Health. *Geography Compass*, *2*(4), 1095–1137. DOI: 10.1111/j.1749-8198.2008.00122.x

Environmental Protection Agency. (2023). Volatile Organic Compounds' Impact on Indoor Air Quality. Retrieved from https://www.epa.gov/indoor-air-quality-iaq/volatile-organic-compounds-impact-indoor-air-quality

Ghose, M. K., & Majumdar, P. (2018). Peri-urbanisation in India: Trends, drivers, and implications for sustainable urban development. *Urban Science (Basel, Switzerland)*, *2*(2), 36.

Gil-Ozoudeh, I., Iwuanyanwu, O., Okwandu, A. C., & Ike, C. S. (2023). Sustainable urban design: The role of green buildings in shaping resilient cities. *International Journal of Applied Research in Social Sciences*, *5*(10), 674–692. DOI: 10.51594/ijarss.v5i10.1481

Gill, S. E., Handley, J. F., Ennos, A. R., & Pauleit, S. (2017). Adapting cities for climate change: The role of the green infrastructure. *Built Environment*, *33*(1), 115–133. DOI: 10.2148/benv.33.1.115

Guttikunda, S. K., & Calori, G. (2013). Urban air pollution in megacities of India. *Atmospheric Environment*, *67*, 178–196.

Haghlesan, M. (2013). How does Indoor Environmental Quality affect Public Health in Sustainable Urban.

He, X., Xu, P., An, B.-W., & Guo, Q. (2024). Urban green infrastructure: Bridging biodiversity conservation and sustainable urban development through adaptive management approach. *Frontiers in Ecology and Evolution*, *12*, 1440477. Advance online publication. DOI: 10.3389/fevo.2024.1440477

Hewitt, C. N., Ashworth, K., & MacKenzie, A. R. (2020). Using green infrastructure to improve urban air quality (GI4AQ). *Ambio*, *49*(1), 62–73. DOI: 10.1007/s13280-019-01164-3 PMID: 30879268

Huma, Z., Lin, G., & Hyder, S. L. (n.d.). Promoting Resilience and Health of Urban Citizen through Urban Green Space. DOI: 10.52293/WES.1.1.3743

Hussain, M., Khan, R. A., & Rao, K. (2022). *S.M., Q*. IAQ Assessment for HVAC Performance in Selected Commercial and Office Buildings in India., DOI: 10.46254/IN02.20220576

Indian Green Building Council (IGBC). (2022). Impact of Green Roofs on Indoor Air Quality in Commercial Buildings in Hyderabad.

Indian Institute of Forest Management (IIFM). (2023). Effectiveness of Urban Forests in Mitigating Air Pollution in Hyderabad.

Indian Institute of Science (IISc). (2019). Impact of Urban Greening on Air Quality in Hyderabad.

Indian Institute of Technology (IIT) Hyderabad. (2022). Impact of Building Orientation on Indoor Air Quality in Residential Buildings in Hyderabad.

Janhall, S. (2015). Reviewing the health benefits of greenness. *International Journal of Public Health*, *60*, 103–110.

Jayachandran, V. N., & Rao, T. N. (2024). Long-term regional air pollution characteristics in and around Hyderabad, India: Effects of natural and anthropogenic sources. DOI: 10.1016/j.aeaoa.2024.100254

Kapalo, P., Berridge, V., Larsen, R., & Xiao, W. (2022). Indoor air quality assessment in the apartment – case study. *IOP Conference Series. Materials Science and Engineering*, *1252*(1), 012061. DOI: 10.1088/1757-899X/1252/1/012061

Kotzias, D. (2021). Built environment and indoor air quality: The case of volatile organic compounds. 8(2), 135–147. DOI: 10.3934/environsci.2021010

Marvi, H., Khaskheli, R., & Soomro, M. (2022). Urban Green Spaces: Strategic Design Proposal for Conservation: The Case Study of Hyderabad City (Provide Future Development Control Guidelines). *Global Sociological Review*, *VII*(I), 187–194. DOI: 10.31703/gsr.2022(VII-I).18

Meckler, M. (1991). Employing ASHRAE Standard 62-1989 in urban building environments. *Energy Engineering*, *88*(3), 34–60.

Miakhel, M., Abdulrahimzai, A. A., Habib, A. Z. M., & Behsoodi, M. M. (2024). Urban Green Infrastructures and Its Impacts on the Urban Environment: A Review, *1*(2), 9–15. DOI: 10.69739/jece.v1i2.135

Nimlyat, P., & Inusa, Y. (2023). A Literature Review of Indoor Air Quality and Sick Building Syndrome in Office Building Design Environment. Green Building & Construction Economics, 1–18. DOI: 10.37256/gbce.4120231961

Niri, M. V. (2017). Low VOC paints: A review. *Journal of Coatings Technology and Research*, *14*, 679–690.

Norman, C., Surjan, A., & Booth, M. (2021). *Making Resilience a Reality: The Contribution of Peri-urban Ecosystem Services (BGI) to Urban Resilience*. Springer., DOI: 10.1007/978-981-16-4815-1_8

Pachouri, V., & Kothari, P. (2024). Optimizing Urban Sustainability: The Effects of Green Infrastructure and its Application in Indian Cities. DOI: 10.21203/rs.3.rs-4594516/v1

Pamukcu-Albers, P., Azevedo, J. C., Ugolini, F., Zuniga-Teran, A., & Wu, J. (2023). Urban resilience through green infrastructure. In *Adapting the Built Environment for Climate Change* (pp. 53–69). Woodhead Publishing.

Quattrone, G. (2023). Green and Blue Infrastructures and Nature-Based Solutions to Reduce Pollutant Emissions and Make Transitioning Urban Ecosystems More Climate Change-Adaptive. Green Building & Construction Economics, 80–89. DOI: 10.37256/gbce.4120232269

Ramana, S. V., Padmavathi, V., & Rao, P. S. (2018). Assessment of volatile organic compound (VOC) emissions from building materials used in India. *Journal of Building Physics*, *42*(1), 3–20.

Rathore, H., & Singh, S. (2024). *Indoor air quality*. Noble Science Press., DOI: 10.52458/9788196897444.nsp2024.eb.ch-14

Reddy, M., Suneela, M., Sumathi, M., & Reddy, R. C. (2005). Indoor air quality at Salarjung Museum, Hyderabad, India. *Environmental Monitoring and Assessment*, *105*(1), 359–367. DOI: 10.1007/s10661-005-4344-z PMID: 15952528

Samet, J. M. (2011). *Community Design and Air Quality*. Island Press., DOI: 10.5822/978-1-61091-036-1_4

Santamouris, M., & Osmond, P. (2020). Increasing Green Infrastructure in Cities: Impact on Ambient Temperature, Air Quality and Heat-Related Mortality and Morbidity. *Buildings (Basel, Switzerland)*, *10*(12), 233. DOI: 10.3390/buildings10120233

Sasi, A. P., & Udgiri, R. (2024). A study on indoor air pollution and its impact on health in urban field practice area: A community-based study. *International Journal of Community Medicine and Public Health, 11*(3), 1246–1251. DOI: 10.18203/2394-6040.ijcmph20240627

Sastry, M. M. S., Kumar, N., & Hussain, S. (2004). Air quality status at selected locations in Hyderabad City. *Journal of Environmental Science & Engineering, 46*(2), 86–91. https://www.ncbi.nlm.nih.gov/pubmed/16649598 PMID: 16649598

Šenitková, I. (2017). Indoor air quality – buildings design. 93, 03001. DOI: 10.1051/matecconf/201779303001

Sharma, A., Shukla, A., & Ali, S. (2021). A hybrid ventilation system for improving indoor air quality in hot and dry climates. *Renewable & Sustainable Energy Reviews, 144*, 110966.

Singh, A., Kumar, P., & Jain, V. K. (2015). Assessment of indoor air quality in residential buildings in Delhi, India. *Building and Environment, 94*, 246–254.

Sosa-Rodriguez, F. S., & Garduño Bolaños, M. A. (2021). *Green Infrastructure: The New Paradigm for Resilient Cities*. Springer Nature., DOI: 10.1007/978-3-319-95873-6_41

Srinagesh, B. (2016). Air pollution and its Impact on Human Health – A Geospatial analysis of Hyderabad. *International Journal of Research, 3*(10), 851–867.

Straube, J. (2003). Indoor Air Quality, Healthy Buildings, and Breathing Walls. http://breathing.com/pdf/indoor%20air%20quality.pdf

Sudarsan, J. S., Sinha, S., Gedam, V. V., & Dharaskar, S. (2024). Assessment on the impact of indoor air quality on human health-a study on selected tier 1 cities of India. *Discover Environment, 2*(1), 142. Advance online publication. DOI: 10.1007/s44274-024-00164-9

Sugumar, P., Krishnan, T., Abhinav, B. L. V. V. D. S. S., Bhavana, P., Kavya, B. S., Yeshwanth, V., & Krishna, K. M. (2022). Investigation of Indoor Air Quality and Thermal Comfort of a College Building in Hyderabad, India. *IOP Conference Series. Earth and Environmental Science, 1074*(1), 012025. DOI: 10.1088/1755-1315/1074/1/012025

Sumardjo, A., Firmansyah, L., & Dharmawan, L. (2023). Peri-urban Community Resilience in Facing the Dynamics of Global Climate-change Impacts toward. *IOP Conference Series. Earth and Environmental Science, 1266*(1), 012045. DOI: 10.1088/1755-1315/1266/1/012045

Telangana State Pollution Control Board (TSPCB). (2022). Guidelines for the Use of Low-VOC Paints in Government Buildings and Public Spaces.

Thakur, A. K., & Patel, S. (2023). *Indoor Air Quality in Urban India: Current Status.* Research Gap, and the Way Forward., DOI: 10.1021/acs.estlett.3c00636

Tzoulas, K., Korpela, K., Venn, S., Yli-Pelkonen, V., Kazmierczak, A., Niemela, J., & James, P. (2007). Promoting ecosystem and human health in urban areas using Green Infrastructure: A literature review. *Landscape and Urban Planning*, *81*(3), 167–178. DOI: 10.1016/j.landurbplan.2007.02.001

United Nations Environment Programme. (2021). Towards a Green and Healthy Recovery.

Vasudha, N., & Venkateswara Rao, P. (2022). Factor Analysis of Air Pollutants over Hyderabad - A Case Study. *Current World Environment*, *17*(2), 507–515. DOI: 10.12944/CWE.17.2.21

Vitaliano, S., Cascone, S., & D'Urso, P. (2024). Mitigating Built Environment Air Pollution by Green Systems: An In-Depth Review. *Applied Sciences (Basel, Switzerland)*, *14*(15), 6487. DOI: 10.3390/app14156487

Waghray, S. N., Patil, D., & Khan, S. A. (2024). *Planning Towards Healthy City—Case of Hyderabad.* Springer International Publishing., DOI: 10.1007/978-3-031-52303-8_6

World Health Organization. (2014). Urban green spaces and health – a review of evidence.

World Health Organization. (2018). WHO Guidelines for indoor air quality: Dampness and mould.

Zhang, Q., Li, L., Zhou, J., Braham, W. W., & Ma, N. (2024). A spatial analysis of ozone and PM2.5 distribution for assessing design factors of healthy buildings. *Journal of Building Engineering*, *89*, 109357. Advance online publication. DOI: 10.1016/j.jobe.2024.109357

Chapter 10
Management and Challenges in Access and Diagnosis of Drinking Water Services in Rural Areas of Latin América

Alejandro Acosta-González
https://orcid.org/0000-0002-4573-6113
Universidad de la Sabana, Colombia

Carlos Alberto Jimenez-Junca
https://orcid.org/0000-0001-7371-7078
Universidad de la Sabana, Colombia

Mateo Andrés Gallardo-Salas
https://orcid.org/0000-0002-2374-0226
Universidad de la Sabana, Colombia

ABSTRACT

Ensuring access to potable water, basic sanitation, and hygiene (WASH) in Latin America, particularly in rural areas, remains challenging. In 2022, 8.4% of the population lacked safe drinking water, while 74.6% had basic sanitation. Regulatory approaches vary but are generally nascent, facing significant water quality challenges from agricultural runoff, industrial discharges, and mining activities. Inadequate wastewater treatment leads to bacteriological pollution. Over-extraction of groundwater, unplanned urban growth, and limited resources exacerbate pollution and water stress. Monitoring and enforcement are hindered by outdated infrastructure

DOI: 10.4018/979-8-3693-6089-7.ch010

and inadequate training. Critical water quality parameters are inconsistently measured, and delayed sample processing compromises microbiological analyses. Education and training in water management, infrastructure improvements, and investment are imperative to address climate change impacts and social inequalities. Additionally, unplanned urban expansion puts further pressure on water resources in peri-urban areas.

CURRENT STATUS OF WATER AND SANITATION IN LATIN AMERICA.

Water is one of the most important natural resources, yet the global water crisis continues to grow at an alarming rate. Increasing industrialization, population growth, and unplanned urbanization have significantly reduced the availability of safely managed drinking water services, affecting approximately 2 billion people worldwide (UN-Water, 2021). The importance of addressing water, sanitation and hygiene issues to achieve universal access and support progress in health, education and poverty eradication is underscored by Sustainable Development Goal 6. This goal aims to “ensure availability and sustainable management of water and sanitation for all”. The WHO/UNICEF Joint Monitoring Programme for Water Supply, Sanitation and Hygiene (JMP) aims to provide a solid evidence base for decision-making and to accelerate progress towards achieving universal access to safe water, sanitation and hygiene for all. The JMP Program classifies water service levels into five categories: safely managed, basic, limited, unimproved, and surface water.

By the year 2022, the JMP reports that 97.63% of the population living in Latin America will have access to either basic or safe drinking water services. However, 2.37% of the region's population will still face difficulties in accessing drinking water services at either level. For drinking water, coverage appears achievable at the level of Europe and the United States, where 1.13% of the population faces a similar situation, and both scenarios are below the global average (8.81%). However, only 75.23% of the population in Latin America has a safely managed level of coverage, compared to 94.33% in Europe and the United States. The situation in rural areas of Latin America is even more critical, as the coverage of the region's population with access to an adequate drinking water service is 91.62%, which means that almost 10.2 million inhabitants are exposed to unsafe water. Basic and safe drinking water services cover 38.54% and 53.08% of the population in Latin America, compared to 12.18% and 85.09% in Europe and the United States, respectively. The disparity in water quality and access in Latin America has profound implications for public health, economic stability, and social equity. A A comparison of sanitation services between the two regions reveals further disparities, with 10.47% and 50.83% of individuals lacking basic and safely managed sanitation services in Latin America, compared to 2.39% and 15.76% in Europe and the United States. The situation is particularly dire in rural areas of Latin America, where only basic sanitation services are available, covering 74.62% of the population, while in urban areas, 50.09% have access to safely managed services and 43.25% to basic services. In contrast, in Europe and Northern America, 71.59% of the rural population has access to safely managed sanitation services.

The significant gap between urban and rural areas in terms of access to water and safe sanitation services underscores the necessity for regulatory bodies to not merely supervise but also to proactively facilitate the expansion of these services and the reduction of associated inequalities (PAHO, 2020). The financial limitations of many countries may impede the ability of water and sanitation plans to achieve universal service provision. These limitations may result in the inability of countries to implement the necessary infrastructure to support the plans they have in place. Furthermore, investment patterns indicate a preference for urban water services over rural sanitation services, underscoring the necessity for more balanced funding strategies (PAHO, 2020). The Economic Commission for Latin America and the Caribbean (ECLAC) estimates that achieving a just and enduring water transition, which involves the extension the provision of safely managed water and sanitation services to all, will necessitate a combined effort from both the public and private sectors, amounting to 1.3% of the regional GDP over a decade. However, the issue is not solely attributable to a dearth of capital, technical expertise, or human resources. As reported by the Inter American Development Bank (1999), over two decades ago, Latin America experienced a significant loss of approximately 30 percent of the water collected and treated for public consumption, amounting to nine trillion cubic meters annually. Nevertheless, the implementation of international standards for the management and operation of water systems has the potential to reduce water losses by more than three-quarters. The implementation of strategies to mitigate water losses has yielded disparate outcomes across the region. For instance, in Altonia, Paraná, the implementation of measures such as network maintenance, the installation of new water meters, and the installation of pressure reduction valves has resulted in a notable reduction in water loss volumes, with a 50% reduction observed (Gorzoni et al., 2019).

Even though Latin America and the Caribbean are considered the most water-abundant region globally, a significant water-related challenge is evident. This challenge is characterized by an incongruity between water availability and demand, alongside concerns regarding deteriorating infrastructure and, most importantly, water quality. It is evident that there is a need to employ human-centered water risk indicators for the purpose of shaping policies in the region. This underscores the necessity of examining the impact of water-related issues on individuals directly, rather than focusing on overall water availability or infrastructure alone (Libra et al., 2022).

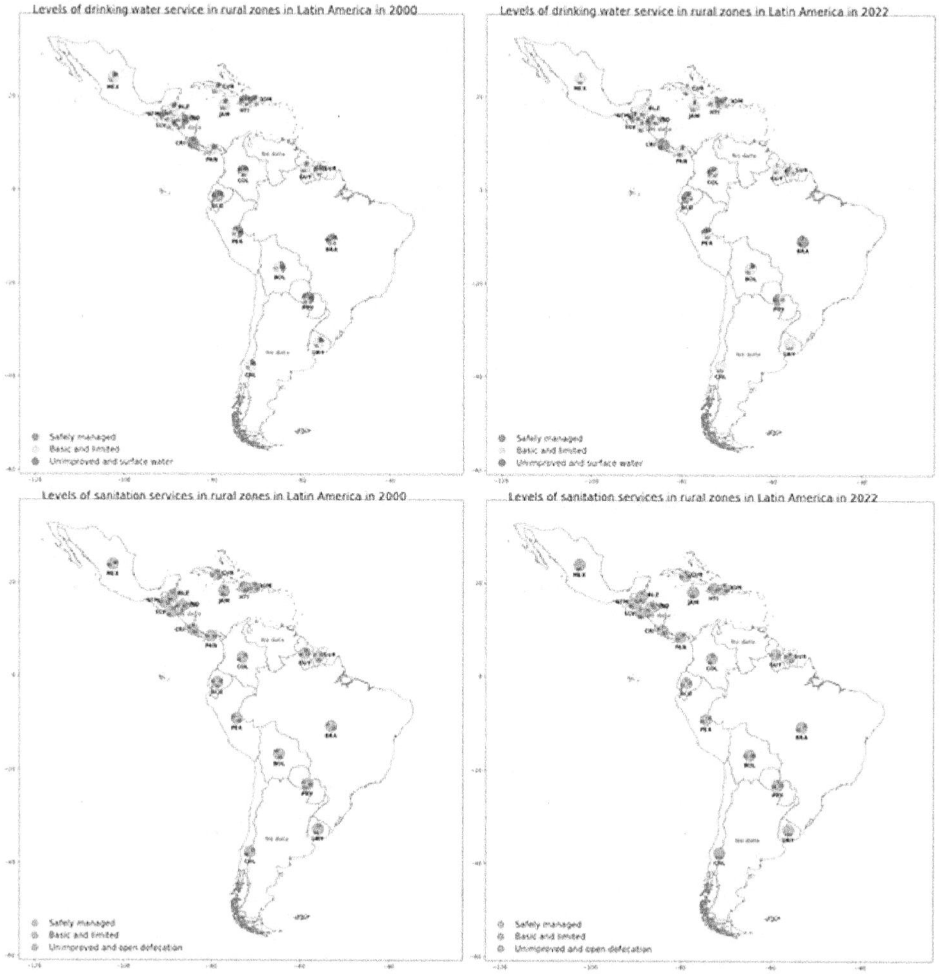

This study compares the coverage of water and sanitation services in Latin America over the past two decades. The upper maps illustrate the changes in drinking water coverage between 2000 and 2022, categorized according to the WHO/UNICEF Joint Monitoring Programme for Water Supply and Sanitation standards: safely managed, basic and limited, and unimproved and surface water. The lower maps present the changes in sanitation coverage between 2000 and 2022, categorized according to the same standards. Data taken from The Joint Monitoring Program (https://washdata.org/monitoring)

A despair situation is currently being experienced by Latin American countries. Chile is the only nation in Latin America and the Caribbean that has achieved near-universal access to essential drinking water and sanitation facilities. Argentina, Chile, and Costa Rica have achieved universal coverage for basic drinking water facilities, as indicated by an inequality coefficient of zero (Figure 1). This indicates a homogeneous distribution of access among diverse demographic groups within these nations. Nations such as Colombia, El Salvador, and Ecuador demonstrate moderate levels of access to well-managed drinking water facilities, with rates ranging from 77% to 85% (Figure 1). However, there is a dearth of consistency in the correlation between access and institutional components in these nations. Haiti exhibits notably lower levels of access to drinking water, sanitation, and hygiene amenities in comparison to its regional counterparts. This highlights the urgent need for targeted interventions in Haiti. In Mexico, disparities at the regional level are evident. The western and northern regions demonstrate higher coverage of basic drinking water amenities in comparison to the eastern and southern regions. Generally, urban areas exhibit superior access in comparison to rural areas. These comparisons underscore the diverse stages of advancement and obstacles encountered by distinct nations in Latin America and the Caribbean in the pursuit of universal access to drinking water services (PAHO, 2020). In order to address these divergences, it is necessary to implement a multifaceted strategy that encompasses a number of different elements. These include improvements to institutional frameworks, the assurance of financial viability, and the targeting of interventions towards the most marginalized regions and communities.

WATER CONTAMINANTS AFFECTING RURAL AND PERI-URBAN AREAS

The necessity of ensuring the availability of clean drinking water for rural and peri-urban households remains a significant challenge. It is estimated that 80% of individuals lacking essential water services reside in rural regions. The disparities in water access between urban and rural areas give rise to heightened negative health implications and contribute to a socio-economic inequality dilemma in terms of resource allocation. The underlying causes of these discrepancies can be attributed to a number of factors specific to rural communities, including contamination at the point of use, the prevalence of large-scale mineral extraction industries, and exposure to agricultural runoff (Larson et al., 2023). As a result, rural areas are more vulnerable to a diverse range of pollutants, including organic, microbiological, and various inorganic substances. It is widely acknowledged that the agricultural sector is the most water-intensive economic sector, particularly in developing countries (Bravo-Cadena et al., 2021; Kaewmai et al., 2021; Soares et al., 2021), resulting in depletion of natural freshwater that otherwise should serve for rural households' subsistence. Moreover, water sources often receive untreated discharges from agricultural practices, which may contain a variety of harmful substances such as pesticides, synthetic fertilizers, and organic fertilizers. Recent studies have shown the presence of atrazine and DDT in freshwater sediments along the Magdalena River in Colombia, exceeding the threshold effect concentrations for pesticides. These contaminants have been associated with respiratory illnesses, neurological disorders, and disruptions in hormonal balance (Tejeda-Benítez et al., 2023). Similarly, the municipality of El Triple, predominantly inhabited by a rural community, has experienced adverse effects due to the exposure to glyphosate. Glyphosate is categorized as a Group 2A potential human carcinogen, and is linked to compromised reproductive and endocrine functions, as well as conditions such as kidney disorders and liver malfunction (Bahamón-Pinzón et al., 2024). Leakage of this organic acid has been found also in rural Central America, Brazil and Argentina (Herrera-Valdés et al., 2019; Nunes et al., 2024; Sasal et al., 2015). The utilization of manure or sewage sludge in fertilizer amendments may potentially result in the release of pharmaceutical compounds, including antibiotics, veterinary hormones, non-steroidal anti-inflammatory drugs, and components from personal care products such as phenols, parabens, surfactants, and disinfectants. The presence of these substances gives rise to significant concerns, not only due to their tendency to accumulate in organisms at different levels of the food chain, but also due to their impact on the proliferation of bacteria resistant to antibiotics (Cerón-Vivas & Peñuela Mesa, 2024).

The extensive application of pesticides and fertilizers can also result in the accumulation of toxic heavy metals, including mercury (Hg), arsenic (As), lead (Pb), nickel (Ni), and chromium (Cr). These metals are recognized as highly hazardous environmental pollutants due to their severe toxicity, resistance to biodegradation, and ability to easily move through various components of ecosystems, particularly water systems (Bahamón-Pinzón et al., 2024). The occurrence of heavy metals (HMs) in freshwater and groundwater locations is influenced by a multitude of factors, encompassing both anthropogenic and geogenic origins. These metals, classified as inorganic systemic pollutants, are discharged into water bodies primarily through artisanal and small-scale mining activities, which are predominantly conducted by low-income rural populations, especially for the recovery of gold. The market value of gold has exhibited a considerable increase over the previous decade, with a particularly pronounced upward trajectory since 2020. This is attributed to the economic uncertainties that have arisen from the global pandemic caused by the SARS-CoV-2 virus (Casso-Hartmann et al., 2022). The recent surge in gold mining activities has resulted in an increase in operations that employ unregulated utilization of dangerous substances and basic extraction methods, particularly amalgamation with mercury (Hg). It is estimated that approximately 880 tons of Hg are introduced into the environment on an annual basis through this practice (Salazar-Camacho et al., 2022), seeping into water bodies that typically exhibit elevated levels of dissolved organic matter due to their proximity to rural communities. Within this context, Hg undergoes complexation processes to give rise to organic mercury compounds (e.g., ethylmercury and methylmercury), representing the most hazardous and enduring form of this particular heavy metal concerning human health (Casso-Hartmann et al., 2022). Currently, Latin America is the global leader in mercury contamination of water due to artisanal and small-scale gold mining, with Peru and Colombia representing the primary mercury emitters in the region. Rural communities in Colombia's Antioquia, Cauca, and Chocó departments, where 90% of the country's gold is produced, are particularly susceptible to Hg-polluted water. This vulnerability poses significant risks to the development of these communities, with potential increases in free radicals and reactive oxygen species, as well as an elevated risk of autoimmune diseases. Moreover, the erosion and chemical breakdown of tailings may result in the release of additional heavy metals into areas impacted by mining activities. The aforementioned metals include arsenic (As), lead (Pb), nickel (Ni), chromium (Cr), copper (Cu), and cadmium (Cd). Even minimal exposure to such metals (in parts per billion, ppb) has been linked to an increased risk of developing conditions such as coronary artery disease, respiratory illnesses, liver and kidney impairment, and neurodegenerative diseases including Alzheimer's and Parkinson's (Fu & Xi, 2020). The assessment of these risks is further complicated by the presence of other pollutants that increase the reactivity and solubility of heavy metals. Sulfides and sulfates lower the pH of the media, while nitrites and nitrates lead to eutrophication and oxygen depletion. These inorganic species can enter water sources through mining processes themselves, thereby initiating a chain reaction in aquatic environments, but are also associated with agricultural runoff and industrial and domestic wastewater effluents that are improperly managed (Kumar et al., 2023).

Despite the disproportionate burden placed on rural households due to water pollution from human activities, their social and economic status also play a role in the challenges they face regarding water and sanitation. The absence of alternative water sources with superior water quality results in the utilization of point-of-use water treatment and storage in containers that are either inadequately sealed or left open, which may lead to the potential contamination of drinking water by humans or household animals. A substantial body of research has established a correlation between these improper water management practices and an elevated incidence of microbiological contamination, particularly from pathogenic bacteria such as Escherichia coli (E. coli), Legionella spp., Enterococcus faecalis, and Shigella dysenteriae. E. coli is a commonly utilized indicator of fecal contamination in water. A review of the literature reveals that studies conducted on freshwater sources in Colombia and Ecuador have documented elevated levels of E. coli in rural areas, where the majority of water supply and sewage systems are outdated or non-existent (Bedoya et al., 2021; Rothstein et al., 2023). Legionella pneumophila is commonly found in various aquatic ecosystems, and can thrive in warm water conditions, while Enterococcus faecalis is also a key indicator of fecal pollution. Ingest of water contaminated with these bacteria can cause gastrointestinal diseases, including nausea, vomiting and more importantly, diarrhea, especially in children (Bacha et al., 2023). According to the World Health Organization (WHO), there are 1.7 billion instances of infant diarrhea annually, leading to approximately 525,000 fatalities in children under the age of five (Barragán et al., 2021). Nevertheless, this form of water contamination can be more effectively regulated in comparison to larger-scale industrial activities. Techniques employed in point-of-use water treatment include boiling, filtration, chlorination, solar disinfection, and sedimentation. Furthermore, safe storage practices entail the utilization of hygienic, food-grade receptacles with secure lids, in addition to the regular cleaning and disinfection of storage vessels (Tamene et al., 2022; Wu et al., 2021).

Climate change significantly impacts water quality in rural areas of Latin America through various mechanisms, exacerbating existing vulnerabilities and creating new challenges. Rising temperatures and altered precipitation patterns, as documented by the Intergovernmental Panel on Climate Change (IPCC), lead to increased water stress and variability in water availability, which directly affect water quality. In Central America, for instance, higher average temperatures and more frequent droughts result in higher water stress and a greater frequency of extreme weather events such as tropical storms, hurricanes, floods, and landslides, all of which pose significant challenges to rural water supply and sanitation (Rita et al., 2012). These climatic changes can lead to contamination of water sources, as increased sediment load, nutrient availability, and dissolved organic carbon disrupt the delicate ecological balance of water bodies, causing periodic phytoplankton blooms and altering dissolved oxygen levels, which can reach perilous levels (Yadava et al., 2022). In Latin America, the impacts of climate change on water resources are compounded by the region's dependency on natural resources and exposure to other stressors like globalization and restricted fiscal policies, making rural populations disproportionately vulnerable (Diaz et al., 2011). For example, in the Andean watershed basins, rural producers face significant challenges due to present and past climate variations, which affect local water resources and their adaptive capacities. Furthermore, the integration of climate change and rural water supply and sanitation policies is crucial to increase resilience to current and future climate conditions (Rita et al., 2012).

LIMITATIONS FOR DEPLOYMENT OF WATER TREATMENT TECHNOLOGIES

The implementation of water treatment in rural regions of Latin America is confronted with a plethora of challenges, originating from technical, social, and regulatory factors. The lack of access to cutting-edge water treatment technologies and infrastructure presents a significant challenge in providing clean and safe water to rural communities. These challenges are further compounded by the prevalence of social inequalities in rural areas, including substandard human development, restricted healthcare availability, and financial limitations, all of which impede efforts to enhance water treatment systems (Bacha et al., 2023). In response to this situation, rural communities have adopted a variety of rudimentary treatment options that usually have proven ineffective in improving water quality. One illustrative example is the potential formation of significant levels of toxic byproducts when chlorine is administered at incorrect dosages, particularly in water with a high organic substance content. (Casso-Hartmann et al., 2022). Moreover, the complex composition of the aforementioned pollutants calls for the development of efficient and cost-effective wastewater treatment technologies that can be easily accessible to rural households. Among the potential solutions to this issue, adsorptive membranes are of particular interest, with numerous studies indicating that materials derived from residual biomass are capable of eliminating a broad spectrum of heavy metals within complex matrices (Gallardo Salas et al., 2024). Conversely, the regulatory framework pertaining to water management and quality introduces additional challenges, particularly as a consequence of the implementation of international guidelines without due consideration of specific contextual factors. For example, conventional analytical techniques employed for the assessment of total mercury necessitate supplementary preparatory procedures to eliminate the organic constituents from samples, whereas rural drinking water sources frequently exhibit elevated levels of organic substances. This methodological bias has the potential to result in an underestimation of the measured concentrations of total mercury, due to the overlooking of its organic state (Casso-Hartmann et al., 2022). Furthermore, the political of water governance in Latin America is of paramount importance regarding the management of rural water resources. The delegation of decision-making authority to local and community-based water authorities represents a legal strategy employed by governments to integrate rural water management within national frameworks. Nevertheless, the efficacy of these approaches is contingent upon the resolution of existing knowledge gaps through the implementation of evidence-based studies on water initiatives in developing nations (Bacha et al., 2023; UN-Water, 2021).

Water Regulatory Frameworks in Latin America

In Latin America, as in the rest of the world, the accessibility of water and the administration of this resource are integral aspects of water governance. The concept of water governance has undergone a significant evolution throughout history, in response to the varying perspectives of the various organizations that have studied it. The World Water Association offers a definition of water governance that encompasses the following key elements: "The range of political, social, economic and administrative systems implemented to develop and manage water resources" (Fundación Aquae, 2022). In general, the implementation of regulations within the drinking water sector across Latin America is still in its nascent stages. A considerable number of regulators in the region operate independently from the service providers, thereby demonstrating a notable degree of autonomy. Nevertheless, it should be noted that not all regulators are empowered to set tariffs, which is a crucial aspect for the effective management of resources. The autonomy enables the making of unbiased decisions, which is crucial for the long-term investment in water and sanitation. Nevertheless, only a minority of regulators have independent funding or the authority to manage their personnel without external permissions (PAHO, 2020).

While regulatory approaches vary significantly among countries, they can be broadly classified into three categories. The first category comprises smaller unitary nations, where national regulation is prevalent and is split evenly between sector-specific and multisectoral approaches. The second category includes larger unitary nations, which are characterized by a mix of national and sector-specific regulation, with one exception employing multisectoral regulation. The third category comprises federal states, which feature subnational, sector-specific, and multisectoral regulatory frameworks. The multifaceted nature of water governance allows for considerable variation across different countries, influenced by a range of factors including economic, cultural, and traditional political norms, as well as the actions of legislative bodies. In some countries, politicians and the bureaucracy engage in a process of bargaining with the law, effectively transferring legislative authority to the executive branch and thereby establishing a leadership role for the latter. In contrast, in other countries, the actions of parliamentarians, who prioritize legislative authority, have a substantial impact on the legislative process. An indispensable element of governance is the establishment of a framework, both institutional and administrative, that enables stakeholders with disparate interests to engage in peaceful dialogue and reach agreements to collaborate and synchronize their efforts. Moreover, a binding arbitration mechanism is necessary to resolve intractable conflicts. It would be optimal for such a mechanism to exist within the government and the judicial system, or alternatively, within the framework of the United Nations and international multilateral agreements (Rogers & Hall, 2006).

The concept of water governance encompasses four dimensions: political, economic, social, and environmental. The political and social dimensions are of particular concern in Latin America, as they pertain to the processes of decision-making and the question of equitable access to resources. The political element necessitates the establishment of social participation mechanisms through which matters pertaining to competition for water resources can be deliberated. Furthermore, it requires the decentralization of decision-making processes and the incorporation of other levels of government (Grupo de Buena Governanza, 2012). In this sense, the importance of stakeholder participation in the sustainable management of water resources is increasingly being recognized. This is evident in the growing number of public management processes that incorporate mechanisms for user and civil society participation, with the aim of improving governance and addressing the impacts of climate change (Valer, 2023). The phenomenon of social inequality serves to exacerbate the issue of water poverty in Latin America, particularly in peri-urban areas. This is due to the fact that those belonging to the lowest socioeconomic strata are compelled to pay a greater sum for water, a consequence of the lack of uninterrupted distribution. Furthermore, disparities in water usage and utilization contribute to the intensification of social inequality. The social dimension entails the empowerment of vulnerable groups and the guarantee of their involvement in decisions pertaining to access to water and climate change adaptation measures. The economic dimension is concerned with the optimization of efficiency and cost recovery, while ensuring that the social and environmental objectives of the countries in question are not compromised. This encompasses the formulation of incentives to encourage the adoption of sustainable practices in water use and management, as well as the resolution of the sector's long-term financing requirements. In conclusion, the environmental dimension necessitates an integrated approach, recognizing that "hydric systems" are part of the "environmental system" and that they interact with "social systems" (Grupo de Buena Governanza, 2012).

The governance of rural water resources in Latin America exhibits considerable variation across countries, reflecting a complex interplay between stakeholders, regulatory frameworks, and community management practices (Rodríguez et al., 2022). Additionally, the governance of these resources is a highly contested domain, shaped by conflicting priorities between communities, states, companies, and conservationists. This contestation gives rise to a dynamic process of formulating and contesting values, procedures, and practices that shape the access and control over natural resources (de Castro et al., 2016). A crucial component of effective water governance is the presence of a comprehensive and efficient regulatory framework that fosters collaboration and communication among key stakeholders. In consideration of the distinctive characteristics and historical evolution of water resource management in rural regions across Latin America, it is evident that the legislative landscape pertaining to water is highly variable. As indicated in Table 1, fourteen Latin American countries have enshrined the right of access to water in their political constitutions. These constitutions include one or more articles that explicitly recognize the fundamental right of access to water and/or the obligation of the state to guarantee access to water resources. It is also observed that the majority of countries in the region have a comprehensive water law that governs the administration of water resources. Nevertheless, only nine countries have explicit regulations pertaining to access to water in rural areas. An illustrative case is that of Peru, which has produced 13 legal documents pertaining to water in rural areas over the past 12 years.

Table 1. Water regulation in rural areas in Latin American countries (adapted from Rodríguez et al. (2022) and Organización de las Naciones Unidas para la Alimentación y la Agricultura (FAO) (2024)). ND: Not defined.

Country	Water Regulation	Explicit water regulation for rural areas
Argentina	Law 25688 (2003) "Environmental water management regime": minimum environmental budgets for the preservation of water, its use and rational use	ND
Bolivia	- Political Constitution (2009): Art. 16 universal right to water, Art. 20 universal and equitable right to drinking water and sewerage - Law 2066 (2000) "Law of Provision of Potable Water and Sanitary Sewerage Services" - Regulation Law 1333 of the Environment (1992):	ND
Brazil	- Political Constitution (1988): Art. 21 competence of Federal Government to establish a national water resource management system and define criteria for granting rights to the use of water - Federal Law 9433 (1997) establishes the Brazilian National Water Resources Policy - Law 9984 (2000): creation of the National Water and Basic Sanitation Agency (ANA)	- Law No. 22.384 (2023) establishing the State Rural Sanitation Program, the guidelines and conditions for the provision of public sanitation services basic sanitation of water supply and sewage in communities settled in rural zones and areas in the State of Goiás - Law No. 23.102 (2018) creating the State policy to support the construction of cisterns in rural areas of the State (Minas Gerais)
Chile	- Water code (1981): Defines the types of water and establishes what refers to the domain and use of this resource - Decree 90 (2000): Establishes the emission standard for the regulation of pollutants associated with the discharge of liquid waste to marine and continental surface waters	Law N° 20.998 (2016): Regulates Rural water and sanitation Services
Colombia	- Political Constitution (1991): Art. 366 access to drinking water is a social purpose of the State, as well as environmental sanitation - Law 99 (1993) and Decree 1073 (2015): Establish a series of rules that govern the sustainable use and exploitation of water resources	- Resolution N° 768/CRA (2016): Adopts the model of uniform conditions of the contract for the provision of domiciliary public utilities of aqueduct and/or sewerage, for providers with more than 5,000 subscribers and/or users in rural or urban areas. - Decree No. 1898 (2016): Amends the Sole Regulatory Decree of the Housing, City and Territory Sector, in relation to differential schemes for the provision of water, sewerage and sanitation services in rural areas. - Decree N° 1688 (2020): Amends Decree N° 1077, Sole Regulatory Decree of the Housing, City and Territory Sector, in relation to the provision of water infrastructure for human and domestic consumption or basic sanitation in rural areas and its direct delivery to organized beneficiary communities, in accordance with the differential schemes defined by the Government.

continued on following page

Table 1. Continued

Country	Water Regulation	Explicit water regulation for rural areas
Costa Rica	- Political Constitution: Art. 50 "Every person has the human, basic and inalienable right of access to drinking water, as an essential good for life". - Law 276 (1942, modified in 2012): Management of water resources - Decree 31545-S-MINAE: Regulates the treatment and disposal of wastewater	ND
Cuba	- Political Constitution (2019): Art. 76 establishes that everyone has the right to water and that the State creates the conditions to guarantee access to drinking water and sanitation - Law 124 "Land Waters Law" (2017): orders the integrated management of terrestrial waters	ND
Ecuador	- Political Constitution (2008): Art. 3 it is a primary duty of the State to guarantee water for its inhabitants Art. 12 The human right to water is fundamental and inalienable - Organic Law of water resources uses and use of water (2014): Aims to guarantee the human right to water, and regulate the management of water resources, their uses and exploitation	- Agreement No. 69 (2007): Management Unit of the Drinking Water and Sanitation Program for Rural Communities and Small Municipalities - Resolution Nº DIR-ARCA-RG-003 (2016): Technical regulations for the evaluation and diagnosis of the provision of public drinking water and/or sanitation services in urban and rural areas.
El Salvador	- Decree 233 (1998): dictates the Environmental Law that aims at the protection, conservation and recovery of the environment - Water Resources Law (2022): prohibits the privatization of water and recognized the access to water and sanitation as a human right	ND
Guatemala	- Political Constitution (1985): Art. 127 "All water is property of the public domain, inalienable and imprescriptible; Art. 128 The use of water for economic development purposes is at the service of the community and not of any private person - Governmental Agreement 236 (2006): Regulation of the Discharges and Reuse of Residual Waters and the disposal of sludge. Authorizes and defines the limits of water reuse for agricultural irrigation, irrigation of edible crops, irrigation of aquaculture, pastures and other crops, and recreational reuse	ND
Honduras	General Water Law (Decree 181-2009): Establishes the principles and regulations applicable to the adequate management of water for integrated management of water resources at the national level	ND
México	- Political Constitution (1917): Art. 4 human right to access to water, Art. 27 the waters belong to the nation, and that the State oversees regulating their use through concessions based on the laws, Art. 115 municipalities oversee public drinking water services - National Water Law (1991), modified in 2023: Aims to strengthen water management, and allow greater social participation of local communities, recognizing community water management - NOM-003-ECOL (1997): establishes the maximum permissible limits of contaminants for treated wastewater that is reused in public services, divided into services to the public with direct contact and with indirect or occasional contact	Yucatan: Law on Drinking Water Supply in Rural Areas of the State of Yucatan (1975)
Nicaragua	- Political Constitution (1987): Art. 105 the State must promote, facilitate and regulate access to water - Law 620 "General Law of National Waters" (2007): aims to establish the institutional legal framework to manage, conserve, develop, use and sustainable use and preservation in quantity and quality of all that is water in the country, while guaranteeing the protection of other natural resources, ecosystems and the environment	Nicaraguan Technical Standard on the design of rural drinking water supply systems (1999)

continued on following page

Table 1. Continued

Country	Water Regulation	Explicit water regulation for rural areas
Panamá	- Political Constitution (1972): Art. 120 The State will regulate, supervise and apply the necessary measures to guarantee the rational use and use of water. - Law Decree No. 2 (1997): the regulatory and institutional framework for the provision of drinking water and sanitary sewerage services	- Resolution N° 713 (2020): Approves the Manual of Good Environmental Practices for aqueducts and rural sanitation systems - Decree No. 1839 (2014): Dictates the new regulatory framework of the Rural Aqueduct Management Boards (JAARs) as bodies co-responsible with the State for the administration, operation, maintenance and expansion of rural drinking water supply systems. - Resolution No. 305 (2019): Transitorily exonerates the Rural Aqueduct Administration Boards (JAARs) to make the payments regulated by the Ministry of Environment.
Paraguay	- Political Constitution (1992): Art. 163 establishes that it is the responsibility of the departmental government to coordinate its activities with the municipalities drinking water services - Law 3239 "Water Resources Law" (2007): regulates the management of the waters of the national territory	Decree No. 3189 (2019): Whereby the "National Strategic Committee for the Implementation of the Rural Water and Sanitation Information System (SIASAR)" is created, and functions are assigned to it.
Perú	- Political Constitution (1993): Art. 7-A declares that the State recognizes the right of everyone to access drinking water and guarantees human consumption over other uses. In addition, the State promotes sustainable water management - Law 29338 "Water Resources Law" (2019): the law and its regulations regulate the use and management of water resources - Supreme Decree No. 005-2011-AG (2011): regulates the reuse of wastewater treated by a person other than the owner of the treatment system to protect and preserve the quality of natural water sources	- Resolution N° 201-2012-VIVIENDA (2012): Modifies Resolution N° 108-2011-VIVIENDA, Guidelines for the formulation of water and sanitation programs or projects for rural population centers. - Supreme Decree N° 007-2013-VIVIENDA (2013): Amends Supreme Decree N° 002-2012-VIVIENDA, National Rural Sanitation Program. - Resolution N° 013-2017-VIVIENDA (2017): Operations Manual of the National Rural Sanitation Program (NRSP) - Resolution N° 263-2017-VIVIENDA (2017): Approves the specific methodologies for the formulation and evaluation of sanitation investment projects for urban and rural areas at the three levels of government - Resolution No. 078-2019-VIVIENDA (2019): Strategy to increase the percentage of rural households with access to chlorinated water in rural areas of Peru. - Resolution N° 015-2020-SUNASS (2020): Regulations on the Quality of Sanitation Services Provided by Community Organizations in Rural Areas. - Resolution N° 015-2017-VIVIENDA (2017): Promotes the training of young professionals committed to contributing to access to water with quality and sufficiency to populations in rural and urban areas. - Resolution No. 189-2017-VIVIENDA (2017) Amends the Guidelines for the formulation of water and sanitation programs or projects for populated centers in rural areas and the Guide of Technological Options for Water Supply Systems for Human Consumption and Sanitation in Rural Areas. - Resolution N° 192-2018-VIVIENDA (2018): Technical Design Standard: Technological Options for Sanitation Systems in Rural Areas. - Resolution N° 063-2017-VIVIENDA (2017): Approves the document "Technical Instruments to Obtain Information on Sanitation Services in Rural Areas" and the Computer Application "Diagnostic System on Water Supply and Sanitation in Rural Areas". - Ministerial Resolution N° 103-2022- MIDIS (2022): Approval of the list of targeted population centers for the implementation of interventions for rehabilitation, replacement, operation and maintenance of water and sanitation systems in rural population centers "Agua+". - Supreme Decree N° 002-2012-VIVIENDA (2012): National Rural Sanitation Program - Legislative Decree No. 1274 (2016): Regulates the execution of interventions for rehabilitation, replacement, operation and maintenance of water and sanitation systems in rural areas of the country - "AGUA +".

continued on following page

Table 1. Continued

Country	Water Regulation	Explicit water regulation for rural areas
Uruguay	Political Constitution (2004): Art. 47 "Access to drinking water and access to sanitation are fundamental human rights... the sustainable management, in solidarity with future generations, of water resources and the preservation of the hydrological cycle, which are matters of general interest. Users and civil society will participate in all levels of planning, management and control of water resources" - Law 18610 "National Water Policy Law" (2009): establishes the guidelines for the management of water resources and the universalization of drinking water and sanitation services - Decree 253 (1979): standards to prevent environmental pollution by controlling water pollution.	ND
Venezuela	Political Constitution (1999): Art. 178 establishes that the municipality is responsible for managing and administering the drinking water, sewerage, channeling and disposal of sewage services - Water Law (2007): establishes the provisions that govern the integral management of water	ND

DIFFICULTIES IN WATER GOVERNANCE IN LATIN AMERICA

Notwithstanding the existence of regulatory frameworks for water resource management, these are insufficient to guarantee adequate water governance. In addition to the aforementioned factors, other elements within the countries and regions themselves impede effective management. For example, the use of water for agriculture, which in the region consumes approximately 70% of renewable water resources, frequently results in rural areas lacking sufficient access to safe drinking water (Rodríguez et al., 2022). This is a consequence of the appropriation of water resources by agribusiness, which has established new territories and agricultural frontiers with a mercantilist approach, affecting the local landscape and leading to conflicts in the social organization of the territory (Zeni et al., 2019).

Another difficulty for adequate water governance is the lack of political commitment, scarce management tools or budgetary deficit of local and regional governments to fulfill their role as representatives of the state in water governance. Thus, despite the existence in many countries of river basin organizations, stakeholders sometimes tend to bypass basin committees during crises, seeking support through other channels, indicating limited effectiveness of the committees in fostering adaptive water governance (Trimble et al., 2022). Furthermore, the municipal authorities that share a given watershed exhibit a range of organizational, coordinating, and commitment levels (Pachoud, 2020). The adoption of watersheds as a management unit for governance has, therefore, become a point of contention, as it does not align with the traditional political-administrative boundaries (Murillo-Bermúdez & Abreu, 2020). Other element is the presence of hidden actors (those who are not recognized by governments), who play a determining role in territorial development and water resource management, disrupting the functioning of the state's water governance (Figueroa-Benitez et al., 2023).

Given the absence of a governance model that is universally effective across the continent and able to meet the specific demands of local contexts, general reference frameworks have been proposed as a means of facilitating adaptation to the particularities of different territories. The following examples illustrate various governance models in Latin America:

1. Intermunicipal Cooperation (IMC) Intermunicipal cooperation is regarded as a promising governance arrangement for the transition towards a water circular economy (WCE) due to its potential to facilitate the reconciliation of interagency interests, stakeholder participation, and effective land use for water management (Riazi et al., 2022).
2. Agricultural organizations serve as governance agents. Territorial governance represents a promising development strategy for rural areas, integrating diverse actors around common interests and affording a preponderant role to producer organizations that serve as key agents for unifying leadership and overcoming market barriers. In accordance with these principles, a governance model pertaining to the coffee-producing region of 92 municipalities in western Honduras is underscored. This model comprises four elements: cooperatives, rural boards, production parameters, and public goods. These elements interact endogenously, thereby fostering a virtuous circle for rural development (Palma et al., 2020).
3. The Rural Water and Sanitation Information System (SIASAR) is a tool designed to facilitate water governance. SIASAR is a joint initiative initiated by the governments of Honduras, Nicaragua, and Panama. Its strategic objective is to develop a comprehensive, updated, and reliable information tool on rural water supply and sanitation services in a country (SIASAR, 2017). This tool is being employed in other Latin American countries (Bolivia, Brazil, Colombia, Costa Rica, Mexico, Paraguay, Peru, and the Dominican Republic) as an information system that enables the systematic aggregation of data from water treatment plants and community water supply and sanitation stakeholders (Machado et al., 2020).
4. Poor management practices, rather than resource scarcity, are a major contributor to water crises in the region. Implementing integrated water resources management (IWRM) could significantly improve water governance, but this requires better coordination, stakeholder engagement, and the use of tools like the Freshwater Health Index (FHI) to assess and address governance issues (Ometto Bezerra et al., 2021). The Freshwater Health Index (WHI) is a tool designed for the assessment of water governance. This tool assesses the health of

a watershed by elucidating the interconnections between water ecosystems, the benefits they confer upon humanity, and the governance systems that regulate them (Conservation International, 2017). This index has been instrumental in evaluating some basins in Latin America, providing a foundation for diagnosing water governance in these basins (Bezerra et al., 2022).

Perspectives

Social and economic inequalities limit access to basic services, including safe drinking water, compounded by a lack of investment and political interest. The uncontrolled growth of cities and the expansion of development and industrial activities exert high pressure on peri-urban water resources, reducing the availability and quality of water for rural communities. Yet, governmental response to mitigate the impacts of climate change on water resources remains inadequate. There is a critical need for education and training in water management and water quality diagnostic techniques as many rural communities do not have the knowledge or resources to conduct adequate water quality testing. The region suffers from extreme climate variability, including drought and flood events that can affect both water availability and water quality. However, the impact on the water quality is unknown. Governments do little to address the challenges required to mitigate the impacts of climate change. Despite the existence of promising initiatives and frameworks, the governance of water in rural Latin America remains a multifaceted challenge that requires continued efforts in legislation, community management, stakeholder participation, and the implementation of integrated approaches to ensure sustainable and equitable access to water.

Acknowledgments: We extend our heartfelt gratitude to everyone who contributed to the project "DPAAPU - Diretrizes, Planos, Ações em Áreas Periurbanas: Ecossistemas num Desenvolvimento Equitativo" (422RT0129). Special thanks to our colleagues and collaborators for their invaluable insights and support.

Conflicts of Interest: The authors declare no conflicts of interest.

REFERENCES

Bacha, L., da Silva Bandeira, M., Lima, V. S., Ventura, R., de Rezende, C. E., Ottoni, A. B., Tschoeke, D., Cosenza, C., Thompson, C., & Thompson, F. (2023). Current Status of Drinking Water Quality in a Latin American Megalopolis. *Water (Basel), 15*(1), 165. Advance online publication. DOI: 10.3390/w15010165

Bahamón-Pinzón, D., Vélez-Torres, I., Estes, S. L., Lee, C., Moore, A., Bridges, W., Carraway, E., Blazer, H., Gutiérrez Zapata, H. M., & Vanegas, D. (2024). Confined within a sugarcane monoculture: A participatory assessment of water pollution and potential health risks in the community of El Tiple, Colombia. *The Science of the Total Environment, 946*(174072), 174072. Advance online publication. DOI: 10.1016/j.scitotenv.2024.174072 PMID: 38897454

Barragán, J. L. M., Cuesta, L. D. I., & Susa, M. S. R. (2021). Quantitative microbial risk assessment to estimate the public health risk from exposure to enterotoxigenic E. coli in drinking water in the rural area of Villapinzon, Colombia. *Microbial Risk Analysis, 18*(100173), 100173. Advance online publication. DOI: 10.1016/j.mran.2021.100173

Bedoya, K., Galeano, L., Hincapié, M. M., Mesa, J. A., & Alzate, J. F. (2021). Bacterial diversity analysis of freshwater sources for human use in rural areas of the tropical Andean region of Colombia. *Infectio : Revista de la Asociacion Colombiana de Infectologia, 26*(1), 11–18. DOI: 10.22354/in.v26i1.988

Bezerra, M. O., Vollmer, D., Acero, N., Marques, M. C., Restrepo, D., Mendoza, E., Coutinho, B., Encomenderos, I., Zuluaga, L., Rodríguez, O., Shaad, K., Hauck, S., González, R., Hernandéz, F., Montelongo, R., Torres, E., & Serrano, L. (2022). Operationalizing Integrated Water Resource Management in Latin America: Insights from Application of the Freshwater Health Index. *Environmental Management, 69*(4), 815–834. DOI: 10.1007/s00267-021-01446-1 PMID: 33693960

Bravo-Cadena, J., Pavón, N. P., Balvanera, P., Sánchez-Rojas, G., & Razo-Zarate, R. (2021). Water availability–demand balance under climate change scenarios in an overpopulated region of Mexico. *International Journal of Environmental Research and Public Health, 18*(4), 1–16. DOI: 10.3390/ijerph18041846 PMID: 33672845

Casso-Hartmann, L., Rojas-Lamos, P., McCourt, K., Vélez-Torres, I., Barba-Ho, L. E., Bolaños, B. W., Montes, C. L., Mosquera, J., & Vanegas, D. (2022). Water pollution and environmental policy in artisanal gold mining frontiers: The case of La Toma, Colombia. *The Science of the Total Environment, 852*(158417), 158417. Advance online publication. DOI: 10.1016/j.scitotenv.2022.158417 PMID: 36055504

Cerón-Vivas, A., & Peñuela Mesa, G. A. (2024). Environmental risk assessment of pharmaceutical pollutants in the Oro River Sub-basin (Colombia). *Environmental Research, 252*(118961), 118951. Advance online publication. DOI: 10.1016/j.envres.2024.118951 PMID: 38688417

Conservation International. (2017). The Freshwater Health Index. https://reports.freshwaterhealthindex.org/

de Castro, F., Hogenboom, B., & Baud, M. (2016). Environmental governance in Latin America. In Palgrave Macmilan (1st Editio). DOI: 10.1007/978-1-137-50572-9

Diaz, H., Garay-Fluhmann, R., McDowell, J., Montaña, E., Reyes, B., and Salas, S. (2011). Vulnerability of Andean Communities to Climate Variability and Climate Change. 209-223. DOI: 10.1007/978-3-642-22266-5_13

Figueroa-Benitez, A., Nagheeby, M., Figueroa, A., & Amezaga, J. (2023). Disrupted water governance in the shadows: Revealing the role of hidden actors in the Upper Cauca River Basin in Colombia. *Frontiers in Water, 5*, 801171. Advance online publication. DOI: 10.3389/frwa.2023.801171

Fu, Z., & Xi, S. (2020). The effects of heavy metals on human metabolism. *Toxicology Mechanisms and Methods, 30*(3), 167–176. DOI: 10.1080/15376516.2019.1701594 PMID: 31818169

Fundación Aquae. (2022). ¿Qué es la gobernanza del agua? https://www.fundacionaquae.org/wiki/gobernanza-agua/

Gallardo Salas, M. A., Mendoza-Castillo, D. I., Bonilla-Petriciolet, A., & Jiménez-Junca, C. (2024). Functionalized activated carbon with whey protein amyloid fibrils for adsorption of arsenic from water. *Environmental Nanotechnology, Monitoring & Management, 22*(100956), 100956. Advance online publication. DOI: 10.1016/j.enmm.2024.100956

Gorzoni, V. A. S., Pereira, P. P., Lautenschlager, S. R., & Okawa, C. M. P. (2019). Measures for reduction of the water losses in the distribution network: A case study on the municipality of Altônia/PR. Revista Eletrônica Em Gestão. *Educação e Tecnologia Ambiental, 23*(10), 10. Advance online publication. DOI: 10.5902/2236117038533

Grupo de Buena Governanza. (2012). Hacia una buena gobernanza para la gestión integrada de los recursos hídricos documento temático de las Américas.

Herrera-Valdés, R., Almaguer-López, M. A., Orantes-Navarro, C. M., López-Marín, L., Brizuela-Díaz, E. G., Bayarre-Vea, H., Silva-Ayçaguer, L. C., Orellana de Figueroa, P., Smith-González, M., Chávez-Muñoz, Y., & Bacallao-Méndez, R. (2019). Epidemic of Chronic Kidney Disease of Nontraditional Etiology in El Salvador: Integrated Health Sector Action and South-South Cooperation. *MEDICC Review*, *21*(4), 46–52. DOI: 10.37757/MR2019.V21.N4.8 PMID: 32335569

Inter American Development Bank. (1999). *Spilled Water*. Institutional Commitment in the Provision of Water Services., DOI: 10.18235/0012351

Kaewmai, R., Grant, T., Mungkalasiri, J., & Musikavong, C. (2021). Assessing the water scarcity footprint of food crops by growing season available water remaining (AWARE) characterization factors in Thailand. *The Science of the Total Environment*, *763*(143000), 143000. Advance online publication. DOI: 10.1016/j.scitotenv.2020.143000 PMID: 33190890

Kumar, V., Sharma, M., Sondhi, S., Kaur, K., Sharma, D., Sharma, S., & Utreja, D. (2023). Removal of Inorganic Pollutants from Wastewater: Innovative Technologies and Toxicity Assessment. *Sustainability (Basel)*, *15*(23), 16376. Advance online publication. DOI: 10.3390/su152316376

Larson, A. J., Haver, S., Hattendorf, J., Salmon-Mulanovich, G., Riveros, M., Verastegui, H., Mäusezahl, D., & Hartinger, S. M. (2023). Household-level risk factors for water contamination and antimicrobial resistance in drinking water among households with children under 5 in rural San Marcos, Cajamarca, Peru. *One Health*, *16*(100482), 100482. Advance online publication. DOI: 10.1016/j.onehlt.2023.100482 PMID: 36655146

Libra, J. M., Marinus Collaer, J. S., Datshkovsky, D., & Pérez-Urdiales, M. (2022). Scarcity in the Land of Plenty.

Machado, A. V. M., Nogueira, M. T., Alves, L. M. C., Quindeler, N. da S., Silva, J. D. C. D., Aranha, P. A. P., Gonçalves, R. P., & Siqueira, N. L. S. (2020). Assessment of community-managed water systems in rural areas of espírito santo, brazil, using the siasar tool. *Revista Ambiente & Água*, *15*(5), 1–19. DOI: 10.4136/ambi-agua.2517

Murillo-Bermúdez, L. F., & De Abreu, A. E. S. (2020). La gestión del recurso hídrico en Brasil y Colombia, una comparación de sus instrumentos. *Gestion y Ambiente*, *22*(2), 173–190. DOI: 10.15446/ga.v22n2.82554

Nunes, R. F. N., Marciano, L. P. A., Oliveira, G. S., Cardoso, N. S., Paula, F. B. de A., Sarpa, M., & Martins, I. (2024). Glyphosate contamination of drinking water and the occurrence of oxidative stress: Exposure assessment to rural Brazilian populations. *Environmental Toxicology and Pharmacology*, *108*(104476), 104476. Advance online publication. DOI: 10.1016/j.etap.2024.104476 PMID: 38796121

Ometto Bezerra, M., Vollmer, D., Acero, N., Marques, M. C., Restrepo, D., Mendoza, E., Coutinho, B., Encomenderos, I., Zuluaga, L., Rodríguez, O., Shaad, K., Hauck, S., González, R., Sánchez Hernández, F. X., Montelongo, R., Torres, E., & Serrano, L. (2021). Operationalizing Integrated Water Resource Management in Latin America: Insights from Application of the Freshwater Health Index. *Environmental Management*, •••, 1–20. DOI: 10.1007/s00267-021-01446-1 PMID: 33693960

Organización de las Naciones Unidas para la Alimentación y la Agricultura (FAO). (2024). Bases de datos de FAOLEX: Perfiles de país. https://www.fao.org/faolex/country-profiles/es/

Pachoud, C. (2020). The quality of territorial governance: An assessment of institutional arrangements. The case of the Serrano cheese production in the Campos de Cima da Serra, Southern Brazil. *Journal of the Geographical Society of Berlin*, *151*(1), 23–36. DOI: 10.12854/erde-2020-424

PAHO. (2020). 2030 Agenda for Drinking Water, Sanitation and Hygiene in Latin America and the Caribbean: A Look from the Human Rights Perspective. DOI: 10.37774/9789275121115

Palma, O. M., Díaz-Puente, J. M., & Yagüe, J. L. (2020). The role of coffee organizations as agents of rural governance: Evidence from western Honduras. *Land (Basel)*, *9*(11), 1–17. DOI: 10.3390/land9110431

Riazi, F., Fidélis, T., & Teles, F. (2022). Governance Arrangements for Water Reuse: Assessing Emerging Trends for Inter-Municipal Cooperation through a Literature Review. *Water (Basel)*, *14*(18), 2789. Advance online publication. DOI: 10.3390/w14182789

Rita, E., Cestti., Jorge, Jose, Escurra., Irina, I., Klytchnikova., Stefano, P., Pagiola. (2012). Climate change impacts on water resources and adaptation in the rural water supply and sanitation sector in Nicaragua. 1-53.

Rodríguez, C., García, B., Pinto, C., Sánchez, R., Serrano, J., & Leiva, E. (2022). Water Context in Latin America and the Caribbean: Distribution, Regulations and Prospects for Water Reuse and Reclamation. *Water (Basel)*, *14*(21), 3589. Advance online publication. DOI: 10.3390/w14213589

Rogers, P., & Hall, A. (2006). Gobernabilidad Efectiva del Agua. In Global Water Partnership: Vol. Vol.7. https://www.cepal.org/samtac/noticias/documentosdetrabajo/0/23420/GWP00504.pdf

Rothstein, A. P., Jesser, K. J., Feistel, D. J., Konstantinidis, K. T., Trueba, G., & Levy, K. (2023). Population genomics of diarrheagenic Escherichia coli uncovers high connectivity between urban and rural communities in Ecuador. *Infection, Genetics and Evolution, 113*(105476), 105476. Advance online publication. DOI: 10.1016/j.meegid.2023.105476 PMID: 37392822

Salazar-Camacho, C., Salas-Moreno, M., Marrugo-Madrid, S., Paternina-Uribe, R., Marrugo-Negrete, J., & Díez, S. (2022). A human health risk assessment of methylmercury, arsenic and metals in a tropical river basin impacted by gold mining in the Colombian Pacific region. *Environmental Research, 212*(113120), 113120. Advance online publication. DOI: 10.1016/j.envres.2022.113120 PMID: 35339468

Sasal, M. C., Demonte, L., Cislaghi, A., Gabioud, E. A., Oszust, J. D., Wilson, M. G., Michlig, N., Beldoménico, H. R., & Repetti, M. R. (2015). Glyphosate loss by runoff and its relationship with phosphorus fertilization. *Journal of Agricultural and Food Chemistry, 63*(18), 4444–4448. DOI: 10.1021/jf505533r PMID: 25775388

SIASAR. (2017). SIASAR. https://globalsiasar.org/es

Soares, R. B., da Silva, S. M. O., & Filho, F. (2021). Macroeconomic accounting of water resources: An input-output approach to linkage analysis and impact indicators applied to the state of ceará, brazil. *Water (Basel), 13*(6), 869. Advance online publication. DOI: 10.3390/w13060869

Tamene, A., Habte, A., Woldeyohannes, D., Tamrat, H., Endale, F., Eajo, T., & Afework, A. (2022). Water treatment at the point-of-use and treatment preferences among households in Ethiopia: A contemporaneous systematic review and meta-analysis. *PLoS One, 17*(10), e0276186. Advance online publication. DOI: 10.1371/journal.pone.0276186 PMID: 36301990

Tejeda-Benítez, L., Noguera, K., Aga, D., & Olivero-Verbel, J. (2023). Pesticides in sediments from Magdalena River, Colombia, are linked to reproductive toxicity on Caenorhabditis elegans. *Chemosphere, 339*(139602), 139602. Advance online publication. DOI: 10.1016/j.chemosphere.2023.139602 PMID: 37480944

Trimble, M., Olivier, T., Anjos, L. A. P., Tadeu, N. D., Giordano, G., Mac Donnell, L., Laura, R., Salvadores, F., Santana-Chaves, I. M., Torres, P. H. C., Pascual, M., Jacobi, P. R., Mazzeo, N., Zurbriggen, C., Garrido, L., Jobbágy, E., & Pahl-Wostl, C. (2022). How do basin committees deal with water crises? Reflections for adaptive water governance from South America. *Ecology and Society*, *27*(2), art42. Advance online publication. DOI: 10.5751/ES-13356-270242

UN-Water. (2021). Summary Progress Update 2021 : SDG 6 — water and sanitation for all. In UN-Water.

Valer, J. O. (2023). Participation in water resources management in Latin America 2017-2022: A systematic review. International Seven Journal of Multidisciplinary, 1–18. DOI: 10.56238/devopinterscie-144

Wu, J., Cao, M., Tong, D., Finkelstein, Z., & Hoek, E. M. V. (2021). A critical review of point-of-use drinking water treatment in the United States. *NPJ Clean Water*, *4*(40), 40. Advance online publication. DOI: 10.1038/s41545-021-00128-z

Yadava, P. K., Kumar, H., Singh, A., Kumar, V., & Verma, S. (2023). Impact of climate change on water quality and its assessment. In *Visualization Techniques for Climate Change with Machine Learning and Artificial Intelligence* (pp. 39–54). Elsevier.

Zeni, V. L. F., Scheibe, L. F., Zeni, E., & Vignatti, M. A. P. (2019). As marcas do agronegócio sobre o território das águas da Bacia do Prata. *Geosul*, *34*(71), 640–664. DOI: 10.5007/1982-5153.2019v34n71p640

Chapter 11
Reframing Urban Resilience:
Integrating Climate Adaptation With Sustainable Development

Seyda Emekci
https://orcid.org/0000-0002-5470-6485
Ankara Yildirim Beyazit University, Turkey

ABSTRACT

The chapter examines urban resilience as a proactive strategy linking climate adaptation with sustainable urban planning. Cities are both major contributors to and highly affected by climate change, requiring integrated responses. The study reviews key approaches such as heat island mitigation, green infrastructure, adaptive planning, and decentralized governance. Technical solutions like cool roofs, permeable surfaces, and urban greening are highlighted. Barriers including institutional gaps, cultural resistance, and challenges in measuring resilience are also discussed. The findings emphasize the need for flexible, multi-level planning models that embed resilience into long-term urban development frameworks.

INTRODUCTION

Anthropogenic climate change poses a systemic risk to urban life; it produces dynamic interactions between physical infrastructure, ecological systems, and socio-political institutions (IPCC, 2020). As spatially concentrated and resource-intensive systems, cities are especially susceptible to climate-induced risks such as increasingly hot temperatures, frequent extreme climatic events and infrastructure overload (European Environment Agency, 2017). Meanwhile, cities are believed to

DOI: 10.4018/979-8-3693-6089-7.ch011

consume 60–80% of global energy and to produce 70% of GHG emissions worldwide, thus also being at the core of the processes of climate change acceleration (UN-HABITAT, 2011; EC, 2016).

This feedback also exacerbates the rapid urbanization. By 2018, 55% of the world population was living in urban areas, a percentage expected to increase to 68% by 2050 and 73% in Europe (United Nations, 2018). This agglomeration of people and goods is what makes cities particularly vulnerable, especially if you factor in aging infrastructure, socio-economic disparity and disjointed systems of governance. European cities are particularly relevant as they are responsible for 69% of European GHG emissions, demonstrating an acute necessity for territorially embedded and cross-cutting climate action (European Commission, 2011).

In such a perspective, urban resilience emerges as an integrative approach including both anticipatory adaptation, anticipatory adaptation (Hunt & Watkiss, 2011a), and long term sustainability. That is, it relates not only to the capability of urban systems to rebound from climate-driven perturbations, however to reconfigure, to learn, and to change in the uncertain circumstances (Leichenko, 2011a). Resilience thinking does not limit the discussion to risk containment but it covers spatial morphology, governance architecture, energy shift, and social equity.

This chapter takes a multidimensional approach to explore the ways of which resilience-based planning approaches may implement climate adaptations into a broader sustainable urban development plan. Drawing upon empirical evidence, technological interventions and institutional designs, the paper seeks to address the process by which cities may evolve from weakness to adaptive capacity, through inclusive and scalable mechanisms of planning. In so doing, the chapter is adding to the growing conversation on climate-resilient urban futures, with emphasis on the strategic fit of resilience, sustainability and innovation.

LITERATURE REVIEW

The notion of urban resilience has seen substantial transformation in the last two decades from a hazard-based perspective to a more comprehensive approach encompassing environmental, spatial and institutional dimensions (Leichenko, 2011b; Boyd et al., 2008). In its original framing, resilience focused mainly on the ability of cities and systems to absorb shocks and return to a previous state. Nevertheless, recent literature tends to view resilience more as a process rather than a state that is characterised by transformation, adaptation, and learning in the face of uncertainty (Pelling, 2003; Jabareen, 2013).

There is now a developing literature that explicitly relates urban resilience to climate adaptation, acknowledging the relationships between urban form, styles of governance and socio-spatial vulnerabilities (Crichton, 2007; Hunt & Watkiss, 2011b). Especially in rapidly urbanizing and climate-sensitive (semi-)peripheries, resilience is articulated not just as a protective measure but as a facilitator for the long-term pathways for sustainability transitions.

Spatial structure and urban form are often referred to as key factors for a city's adaptive capacity. According to Jabareen (2006), the structural form of cities based on density, land use mix, connectivity, and ecological integration has a profound effect on climate risk exposure and responses. Planning approaches for lower the UHI effect and improving outdoor thermal comfort (Gartland 2008; Gill et al. 2007) include increasing the density, achieving a mixed land-use, and increasing green infrastructure.

At the same time urban governance has become increasingly prominent. Building resilience effectively demands decentralised, participatory and flexible governance systems that are able to incorporate climate knowledge into planning practices (Bulkeley 2010). Waters et al. (2014) stress that the resilience programmes are generally weakened by institutional fragmentation, low administrative capacity and lack of coordination. In addition, socio-cultural norms and regional disparities (e.g., in gender roles, traditional land tenure systems) can limit the ability to implement adaptive strategies (Kamal et al., 2018; Mersha & Van Laerhoven, 2016).

Technological solutions are also part of urban resilience strategies. In the past, field studies have been conducted to evaluate the effectiveness of interventions, which include cool roofs, reflective pavements and vegetative cover over urban heat islands as well as how effective they are in reducing urban vulnerability. As an example, processes of Georgescu et al. (2014) show how white roofs, as compared to green roofs, are beneficial for future climate scenarios, and Stone et al. (2014) project the heat-related mortality benefit from combined greening and albedo increasing on U.S. cities.

Although a great deal of work has been done, there are still a number of challenges surrounding the operationalisation of resilience. These range from the absence of standardised measurement for resilience building (Jacot des Combes et al., 2019) to institutional inertia, and the clash between short-term political direction versus long-term climate planning. The literature also highlights the importance of integrative approaches – one that integrates the technical, spatial and social dimensions of resilience and does not simply continue improving a system or making adjustments (Leichenko, 2011a; Jabareen, 2013).

Overall, the literature confirms that urban resilience is not a fixed situation but remains a dynamic and context-specific phenomenon. This effort will require long-term coordination among sectors, scales, and disciplines to build adaptive capacity in the short-term, and to advance climate justice and urban sustainability in the long-term.

METHODOLOGY

This investigation employs a qualitative, integrative methodology grounded in conceptual reflection and cross-disciplinary evidence synthesis. Its central aim is to explore the multifaceted nature of urban resilience, particularly as it intersects with climate change adaptation and the broader imperatives of sustainable urban development. The adopted framework bridges theoretical discourse with real-world observations, seeking to illuminate recurring themes, critical gaps, and pragmatic strategies within resilience-oriented planning paradigms.

-Research Design

The study is anchored in an interpretive research design, drawing on a multi-scalar analytical lens. It conducts a structured and selective review of peer-reviewed literature, institutional policy documents, and documented case studies that engage with themes of urban resilience, climate adaptation strategies, mitigation of urban heat, and sustainability in planning. Primary reference materials include authoritative publications such as those issued by the IPCC (2020), UN-HABITAT (2011), and the European Commission (2011), alongside datasets and assessments from recognized bodies including NOAA (Arndt, 2014), and the IMF (2023), among others.

-Data Collection and Selection Criteria

A targeted literature review was carried out via academic databases including Scopus, Web of Science, and Google Scholar. Selection was guided by strict inclusion criteria, notably:

- Publications released between 2006 and 2023,
- Studies explicitly addressing the intersection of urban resilience and climate adaptation,
- Empirical investigations focusing on spatial, technical, or institutional interventions in urban contexts,

- Case-based research demonstrating tangible environmental outcomes, such as reductions in surface temperature or climate-related mortality.

Additionally, secondary data—comprising modeling studies from Georgescu et al. (2014), temperature simulations by Gill et al. (2007), and intervention impact assessments from Stone et al. (2014)—were meticulously analyzed to evaluate the efficacy of different resilience-building strategies across a variety of projected climate scenarios.

-Analytical Framework

The analytical approach relies on a thematic synthesis method to distill foundational principles, recurring obstacles, and novel approaches from the reviewed literature. The synthesis is organized along four key thematic dimensions:

- Urban form and spatial resilience,
- Institutional governance and adaptive capacity,
- Technological responses to urban heat island effects,
- Metrics and frameworks for evaluating resilience effectiveness.

This structure enables a comparative, multi-contextual analysis of how resilience is conceptualized and operationalized across varying urban and governance settings. The thematic organization of findings supports the formulation of actionable planning guidelines and forward-looking policy recommendations.

Climate Change and the Urban Paradox

Cities present a unique contradiction in the climate discourse—while they are pivotal drivers of global climate change, they are also acutely susceptible to its adverse consequences. This duality, often encapsulated by the term "urban paradox" (Bulkeley, 2010; Revi et al., 2014), underscores a fundamental tension at the heart of contemporary urbanization. On one side, urban environments are accountable for a significant portion of global greenhouse gas (GHG) emissions. Their dense infrastructures, sprawling transport systems, and energy-intensive economic operations collectively render them substantial contributors to climate-altering emissions. As highlighted by UN-Habitat (2011), urban areas are responsible for around 70% of global CO_2 emissions and approximately 75% of total energy consumption, despite covering a mere fraction—less than 2%—of the Earth's terrestrial area.

Figure 1. The Urban Paradox of Climate Change

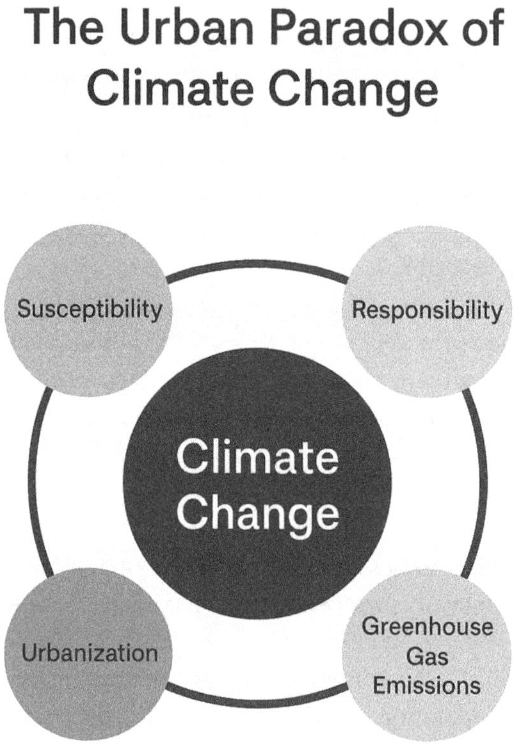

Source: Adapted by the author based on UN-Habitat (2011), European Environment Agency (2017), and United Nations (2018).

Conversely, cities stand at the frontline of climate vulnerability. Climate-induced phenomena such as prolonged heatwaves, intensified flooding, freshwater scarcity, and rising sea levels have a disproportionate impact on urban settlements (IPCC, 2014; IPCC, 2022). Of particular concern is the urban heat island (UHI) effect, which intensifies ambient temperatures in densely constructed zones, thereby aggravating public health challenges and escalating the demand for cooling infrastructure (Oke, 1982; Santamouris, 2015). These risks are especially pronounced in rapidly expanding metropolitan regions where informal housing, infrastructural deficits, and socio-economic inequalities amplify exposure and limit adaptive capacity (Dodman et al., 2019).

Furthermore, the distribution of climate risks within cities is far from equitable. Existing patterns of urban inequality serve to magnify these impacts, with marginalized populations—such as low-income households, elderly residents, and migrant groups—often confined to high-risk zones lacking basic services and resilient infrastructure (Satterthwaite et al., 2009; Anguelovski et al., 2016).

The scale and speed of urbanization add another layer of complexity. With projections indicating that nearly 68% of the global population will reside in urban areas by 2050, up from 55% in 2018 (United Nations, 2018), cities are under immense pressure to manage spatial expansion, service provision, and governance. This demographic transition intensifies the urgency of embedding climate adaptation within urban policy and planning frameworks.

Addressing this paradox requires a strategic synthesis of mitigation and adaptation. Cities must concurrently curtail their ecological footprints while bolstering their adaptive capacities. Achieving this balance depends on integrative approaches that span governance, policy, and design—emphasizing cross-sector collaboration, inclusive decision-making processes, and transformative planning models (Romero-Lankao et al., 2018; Leichenko, 2011).

CONTEMPORARY APPROACHES TO URBAN CLIMATE CHANGE ADAPTATION AND RESILIENCE

As climate-related hazards intensify in both frequency and severity, cities around the world are compelled to adopt integrated approaches aimed at boosting urban resilience. In recent academic discourse, resilience is no longer interpreted merely as the ability to recover from shocks. Instead, it is now seen as a proactive, forward-looking capacity to adapt, transform, and even thrive under increasingly complex and interlinked risks (Leichenko, 2011b; Pelling, 2003). This reconceptualization, especially relevant in urban environments, calls for the coordination of spatial planning, institutional frameworks, and technological innovation to support immediate responsiveness while securing long-term sustainability.

The notion of the "resilient city" has gained significant traction in this context. It emphasizes the capacity of urban systems to endure and reorganize in response to stressors such as heatwaves, flooding, and the depletion of critical resources (Boyd et al., 2008). Contemporary adaptation strategies, therefore, extend beyond mere infrastructural concerns to also embrace institutional adaptability and social justice (Crichton, 2007; Bulkeley, 2010).

-Strategic Approaches

Among the core strategies to bolster urban resilience are the mitigation of Urban Heat Island (UHI) effects, the development of sustainable urban configurations, and the implementation of decentralized, clean energy systems. Addressing UHI involves a suite of techniques, including increasing surface reflectivity through cool roofs and pavements, promoting vegetative cooling with green infrastructure, and minimizing anthropogenic heat emissions (Gartland, 2008).

Energy strategies likewise play a pivotal role in shaping adaptive capacity. By turning to locally sourced and renewable energy, cities can reduce their reliance on fossil fuels—an especially crucial step for regions grappling with energy insecurity (UNIDO, 2009). Moreover, distributed renewable systems offer critical redundancy, making urban energy networks more resilient to central grid disruptions.

In terms of spatial planning, embedding flexibility and ecological considerations into design frameworks is essential. Jabareen (2013) introduces a "planning with uncertainty" approach that encourages urban designers to anticipate multiple and uncertain climate futures. Compact, mixed-use urban development has also been shown to reduce exposure, increase mobility, and promote efficient use of resources (Jabareen, 2006).

Figure 2. Projected Temperature Reductions by Roof Type (2100)

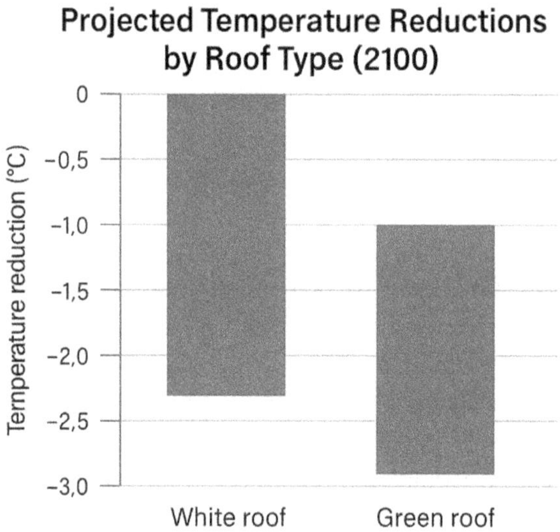

Source: Georgescu et al. (2014)

Effective governance is equally foundational to resilience. Achieving meaningful outcomes requires multilevel coordination, inclusive stakeholder engagement, and institutional mechanisms that support iterative learning and adaptive policymaking (Bulkeley, 2010).

Challenges in Operationalizing Urban Resilience

While there is growing agreement about the necessity of resilience, substantial barriers continue to hinder its practical realization. Institutional fragmentation is among the most persistent issues, where siloed agencies and overlapping mandates obstruct cohesive policy implementation (Waters et al., 2014). In addition, many urban resilience initiatives suffer from the absence of clear evaluative metrics, complicating the ability to assess progress or compare different interventions (Jacot des Combes et al., 2019).

Social and cultural dynamics further complicate the landscape. In various contexts, entrenched belief systems, traditional norms, and gendered hierarchies can limit the adoption of resilience measures (Kamal et al., 2018; Mersha & Van Laerhoven, 2016). Compounding these issues, political and economic priorities often skew toward short-term gains, threatening the continuity and scaling of adaptation efforts.

Innovations and Empirical Evidence

Technological innovation continues to offer promising avenues for reducing urban vulnerabilities. For instance, empirical studies show that cool roofs and pavements can lead to substantial drops in surface temperatures and energy usage (Gartland, 2008). Modeling research by Georgescu et al. (2014) found that white roofs consistently outperformed green roofs across multiple U.S. metropolitan areas in terms of heat mitigation, highlighting their potential for long-term climate benefits.

Figure 3. Surface Temperature Reduction via Urban Greening

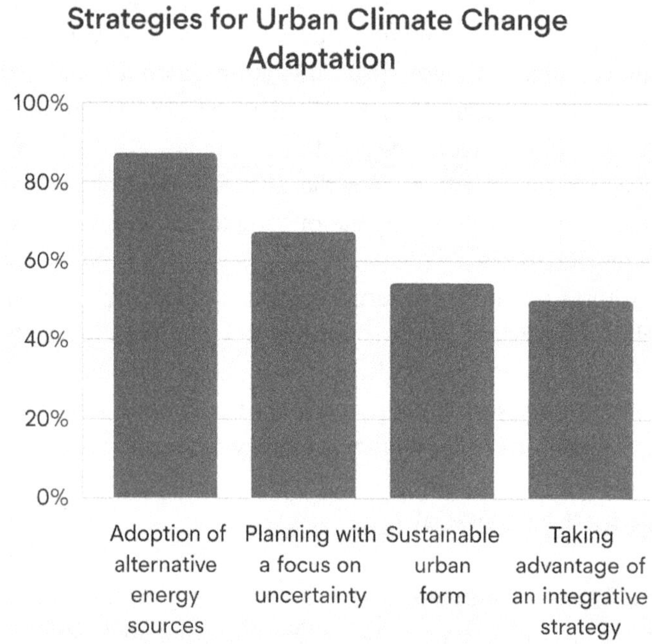

Source: Gill et al. (2007)

Similarly, Gill et al. (2007) demonstrated that a modest 10% increase in green coverage across Greater Manchester could lead to temperature reductions ranging from 1.7°C to 3.7°C in densely developed zones. Stone et al. (2014) further underscored the effectiveness of combining vegetation and reflective materials, finding that such strategies could meaningfully reduce future heat-related mortality in cities like Atlanta and Philadelphia by mid-century.

Figure 4. Combined Strategy Effects on Mortality Risk

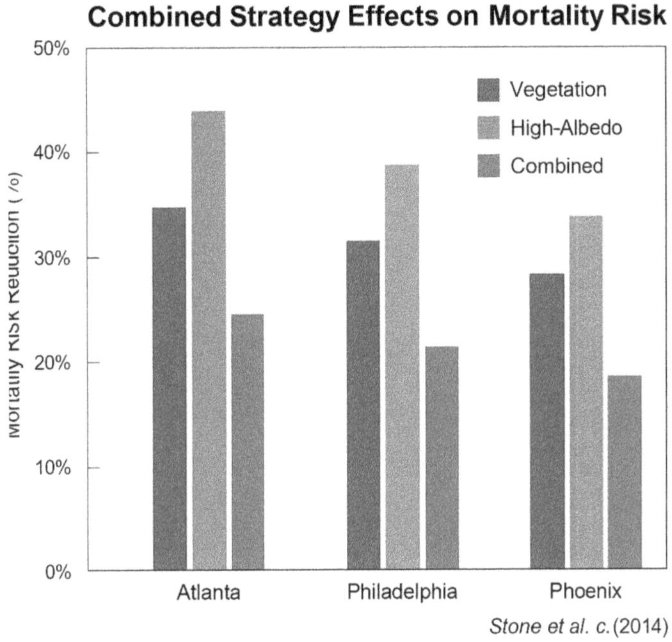

Source: Stone et al. (2014)

These findings collectively reinforce the value of integrating nature-based solutions and surface albedo enhancements into urban adaptation planning. They also highlight the necessity of context-specific modeling and scenario-based approaches to guide effective interventions.

DISCUSSION

The preceding synthesis illustrates the conceptual depth and real-world complexities involved in implementing urban resilience strategies. Building on the thematic analysis framework used in the research methodology, the discussion here integrates empirical and theoretical perspectives into a comprehensive understanding of resilience as a multidimensional construct.

First and foremost, the spatial configuration of cities and land-use decisions emerge as foundational levers in climate adaptation. Compact urban forms and increased vegetation not only mitigate UHI effects but also yield ancillary benefits, including improved energy performance and public health outcomes (Gill et al., 2007; Jabareen, 2006).

Second, institutional flexibility and responsive governance—particularly at local and metropolitan levels—are critical for resilience-building. Adaptive governance, marked by decentralization, cross-sectoral collaboration, and stakeholder inclusion, tends to produce more sustainable and equitable results (Bulkeley, 2010; Waters et al., 2014).

Figure 5. Intersections of Resilience Components

Source: Synthesized and adapted from Leichenko (2011a), Jabareen (2013), and Bulkeley (2010).

Third, technological tools must be embedded in a nuanced, place-sensitive planning framework. Innovations such as high-albedo surfaces, green infrastructure, and decentralized energy systems offer substantial promise, but their effectiveness depends on robust data and long-term planning horizons (Georgescu et al., 2014; Stone et al., 2014).

Yet, translating these insights into actionable, scalable solutions remains challenging. The lack of standardized metrics for evaluating resilience efforts hampers comparative learning and accountability. Furthermore, systemic inertia and sociopolitical constraints—especially in low-resource or politically fragmented settings—continue to slow progress.

To move forward, the resilience discourse must extend beyond purely technical interventions to embrace a systems-thinking approach that incorporates social justice, institutional reform, and holistic integration. Ultimately, urban resilience is best understood not as a static endpoint but as a dynamic, evolving process—deeply embedded in broader efforts to create cities that are not only sustainable, but also inclusive and just.

CONCLUSION

This chapter highlights the essential role of urban resilience as a strategic response to the intertwined challenges of climate change, rapid urban growth, and socio-spatial inequality. Building on insights from diverse fields and grounded in empirical data, it shows that true resilience goes beyond physical adaptation—it emerges from the intersection of thoughtful spatial planning, institutional shifts, technological progress, and inclusive governance.

The findings point to the value of compact city layouts, expanded green networks, and decentralized energy systems in boosting adaptive capacity while also enhancing urban livability and environmental performance. When nature-based solutions and reflective technologies are tailored to local climate data, they can measurably reduce urban heat and related health risks.

Yet, issues like fragmented institutions, weak evaluation methods, and cultural barriers continue to hinder progress. Addressing these challenges demands a broader rethinking of resilience—not as a fixed goal, but as an evolving, learning-driven process shaped by local contexts.

Embedding resilience into the core of urban planning calls for long-term commitment aligned with principles of climate justice, sustainability, and inclusive development. Through adaptive, multi-level, and integrative planning, cities can shift from vulnerability toward resilience and long-term transformation.

Policy Implications and Recommendations

-**Integrate Resilience into Urban Development:** Resilience must become a foundational element in how cities plan, invest, and govern. From zoning codes to infrastructure funding, policies should promote climate-smart designs—emphasizing green infrastructure and buildings that respond to changing climate conditions.

-**Promote Decentralized, Inclusive Governance:** City leaders need to embrace participatory models that bring local voices into the room—especially grassroots organizations, marginalized communities, and neighborhood stakeholders—to co-create adaptive strategies that work on the ground.

-Build Technical Expertise and Data Systems: Investing in tools like climate modeling, GIS-based vulnerability assessments, and resilience metrics is essential. These systems empower governments to make more adaptive and informed decisions in the face of evolving risks.
-Advance Nature-Based, Low-Carbon Approaches: Cities should prioritize green, multi-functional spaces and water-sensitive urban design, paired with clean energy systems. These strategies offer dual benefits—supporting both environmental sustainability and community health.
-Foster Institutional Alignment: Coordination is key. Establishing mechanisms that bridge fragmented agencies and align sectoral policies will help urban regions—especially those crossing jurisdictional lines—work toward shared climate goals.

Future Research Directions

Research going forward should delve into:

- The long-term effects of integrated resilience efforts across varied urban environments, offering insight into what truly works over time.
- Comparative case studies that span different climates and governance models to understand which adaptation strategies can be scaled or replicated.
- Frameworks focused on equity, probing how adaptation measures impact vulnerable groups and whether they help close or widen urban disparities.
- Financial innovation in resilience—like public-private partnerships or green bonds—that could make large-scale adaptation more feasible.
- Cross-disciplinary approaches that marry climate science with urban design and social innovation, ensuring adaptation strategies are both resilient and just.

REFERENCES

Anguelovski, I., Carmin, J., Agyeman, J., Schlosberg, D., & Huxley, M. (2016). Urban climate justice. *Journal of Planning Education and Research*, *36*(3), 333–348. DOI: 10.1177/0739456X16645166

Boyd, E., Osbahr, H., Ericksen, P. J., Tompkins, E. L., Lemos, M. C., & Miller, F. (2008). Resilience and 'climatizing' development: Examples and policy implications. *Development*, *51*(3), 390–396. DOI: 10.1057/dev.2008.32

Bulkeley, H. (2010). Cities and the governing of climate change. *Annual Review of Environment and Resources*, *35*(1), 229–253. DOI: 10.1146/annurev-environ-072809-101747

Crichton, D. (2007). What can cities do to increase resilience? *Philosophical Transactions of the Royal Society A: Mathematical, Physical and Engineering Sciences*, *365*(1860), 2731–2739.

Dodman, D., Leck, H., Rusca, M., & Colenbrander, S. (2019). African urbanisation and urbanism: Implications for risk accumulation and reduction. *International Journal of Disaster Risk Reduction*, *26*, 7–15. DOI: 10.1016/j.ijdrr.2017.06.029

European Commission. (2011). *Cities of tomorrow: Challenges, visions, ways forward*. Directorate-General for Regional Policy.

European Environment Agency. (2017). *Climate change, impacts and vulnerability in Europe 2016: An indicator-based report* (EEA Report No. 1/2017).

Gartland, L. (2008). *Heat islands: Understanding and mitigating heat in urban areas*. Earthscan.

Georgescu, M., Morefield, P. E., Bierwagen, B. G., & Weaver, C. P. (2014). Urban adaptation can roll back warming of emerging megapolitan regions. *Proceedings of the National Academy of Sciences of the United States of America*, *111*(8), 2909–2914. DOI: 10.1073/pnas.1322280111 PMID: 24516126

Gill, S. E., Handley, J. F., Ennos, A. R., & Pauleit, S. (2007). Adapting cities for climate change: The role of the green infrastructure. *Built Environment*, *33*(1), 115–133. DOI: 10.2148/benv.33.1.115

Hunt, A., & Watkiss, P. (2011a). Climate change impacts and adaptation in cities: A review of the literature. *Climatic Change*, *104*(1), 13–49. DOI: 10.1007/s10584-010-9975-6

Hunt, A., & Watkiss, P. (2011b). Identifying and assessing adaptation options in urban areas. In Satterthwaite, D. (Ed.), *Adapting cities to climate change* (pp. 123–143). Earthscan.

IPCC. (2014). *Climate Change 2014: Impacts, Adaptation, and Vulnerability. Part A: Global and Sectoral Aspects.* Contribution of Working Group II to the Fifth Assessment Report of the Intergovernmental Panel on Climate Change. Cambridge University Press.

IPCC. (2020). *Climate Change and Land: An IPCC Special Report.* Retrieved from https://www.ipcc.ch/srccl/

IPCC. (2022). [*Impacts, Adaptation and Vulnerability.* Working Group II Contribution to the Sixth Assessment Report of the IPCC.]. *Climatic Change*, •••, 2022.

Jabareen, Y. (2006). Sustainable urban forms: Their typologies, models, and concepts. *Journal of Planning Education and Research*, *26*(1), 38–52. DOI: 10.1177/0739456X05285119

Jabareen, Y. (2013). Planning the resilient city: Concepts and strategies for coping with climate change and environmental risk. *Cities (London, England)*, *31*, 220–229. DOI: 10.1016/j.cities.2012.05.004

Jacot des Combes, H., Mitchell, D., & Wisner, B. (2019). Measuring urban resilience: Are we asking the right questions? *International Journal of Disaster Risk Reduction*, *37*, 101–128.

Kamal, A. S. M., Hassan, S. M., & Adnan, M. S. G. (2018). Climate change adaptation policy and practice in Bangladesh: An empirical review. *Environmental Development*, *25*, 56–66.

Leichenko, R. (2011a). Climate change and urban resilience. *Current Opinion in Environmental Sustainability*, *3*(3), 164–168. DOI: 10.1016/j.cosust.2010.12.014

Leichenko, R. (2011b). Resilience and the neoliberal city: A critical perspective. *Cities (London, England)*, *28*(4), 235–240.

Mersha, A. A., & Van Laerhoven, F. (2016). The interplay between planned and autonomous adaptation in response to climate change: Insights from rural Ethiopia. *World Development*, *84*, 155–169.

Oke, T. R. (1982). The energetic basis of the urban heat island. *Quarterly Journal of the Royal Meteorological Society*, *108*(455), 1–24. DOI: 10.1002/qj.49710845502

Pelling, M. (2003). *The vulnerability of cities: Natural disasters and social resilience.* Earthscan.

Romero-Lankao, P., Gnatz, D. M., & Sperling, J. (2018). Examining urban adaptation and transformation through the lens of justice. *Environmental Research Letters*, *13*(8), 084008.

Santamouris, M. (2015). Analyzing the heat island magnitude and characteristics in one hundred Asian and Australian cities and regions. *The Science of the Total Environment*, *512–513*, 582–598. DOI: 10.1016/j.scitotenv.2015.01.060 PMID: 25647373

Satterthwaite, D., Huq, S., Pelling, M., Reid, H., & Romero-Lankao, P. (2009). *Adapting to climate change in urban areas: The possibilities and constraints in low- and middle-income nations*. IIED Working Paper.

Stone, B., Vargo, J., Liu, P., DeLucia, A., Trail, M., Hu, Y., & Russell, A. (2014). Avoided heat-related mortality through climate adaptation strategies in three US cities. *PLoS One*, *9*(6), e100852. DOI: 10.1371/journal.pone.0100852 PMID: 24964213

UN-Habitat. (2011). *Cities and Climate Change: Global Report on Human Settlements*. United Nations Human Settlements Programme.

UN-Habitat. (2021). *World Cities Report 2020: The Value of Sustainable Urbanization*. United Nations Human Settlements Programme.

UNIDO. (2009). *Scaling up renewable energy in Africa*. United Nations Industrial Development Organization.

United Nations. (2018). *World Urbanization Prospects: The 2018 Revision*. Department of Economic and Social Affairs.

Waters, E., Barnett, J., & Puleston, A. (2014). Contrasting perspectives on barriers to climate change adaptation in Australia. *Climate Policy*, *14*(5), 572–588.

Compilation of References

Adams, R., Jeanrenaud, S., Bessant, J., Overy, P., & Denyer, D. (2012). *Innovating for Sustainability. A Systematic Review of the Body of Knowledge*. Network for Business Sustainability.

Administrative Staff College of India (ASCI). (2020). Study on the Impact of Mechanical Ventilation on Indoor Air Quality in Residential Buildings in Hyderabad.

Adugbila, E. J., Martinez, J. A., & Pfeffer, K. (2023). Road infrastructure expansion and socio-spatial fragmentation in the peri-urban zone in Accra, Ghana. *Cities (London, England)*, *133*, 104154. DOI: 10.1016/j.cities.2022.104154

Aguilera, B., Rodríguez, E., & Gómez, D. (2018). Definició d'infraestructures verdes: Una proposta metodològica integrada a través d'una anàlisi espacial. *Documents d'Analisi Geografica*, *66*(2), 313–337. DOI: 10.5565/rev/dag.419

Ahani, S., & Dadashpoor, H. (2021). A review of domains, approaches, methods and indicators in peri-urbanization literature. *Habitat International*, *114*, 102387. DOI: 10.1016/j.habitatint.2021.102387

Ahmed, S. (2018). *Vivir una vida feminista*. Ediciones Bellaterra.

Ahn, M., Kang, J., & Hustvedt, G. (2016). A model of sustainable household technology acceptance. *International Journal of Consumer Studies*, *40*(1), 83–91. DOI: 10.1111/ijcs.12217

Aiking, H., & de Boer, J. (2020). The next protein transition. *Trends in Food Science & Technology*, *105*, 515–522. DOI: 10.1016/j.tifs.2018.07.008 PMID: 38620223

Alberti, M. (1996). Measuring urban sustainability. *Environmental Impact Assessment Review*, *16*(4-6), 381–424. DOI: 10.1016/S0195-9255(96)00083-2

Alcaldía Mayor de Bogotá (2021*). Decreto 555 por medio del cual se adopta la revisión general del Plan de Ordenamiento Territorial de Bogotá DC.*

Alcaldía Mayor de Bogotá. (2021). Plan de Ordenamiento Territorial Bogotá Reverdece 2022- 2035. Recuperado de https://bogota.gov.co/bog/pot-2022-2035/

Alcantar García, É. (2020). Ciudad Satélite: El habitar moderno de las clases medias mexicanas. *Academia XXII*, *11*(22), 22. Advance online publication. DOI: 10.22201/fa.2007252Xp.2020.22.77411

Alfonso-Roa, Ó., & Amézquita, L. (2017). La Segmentación del mercado residencial formal en la zona metropolitana de Bogotá en la última década. In *Ó. Alfonso-Roa, Bogotá en la Encrucijada del Desorden. Estructuras sociespaciales y gobernabilidad me-tropolitana (págs* (pp. 83–120). Universidad Externado de Colombia. DOI: 10.4000/books.uec.1875

Al-Saedi, K., Al-Emran, M., Ramayah, T., & Abusham, E. (2020). Developing a general extended UTAUT model for M-payment adoption. *Technology in Society*, *62*, 101293. DOI: 10.1016/j.techsoc.2020.101293

Alshehhi, A., Nobanee, H., & Khare, N. (2018). The impact of sustainability practices on corporate financial performance: Literature trends and future research potential. *Sustainability (Basel)*, *10*(2), 494. DOI: 10.3390/su10020494

Álvarez Jaramillo, J., Zartha Sossa, J. W., & Orozco Mendoza, G. L. (2018). Barriers to sustainability for small and medium enterprises in the framework of sustainable development—Literature review. *Business Strategy and the Environment*, *10*(1), 1.

Amit, R., & Zott, C. (2012). Creating value through business model innovation. *MIT Sloan Management Review*, *53*(3), 41–49.

Andrade, G., Remolina, F., & Wiesner, D. (2013). Assembling the pieces: A framework for the integration of multi-functional ecological main structure in the emerging urban region of Bogotá, Colombia. *Urban Ecosystems*, *16*(4), 723–739. DOI: 10.1007/s11252-013-0292-5

Anelli, R. L. S. (2018). Planning São Paulo. Planum The Journal of Urbanism, 36(1).

Anguelovski, I., Carmin, J., Agyeman, J., Schlosberg, D., & Huxley, M. (2016). Urban climate justice. *Journal of Planning Education and Research*, *36*(3), 333–348. DOI: 10.1177/0739456X16645166

Anser, M. K., Yousaf, Z., & Zaman, K. (2020). Green technology acceptance model and green logistics operations: To see which way the wind is blowing. *Frontiers in Sustainability*, *1*(3), 1–9. DOI: 10.3389/frsus.2020.00003

Ansoff, H. I. (1957). Strategies for diversification. *Harvard Business Review*, *35*(5), 113–124.

Anwar, M., Shah, S. Z. A., & Khan, S. Z. (2018). The role of personality in SMEs internationalization: Empirical evidence. *Rev. Int. Bus. Strategy*, *28*(2), 258–282. DOI: 10.1108/RIBS-12-2017-0113

Aragón-Correa, J. A., Hurtado-Torres, N., Sharma, S., & Garcia-Morales, V. J. (2008). Environmental strategy and performance in small firms: A resource-based perspective. *Journal of Environmental Management*, *86*(1), 88–103. DOI: 10.1016/j.jenvman.2006.11.022 PMID: 17239519

Araque, A., Cantor, L., & Moreno, P. (2022). Norma y precio del suelo urbano en la ciudad de Bogotá. *EURE* 48(143), 1-22. https://dx.doi.org/.DOI: 10.7764/EURE.48.143.13

Arellano, R., & Roca, C. J. (2016). Identifying urban heat island: the Barcelona case. In Back to the Sense of the City: International Monograph Book. En *Back to the Sense of the City: International Monograph Book* (págs. 798-812). Centre de Política de Sòl i Valoracions. DOI: 10.5821/ctv.8130

Arguedas Marín, M. P. (2022). *Propuesta metodológica para identificar sitios prioritarios para restaurar ecosistemas con fines de protección del recurso hídrico: estudio de caso de la microcuenca del Río Cacao*. Atenas.

Asadi-Shekari, Z., Moeinaddini, M., & Shah, M. Z. (2013). Non-motorised level ofservice: Addressing challenges in pedestrian and bicycle level of service. *Transport Reviews*, *33*(2), 166–194. DOI: 10.1080/01441647.2013.775613

Ascue Cuba, J. C. (2018). La vulnerabilidad de ecosistemas frágiles en ciudades altoandinas. caso: microcuenca huancaro, Distrito de Santiago–Cusco y el desarrollo sostenido urbano marginal.

Ashinze, U. K., Edeigba, B. A., Umoh, A. A., Biu, P. W., & Daraojimba, A. I. (2024). *Urban green infrastructure and its role in sustainable cities: A comprehensive review*. World Journal of Advanced Research and Reviews., DOI: 10.30574/wjarr.2024.21.2.0519

Aşıcı, G. (2023). Kır-kent çeperinin iklim değişikliği perspektifinden incelenmesi: Denizli örneği (Master's thesis).

Aurich, J. C., Fuchs, C., & Wagenknecht, C. (2006). Life cycle oriented design of technical product–service systems. *Journal of Cleaner Production*, *14*(17), 1480–1494. DOI: 10.1016/j.jclepro.2006.01.019

Awan, U., Arnold, M. G., & Golgeci, I. (2020). Enhancing green product and process innovation: Towards an integrative framework of knowledge acquisition and environmental investment. *Business Strategy and the Environment*, •••, 1–13. DOI: 10.1002/bse.2684

Ayuntamiento de Mérida. (2014). *Acuerdo en el que el Ayuntamiento de Mérida aprueba crear el Instituto Municipal de Planeación*. IMPLAN.

Bacha, L., da Silva Bandeira, M., Lima, V. S., Ventura, R., de Rezende, C. E., Ottoni, A. B., Tschoeke, D., Cosenza, C., Thompson, C., & Thompson, F. (2023). Current Status of Drinking Water Quality in a Latin American Megalopolis. *Water (Basel)*, *15*(1), 165. Advance online publication. DOI: 10.3390/w15010165

Bahamón-Pinzón, D., Vélez-Torres, I., Estes, S. L., Lee, C., Moore, A., Bridges, W., Carraway, E., Blazer, H., Gutiérrez Zapata, H. M., & Vanegas, D. (2024). Confined within a sugarcane monoculture: A participatory assessment of water pollution and potential health risks in the community of El Tiple, Colombia. *The Science of the Total Environment*, *946*(174072), 174072. Advance online publication. DOI: 10.1016/j.scitotenv.2024.174072 PMID: 38897454

Barney, J. (1991). Firm resources and sustained competitive advantage. *J. Manag.*, 17, 99–120. Baumard, P., & Starbuck, W. H. (2005). Learning from failures: Why it may not happen. *Long Range Planning*, *38*(3), 281–298. DOI: 10.1016/j.lrp.2005.03.004

Barragán, J. L. M., Cuesta, L. D. I., & Susa, M. S. R. (2021). Quantitative microbial risk assessment to estimate the public health risk from exposure to enterotoxigenic E. coli in drinking water in the rural area of Villapinzon, Colombia. *Microbial Risk Analysis*, *18*(100173), 100173. Advance online publication. DOI: 10.1016/j.mran.2021.100173

Bassul, J. R. (2010). City statute: Building a law. In *The city statute: A commentary* (pp. 71–90). Ministry of Cities, Cities Alliance.

Bedoya, K., Galeano, L., Hincapié, M. M., Mesa, J. A., & Alzate, J. F. (2021). Bacterial diversity analysis of freshwater sources for human use in rural areas of the tropical Andean region of Colombia. *Infectio : Revista de la Asociacion Colombiana de Infectologia*, *26*(1), 11–18. DOI: 10.22354/in.v26i1.988

Belge, Z. S. (2012). Increasing walkability capacity of historic city centers: The case of Mersin (Master's thesis, Middle East Technical University).

Belge, Z. S., & Akkar Ercan, Z. M. (2017). Daha Yaşanabilir Kentler İçin Mikro Ölçek Bir Yürünebilirlik Modeli.

Belge, Z. S., & Ercan, M. A. (2022). Mobility and the Role of Pedestrian in the Making of Public Space: The Case Study of Mersin. *Transportation Research Procedia*, *60*, 386–393. DOI: 10.1016/j.trpro.2021.12.050

Bezerra, M. O., Vollmer, D., Acero, N., Marques, M. C., Restrepo, D., Mendoza, E., Coutinho, B., Encomenderos, I., Zuluaga, L., Rodríguez, O., Shaad, K., Hauck, S., González, R., Hernandéz, F., Montelongo, R., Torres, E., & Serrano, L. (2022). Operationalizing Integrated Water Resource Management in Latin America: Insights from Application of the Freshwater Health Index. *Environmental Management*, *69*(4), 815–834. DOI: 10.1007/s00267-021-01446-1 PMID: 33693960

Biljecki, F., Ledoux, H., & Oosterom, P. V. (2013). Transportation mode-based segmentation and classification of movement trajectories. *International Journal of Geographical Information Science*, *27*(2), 385–407. Advance online publication. DOI: 10.1080/13658816.2012.692791

Binder, J., & Matern, A. (2020). Mobility and social exclusion in peripheral regions. *European Planning Studies*, *28*(6), 1049–1067. Advance online publication. DOI: 10.1080/09654313.2019.1689926

Blatter, J. (2008). Case study. In L. Given (Ed.). *The SAGE Encyclopedia of qualitative research methods*. V.1 y 2. Estados Unidos: SAGE Publications, Inc.

Block, A., Gellrich, M., & Russ, C. (2021). Effects of the COVID-19 Pandemic on SME sustainability: Case study of car dealerships in Switzerland | Block | European Journal of Applied Business and Management. *European Journal of Applied Business and Management*, *7*(1). Retrieved April 24, 2021, from https://nidisag.isag.pt/index.php/IJAM/article/view/547

Bocarejo, J. P., Portilla, I., & Meléndez, D. (2016). Social fragmentation as a consequence of implementing a Bus Rapid Transit system in the city of Bogotá. *Urban Studies (Edinburgh, Scotland)*, *53*(8), 1617–1634. DOI: 10.1177/0042098015588739

Bolay, J.-C., Pedrazzini, Y., Rabinovich, A., Catenazzi, A., & García Pleyán, C. (2005). Urban environment, spatial fragmentation and social segration in Latin America: Where does innovation lie? *Habitat International*, *29*(4), 627–645. DOI: 10.1016/j.habitatint.2004.05.003

Boons, F., & Lüdeke-Freund, F. (2013). Business models for sustainable innovation: State-of-the-art and steps towards a research agenda. *Journal of Cleaner Production*, *45*, 9–19. DOI: 10.1016/j.jclepro.2012.07.007

Bos-Brouwers, H. (2009). Corporate sustainability and innovation in SMEs: Evidence of themes and activities in practice. *Business Strategy and the Environment*, *19*(7), 417–435. DOI: 10.1002/bse.652

Bossle, M.B., De Barcellos, M.D., Vieira, L.M. and Sauvee, L. (2016), The drivers for adoption of eco-innovation, *Journal of Cleaner Production*, Vol. 113 No. 2014, pp. 861-872.

Bourne, L. S., & Simmons, J. (2003). NEW FAULT LINES? RECENT TRENDS IN THE CANADIAN URBAN SYSTEM AND THEIR IMPLICATIONS FOR PLANNING AND PUBLIC POLICY. *Canadian Journal of Urban Research*, *12*(1), 22–47. https://www.jstor.org/stable/44387635

Boyd, E., Osbahr, H., Ericksen, P. J., Tompkins, E. L., Lemos, M. C., & Miller, F. (2008). Resilience and 'climatizing' development: Examples and policy implications. *Development*, *51*(3), 390–396. DOI: 10.1057/dev.2008.32

Bragos, O., Latour, M., Mazzaro, P., & Ochoa, A. (2016): Suburban sprawl in the metropolitan region of Rosario. And sustainable urban development? En: NALARs Jurnalarsitektur, Vol. 15, Nº 3.

Brandes, T., & Emary, C. (2016). Feedback control of waiting times. *Physical Review. E*, *93*(4), 042103. Advance online publication. DOI: 10.1103/PhysRevE.93.042103 PMID: 27176250

Bravo-Cadena, J., Pavón, N. P., Balvanera, P., Sánchez-Rojas, G., & Razo-Zarate, R. (2021). Water availability–demand balance under climate change scenarios in an overpopulated region of Mexico. *International Journal of Environmental Research and Public Health*, *18*(4), 1–16. DOI: 10.3390/ijerph18041846 PMID: 33672845

Brea-Martínez, G., & Dribe, M. (2024). Economic Inequality and Social Mobility. Oxford University Press EBooks. DOI: 10.1093/oso/9780197761090.003.0003

Brito, M. (2008). *Más allá de la dicotomía: la distinción entre lo público, lo privado y lo doméstico. Tesis de Maestría. Universidad Autónoma Metropolitana*. Unidad Iztapalapa.

Brovarone, E. V. (2021). Accessibility and mobility in peripheral areas: A national place-based policy. *European Planning Studies*. Advance online publication. DOI: 10.1080/09654313.2021.1894098

Bucheli Guevara, J. F. (2019). Living Together: A Capability Approach to Spatially Segregated Areas of Bogota [Doctoral dissertation]. University of Cambridge.

Bulkeley, H. (2010). Cities and the governing of climate change. *Annual Review of Environment and Resources*, *35*(1), 229–253. DOI: 10.1146/annurev-environ-072809-101747

Butler, J. (2010). *Marcos de guerra. Las vidas lloradas*. Paidós.

Buxton, M. (2022). Connecting peri-urban theory with policy: Implications for practice. In P. Pereira, E. Gomes, & J. Rocha (Eds.), Mapping and Forecasting Land Use (pp. 55-94). Elsevier. https://doi.org/DOI: 10.1016/B978-0-323-90947-1.00005-3

Cabnal, L. (2015). *Lorena Cabnal. Feminista comunitaria*. https://suds.cat/experiencies/857-2/

Cabnal, L. (2010). *Feminismos diversos: el feminismo comunitario*. ACSUR-Las Segovias.

Caffentzis, G., & Federici, S. (2013). Comunes contra y más allá del capitalismo. In Menendez, M., & Conze, C. (Eds.), *La Vida en el centro. Feminismo, reproducción y tramas comunitarias*. Bajo Tierra Ediciones.

Calisto Friant, M., & Langmore, J. (2015). The Buen Vivir: A policy to survive the Anthropocene? *Global Policy*, *6*(1), 64–71. DOI: 10.1111/1758-5899.12187

Cao, M., Zhang, Y., Zhang, Y., Li, S., & Hickman, R. (2019). *Using different approaches to evaluate individual social equity in transport. A Companion to Transport*. Space and Equity., DOI: 10.4337/9781788119825.00024

Carmona, M. (2021). *Public places urban spaces: The dimensions of urban design*. Routledge., DOI: 10.4324/9781315158457

Carrilho, J., & Trindade, J. (2022). Sustainability in Peri-Urban Informal Settlements: A Review. *Sustainability (Basel)*, *14*(13), 7591. DOI: 10.3390/su14137591

Carspecken, P. F. (2008). Critical research. In L. Given (Ed.). *The SAGE Encyclopedia of qualitative research methods*. V.1 y 2. Estados Unidos: SAGE Publications, Inc.

Casais, N., & Grau Valldosera, F. (2023). Infrastructural peripheries in the city-region: Airport spatial influences. In Richards, S., Schmidt, R.III, Sanliturk, C., & Palaiologou, F. (Eds.), *Region* (pp. 271–294). Routledge., https://www.lboro.ac.uk/departments/abce/ahra2021-region/

Cassiers, T., & Kesteloot, C. (2012). Socio-spatial Inequalities and Social Cohesion in European Cities. *Urban Studies (Edinburgh, Scotland)*, *49*(9), 1909–1924. DOI: 10.1177/0042098012444888

Cass, N., Shove, E., & Urry, J. (2003). *Changing infrastructures, measuring socio-spatial inclusion/exclusion: final report to the Department for Transport*. Lancaster University.

Casso-Hartmann, L., Rojas-Lamos, P., McCourt, K., Vélez-Torres, I., Barba-Ho, L. E., Bolaños, B. W., Montes, C. L., Mosquera, J., & Vanegas, D. (2022). Water pollution and environmental policy in artisanal gold mining frontiers: The case of La Toma, Colombia. *The Science of the Total Environment*, *852*(158417), 158417. Advance online publication. DOI: 10.1016/j.scitotenv.2022.158417 PMID: 36055504

Castillo Haeger, C. A. (2010). La organización del espacio lacustre: desde la superación del planeamiento sectorial (Doctoral dissertation, Arquitectura).

Castillo Mejía, A. M. (2013). Dinámica de las construcciones por usos de la localidad de Suba en los años 2002 y 2012. https://www.catastrobogota.gov.co/sites/default/files/archivos/suba.pdf

Cebey, G. (2016, mayo 9). Insurgentes 300: Un fantasma de la modernidad. Letras Libres. https://letraslibres.com/revista-espana/insurgentes-300-un-fantasma-de-la-modernidad/

CEPAL. (2023). Las ciudades y la vivienda brindan una oportunidad para transformar el modelo de desarrollo de América Latina y el Caribe hacia uno más inclusivo, igualitario y sostenible. Obtenido de https://www.cepal.org/es/noticias/ciudades-la-vivienda-brindan-oportunidad-transformar-modelo-desarrollo-america-latina

Cerdán Verástegui, A., González Arreola, M. A., & Velasco Sánchez, E. (2006). IV. La reforma en marcha, 2001-2006. In *El proceso de modernización en el INFONAVIT, 2001-2006: Estrategia, redes y liderazgo* (pp. 101–266). El Colegio de México.

Cerón-Vivas, A., & Peñuela Mesa, G. A. (2024). Environmental risk assessment of pharmaceutical pollutants in the Oro River Sub-basin (Colombia). *Environmental Research*, *252*(118961), 118951. Advance online publication. DOI: 10.1016/j.envres.2024.118951 PMID: 38688417

Cervero, R. (2014). Transport Infrastructure and the Environment in the Global South: Sustainable Mobility and Urbanism. *Jurnal Perencanaan Wilayah Dan Kota*, *25*(3), 174–191. DOI: 10.5614/jpwk.2015.25.3.1

Cervero, R., Sarmiento, O. L., Jacoby, E., Gomez, L. F., & Neiman, A. (2009). Influences of built environments on walking and cycling: Lessons from bogotá. *International Journal of Sustainable Transportation*, *3*(4), 203–226. DOI: 10.1080/15568310802178314

Chardigny, J.-M., & Walrand, S. (2016). Plant protein for food: Opportunities and bottlenecks. OCL *Oilseeds Fats Crop. Lipids* 23, 6p

Chege, S. M., & Wang, D. (2020a). The influence of technology innovation on SME performance through environmental sustainability practices in Kenya. *Technology in Society*, *60*, 101210. DOI: 10.1016/j.techsoc.2019.101210

Chen, Y. S. (2008). The driver of green innovation and green image - Green core competence. *Journal of Business Ethics*, *81*(3), 531–543. DOI: 10.1007/s10551-007-9522-1

Chen, Y., Salike, N., Luan, F., & He, M. (2016). Heterogeneous effects of inter- and intra-city transportation infrastructure on economic growth: Evidence from Chinese cities. *Cambridge Journal of Regions, Economy and Society*, rsw019. Advance online publication. DOI: 10.1093/cjres/rsw019

Chiou, T. Y., Chan, H. K., Lettice, F., & Chung, S. H. (2011). The influence of greening the suppliers and green innovation on environmental performance and competitive advantage in Taiwan. *Transportation Research Part E, Logistics and Transportation Review*, *47*(6), 822–836. DOI: 10.1016/j.tre.2011.05.016

Choi, D., & Johnson, K. K. P. (2019). Influences of environmental and hedonic motivations on intention to purchase green products: An extension of the theory of planned behavior. *Sustainable Production and Consumption*, *18*, 145–155. DOI: 10.1016/j.spc.2019.02.001

Cielo, C. (2023). Reproducción ampliada de la vida. economía feminista y ecología política. [Clase No. 2]. *Diplomado en Economía popular y feminista*. Buenos Aires: Clacso.

Cielo, C., (2016). Aportes de la economía feminista para el análisis del capitalismo contemporáneo. *Revista Acadêmica (Pontifícia Universidade Católica do Paraná)*, •••, 157–175.

Colectiu-Punt 6. (2019). *Urbanismo feminista. Por una transformación radical de los espacios de vida.* Barcelona: Virus Editorial.

Comune di Milano. (2023). *Piano dei Servizi: Schede dei Nuclei di Identità Locale - Dal NIL 1 al NIL 15*. Comune di Milano.

Connolly, P. (2014). La ciudad y el hábitat popular: Paradigma latinoamericano. In B, Ramírez & E. Pradilla (Eds.). *Teorías sobre la ciudad en América Latina*, (397-441). Ciudad de México, México: Universidad Autónoma Metropolitana.

Conservation International. (2017). The Freshwater Health Index. https://reports.freshwaterhealthindex.org/

Corporación Regional Autónoma. (2006). Elaboración del Diagnóstico, Prospectiva y Formulación de la Cuenca Hidrográfica del Río Bogotá - Subcuenca Río Chicú. Obtenido de Subcuenca Rio Chicú: https://www.car.gov.co/vercontenido/55

Crenshaw, K. (1989). Race, Reform and Retrenchment: Transformation and Legitimation in Anti-Discrimination Law, *Harvard Law Review*,101, pp. 1.331-1.387.

Crevoisier, O., & Rime, D. (2021). Anchoring Urban Development: Globalisation, Attractiveness and Complexity. *Urban Studies (Edinburgh, Scotland)*, *58*(1), 36–52. DOI: 10.1177/0042098019889310

Crichton, D. (2007). What can cities do to increase resilience? *Philosophical Transactions of the Royal Society A: Mathematical, Physical and Engineering Sciences, 365*(1860), 2731–2739.

D'Albergo, E. (2010). Urban issues in nation-state agendas: A comparison in Western Europe. *Urban Research & Practice*, *3*(2), 138–158. DOI: 10.1080/17535069.2010.481220

D'Ambrosio, C., & Rodrigues, R. I. (2008). Deprivation in the São Paulo Districts: Evidence from 2000. *World Development*, *36*(6), 1094–1112. DOI: 10.1016/j.worlddev.2007.10.007

de Castro, F., Hogenboom, B., & Baud, M. (2016). Environmental governance in Latin America. In Palgrave Macmilan (1st Editio). DOI: 10.1007/978-1-137-50572-9

de Garay, G. (2010). Recordando el futuro de la Ciudad de México. Testimonios orales de sus arquitectos, 1940-1990. *Alteridades (El Parque)*, *20*(39), 11–28.

De Vidovich, L., & Scolari, G. (2022). Seeking polycentric post-suburbanization: A view from the urban region of Milan. *Urban Geography*, *43*(1), 123–133. DOI: 10.1080/02723638.2020.1858587

Decreto por el que se reestructura la Comisión para la Regularización de la Tenencia de la Tierra para transformarse en el Instituto Nacional del Suelo Sustentable. (2016). https://www.dof.gob.mx/nota_detalle.php?codigo=5465842&fecha=16/12/2016#gsc.tab=0

Dede, M., Asdak, C., & Setiawan, I. (2022). Spatial-ecological approach in cirebon's peri-urban regionalization. *IOP Conference Series. Earth and Environmental Science*, *1089*(1), 012080. DOI: 10.1088/1755-1315/1089/1/012080

Demazière, C. (2018). Strategic Spatial Planning in a Situation of Fragmented Local Government: The Case of France. DisP - The Planning Review, 54(2), 58–76. DOI: 10.1080/02513625.2018.1487645

Departamento Administrativo Nacional de Estadísitca- DANE. (2018). Censo de Población y Vivienda. Recuperado el 19 de 09 de 2019, de http://systema59.dane .gov.co/bincol/RpWebEngine.exe/Portal?BASE=CNPVBASE4V2&lang=esp

Departamento Administrativo Nacional de Estadística (DANE). (2005). Censo general 2005. Recuperado de https://www.dane.gov.co/index.php/estadisticas-por -tema/demografia-y-poblacion/censo-general-2005-1

Diario Oficial de la Federación. (1985, agosto 19). Reglamento Interior de la Secretaria de Desarrollo Urbano y Ecología. https://www.dof.gob.mx/nota_detalle.php ?codigo=4758477&fecha=19/08/1985#gsc.tab=0

Diaz, H., Garay-Fluhmann, R., McDowell, J., Montaña, E., Reyes, B., and Salas, S. (2011). Vulnerability of Andean Communities to Climate Variability and Climate Change. 209-223. DOI: 10.1007/978-3-642-22266-5_13

Díaz-García, C., González-Moreno, Á., & Sáez-Martínez, F. J. (2015). Eco-innovation: Insights from a literature review. *Innovation (North Sydney, N.S.W.)*, *17*(1), 6–23. DOI: 10.1080/14479338.2015.1011060

Diaz, J., & Torno, C. (2021). *Debates picantes de los feminismos populares. Estado y Autonomía*. Madre Selva.

Dirección de Análisis y Diseño Estratégico. (2022). Diagnostico Local de Suba. https://www.integracionsocial.gov.co/images/_docs/entidad/11_Diagnostico_Local _Suba_2021_VF_.pdf

Directiva Europea del Paisaje. (2000). *Convenio Europeo del Paisaje*.

Dodman, D., Leck, H., Rusca, M., & Colenbrander, S. (2019). African urbanisation and urbanism: Implications for risk accumulation and reduction. *International Journal of Disaster Risk Reduction*, *26*, 7–15. DOI: 10.1016/j.ijdrr.2017.06.029

Dong, J. Q., Karhade, P. P., Rai, A., & Xu, S. X. (2021). How firms make information technology investment decisions: Toward a behavioral agency theory. *Journal of Management Information Systems*, *38*(1), 29–58. DOI: 10.1080/07421222.2021.1870382

Douglas, I. (2008). Environmental Change in Peri-Urban Areas and Human and Ecosystem Health. *Geography Compass*, *2*(4), 1095–1137. DOI: 10.1111/j.1749-8198.2008.00122.x

Doyle, M. W., & Havlick, D. G. (2009). Infrastructure and the Environment. *Annual Review of Environment and Resources*, *34*(1), 349–373. Advance online publication. DOI: 10.1146/annurev.environ.022108.180216

Dubey, R., Gunasekaran, A., & Samar Ali, S. (2015). Exploring the relationship between leadership, operational practices, institutional pressures and environmental performance: A framework for green supply chain. *International Journal of Production Economics*, *160*, 120–132. DOI: 10.1016/j.ijpe.2014.10.001

Dupont, V. (Ed.). (2005). *Peri-urban dynamics: population, habitat and environment on the peripheries of large Indian metropolises: a review of concepts and general issues*. New Delhi: Centre de sciences humaines.

Eccles, R. G., Ioannou, I., & Serafeim, G. (2014). The impact of corporate sustainability on organizational processes and performance. *Management Science*, *60*(11), 2835–2857. DOI: 10.1287/mnsc.2014.1984

Elizalde, S. (2008). Debates sobre la experiencia. Un recorrido por la teoría y la praxis feminista. *Oficios terrestres*, (23), 18 – 30.

El-Kassar, A. N., & Singh, S. K. (2019). Green innovation and organizational performance: The influence of big data and the moderating role of management commitment and HR practices. *Technological Forecasting and Social Change*, *144*, 483–498. DOI: 10.1016/j.techfore.2017.12.016

Elkington, J. (1994). Towards the Sustainable Corporation: Win–win–win Business Strategies for Sustainable Development. *California Management Review*, *36*(2), 90–100. DOI: 10.2307/41165746

Engels, J. I. (2016). Infrastructure and Fragmentation: The Limits of the Integration Paradigm. In Schiefelbusch, M. (Ed.), *In Linking Networks: The Formation of Common Standards and Visions for Infrastructure Development* (1st ed., pp. 19–34). Routledge., DOI: 10.4324/9781315592497

Environmental Protection Agency. (2023). Volatile Organic Compounds' Impact on Indoor Air Quality. Retrieved from https://www.epa.gov/indoor-air-quality-iaq/volatile-organic-compounds-impact-indoor-air-quality

Eraydın, Z. (2016). Kentsel Markalaşma Stratejilerinin Kent Belleği ve Kent İmgesi Üzerine Etkileri: Ankara Örneği. İdealkent, 7(20), 830-855.

Ercan, M. A., & Belge, Z. S. (2020). *Measuring Walkability for More Liveable and Sustainable Cities: The Case of Mersin City Centre*. Urbanism and the New Habitat.

Escobar, A. (2015). Development, critiques of. In G. D'Alisa, F., Demaria, G. & Kallis, G. (eds), *Degrowth. A vocabulary for a new era*, (pp. 29–32), Abingdon & New York, NY: Routledge.

Etzion, D. (2007). Research on organizations and the natural environment, 1992-Present: A review. *Journal of Management*, *33*(4), 637–664. DOI: 10.1177/0149206307302553

European Commission. (2011). *Cities of tomorrow: Challenges, visions, ways forward*. Directorate-General for Regional Policy.

European Environment Agency. (2017). *Climate change, impacts and vulnerability in Europe 2016: An indicator-based report* (EEA Report No. 1/2017).

Evans, G. (2009). Accessibility, Urban Design and the Whole Journey Environment. *Built Environment*, *35*(3), 365–385.

Ewing, R., & Handy, S. (2009). Measuring the unmeasurable: Urban design qualities related to

Ewing, R., & Clemente, O. (2013). *Measuring Urban Design: Metrics for Livable Places*. Island Press. DOI: 10.5822/978-1-61091-209-9

Fadaei, A. (2018). Formal-informal nexus in academic debates: A literature review. *Territorio*, (84), 167–174. DOI: 10.3280/TR2018-084023

FAO. (2014). Conference outcome document: Rome declaration on nutrition. In Proceedings of the Second International Conference on Nutrition, Rome, Italy, 19–21 November 2014.

Fasolin, L. H., Pereira, R. N., Pinheiro, A. C., Martins, J. T., Andrade, C., Ramos, O., & Vicente, A. (2019). Emergent food proteins–Towards sustainability, health and innovation. *Food Research International*, *125*, 108586. DOI: 10.1016/j.foodres.2019.108586 PMID: 31554037

Fatoki, O. (2019). Green marketing orientation and environmental and social performance of hospitality firms in South Africa. *Foundations of Management*, *11*(1), 277–290. DOI: 10.2478/fman-2019-0023

Fedeli, V. (2022). National Urban Policies in Europe, a Contrasted and Fragmented Picture or a Shared Social Construction? In Gelli, F., & Basso, M. (Eds.), *Identifying Models of National Urban Agendas, Comparative Studies of Political Agendas*. Springer Nature Switzerland AG., DOI: 10.1007/978-3-031-08388-4_10

Federici, S. (2010). *Calibán y la bruja. Mujeres, cuerpo y acumulación originaria.* Madrid: traficantes de sueños.

Federici, S. (2022). *Ir más alla de la piel repensar, rehacer y reinvidicar el cuerpo en el capitalismo contemporaneo*. Madrid: Traficantes de sueños.

Feria, T. J., & Ramos, J. S. (2017). Naturaleza y ciudad. Perspectivas para la ordenación de la infraestructura verde en los planes territoriales metropolitanos en España. *Boletín de la Asociación de Geógrafos Españoles*, *74*(74), 117–141. DOI: 10.21138/bage.2447

Fernandes, E. (2018). A Produção Socioeconômica, Política e Jurídica da Informalidade Urbana. Instituto Polis. Retrieved from https://abrir.link/hNfgq

Fichter, K., Beucker, S., Noack, T., & Springer, S. (2007). Entstehungspfade von Nachhaltigkeitsinnovationen. *Fallstudien und Szenarien zu Einflussfaktoren, Schlüsselakteuren und Internetunterstützung* [Development pathways of sustainable innovation: Case studies and scenarios of influencing factors]. Stuttgart: Fraunhofer IRB-Verlag (nova-net Werkstattreihe).

Figueroa-Benitez, A., Nagheeby, M., Figueroa, A., & Amezaga, J. (2023). Disrupted water governance in the shadows: Revealing the role of hidden actors in the Upper Cauca River Basin in Colombia. *Frontiers in Water*, *5*, 801171. Advance online publication. DOI: 10.3389/frwa.2023.801171

Fisher, W. S.. (2001). *Urban lake ecosystems: A multidisciplinary approach to understanding their ecology and management*. Springer Science & Business Media.

Fitriasari, F. (2020). How do small and medium enterprise (SME) survive the COVID-19 outbreak? *Jurnal Inovasi Ekonomi*, *5*(02). Advance online publication. DOI: 10.22219/jiko.v5i3.11838

Forsyth, A. (2012). Defining Suburbs. *Journal of Planning Literature*, *27*(3), 270–281. DOI: 10.1177/0885412212448101

Forsyth, A. (2015). What is a walkable place? The walkability debate in urban design. *URBAN DESIGN International*, *20*(4), 274–292. DOI: 10.1057/udi.2015.22

Forsyth, A., & Krizek, K. (2010). Promoting Walking and Bicycling: Assessing the Evidence to Assist Planners. *Built Environment*, *36*(4), 429–446. DOI: 10.2148/benv.36.4.429

Forsyth, A., & Southworth, M. (2008). Cities afoot—Pedestrians, walkability, and urban design. *Journal of Urban Design*, *13*(1), 1–3. DOI: 10.1080/13574800701816896

Forsyth, A., & Southworth, M. (2008). *Guest Editorial: Cities Afoot—Pedestrians*. Walkability and.

Fraser, N. (2014). Tras la morada oculta de Marx. Por una concepción ampliada del capitalismo. *New Left Review*, (86), 57–86.

Friedmann, J. (1987). *Planning in the Public Domain: From Knowledge to Action*. Princeton University Press.

Fukuda-Hayakawa, I. (2010). Planeación urbana en Curitiba. Quivera Revista de Estudios Territoriales, 12(1), Article 1.

Fundación Aquae. (2022). ¿Qué es la gobernanza del agua? https://www.fundacionaquae.org/wiki/gobernanza-agua/

Füssel, H. M. (2007). Adaptation planning for climate change: Concepts, assessment approaches, and key lessons. *Sustainability Science*, *2*(2), 2. DOI: 10.1007/s11625-007-0032-y

Fu, Z., & Xi, S. (2020). The effects of heavy metals on human metabolism. *Toxicology Mechanisms and Methods*, *30*(3), 167–176. DOI: 10.1080/15376516.2019.1701594 PMID: 31818169

Gago, V. (2019). *La potencia feminista o el deseo de cambiarlo todo*. Madrid: traficantes de sueños.

Galbreath, J. (2019). Drivers of green innovations: The impact of export intensity, women leaders, and absorptive capacity. *Journal of Business Ethics*, *158*(1), 47–61. DOI: 10.1007/s10551-017-3715-z

Gallardo Salas, M. A., Mendoza-Castillo, D. I., Bonilla-Petriciolet, A., & Jiménez-Junca, C. (2024). Functionalized activated carbon with whey protein amyloid fibrils for adsorption of arsenic from water. *Environmental Nanotechnology, Monitoring & Management*, *22*(100956), 100956. Advance online publication. DOI: 10.1016/j.enmm.2024.100956

García Galindo, W., & Carrero Barón, D. F. (2017). Dinámica Inmobiliaria Bogotá - Región. https://www.catastrobogota.gov.co/sites/default/files/Dinamica%20Inmobiliaria%20Bogota%20Region%202017%20-%202020_20210331_VersionDiseno_v1_20210520.pdf

García-Ramón, M. (2019). La Geografía del género. In Monk, J., Prats, M., & Veleda, S. (Eds.), *María Dolors García-Ramon. Geografía y género, disidencia e innovación*. Icaria Editorial.

Gartland, L. (2008). *Heat islands: Understanding and mitigating heat in urban areas*. Earthscan.

Geneletti, D., La Rosa, D., Spyra, M., & Cortinovis, C. (2017). A review of approaches and challenges for sustainable planning in urban peripheries. *Landscape and Urban Planning*, *165*, 231–243. DOI: 10.1016/j.landurbplan.2017.01.013

Geneletti, D., & Zardo, L. (2016). Ecosystem-based adaptation in cities: An analysis of European urban climate adaptation plans. *Land Use Policy*, *50*, 38–47. DOI: 10.1016/j.landusepol.2015.09.003

Geng, R., Mansouri, S. A., & Aktas, E. (2017). The relationship between green supply chain management and performance: A meta-analysis of empirical evidences in Asian emerging economies. *International Journal of Production Economics*, *183*, 245–258. DOI: 10.1016/j.ijpe.2016.10.008

Georgescu, M., Morefield, P. E., Bierwagen, B. G., & Weaver, C. P. (2014). Urban adaptation can roll back warming of emerging megapolitan regions. *Proceedings of the National Academy of Sciences of the United States of America*, *111*(8), 2909–2914. DOI: 10.1073/pnas.1322280111 PMID: 24516126

Ghose, M. K., & Majumdar, P. (2018). Peri-urbanisation in India: Trends, drivers, and implications for sustainable urban development. *Urban Science (Basel, Switzerland)*, *2*(2), 36.

Giannotti, E., Vásquez, A., Galdámez, E., Velásquez, P., & Devoto, C. (2021). Planificación de infraestructura verde para la emergencia climática: Aprendizajes desde el proyecto" Stgo+", Santiago de Chile. *Cuadernos de Geografia*, *30*(2), 359–375. DOI: 10.15446/rcdg.v30n2.88749

Gifreu, F. J. (2018). Ciudades adaptativas y resilientes ante el cambio climático. Estrategias locales para contribuir a la sostenibilidad urbana. *Revista Aragonesa de Administración Pública*, *52*(52), 102–158. DOI: 10.71296/raap.129

Gil-Alonso, F., & López-Villanueva, C. (2023). Metropolitan Spatial Reconfiguration and the Mobility Transition: Sustainability Challenges in the Fragmented City. In *Urban Dynamics in the Post-pandemic Period: Tourist Spaces and Urban Centres* (pp. 305–324). Springer International Publishing.

Gilbert, A. (2007). The Return of the Slum: Does Language Matter? *International Journal of Urban and Regional Research*, *31*(4), 697–713. DOI: 10.1111/j.1468-2427.2007.00754.x

Gil-Grandet, N. (2019). El borde urbano un concepto dinámico e integral para el estudio de los espacios urbano regionales. *Revista Latinoamericana de Estudiantes de Geografía*, 6. Obtenido de https://releg.org/pdf/releg2019n6_pp10-20.pdf

Gill, S. E., Handley, J. F., Ennos, A. R., & Pauleit, S. (2017). Adapting cities for climate change: The role of the green infrastructure. *Built Environment*, *33*(1), 115–133. DOI: 10.2148/benv.33.1.115

Gil-Ozoudeh, I., Iwuanyanwu, O., Okwandu, A. C., & Ike, C. S. (2023). Sustainable urban design: The role of green buildings in shaping resilient cities. *International Journal of Applied Research in Social Sciences*, *5*(10), 674–692. DOI: 10.51594/ijarss.v5i10.1481

Gladwin, T. N., Kennelly, J. J., & Krause, T. S. (1995). Shifting Paradigms for Sustainable Development: Implications for Management Theory and Research. *Academy of Management Review*, *20*(4), 874–907. DOI: 10.2307/258959

Global Innovation Index. (2018). *Key findings report*. https://www.globalinnovationindex.org/about-gii#keyfindings

Gobierno del Estado de Yucatán. (1962). Ley Sobre el Régimen de Propiedad y Condominio Inmobiliario del Estado de Yucatán. https://docs.mexico.justia.com/estatales/yucatan/ley-sobre-el-regimen-de-propiedad-y-condominio-inmobiliario-del-estado-de-yucatan.pdf

Gobierno del Estado de Yucatán. (1985). Ley de Fraccionamientos del Estado de Yucatán. https://www.poderjudicialyucatan.gob.mx/digestum/marcoLegal/02/2012/DIGESTUM02073.pdf

Gobierno del Estado de Yucatán. (2010, diciembre 7). Ley de Desarrollos Inmobiliarios del Estado de Yucatán. https://www.poderjudicialyucatan.gob.mx/digestum/marcoLegal/02/2012/DIGESTUM02098.pdf

Gobierno del Estado de Yucatán. (2012). Reglamento de la Ley de Desarrollos Inmobiliarios del Estado de Yucatán. https://www.poderjudicialyucatan.gob.mx/digestum/marcoLegal/05/2012/DIGESTUM05044.pdf

Gobierno del Estado de Yucatán. (2014). Ley sobre el Régimen de Propiedad en Condominio del Estado de Yucatán. https://www.congresoyucatan.gob.mx/storage/legislacion/leyes/45e8dfc61af9521fa5b579bce956a7d7_2024-01-17.pdf

González Bernáldez, F. (2014). *Invitación al paisaje: Ensayos sobre el paisaje*. Abada Editores.

Goodman, J., Korsunova, A., & Halme, M. (2017). Our collaborative future: Activities and roles of stakeholders in sustainability-oriented innovation. *Business Strategy and the Environment*, *26*(6), 731–753. DOI: 10.1002/bse.1941

Gorzoni, V. A. S., Pereira, P. P., Lautenschlager, S. R., & Okawa, C. M. P. (2019). Measures for reduction of the water losses in the distribution network: A case study on the municipality of Altônia/PR. Revista Eletrônica Em Gestão. *Educação e Tecnologia Ambiental*, *23*(10), 10. Advance online publication. DOI: 10.5902/2236117038533

Gottero, E., Larcher, F., & Cassatella, C. (2023). Defining and Regulating Peri-Urban Areas through a Landscape Planning Approach: The Case Study of Turin Metropolitan Area (Italy). *Land (Basel)*, *12*(1), 217. DOI: 10.3390/land12010217

Grau Biosca, E. (2014). Saber que alguien lo escucha. El método de la narrativa en la investigación La verdad de las mujeres. Víctimas del conflicto armado en Colombia. In Mendia Azkue, I., Luxán, M., Legarreta, M., Guzmán, G., Zirion, I., & Azpiazu Carballo, J. (Eds.), *Otras formas de (re)conocer. Reflexiones, herramientas y aplicaciones desde la investigación feminista* (pp. 147–160). Hegoa.

Grupo de Buena Governanza. (2012). Hacia una buena gobernanza para la gestión integrada de los recursos hídricos documento temático de las Américas.

Gudynas, E. (2011). Buen vivir: Germinando alternativas al desarrollo. *América Latina en Movimiento – ALAI-*, 462, 1-20.

Gutiérrez, R. (2017*). Horizontes comunitario-populares. Producción de lo común más allá de las políticas estado-céntricas.* Madrid: Traficantes de sueños.

Gutiérrez, J. (2009). Transport and Accessibility. DOI: 10.1016/B978-008044910-4.01030-0

Guttikunda, S. K., & Calori, G. (2013). Urban air pollution in megacities of India. *Atmospheric Environment*, *67*, 178–196.

Guzmán, A. (2019). *Descolonizar la memoria. Descolonizar los feminismos*. Tarpuna Muya.

Guzman, L. A., Oviedo, D., & Bocarejo, J. P. (2017). City profile: The Bogotá Metropolitan Area that never was. *Cities (London, England)*, *60*, 202–215. DOI: 10.1016/j.cities.2016.09.004

Haeger, R. (2010). La planificación del espacio lacustre. Una aproximación conceptual a la elaboración de planes de ordenación de ámbitos lacustres. *Boletín de la Asociación de Geógrafos Españoles*, (53), 127–151.

Haghlesan, M. (2013). How does Indoor Environmental Quality affect Public Health in Sustainable Urban.

Hall, J., & Wagner, M. (2012). Integrating sustainability into firms' processes: Performance effects and the moderating role of business models and innovation. *Business Strategy and the Environment*, *21*(3), 183–196. DOI: 10.1002/bse.728

Halme, M., & Korpela, M. (2014). Responsible innovation toward sustainable development in small and medium-sized enterprises. A resource perspective. *Business Strategy and the Environment*, *23*(8), 547–566. DOI: 10.1002/bse.1801

Han & Chen (2021) 800 Survey TRA To uncover the antecedents of eco-innovation adoption by SMEs in Myanmar Customer demands, Environmental concerns and regulations, Rivalry pressures, Eco-innovation adoption, and Firm innovation capabilities.

Handy, S. (2020). Is accessibility an idea whose time has finally come? *Transportation Research Part D, Transport and Environment*, *83*, 102319. DOI: 10.1016/j.trd.2020.102319

Hanelt, A., Busse, S., & Kolbe, L. M. (2016). Driving business transformation toward sustainability: Exploring the impact of supporting IS on the performance contribution of eco-innovations. *Information Systems Journal*, *27*(4), 463–502. DOI: 10.1111/isj.12130

Hansen, E., Große-Dunker, F., & Reichwald, R. (2009). Sustainable innovation cube—A framework to evaluate sustainability-oriented innovations. *International Journal of Innovation Management*, *13*(4), 683–713. DOI: 10.1142/S1363919609002479

Hansen, W. G. (1959). How accessibility shapes land use. *Journal of the American Institute of Planners*, *25*(2), 73–76. DOI: 10.1080/01944365908978307

Haoran, Y., Cong, W., & Youyang, Y. (2022). The Spatial Structure Evolution of China's High-Speed Rail Network and Its Impacts on Real Estate Investment. *Applied Spatial Analysis and Policy*, *15*(1), 49–69. Advance online publication. DOI: 10.1007/s12061-021-09390-7

Harris, R. (2001). The Knowledge-based Economy: Intellectual Origins and New Economic Perspectives. *International Journal of Management Reviews*, *3*(1), 21–40. DOI: 10.1111/1468-2370.00052

Hart, S. L., Milstein, M. B., & Caggiano, J. (2003). Creating sustainable value [and executive commentary]. *The Academy of Management Executive (1993–2005)*, 17(2), 56.

Hasan, Z., & Ali, N. A. (2015). The impact of green marketing strategy on the firm's performance in Malaysia. *Procedia: Social and Behavioral Sciences, 172*, 463–470. DOI: 10.1016/j.sbspro.2015.01.382

Hasselwander, M., Nieland, S., Dematera-Contreras, K., & Goletz, M. (2023). MaaS for the masses: Potential transit accessibility gains and required policies under Mobility-as-a-Service. DOI: 10.1016/j.multra.2023.100086

Hellström, T. (2007). Dimensions of environmentally sustainable innovation: The structure of eco-innovation concepts. *Sustainable Development (Bradford), 15*(3), 148–159. DOI: 10.1002/sd.309

Henchion, M., Hayes, M., Mullen, A. M., Fenelon, M., & Tiwari, B. (2017). Future protein supply and demand: Strategies and factors influencing a sustainable equilibrium. *Foods, 6*(7), 53. DOI: 10.3390/foods6070053 PMID: 28726744

Hernández Aja, A. (2009). La protección del paisaje en la ordenación territorial y urbanística: instrumentos y técnicas para su aplicación. Revista Catalana de Derecho Ambiental, 1(1).

Hernández-Garcia, J. (2016). Hábitat popular, un modo alternativo de producción de espacio para América Latina? In Hernández, I. (Ed.), *Estética de los mundos posibles: inmersión en la vida artificial, las artes y las practicas urbanas* (pp. 245–258). Pontificia Universidad Javeriana.

Herrera-Valdés, R., Almaguer-López, M. A., Orantes-Navarro, C. M., López-Marín, L., Brizuela-Díaz, E. G., Bayarre-Vea, H., Silva-Ayçaguer, L. C., Orellana de Figueroa, P., Smith-González, M., Chávez-Muñoz, Y., & Bacallao-Méndez, R. (2019). Epidemic of Chronic Kidney Disease of Nontraditional Etiology in El Salvador: Integrated Health Sector Action and South-South Cooperation. *MEDICC Review, 21*(4), 46–52. DOI: 10.37757/MR2019.V21.N4.8 PMID: 32335569

Herrero, Y. (2011). *Cambiar las gafas para mirar el mundo. Una nueva cultura de la sostenibilidad*. Madrid: libros en acción.

Hesse-Biber, S. N. (2008) Feminist research. In L. Given (Ed.). *The SAGE Encyclopedia of qualitative research methods*. V.1 y 2. Estados Unidos: SAGE Publications, Inc.

Hewitt, C. N., Ashworth, K., & MacKenzie, A. R. (2020). Using green infrastructure to improve urban air quality (GI4AQ). *Ambio, 49*(1), 62–73. DOI: 10.1007/s13280-019-01164-3 PMID: 30879268

He, X., Xu, P., An, B.-W., & Guo, Q. (2024). Urban green infrastructure: Bridging biodiversity conservation and sustainable urban development through adaptive management approach. *Frontiers in Ecology and Evolution*, *12*, 1440477. Advance online publication. DOI: 10.3389/fevo.2024.1440477

Hidalgo, G. M. (2017). Las ciudades como objetivo de desarrollo sostenible. *Boletín IEEE*, *5*, 22–32.

Hidayati, I., Yamu, C., & Tan, W. (2019). The Emergence of Mobility Inequality in Greater Jakarta, Indonesia: A Socio-Spatial Analysis of Path Dependencies in Transport–Land Use Policies. *Sustainability (Basel)*, *11*(18), 5115. DOI: 10.3390/su11185115

Historia_del_Infonavit.pdf. (s. f.). Recuperado 22 de junio de 2024, de https://portalmx.infonavit.org.mx/wps/wcm/connect/7cf006d4-1466-48fe-88eb-78bc920a0624/Historia_del_Infonavit.pdf?MOD=AJPERES&CONVERT_TO=url&CACHEID=ROOTWORKSPACE-7cf006d4-1466-48fe-88eb-78bc920a0624-naAruF

Hojnik, J., & Ruzzier, M. (2016). The Driving Forces of Process Eco-innovation and Its Impact on Performance: Insights from Slovenia. *Journal of Cleaner Production*, *133*, 812–825. DOI: 10.1016/j.jclepro.2016.06.002

https://isla.merida.gob.mx/serviciosinternet/normatividad/files/Acuerdos/ACUERDO_IMPLAN.pdf

Huhtala, J., Mattila, P., Sihvonen, A., & Tikkanen, H. (2014). Barriers to innovation diffusion in industrial networks – a systematic combining approach. In Woodside, A., Pattison, H., & Marshall, R. (Eds.), *Field Guide For Business-To-Business Case Study Research (Advances in Business Marketing and Management)* (Vol. 21). Emerald. DOI: 10.1108/S1069-096420140000021002

Huma, Z., Lin, G., & Hyder, S. L. (n.d.). Promoting Resilience and Health of Urban Citizen through Urban Green Space. DOI: 10.52293/WES.1.1.3743

Hunt, A., & Watkiss, P. (2011a). Climate change impacts and adaptation in cities: A review of the literature. *Climatic Change*, *104*(1), 13–49. DOI: 10.1007/s10584-010-9975-6

Hunt, A., & Watkiss, P. (2011b). Identifying and assessing adaptation options in urban areas. In Satterthwaite, D. (Ed.), *Adapting cities to climate change* (pp. 123–143). Earthscan.

Hussain, M., Khan, R. A., & Rao, K. (2022). *S.M., Q*. IAQ Assessment for HVAC Performance in Selected Commercial and Office Buildings in India., DOI: 10.46254/IN02.20220576

IBGE. (2022). *Brazilian Census of 2022*. IBGE.

IDECA -Infraestructura de Datos Espaciales de Catastro Distrital-. (2021). *Cartografía básica*. https://www.ideca.gov.co/

IDOM. (2018). *Estudio del crecimiento y evolución de la huella urbana para Bogotá Región*.

IGAC -Instituto Geográfico Agustín Codazzi-. (1977). *Fotografía aérea 1977*

Indian Green Building Council (IGBC). (2022). Impact of Green Roofs on Indoor Air Quality in Commercial Buildings in Hyderabad.

Indian Institute of Forest Management (IIFM). (2023). Effectiveness of Urban Forests in Mitigating Air Pollution in Hyderabad.

Indian Institute of Science (IISc). (2019). Impact of Urban Greening on Air Quality in Hyderabad.

Indian Institute of Technology (IIT) Hyderabad. (2022). Impact of Building Orientation on Indoor Air Quality in Residential Buildings in Hyderabad.

INSUS. (2023). Manual de procedimientos para la integración y actualización del inventario nacional de suelo del INSUs. SEDATU. http://insus.gob.mx/transparencia/Normateca/nis/Manual-integracion-acutalizacion-INS.pdf

Inter American Development Bank. (1999). *Spilled Water*. Institutional Commitment in the Provision of Water Services., DOI: 10.18235/0012351

IPCC. (2014). *Climate Change 2014: Impacts, Adaptation, and Vulnerability. Part A: Global and Sectoral Aspects*. Contribution of Working Group II to the Fifth Assessment Report of the Intergovernmental Panel on Climate Change. Cambridge University Press.

IPCC. (2020). *Climate Change and Land: An IPCC Special Report*. Retrieved from https://www.ipcc.ch/srccl/

IPCC. (2022). [*Impacts, Adaptation and Vulnerability*. Working Group II Contribution to the Sixth Assessment Report of the IPCC.]. *Climatic Change*, •••, 2022.

Iqbal, A., Nazir, H., & Memon, R. M. (2022). Shopping centers versus traditional open street bazaars: A comparative study of user's preference in the city of Karachi, Pakistan. *Frontiers in Built Environment*, *8*, 1066093. Advance online publication. DOI: 10.3389/fbuil.2022.1066093

Iyer, N., & Menezes, R. Barbosa, & Hugo. (2023). Mobility and Transit Segregation in Urban Spaces. DOI: 10.48550/ARXIV.2304.07086

Iyer, N. G., Menezes, R., & Barbosa, H. (2023). Transport and Mobility Segregation in Urban Spaces. *International Journal of Population Data Science*, *8*(3). Advance online publication. DOI: 10.23889/ijpds.v8i3.2268

Izquierdo, R.. (2005). *Cambio climático en los sistemas lacustres de España: impactos, vulnerabilidad y adaptación*. Ministerio de Medio Ambiente.

Jabareen, Y. (2006). Sustainable urban forms: Their typologies, models, and concepts. *Journal of Planning Education and Research*, *26*(1), 38–52. DOI: 10.1177/0739456X05285119

Jabareen, Y. (2013). Planning the resilient city: Concepts and strategies for coping with climate change and environmental risk. *Cities (London, England)*, *31*, 220–229. DOI: 10.1016/j.cities.2012.05.004

Jacot des Combes, H., Mitchell, D., & Wisner, B. (2019). Measuring urban resilience: Are we asking the right questions? *International Journal of Disaster Risk Reduction*, *37*, 101–128.

Jaeger, J. A. G., Raumer, H. S., Esswein, H., Müller, M., & Schmidt-Lüttmann, M. (2007). *Time series of landscape fragmentation caused by transportation infrastructure and urban development: a case study from Baden-Württemberg*., DOI: 10.5751/ES-01983-120122

Janhall, S. (2015). Reviewing the health benefits of greenness. *International Journal of Public Health*, *60*, 103–110.

Janoschka, M. (2016). Gentrificación, desplazamiento, desposesión: Procesos urbanos claves en América Latina. *Revista INVI*, *31*(88), 27–71. DOI: 10.4067/S0718-83582016000300002

Jaramillo, S. (2012). Urbanización informal: Diagnósticos y políticas. Una revisión al debate latinoamericano para pensar líneas de acción actuales. In Salazar, C. (Ed.), *Irregular: Suelo y mercado en América Latina* (pp. 33–83). El Colegio de México.

Jayachandran, V. N., & Rao, T. N. (2024). Long-term regional air pollution characteristics in and around Hyderabad, India: Effects of natural and anthropogenic sources. DOI: 10.1016/j.aeaoa.2024.100254

Jenkins, H. (2009). A 'business opportunity' model of corporate social responsibility for small- and medium-sized enterprises. *Business Ethics (Oxford, England)*, *18*(1), 21–36. DOI: 10.1111/j.1467-8608.2009.01546.x

Johnson, M. W., Christensen, C. M., & Kagermann, H. (2008). Reinventing your business model. *Harvard Business Review*, *86*(12), 51–59.

Kaewmai, R., Grant, T., Mungkalasiri, J., & Musikavong, C. (2021). Assessing the water scarcity footprint of food crops by growing season available water remaining (AWARE) characterization factors in Thailand. *The Science of the Total Environment*, *763*(143000), 143000. Advance online publication. DOI: 10.1016/j.scitotenv.2020.143000 PMID: 33190890

Kamal, A. S. M., Hassan, S. M., & Adnan, M. S. G. (2018). Climate change adaptation policy and practice in Bangladesh: An empirical review. *Environmental Development*, *25*, 56–66.

Kanai, J. M., & Schindler, S. (2022). Infrastructure-led development and the peri-urban question: Furthering crossover comparisons. *Urban Studies (Edinburgh, Scotland)*, *59*(8), 1597–1617. DOI: 10.1177/00420980211064158

Kapalo, P., Berridge, V., Larsen, R., & Xiao, W. (2022). Indoor air quality assessment in the apartment – case study. *IOP Conference Series. Materials Science and Engineering*, *1252*(1), 012061. DOI: 10.1088/1757-899X/1252/1/012061

Karjaluoto, H., & Vaccaro, V. L. (2009). B2B green marketing and innovation theory for competitive advantage. *Journal of Systems and Information Technology*, *11*(4), 315–330. DOI: 10.1108/13287260911002477

Kelly, C. E., Tight, M. R., Hodgson, F. C., & Page, M. W. (2011). A comparison of three methods for assessing the walkability of the pedestrian environment. *Journal of Transport Geography*, *19*(6), 1500–1508. DOI: 10.1016/j.jtrangeo.2010.08.001

Kemp, R. (2010). Eco-innovation: Definition, Measurement and Open Research Issues. *Economics and Politics*, *27*(3), 397–420.

Khanani, R. S. (2019). *The Impact of a road Infrastructure project on Socio-Spatial Interaction and Quality of Life of Planned and Unplanned Fragments in Kisumu City* [Essay (Master)]. University of Twente.

Khanani, R. S., Adugbila, E. J., Martinez, J. A., & Pfeffer, K. (2021). The Impact of Road Infrastructure Development Projects on Local Communities in Peri-Urban Areas: The Case of Kisumu, Kenya and Accra, Ghana. *International Journal of Community Well-being*, *4*(1), 33–53. DOI: 10.1007/s42413-020-00077-4

Kiefer, C. P., Del Río González, P., & Carrillo-Hermosilla, J. (2018). Drivers and barriers of eco-innovation types for sustainable transitions: A quantitative perspective. *Business Strategy and the Environment*, *107*, 103.

Kinoti, M. (2011). Green marketing intervention strategies and sustainable development: A conceptual paper. *International Journal of Business and Social Science*, *2*(23), 263–273.

Klewitz, J., & Hansen, E. (2014). Sustainability-oriented innovation in SMEs: A systematic literature review. *Journal of Cleaner Production*, *65*, 57–75. DOI: 10.1016/j.jclepro.2013.07.017

Klewitz, J., Zeyen, A., & Hansen, E. G. (2012). Intermediaries driving eco-innovation in SMEs: A qualitative investigation. *European Journal of Innovation Management*, *15*(4), 442–467. DOI: 10.1108/14601061211272376

Kneipp, J. M., Gomes, C. M., Bichueti, R. S., Frizzo, K., & Perlin, A. P. (2019). Sustainable innovation practices and their relationship with the performance of industrial companies, *Rev. Gest˜ao*, *26*(2), 94–111. DOI: 10.1108/REGE-01-2018-0005

Koh, P. P., & Wong, Y. D. (2013). Comparing pedestrians' needs and behaviors indifferent land use environments. *Journal of Transport Geography*, *26*, 43–50. DOI: 10.1016/j.jtrangeo.2012.08.012

Kotzias, D. (2021). Built environment and indoor air quality: The case of volatile organic compounds. 8(2), 135–147. DOI: 10.3934/environsci.2021010

Krambeck, H., & Shah, J. J. (2006). The global walkability index. Cambridge, USA: Massachusetts Institute of Technology (MIT).

Kraśnicka, T., Głód, W., & Wronka-Pośpiech, M. (2018). Management innovation, pro-innovation organisational culture and enterprise performance: Testing the mediation effect. *Review of Managerial Science*, *12*(3), 737–769. DOI: 10.1007/s11846-017-0229-0

Kumar, V., Sharma, M., Sondhi, S., Kaur, K., Sharma, D., Sharma, S., & Utreja, D. (2023). Removal of Inorganic Pollutants from Wastewater: Innovative Technologies and Toxicity Assessment. *Sustainability (Basel)*, *15*(23), 16376. Advance online publication. DOI: 10.3390/su152316376

Lambert, M. R., Brans, K. I., Des Roches, S., Donihue, C. M., & Diamond, S. E. (2021). Adaptive evolution in cities: Progress and misconceptions. *Trends in Ecology & Evolution*, *36*(3), 239–257. DOI: 10.1016/j.tree.2020.11.002 PMID: 33342595

Lam, J. S. L., & Li, K. X. (2019). Green port marketing for sustainable growth and development. *Transport Policy*, *84*, 73–81. DOI: 10.1016/j.tranpol.2019.04.011

Langebaek, C. H. (2019). *Los muiscas. La historia milenaria de un pueblo chibcha*. Penguin Random House.

Lang, R., & Knox, P. (2009). The New Metropolis: Rethinking Megalopolis. *Regional Studies*, *43*(6), 789–802. DOI: 10.1080/00343400701654251

Larson, A. J., Haver, S., Hattendorf, J., Salmon-Mulanovich, G., Riveros, M., Verastegui, H., Mäusezahl, D., & Hartinger, S. M. (2023). Household-level risk factors for water contamination and antimicrobial resistance in drinking water among households with children under 5 in rural San Marcos, Cajamarca, Peru. *One Health, 16*(100482), 100482. Advance online publication. DOI: 10.1016/j.onehlt.2023.100482 PMID: 36655146

Lee, J., Arts, J., Vanclay, F., & Ward, J. (2020). Examining the Social Outcomes from Urban Transport Infrastructure: Long-Term Consequences of Spatial Changes and Varied Interests at Multiple Levels. *Sustainability (Basel), 12*(15), 5907. DOI: 10.3390/su12155907

Lee, J., Baig, F., Talpur, M. A. H., & Shaikh, S. (2021). Public intentions to purchase electric vehicles in Pakistan. *Sustainability (Basel), 13*(10), 1–18. DOI: 10.3390/su13105523

Lee, S., & Talen, E. (2014). Measuring walkability: A note on auditing methods. *Journal of Urban Design, 19*(3), 368–388. DOI: 10.1080/13574809.2014.890040

Leichenko, R. (2011a). Climate change and urban resilience. *Current Opinion in Environmental Sustainability, 3*(3), 164–168. DOI: 10.1016/j.cosust.2010.12.014

Leichenko, R. (2011b). Resilience and the neoliberal city: A critical perspective. *Cities (London, England), 28*(4), 235–240.

Leiva, X., & Icaza, R. (2019). *En tiempos de muerte: cuerpos, rebeldías y resistencias*. Cooperativa Editorial Retos.

León, I. M. P. L. A. N. (s. f.). ¿Quiénes somos? - Somos Implan, un puente que construye León hacia el futuro. Recuperado 23 de junio de 2024, de https://www.implan.gob.mx/quienes-somos.php

Levi, L. L., & Guzmán, E. R. (2019). Mario Pani: De la ciudad imaginada a la ciudad habitada. TOPOFILIA, 18, Article 18.

Libra, J. M., Marinus Collaer, J. S., Datshkovsky, D., & Pérez-Urdiales, M. (2022). Scarcity in the Land of Plenty.

Li, L., Msaad, H., Sun, H., Tan, M. X., Lu, Y., & Lau, A. K. W. (2020). Green innovation and business sustainability: New evidence from energy intensive industry in China. *International Journal of Environmental Research and Public Health, 17*(21), 1–18. DOI: 10.3390/ijerph17217826 PMID: 33114610

Lima, J. J. (2001). Socio-spatial segregation and urban form: Belém at the end of the 1990s. *Geoforum, 32*(4), 493–507. DOI: 10.1016/S0016-7185(01)00019-7

Lin, C. Y., & Ho, Y. H. (2011). Determinants of green practice adoption for logistics companies in China. *Journal of Business Ethics*, *98*(1), 67–83. DOI: 10.1007/s10551-010-0535-9

Lindblom, C. E. (1959). The Science of "Muddling Through". *Public Administration Review*, *19*(2), 79–88. DOI: 10.2307/973677

Linder, M., & Williander, M. (2015). Circular business model innovation: Inherent uncertainties. *Business Strategy and the Environment*. Advance online publication. DOI: 10.1002/bse.1906

Liozu, S. M., & Hinterhuber, A. (2017). Is innovation in pricing your next source of competitive advantage? In *Innovation in Pricing* (pp. 29–46). Routledge.

Lipovetsky, G., & Sébastien, C. (2006). Los tiempos hipermodernos (Primera). Anagrama. https://cursoshistoriavdemexico.wordpress.com/wp-content/uploads/2019/07/lipovetsky-gilles-y-sc3a9bastien-charles-los-tiempos-hipermodernos.pdf

López, A. (2022). Agentes, procesos y activismos ciudadanos en la urbanización de áreas de valor medioambiental en Bogotá. *Tesis Doctoral*. Escuela Internacional de Doctorado.

López, M. J. (2015). Des-Bordes urbanos: Un concepto en construcción. *Revista Hábitat y Sociedad*, (8), 15–41. DOI: 10.12795/HabitatySociedad.2015.i8.02

Lotfi, S., & Koohsari, M. J. (2009). Analyzing accessibility dimension of urban quality of life: Where urban designers face duality between subjective and objective reading of place. *Social Indicators Research*, *94*(3), 417–435. DOI: 10.1007/s11205-009-9438-5 PMID: 20390026

Lucchini, L., Langle-Chimal, O., Candeago, L., Melito, L., Chunet, A., Montfort, A., Lepri, B., Lozano-Gracia, N., & Fraiberger, S. (2023). Socioeconomic disparities in mobility behavior during the COVID-19 pandemic in developing countries. ArXiv. Org. DOI: 10.48550/ARXIV.2305.06888

Luethi, S. (2010). Effective deployment of photovoltaics in the Mediterranean countries: Balancing policy risk and return. *Solar Energy*, *84*(6), 1059–1071. DOI: 10.1016/j.solener.2010.03.014

Macedo, J. (2008). Urban land policy and new land tenure paradigms: Legitimacy vs. legality in Brazilian cities. *Land Use Policy*, *25*(2), 259–270. DOI: 10.1016/j.landusepol.2007.08.001

Machado, A. V. M., Nogueira, M. T., Alves, L. M. C., Quindeler, N. da S., Silva, J. D. C. D., Aranha, P. A. P., Gonçalves, R. P., & Siqueira, N. L. S. (2020). Assessment of community-managed water systems in rural areas of espírito santo, brazil, using the siasar tool. *Revista Ambiente & Água*, *15*(5), 1–19. DOI: 10.4136/ambi-agua.2517

Mackinlay, H. (1993). Las reformas de 1992 a la legislación agraria. El fin de la Reforma Agraria mexicana y la privatización del ejido. *Polis (Bologna)*, *1*(1), 1.

Magretta, J. (2002). Why business models matter. *Harvard Business Review*, *80*(5), 86–92. PMID: 12024761

Malano, H., Maheshwari, B., Singh, V. P., Purohit, R., & Amerasinghe, P. (2014). Challenges and opportunities for peri-urban futures. The Safety of Water, Food, Energy and Livability of Cities: Challenges and Opportunities for Peri-Urban Futures, 3-10.

Maletic, M., Maletic, D., Dahlgaard, J., Dahlgaard-Park, S. M., & Gomišcek, B. (2015). Do corporate sustainability practices enhance organizational economic performance? *International Journal of Quality and Service Sciences*, *2015*(7), 184–200. DOI: 10.1108/IJQSS-02-2015-0025

Manes, F., Silli, V., Salvatori, E., Incerti, G., Galante, G., Fusaro, L., & Perrino, C. (2014). Urban ecosystem services: Tree diversity and stability of PM10 removal in the metropolitan area of Rome. *Annali di Botanica*, 4, 19-26., 4, 19-26.

Marando, F., Heris, M. P., Zulian, G., Udías, A., Mentaschi, L., Chrysoulakis, N., Parastatidis, D., & Maes, J. (2022). Urban heat island mitigation by green infrastructure in European Functional Urban Areas. *Sustainable Cities and Society*, *77*(103564), 103564. DOI: 10.1016/j.scs.2021.103564

Marchant Santiago, C., Sánchez Acuña, R., & Monje-Hernández, Y. (2022). Long-Term Features of Cities in Latin America and the Caribbean: Socio-Residential Segregation, Territorial Inequality, and Spatial Fragmentation. In González Pérez, J. M., Irazábal, C., & Lois González, R. C. (Eds.), *The Routledge Handbook of Urban Studies in Latin America and the Caribbean* (Vol. 1, pp. 177–201). Routledge., DOI: 10.4324/9781003132622-10

March, J. G. (1991). Exploration and exploitation in organizational learning. *Organization Science*, *2*(1), 71–87. DOI: 10.1287/orsc.2.1.71

Maricato, E. (1988). The urban reform movement in Brazil. *International Journal of Urban and Regional Research*, *12*(1), 137–138. DOI: 10.1111/j.1468-2427.1988.tb00079.x

Marmolejo, C., Chica, J. E., & Masip, J. (2012). ¿Hacia un sistema de metrópolis españolas policéntricas?: Evolución de la influencia de los subcentros en la distribución de la población. *ACE: Arquitectura. Ciudad y Entorno*, *18*(18), 163–190. DOI: 10.5821/ace.v6i18.2548

Martin, R., Aslesen, H. W., Grillitsch, M., & Herstad, S. J. (2018). Regional innovation systems and global flows of knowledge. In *New avenues for regional innovation systems-theoretical advances, empirical cases and policy lessons*,127-147 DOI: 10.1007/978-3-319-71661-9_7

Martínez, J. G., & Reza, C. M. (2020). Tlatelolco. Decadencia urbana y arquitectónica de un proyecto simbólico del Modernismo – Editorial Restauro Compás y Canto. Revista Gremium. https://editorialrestauro.com.mx/tlatelolco-decadencia-urbana-y-arquitectonica-de-un-proyecto-simbolico-del-modernismo/

Marvi, H., Khaskheli, R., & Soomro, M. (2022). Urban Green Spaces: Strategic Design Proposal for Conservation: The Case Study of Hyderabad City (Provide Future Development Control Guidelines). *Global Sociological Review*, *VII*(I), 187–194. DOI: 10.31703/gsr.2022(VII-I).18

Massey, D. (1994). *Space, place and gender*. University of Minnesota Press.

Mata Olmo, R. (2002). *Manual de paisaje: Guía para la elaboración de estudios del paisaje*. Junta de Andalucía, Consejería de Medio Ambiente.

Matos, B., & Lobo, C. (2023). The Barrier Effect and Pedestrian Mobility/Accessibility on Urban Highways: An Analysis Based on the Belo Horizonte/Minas Gerais/ Brazil Ring Road. *Sustainability (Basel)*, *15*(4), 3408. Advance online publication. DOI: 10.3390/su15043408

Ma, Y. J., Gam, H. J., & Banning, J. (2017). *Perceived ease of use and usefulness of sus-tainability labels on apparel products: Application of the technology acceptance model*. Fashion and Textiles., DOI: 10.1186/s40691-017-0093-1

Mayorga Guzmán, J. M. (2022). Análisis multitemporal de la transformación del paisaje en áreas periurbanas del norte de Bogotá D.C. para el periodo 1956 – 2021. (tesis de maestría). Universidad Distrital Francisco José de Caldas, Recuperado de: http://hdl.handle.net/11349/30659

McDowell, L. (1999). *Género, identidad y lugar: un estudio de las geografías feministas*. Ediciones Cátedra.

Measham, T. G., Preston, B. L., Smith, T. F., Brooke, C., Gorddard, R., Withycombe, G., & Morrison, C. (2011). Adapting to climate change through local municipal planning: Barriers and challenges. *Mitigation and Adaptation Strategies for Global Change*, *16*(8), 889–909. DOI: 10.1007/s11027-011-9301-2

Meckler, M. (1991). Employing ASHRAE Standard 62-1989 in urban building environments. *Energy Engineering*, *88*(3), 34–60.

Méndez, J. G., García-Moreno, L. M., Murillo-Hoyos, J., & Molina, C. J. (2023). Social Inequality in Popular Neighborhoods: A Pre- and Post-Pandemic Perspective from Joint Accessibility. *Sustainability (Basel)*, *15*(13), 10587. Advance online publication. DOI: 10.3390/su151310587

Mérida, I. M. P. L. A. N. (2019). Plan Integral de Movilidad Urbana Sustentable, Nivel Estrategia. *Vision (Basel)*, *2040*, •••. https://isla.merida.gob.mx/serviciosinternet/ordenamientoterritorial/docs/PIMUS_2040.pdf

Mersha, A. A., & Van Laerhoven, F. (2016). The interplay between planned and autonomous adaptation in response to climate change: Insights from rural Ethiopia. *World Development*, *84*, 155–169.

Meyer Falcón, R. (2023, enero 12). 10 años de Sedatu, el reflejo de una transformación. Medium. https://meyerfalcon.medium.com/10-a%C3%B1os-de-sedatu-el-reflejo-de-una-transformaci%C3%B3n-9b81c7a0a909

Miakhel, M., Abdulrahimzai, A. A., Habib, A. Z. M., & Behsoodi, M. M. (2024). Urban Green Infrastructures and Its Impacts on the Urban Environment: A Review, *1*(2), 9–15. DOI: 10.69739/jece.v1i2.135

Migliario González, A., Mazariegos García, D., Rodríguez Lezica, L., & Díaz Lozano, J. (2020). Interseccionalidades en el cuerpo-territorio. In *Cruz Hernández & M. Bayón Jiménez (Coords.). Cuerpos, Territorios y feminismos. Compilación latinoaméricana de teorías, metodología y prácticas políticas* (pp. 63–82). Clacso.

Miles, L. S., Carlen, E. J., Winchell, K. M., & Johnson, M. T. (2021). Urban evolution comes into its own: Emerging themes and future directions of a burgeoning field. *Evolutionary Applications*, *14*(1), 3–11. DOI: 10.1111/eva.13165 PMID: 33519952

Mohan, M., Sati, A. P., & Bhati, S. (2020). Urban sprawl during five decadal period over National Capital Region of India: Impact on urban heat island and thermal comfort. *Urban Climate*, *33*, 100647. DOI: 10.1016/j.uclim.2020.100647

Molyneux, M. (2010). *Justicia de género, ciudadanía y diferencia en América Latina*. Ediciones Universidad de Salamanca.

Monclus, j. Ed. (1998): La ciudad disperas. Suburbanizacion y nuevas periferias. Barcelona, CCCB.

Morales, E. R. (2024). Planned Socio-Spatial Fragmentation: The Normalisation of Gated Communities in Two Mexican Metropolises. *Urban Planning*, *9*, 6879. Advance online publication. DOI: 10.17645/up.6879

Moreno Barón, J. A. (2021). Documento Técnico de Base Plan de Desarrollo Local 2021-2024. http://www.suba.gov.co/sites/suba.gov.co/files/documentos/tabla_archivos/documento_tecnico_de_base_final.pdf

Mortoja, M., Yigitcanlar, T., & Mayere, S. (2020). What is the most suitable methodological approach to demarcate peri-urban areas? A systematic review of the literature. *Land Use Policy*, *95*, 104601. DOI: 10.1016/j.landusepol.2020.104601

Mosquera Becerra, M. J. (2014). Socio-spatial Transformation and Contested Space at the Street Level in Latin America: The Case of Cali, Colombia. DOI: 10.15760/etd.1952

Moura, F., Cambra, P., & Gonçalves, A. B. (2017). Measuring walkability for distinct pedestrian groups with a participatory assessment method: A case study in Lisbon. *Landscape and Urban Planning*, *157*, 282–296. DOI: 10.1016/j.landurbplan.2016.07.002

Mousa, S. K., & Othman, M. (2020). The impact of green human resource management practices on sustainable performance in healthcare organisations: A conceptual framework. *Journal of Cleaner Production*, *243*, 118595. DOI: 10.1016/j.jclepro.2019.118595

Muisyo, P. K., & Qin, S. (2021). Enhancing the FIRM'S green performance through green HRM: The moderating role of green innovation culture. *Journal of Cleaner Production*, *289*, 125720. DOI: 10.1016/j.jclepro.2020.125720

Murillo-Bermúdez, L. F., & De Abreu, A. E. S. (2020). La gestión del recurso hídrico en Brasil y Colombia, una comparación de sus instrumentos. *Gestion y Ambiente*, *22*(2), 173–190. DOI: 10.15446/ga.v22n2.82554

Muxi, Z. (2018). *Mujeres, Casas y Ciudades. Más allá del umbral.* DPR.

MXCity. (2023, febrero 7). Ciudad Satélite, la historia de un suburbio que se proyectó como la ciudad del futuro. MXCity. https://mxcity.mx/2023/02/ciudad-satelite-la-historia-de-un-suburbio-que-se-proyecto-como-la-ciudad-del-futuro/

Nadathur, S., Wanasundara, J., & Scanlin, L. (2017). Proteins in the diet: Challenges in feeding the global population. In *Sustainable Protein Sources* (pp. 1–19). Elsevier. DOI: 10.1016/B978-0-12-802778-3.00001-9

Navas Florián, L. N. (2022). *Sistematización de la experiencia ecofeminista de concertación de una operación comunitaria para la Reserva Natural del Delirio en Bogotá. Trabajo de grado*. Universidad Nacional de Colombia.

Nel.lo. O. (1998): Los confines de la ciudad sin confines. Estructura urbana y límites administrativos de la ciudad difusa. En: Monclús, J. (editor) La ciudad dispersa. Centre de Cultura Contemporània de Barcelona.

Nimlyat, P., & Inusa, Y. (2023). A Literature Review of Indoor Air Quality and Sick Building Syndrome in Office Building Design Environment. Green Building & Construction Economics, 1–18. DOI: 10.37256/gbce.4120231961

Niri, M. V. (2017). Low VOC paints: A review. *Journal of Coatings Technology and Research*, *14*, 679–690.

Nobre, E. A. C. (2018). *Do plano diretor às operações urbanas consorciadas: a ascensão do discurso neoliberal e dos grandes projetos urbanos no planejamento paulistano. Livre Docência*. Faculdade de Arquitetura e Urbanismo/USP., DOI: 10.11606/T.16.2018.tde-27012022-090358

Noci, G., & Verganti, R. (1999). Managing 'green' product innovation in small firms. *R & D Management*, *29*(1), 3–15. DOI: 10.1111/1467-9310.00112

Nogués, S., & Salas-Olmedo, M. H. (2009). Land Use and Transport Integrated Policies in Peripheral Areas.

Norman, C., Surjan, A., & Booth, M. (2021). *Making Resilience a Reality: The Contribution ofPeri-urban Ecosystem Services (BGI) to Urban Resilience*. Springer., DOI: 10.1007/978-981-16-4815-1_8

Nunes, R. F. N., Marciano, L. P. A., Oliveira, G. S., Cardoso, N. S., Paula, F. B. de A., Sarpa, M., & Martins, I. (2024). Glyphosate contamination of drinking water and the occurrence of oxidative stress: Exposure assessment to rural Brazilian populations. *Environmental Toxicology and Pharmacology*, *108*(104476), 104476. Advance online publication. DOI: 10.1016/j.etap.2024.104476 PMID: 38796121

Oke, T. R. (1982). The energetic basis of the urban heat island. *Quarterly Journal of the Royal Meteorological Society*, *108*(455), 1–24. DOI: 10.1002/qj.49710845502

Omri, A. (2020). Technological innovation and sustainable development : Does the stage of development matter? *Environmental Impact Assessment Review*, *83*, 106398. DOI: 10.1016/j.eiar.2020.106398

ONU-Hábitat. (2023, diciembre 4). Yucatán, México, reforma leyes en ordenamiento territorial. https://onuhabitat.org.mx/index.php/yucatan-mexico-actualiza-su-normativa-territorial-y-urbana

Organización de las Naciones Unidas para la Alimentación y la Agricultura (FAO). (2024). Bases de datos de FAOLEX: Perfiles de país. https://www.fao.org/faolex/country-profiles/es/

Ortiz Flores, E. (2016). De Vancouver 1976 a Vancouver 2006. In Internacional del Hábitat, C. (Ed.), *Hábitat I (1976), Hábitat II (1996) & Hábitat III (2016)*. Habitat Internacional Coalition.

Osterwalder, A., Pigneur, Y., & Tucci, C. L. (2005). Clarifying business models: Origins, present, and future of the concept. *Communications of the Association for Information Systems*, *15*, 1–25. DOI: 10.17705/1CAIS.01601

Ostrensky, V. P., Porsse, A. A., & Frota, L. M. (2022). Public Transport and gentrification. Evidence from São Paulo Metro new stations. DOI: 10.1111/rsp3.12536

Pachoud, C. (2020). The quality of territorial governance: An assessment of institutional arrangements. The case of the Serrano cheese production in the Campos de Cima da Serra, Southern Brazil. *Journal of the Geographical Society of Berlin*, *151*(1), 23–36. DOI: 10.12854/erde-2020-424

Pachouri, V., & Kothari, P. (2024). Optimizing Urban Sustainability: The Effects of Green Infrastructure and its Application in Indian Cities. DOI: 10.21203/rs.3.rs-4594516/v1

PAHO. (2020). 2030 Agenda for Drinking Water, Sanitation and Hygiene in Latin America and the Caribbean: A Look from the Human Rights Perspective. DOI: 10.37774/9789275121115

Paisajeo.org. (s.f.). Paisaje y ecología, una relación indisoluble. Recuperado de https://www.ambientebogota.gov.co/todas-las-investigaciones/-/asset_publisher/pibvwzUnZiNr/content/paisajes-sostenibles-una-estrategia-de-cuidado-ambiental

Palma, O. M., Díaz-Puente, J. M., & Yagüe, J. L. (2020). The role of coffee organizations as agents of rural governance: Evidence from western Honduras. *Land (Basel)*, *9*(11), 1–17. DOI: 10.3390/land9110431

Pamukcu-Albers, P., Azevedo, J. C., Ugolini, F., Zuniga-Teran, A., & Wu, J. (2023). Urban resilience through green infrastructure. In *Adapting the Built Environment for Climate Change* (pp. 53–69). Woodhead Publishing.

Pani, M. (1957). México, un problema, una solución. Ciudad Satélite. *Arquitectura México*, *XIII*(60), 198–226.

Pani, Mario, Cuevas, José Luis, Ramos, García, & Domingo, Vila, Victor, & Manero Peón, Enrique. (1953, March). Estudios de planificación sobre Yucatán. *Arquitectura México*, *41*, 5–39.

Pelling, M. (2003). *The vulnerability of cities: Natural disasters and social resilience*. Earthscan.

Pereira, K. C. (2023). O impacto da Lei Federal 13.465 de 2017 sobre usucapião coletivo urbano no tribunal federal da 1ª região: Uma análise dos processos do Estado do Tocantins, Research. *Social Development*, *12*(4), 1–15.

Petrisor, A. (2017). A diversity-based approach to the spatial development of socio-ecological systems. Urbanism. Arhitectură. Construcţii, 143–162. https://api.semanticscholar.org/CorpusID:7105419

Pfannenstein, B., Martínez Jaramillo, J. O., Anacleto Herrera, E. E., Sevilla Villalobos, S., Pfannenstein, B., Martínez Jaramillo, J. O., Anacleto Herrera, E. E., & Sevilla Villalobos, S. (2019). Planificación urbana y la influencia de las urbanizaciones cerradas: El Área Metropolitana de Guadalajara, México. *Economía, Sociedad y Territorio*, *19*(59), 1087–1117. DOI: 10.22136/est20191278

Pioletti, M., & Dalla Vecchia, V. (2022). The Federal Urban Agenda in Brazil: Democratization and Politicization of Planning Practice. In Gelli, F., & Basso, M. (Eds.), *Identifying Models of National Urban Agendas: A View to the Global Transition* (pp. 189–211). Springer Nature Switzerland AG. DOI: 10.1007/978-3-031-08388-4_7

Prasad, D., Alizadeh, T., & Dowling, R. (2022). Smart city place-based outcomes in India: Bubble urbanism and socio-spatial fragmentation. *Journal of Urban Design*, *27*(4), 483–503. DOI: 10.1080/13574809.2021.2022978

Quattrone, G. (2023). Green and Blue Infrastructures and Nature-Based Solutions to Reduce Pollutant Emissions and Make Transitioning Urban Ecosystems More Climate Change-Adaptive. Green Building & Construction Economics, 80–89. DOI: 10.37256/gbce.4120232269

Rahaman, K. R., Lourenço, J. M., & Viegas, J. M. (2012). Perceptions of pedestrians and shopkeepers in European medium-sized cities: Study of Guimarães, Portugal. *Journal of Urban Planning and Development*, *138*(1), 26–34. DOI: 10.1061/(ASCE)UP.1943-5444.0000094

Rajendran, L. P., Raúl, L., Chen, M., Guerrero Andrade, J. C., Akhtar, R., Mngumi, L. E., Chander, S., Srinivas, S., & Roy, M. R. (2024). The 'peri-urban turn': A systems thinking approach for a paradigm shift in reconceptualising urban-rural futures in the global South. *Habitat International*, *146*, 103041. DOI: 10.1016/j.habitatint.2024.103041

Ramana, S. V., Padmavathi, V., & Rao, P. S. (2018). Assessment of volatile organic compound (VOC) emissions from building materials used in India. *Journal of Building Physics*, *42*(1), 3–20.

Ramírez, A. (2003, December). Comisión para la Regularización de la Tenencia de la Tierra (CORETT). Podium Notarial. *Revista Digital de Derecho del Colegio de Notarios de Jalisco, México.*, *28*, 130–133.

Ramos, J. S., & Hurtado, R. C. (2021). Análisis de servicios ecosistémicos para la configuración de una infraestructura verde en el área metropolitana de Sevilla. ACE: *Arquitectura. Ciudad y Entorno*, *16*(46), 9884. DOI: 10.5821/ace.16.46.9884

Rangel Montavo, L. E. (2015). Urbanismo y humedales. Caso de estudio: el humedal" La sabana" desarrollo urbano en la zona noroeste de Chetumal, México.

Rathore, H., & Singh, S. (2024). *Indoor air quality*. Noble Science Press., DOI: 10.52458/9788196897444.nsp2024.eb.ch-14

Reddy, M., Suneela, M., Sumathi, M., & Reddy, R. C. (2005). Indoor air quality at Salarjung Museum, Hyderabad, India. *Environmental Monitoring and Assessment*, *105*(1), 359–367. DOI: 10.1007/s10661-005-4344-z PMID: 15952528

Riazi, F., Fidélis, T., & Teles, F. (2022). Governance Arrangements for Water Reuse: Assessing Emerging Trends for Inter-Municipal Cooperation through a Literature Review. *Water (Basel)*, *14*(18), 2789. Advance online publication. DOI: 10.3390/w14182789

Ribeiro, S. C. L., Daniel, M. N., & Abiko, A. (2016). ZEIS maps: Comparing areas to be earmarked exclusively for social housing in São Paulo city. *Land Use Policy*, *58*, 445–455. DOI: 10.1016/j.landusepol.2016.08.010

Ripio Rodriguez, V. Ferrer Valero, S.; Palomo Cermeño, E. & Duarte Hidalgo, C. (2019). *Feminismo. La historia.* Madrid: Ediciones Akal. S.A

Rita, E., Cestti., Jorge, Jose, Escurra., Irina, I., Klytchnikova., Stefano, P., Pagiola. (2012). Climate change impacts on water resources and adaptation in the rural water supply and sanitation sector in Nicaragua. 1-53.

Rodó de Zarate, M. (2019). Intersectionality. In Orum, A. (Ed.), *The Wiley Blackwell Encyclopedia of Urban and Regional Studies*. John Wiley & Sons Ltd. DOI: 10.1002/9781118568446.eurs0164

Rodríguez, C., García, B., Pinto, C., Sánchez, R., Serrano, J., & Leiva, E. (2022). Water Context in Latin America and the Caribbean: Distribution, Regulations and Prospects for Water Reuse and Reclamation. *Water (Basel)*, *14*(21), 3589. Advance online publication. DOI: 10.3390/w14213589

Rodriguez, C., Lima Sakr, F., Griffiths, S., & Hillier, B. (2012). The relationship of spatial configuration and socio-economic conditions in São Paulo, Brazil. Proceedings: *Eighth International Space Syntax Symposium*, 1–24.

Rogers, P., & Hall, A. (2006). Gobernabilidad Efectiva del Agua. In Global Water Partnership: Vol. Vol.7. https://www.cepal.org/samtac/noticias/documentosdetrabajo/0/23420/GWP00504.pdf

Rokem, J., & Vaughan, L. (2018). Segregation, mobility and encounters in Jerusalem: The role of public transport infrastructure in connecting the 'divided city.'. *Urban Studies (Edinburgh, Scotland)*, *55*(15), 3454–3473. DOI: 10.1177/0042098017691465

Rolnik, R. (2009). Democracia no fio da navalha: Limites e possibilidades para a implementação de uma agenda de reforma urbana no Brasil. *Revista Brasileira de Estudos Urbanos e Regionais*, *11*(2), 31. DOI: 10.22296/2317-1529.2009v11n2p31

Rolnik, R. (2015). *Guerra dos lugares: a colonização da terra e da moradia na era das finanças*. Boitempo.

Rolnik, R. (2017). *La guerra de los lugares. La colonización de la tierra y la vivienda en la era de las finanzas*. Ediciones.

Rolnik, R., & Santoro, P. F. (2014). *Zonas Especiais de Interesse Social (ZEIS) em Cidades Brasileiras: Trajetória Recente de Implementação de um Instrumento de Política Fundiária*. Lincoln Institute., https://www.lincolninst.edu/pt-br/publicacoes-recursos/

Romero-Lankao, P., Gnatz, D. M., & Sperling, J. (2018). Examining urban adaptation and transformation through the lens of justice. *Environmental Research Letters*, *13*(8), 084008.

Rosenzweig, C., Solecki, W., Hammer, S. A., & Mehrotra, S. (2010). Cities lead the way in climate-change action. *Nature*, *467*(7318), 909–911. DOI: 10.1038/467909a PMID: 20962822

Rosik, P., & Wójcik, J. (2022). Transport Infrastructure and Regional Development: A Survey of Literature on Wider Economic and Spatial Impacts. DOI: 10.3390/su15010548

Rothstein, A. P., Jesser, K. J., Feistel, D. J., Konstantinidis, K. T., Trueba, G., & Levy, K. (2023). Population genomics of diarrheagenic Escherichia coli uncovers high connectivity between urban and rural communities in Ecuador. *Infection, Genetics and Evolution*, *113*(105476), 105476. Advance online publication. DOI: 10.1016/j.meegid.2023.105476 PMID: 37392822

Roy, A. (2005). Urban Informality: Toward an Epistemology of Planning. *Journal of the American Planning Association*, *71*(2), 147–158. DOI: 10.1080/01944360508976689

Rueda, S. (2017). La lucha por la mitigación del cambio climático se ganará o se perderá en las ciudades. *Revista Democracia y Gobierno Local*, (37), 10–19.

Ryoo, S. Y., & Koo, C. (2013). Green practices-IS alignment and environmental performance: The mediating effects of coordination. *Information Systems Frontiers*, *15*(5), 799–814. DOI: 10.1007/s10796-013-9422-0

SAHOP. (1981). *Sistema Normativo de Equipamiento Urbano*. Normas Básicas. Secretaría de Asentamientos Humanos y Obras Públicas.

Salas-Olmedo, M. H., García, P., & Gutiérrez, J. (2015). Accessibility and transport infrastructure improvement assessment: The role of borders and multilateral resistance. *Transportation Research Part A, Policy and Practice*, *82*, 110–129. https://doi.org/https://doi.org/10.1016/j.tra.2015.09.009. DOI: 10.1016/j.tra.2015.09.009

Salazar-Camacho, C., Salas-Moreno, M., Marrugo-Madrid, S., Paternina-Uribe, R., Marrugo-Negrete, J., & Díez, S. (2022). A human health risk assessment of methylmercury, arsenic and metals in a tropical river basin impacted by gold mining in the Colombian Pacific region. *Environmental Research*, *212*(113120), 113120. Advance online publication. DOI: 10.1016/j.envres.2022.113120 PMID: 35339468

Salinas Arreortua, L. A. (2022). Financiarización subordinada. El mercado hipotecario de la vivienda social en México. *Investigaciones Geográficas*, *107*, 1–13. DOI: 10.14350/rig.60458

Samet, J. M. (2011). *Community Design and Air Quality*. Island Press., DOI: 10.5822/978-1-61091-036-1_4

Sánchez. (2019). *Aportes desde la agroecología para habitar el Alto Fucha desde la noción de Ecoterritorio: una apuesta de Huertopía para la permanencia en los cerros orientales de Bogotá. Tesis de pregrado*. Universidad Pedagógica Nacional.

Santamouris, M. (2015). Analyzing the heat island magnitude and characteristics in one hundred Asian and Australian cities and regions. *The Science of the Total Environment, 512–513*, 582–598. DOI: 10.1016/j.scitotenv.2015.01.060 PMID: 25647373

Santamouris, M., & Osmond, P. (2020). Increasing Green Infrastructure in Cities: Impact on Ambient Temperature, Air Quality and Heat-Related Mortality and Morbidity. *Buildings (Basel, Switzerland)*, *10*(12), 233. DOI: 10.3390/buildings10120233

São Paulo. (2016a). Cadernos das Subprefeituras: Material de apoio para Revisão Participativa dos Planos Regionais das Subprefeituras - Cidade Tiradentes. Secretaria Municipal de Desenvolvimento Urbano. Retrieved from gestaourbana.prefeitura.sp.gov.br

São Paulo. (2016b). Caderno de Propostas dos Planos Regionais das Subprefeituras: Quadro Analítico. Secretaria Municipal de Desenvolvimento Urbano. Retrieved from gestaourbana.prefeitura.sp.gov.br

São Paulo. (2016c). Decreto nº 56.759, de 7 de janeiro de 2016. São Paulo, SP. Retrieved from https://legislacao.prefeitura.sp.gov.br/leis/decreto-56759-de-07-de-janeiro-de-2016/detalhe

São Paulo. (2016d). Decreto nº 57.377, de 11 de outubro de 2016. São Paulo, SP. Retrieved from https://legislacao.prefeitura.sp.gov.br/leis/decreto-57377-de-11-de-outubro-de-2016/

Sasal, M. C., Demonte, L., Cislaghi, A., Gabioud, E. A., Oszust, J. D., Wilson, M. G., Michlig, N., Beldoménico, H. R., & Repetti, M. R. (2015). Glyphosate loss by runoff and its relationship with phosphorus fertilization. *Journal of Agricultural and Food Chemistry*, *63*(18), 4444–4448. DOI: 10.1021/jf505533r PMID: 25775388

Sasi, A. P., & Udgiri, R. (2024). A study on indoor air pollution and its impact on health in urban field practice area: A community-based study. *International Journal of Community Medicine and Public Health*, *11*(3), 1246–1251. DOI: 10.18203/2394-6040.ijcmph20240627

Sastry, M. M. S., Kumar, N., & Hussain, S. (2004). Air quality status at selected locations in Hyderabad City. *Journal of Environmental Science & Engineering*, *46*(2), 86–91. https://www.ncbi.nlm.nih.gov/pubmed/16649598 PMID: 16649598

Satterthwaite, D., Huq, S., Pelling, M., Reid, H., & Romero-Lankao, P. (2009). *Adapting to climate change in urban areas: The possibilities and constraints in low- and middle-income nations*. IIED Working Paper.

Schaltegger, S., Lüdeke-Freund, F., & Hansen, E. (2012). Business cases for sustainability: The role of business model innovation for corporate sustainability. *International Journal of Innovation and Sustainable Development*, *6*(2), 95–119. DOI: 10.1504/IJISD.2012.046944

Schaltegger, S., & Wagner, M. (2011). Sustainable entrepreneurship and sustainability innovation: Categories and interactions. *Business Strategy and the Environment*, *20*(4), 222–237. DOI: 10.1002/bse.682

Scheyvens, R., Banks, G., & Hughes, E. (2016). The private sector and the SDGs: The need to move beyond 'business as usual. *Sustainable Development (Bradford)*, *24*(6), 371–382. DOI: 10.1002/sd.1623

Schiederig, T., Tietze, F., & Herstatt, C. (2012). Green innovation in technology and innovation management—An exploratory literature review. *R & D Management*, *42*(2), 180–192. DOI: 10.1111/j.1467-9310.2011.00672.x

Schmeidler, K. (2010). Walking as a sustainable transport mode in cities.

Schwaab, J. (2022). Sprawl or compactness? How urban form influences urban surface temperatures in Europe. *City and Environment Interactions*, *16*, 100091. DOI: 10.1016/j.cacint.2022.100091

Sclavi, M., & Buraschi, D. (2022). Participative Democracy and the Art of Listening. Ascolto Attivo srl, Milan.

Sdoukopoulos, A., Pitsiava-Latinopoulou, M., & Politis, I. (2023). Assessing the fragmentation-barrier effect in urban areas: The case study of Thessaloniki, Greece. *IOP Conference Series. Earth and Environmental Science*, *1196*(1), 012078. DOI: 10.1088/1755-1315/1196/1/012078

Secretaría de Gobernación. (1954). *Ley sobre el Régimen de propiedad y Condominio de las Edificaciones Divididas en Pisos, Departamentos, Viviendas o Locales*. Diario Oficial.

Secretaría de Planeación. (2020). Proceso de Revisión del Plan de Ordenamiento Territorial de Bogotá D. C. https://www.sdp.gov.co/sites/default/files/11_suba_-_diagnostico_pot_2020.pdf

Secretaría Distrital de Movilidad. (2020). Informe Preliminar de Rendición de Cuentas Locales: Localidad de Suba. https://www.movilidadbogota.gov.co/web/sites/default/files/Paginas/04-10-2021/informe_preliminar_rdc_gestion_2020_localidad_suba.pdf.pdf

Secretaría Distrital de Planeación. (2009). Conociendo la Localidad de Suba: Diagnóstico de los aspectos físicos, demográficos y socioeconómicos. https://oab.ambientebogota.gov.co/?post_type=dlm_download&p=4145

Secretaría Distrital de Planeación. (2015a). Construyendo una visión regional común entre Bogotá y sus territorios circunvecinos. Colección Integración Regional (Vol. 12). Bogotá D.C.: UNCRD, Secretaria Distrital de Planeación. Obtenido de https://www.sdp.gov.co/gestion-socioeconomica/integracion-regional-y-nacional/publicaciones/construyendo-vision-regional-comun-entre-bogota-y-sus-territorios-circunvecinos

Secretaría Distrital de Planeación. (2015b). Región metropolitana de Bogotá: Una Visión de la Ocupación del Suelo. Bogotá: Alcaldía Mayor de Bogotá. Obtenido de https://www.sdp.gov.co/sites/default/files/region_metropolitana_de_bogota_una_vision_de_la_ocupacion_del_suelo.pdf

SEDATU. (2022). NOM-002-SEDATU-2022, Equipamiento en los instrumentos que conforman el Sistema General de Planeación Territorial. Clasificación, terminología y aplicación. https://www.dof.gob.mx/nota_detalle.php?codigo=5662152&fecha=23/08/2022#gsc.tab=0

Šenitková, I. (2017). Indoor air quality – buildings design. 93, 03001. DOI: 10.1051/matecconf/201779303001

Serrano Romero, R. O. (2019). *Movilidad urbana y espacio público: reflexiones, métodos y contextos*. Universidad Piloto de Colombia.

Sharma, A., Shukla, A., & Ali, S. (2021). A hybrid ventilation system for improving indoor air quality in hot and dry climates. *Renewable & Sustainable Energy Reviews*, *144*, 110966.

Shaw, D. R. (2010). Value creation in multi-level networks: a development of business model theory. In *PACIS 2010 Proceedings*; 25–36.

Shaw, B. J., van Vliet, J., & Verburg, P. H. (2020). The peri-urbanization of Europe: A systematic review of a multifaceted process. *Landscape and Urban Planning*, *196*, 103733. DOI: 10.1016/j.landurbplan.2019.103733

Shebell, E & Moser, S (2019). Planning for the Buen Vivir: socialism, decentralisation and urbanisation in rural Ecuador. *IDPR*, 41(4).

Sherry, J., & Soranno, P. A. (2006). Landscape influences on water chemistry and primary production in lakes and reservoirs. *Landscape Ecology*, *21*(3), 321–336.

SIASAR. (2017). SIASAR. https://globalsiasar.org/es

Silva, S. U. A. (2021). As ZEIS no planejamento de São Paulo: Regulações urbanas e assentamentos informais. *Revista Brasileira de Direito Urbanístico*, *7*(12), 43–84. DOI: 10.55663/rbdu.v7i12.303

Singh, S., Tan, B. C., & Khan, N. (2017). Driving green practice adoption in restaurant sector: Restaurant operator's perspectives - MMU institutional repository. In *Proceedings of the 5th International Conference on Innovation and Entrepreneurship (ICIE 2017)* (pp. 219–226). Academic Conferences and Publishing International Limited. https://shdl.mmu.edu.my/7108/. Accessed 24 April 2021.

Singh, A., Kumar, P., & Jain, V. K. (2015). Assessment of indoor air quality in residential buildings in Delhi, India. *Building and Environment*, *94*, 246–254.

Smith, W. K., & Tushman, M. L. (2005). Managing strategic contradictions: A top management model for managing innovation streams. *Organization Science*, *16*(5), 522–536. DOI: 10.1287/orsc.1050.0134

Soares, R. B., da Silva, S. M. O., & Filho, F. (2021). Macroeconomic accounting of water resources: An input-output approach to linkage analysis and impact indicators applied to the state of ceará, brazil. *Water (Basel)*, *13*(6), 869. Advance online publication. DOI: 10.3390/w13060869

Soja Edward. 2008. Post metrópolis. Estudios críticos sobre las ciudades y las regiones. Madrid. Traficantes de sueños.

Sosa-Rodriguez, F. S., & Garduño Bolaños, M. A. (2021). *Green Infrastructure: The New Paradigm for Resilient Cities*. Springer Nature., DOI: 10.1007/978-3-319-95873-6_41

Speck, J. (2013). *Walkable city: How downtown can save America, one step at a time*. Macmillan.

Spieth, P., Schneckenberg, D., & Ricart, J. E. (2014). Business model innovation – state of the art and future challenges for the field. *R & D Management*, *44*(3), 237–247. DOI: 10.1111/radm.12071

Spoon, S. (2005). What Defines Walkability: Walking Behavior Correlates. DOI: 10.17615/ddw2-sr16

Srinagesh, B. (2016). Air pollution and its Impact on Human Health – A Geospatial analysis of Hyderabad. *International Journal of Research*, *3*(10), 851–867.

Stone, B., Vargo, J., Liu, P., DeLucia, A., Trail, M., Hu, Y., & Russell, A. (2014). Avoided heat-related mortality through climate adaptation strategies in three US cities. *PLoS One*, *9*(6), e100852. DOI: 10.1371/journal.pone.0100852 PMID: 24964213

Straube, J. (2003). Indoor Air Quality, Healthy Buildings, and Breathing Walls. http://breathing.com/pdf/indoor%20air%20quality.pdf

Stubbs, W., & Cocklin, C. (2008). Conceptualizing a 'sustainability business model'. *Organization & Environment*, *21*(2), 103–127. DOI: 10.1177/1086026608318042

Suarez-Daza, F. (2021). Percepciones eco políticas del borde norte de Bogotá, Colombia. (U. d. Andes., Ed.) Obtenido de Universidad de los Andes: http://hdl.handle.net/1992/54023

Sudarsan, J. S., Sinha, S., Gedam, V. V., & Dharaskar, S. (2024). Assessment on the impact of indoor air quality on human health-a study on selected tier 1 cities of India. *Discover Environment*, *2*(1), 142. Advance online publication. DOI: 10.1007/s44274-024-00164-9

Sugumar, P., Krishnan, T., Abhinav, B. L. V. V. D. S. S., Bhavana, P., Kavya, B. S., Yeshwanth, V., & Krishna, K. M. (2022). Investigation of Indoor Air Quality and Thermal Comfort of a College Building in Hyderabad, India. *IOP Conference Series. Earth and Environmental Science*, *1074*(1), 012025. DOI: 10.1088/1755-1315/1074/1/012025

Sukma, N., & Leelasantitham, A. (2022a). A community sustainability ecosystem modeling for water supply business in Thailand. *Frontiers in Environmental Science*, *10*, 940955. DOI: 10.3389/fenvs.2022.940955

Sukma, N., & Leelasantitham, A. (2022b). From conceptual model to conceptual framework: A sustainable business framework for community water supply businesses. *Frontiers in Environmental Science*, *10*, 1013153. DOI: 10.3389/fenvs.2022.1013153

Sumardjo, A., Firmansyah, L., & Dharmawan, L. (2023). Peri-urban Community Resilience in Facing the Dynamics of Global Climate-change Impacts toward. *IOP Conference Series. Earth and Environmental Science*, *1266*(1), 012045. DOI: 10.1088/1755-1315/1266/1/012045

Tamene, A., Habte, A., Woldeyohannes, D., Tamrat, H., Endale, F., Eajo, T., & Afework, A. (2022). Water treatment at the point-of-use and treatment preferences among households in Ethiopia: A contemporaneous systematic review and meta-analysis. *PLoS One*, *17*(10), e0276186. Advance online publication. DOI: 10.1371/journal.pone.0276186 PMID: 36301990

Taşan-Kok, T., & Stead, D. (2013). Analysing the Socio-Spatial Vulnerability to Drivers of Globalisation in Lisbon, Oporto, Istanbul, Stockholm and Rotterdam. In Resilience Thinking in Urban Planning (1st ed., pp. 71–91). Springer Dordrecht. DOI: 10.1007/978-94-007-5476-8_5

Taylor, A., & Helfat, C. E. (2009). Organizational linkages for surviving technological change: Complementary assets, middle management, and ambidexterity. *Organization Science*, *20*(4), 718–739. DOI: 10.1287/orsc.1090.0429

Teece, D. J. (2010). Business models, business strategy and innovation. *Long Range Planning*, *43*(2/3), 172–194. DOI: 10.1016/j.lrp.2009.07.003

Teixeira, C. C. (2018). Os decretos de Habitação de Interesse Social e a flexibilização de parâmetros de uso e ocupação do solo na cidade de São Paulo no período de 1992 a 2016. *PosFAUUSP*, *25*(45), 86–101. DOI: 10.11606/issn.2317-2762.v25i45p86-101

Tejeda-Benítez, L., Noguera, K., Aga, D., & Olivero-Verbel, J. (2023). Pesticides in sediments from Magdalena River, Colombia, are linked to reproductive toxicity on Caenorhabditis elegans. *Chemosphere*, *339*(139602), 139602. Advance online publication. DOI: 10.1016/j.chemosphere.2023.139602 PMID: 37480944

Telangana State Pollution Control Board (TSPCB). (2022). Guidelines for the Use of Low-VOC Paints in Government Buildings and Public Spaces.

Thakur, A. K., & Patel, S. (2023). *Indoor Air Quality in Urban India: Current Status.* Research Gap, and the Way Forward., DOI: 10.1021/acs.estlett.3c00636

Theurillat, T., Rérat, P., & Crevoisier, O. (2015). The real estate markets: Players, institutions and territories. *Urban Studies (Edinburgh, Scotland)*, *52*(8), 1414–1433. DOI: 10.1177/0042098014536238

Thomas, M., Costa, D., & Oliveira, T. (2016). Assessing the role of IT-enabled process virtualization on green IT adoption. *Information Systems Frontiers*, *18*(4), 693–710. DOI: 10.1007/s10796-015-9556-3

Tidd, J., & Bessant, J. R. (2009). *Managing innovation. Integrating technological, market and organizational change* (4th ed.). Wiley.

Tomasiello, D. B., Santos, D. H. M., Oliveira, J. P., Braga, C. G., Pereira, R., Tomasiello, D. B., Santos, D. H. M., Oliveira, J. P., Braga, C. G., & Pereira, R. (2022). A time interval metric for cumulative opportunity accessibility. https://doi.org/DOI: 10.31235/OSF.IO/UX5AH

Trimble, M., Olivier, T., Anjos, L. A. P., Tadeu, N. D., Giordano, G., Mac Donnell, L., Laura, R., Salvadores, F., Santana-Chaves, I. M., Torres, P. H. C., Pascual, M., Jacobi, P. R., Mazzeo, N., Zurbriggen, C., Garrido, L., Jobbágy, E., & Pahl-Wostl, C. (2022). How do basin committees deal with water crises? Reflections for adaptive water governance from South America. *Ecology and Society*, *27*(2), art42. Advance online publication. DOI: 10.5751/ES-13356-270242

Tseng, M. L., Tan, R. R., & Siriban-Manalang, A. B. (2013). Sustainable consumption and production for Asia: Sustainability through green design and practice. *Journal of Cleaner Production*, *40*, 1–5. DOI: 10.1016/j.jclepro.2012.07.015

Tzoulas, K., Korpela, K., Venn, S., Yli-Pelkonen, V., Kazmierczak, A., Niemela, J., & James, P. (2007). Promoting ecosystem and human health in urban areas using Green Infrastructure: A literature review. *Landscape and Urban Planning*, *81*(3), 167–178. DOI: 10.1016/j.landurbplan.2007.02.001

UN-Habitat. (2011). *Cities and Climate Change: Global Report on Human Settlements*. United Nations Human Settlements Programme.

UN-Habitat. (2021). *World Cities Report 2020: The Value of Sustainable Urbanization*. United Nations Human Settlements Programme.

Unidas, N. (2018). *La agenda 2030 y los Objetivos de Desarrollo Sostenible. Una oportunidad para América Latina y el Caribe*. https://repositorio.cepal.org/server/api/core/bitstreams/cb30a4de-7d87-4e79-8e7a-ad5279038718/content

UNIDO. (2009). *Scaling up renewable energy in Africa*. United Nations Industrial Development Organization.

United Nations Environment Programme. (2021). Towards a Green and Healthy Recovery.

United Nations Human Settlements Programme (UN-Habitat). (2022). World Cities Report 2022. https://unhabitat.org/sites/default/files/2022/06/wcr_2022.pdf

United Nations. (1987). Report of the World Commission on Environment and Development: Our Common Future; UN Documents; United Nations: New York, NY, USA.

United Nations. (2016). *New urban green innovation agenda. Draft Resolution Submitted by the President of the General Assembly*. Available online: https://habitat3.org/wp-content/uploads/N1639668-English.pdf (accessed on 24 May 2020).

United Nations. (2018). *World Urbanization Prospects: The 2018 Revision*. Department of Economic and Social Affairs.

Universidad Nacional de Colombia. (18 de abril de 2024). Estructura Ecológica Principal de la Sabana de Bogotá. Instituto de Estudios Urbanos. Obtenido de https://periodico.unal.edu.co/articulos/los-rios-urbanos-son-vitales-en-tiempos-de-escasez-de-agua-por-eso-urge-recuperarlos

UN-Water. (2021). Summary Progress Update 2021 : SDG 6 — water and sanitation for all. In UN-Water.

Valer, J. O. (2023). Participation in water resources management in Latin America 2017-2022: A systematic review. International Seven Journal of Multidisciplinary, 1–18. DOI: 10.56238/devopinterscie-144

Van de Ven. Angle, H. L., & Poole, M. S. (Eds.) (2000/1989). *Research on the Management of Innovations: The Minnesota Studies*. Oxford, New York: Oxford University Press.

Van de Ven. Polley, D., Garud, S., & Venkataraman, S. (2008). *The innovation journey* (2nd ed.). New York: Oxford University Press.

Varkey, A. (2019). A Review of Peri-Urban Definitions. *Land Use Changes and Challenges to Development.*, *39*(I), 111.

Varley, A. (2013). Postcolonialising informality? *Environment and Planning. D, Society & Space*, *31*(1), 4–22. DOI: 10.1068/d14410

Vasudha, N., & Venkateswara Rao, P. (2022). Factor Analysis of Air Pollutants over Hyderabad - A Case Study. *Current World Environment*, *17*(2), 507–515. DOI: 10.12944/CWE.17.2.21

Vega, C. (2020). Rutas de la reproducción y el cuidadopor América Latina. Apropiación, valorización coelctiva y política. In Menendez, M., & Conze, C. (Eds.), *La vida en el centro. Feminismo, reproducción y tramas comunitarias* (pp. 81–144). Bajo Tierra Ediciones, Minerva Ediciones y Escuela de Formación Feminista.

Vitaliano, S., Cascone, S., & D'Urso, P. (2024). Mitigating Built Environment Air Pollution by Green Systems: An In-Depth Review. *Applied Sciences (Basel, Switzerland)*, *14*(15), 6487. DOI: 10.3390/app14156487

Viveros Vigoya, M. (2016). La interseccionalidad: Una aproximación situada a la dominación. *Debate Feminista*, *52*, 1–17. DOI: 10.1016/j.df.2016.09.005

Voss, G. B., & Voss, Z. G. (2013). Strategic ambidexterity in small and medium-sized enterprises: Implementing exploration and exploitation in product and market domains. *Organization Science*, *24*(5), 1459–1477. DOI: 10.1287/orsc.1120.0790

Waghray, S. N., Patil, D., & Khan, S. A. (2024). *Planning Towards Healthy City—Case of Hyderabad.* Springer International Publishing., DOI: 10.1007/978-3-031-52303-8_6

Water & Corporation. (1980). *The urban lake restoration program: Summary report.* U.S. Environmental Protection Agency.

Waters, E., Barnett, J., & Puleston, A. (2014). Contrasting perspectives on barriers to climate change adaptation in Australia. *Climate Policy, 14*(5), 572–588.

Wen, H., Lee, C. C., & Song, Z. (2021). Digitalization and environment: How does ICT affect enterprise environmental performance? *Environmental Science and Pollution Research International, 28*(39), 54826–54841. DOI: 10.1007/s11356-021-14474-5 PMID: 34014481

Wen, Y.. (2014a). A framework for assessing urban ecosystem services: Integrating ecological, economic, and social perspectives. *Ecological Indicators, 45*, 220–231.

Wibowo, S. S., Tanan, N., & Tinumbia, N. (2015). Walkability measures for city area in Indonesia (case study of Bandung). *Journal of the Eastern Asia Society for Transportation Studies, 11*, 1507–1521.

Wicki, S., Hansen, E. G., & Schaltegger, S. (2015). Exploration of Green Technologies in SMEs: the Role of Ambidexterity, Domain Separation and Commercialization, *XXVI ISPIM Innovation Conference*, 14-17 June 2015, Budapest, Hungary.

Winn, M., & Kirchgeorg, M. (2005). The siesta is over: a rude awakening from sustainability myopia. In Sharma, S., & Starik, M. (Eds.), *Corporate Environmental Strategy and Competitive Advantage* (pp. 232–258). Elgar. DOI: 10.4337/9781845426859.00017

World Commission on Environment and Development (WCED). (1987). *Report of the World Commission on Environment and Development: Our Common Future.* WCED, United Nations.

World Health Organization. (2014). Urban green spaces and health – a review of evidence.

World Health Organization. (2018). WHO Guidelines for indoor air quality: Dampness and mould.

Wu, J., Cao, M., Tong, D., Finkelstein, Z., & Hoek, E. M. V. (2021). A critical review of point-of-use drinking water treatment in the United States. *NPJ Clean Water, 4*(40), 40. Advance online publication. DOI: 10.1038/s41545-021-00128-z

Wu, J., Liao, H., Wang, J. W., & Chen, T. (2019). The role of environmental concern in the public acceptance of autonomous electric vehicles: A survey from China. *Transportation Research Part F: Traffic Psychology and Behaviour*, *60*, 37–46. DOI: 10.1016/j.trf.2018.09.029

Yadava, P. K., Kumar, H., Singh, A., Kumar, V., & Verma, S. (2023). Impact of climate change on water quality and its assessment. In *Visualization Techniques for Climate Change with Machine Learning and Artificial Intelligence* (pp. 39–54). Elsevier.

Yasin, M. Y., Yusoff, M. M., Abdullah, J., & Noor, N. (2020, November 29). Hj. Mohd. (2020). Is urban sprawl a threat to sustainable development? A review of characteristics and consequences. *Geografia : Malaysian Journal of Society and Space*, *16*(4). Advance online publication. DOI: 10.17576/geo-2020-1604-05

Yekimov, S., Kluger, V., Sobirov, B., & Ahrorov, F. (2023). Dynamic entropy model of transport flows. DOI: 10.1051/e3sconf/202338905035

Yoo, S., Kumagai, J., Sho, K., & Managi, S. (2024). Impact of high-speed railway on gentrification and regional inequality in Japan. *Transportation Research Part D, Transport and Environment*, *134*, 104346. DOI: 10.1016/j.trd.2024.104346

Yu, P., Yung, E. H. K., Chan, E. H. W., Wong, M. S., Wang, S., & Chen, Y. (2023). An integrated approach for examining urban fragmentation in metropolitan areas: Implications for sustainable urban planning. *Journal of Cleaner Production*, *419*, 138151. DOI: 10.1016/j.jclepro.2023.138151

Zambon, I., Serra, P., Sauri, D., Carlucci, M., & Salvati, L. (2017). Beyond the 'Mediterranean city': Socioeconomic disparities and urban sprawl in three Southern European cities. *Geografiska Annaler. Series B, Human Geography*, *99*(3), 319–337. DOI: 10.1080/04353684.2017.1294857

Zaragocin, S., & Caretta, M. A. (2021). Cuerpo-Territorio: A Decolonial Feminist Geographical Method for the Study of Embodiment. *Annals of the Association of American Geographers*, *111*(5), 1503–1518.

Zasada, I., Fertner, C., Piorr, A., & Nielsen, T. A. (2011). Peri-urbanisation and multifunctional adaptation of agriculture around Copenhagen. *Geografisk Tidsskrift-Danish Journal of Geography,* 111(1), 59-72, 111(1), 59-72.

Zeni, V. L. F., Scheibe, L. F., Zeni, E., & Vignatti, M. A. P. (2019). As marcas do agronegócio sobre o território das águas da Bacia do Prata. *Geosul*, *34*(71), 640–664. DOI: 10.5007/1982-5153.2019v34n71p640

Zhang, Q., Li, L., Zhou, J., Braham, W. W., & Ma, N. (2024). A spatial analysis of ozone and PM2.5 distribution for assessing design factors of healthy buildings. *Journal of Building Engineering*, *89*, 109357. Advance online publication. DOI: 10.1016/j.jobe.2024.109357

Zhang, Q., Yung, E. H. K., & Chan, E. H. W. (2018). Towards Sustainable Neighborhoods: Challenges and Opportunities for Neighborhood Planning in Transitional Urban China. *Sustainability (Basel)*, *10*(2), 406. DOI: 10.3390/su10020406

Zollo, M., Cennamo, C., & Neumann, K. (2013). Beyond what and why: Understanding organizational evolution towards sustainable enterprise models. [https://do]. *Organization & Environment*, *26*(3), 241–259. DOI: 10.1177/1086026613496433

Zott, C., Amit, R., & Massa, L. (2011). The business model: Recent developments and future research. *Journal of Management*, *37*(4), 1019–1042. DOI: 10.1177/0149206311406265

Zubelzu Mínguez, M. J., & Allende Álvarez, F. (2014). *Ordenación del territorio: un enfoque integrador*. Ediciones Mundi-Prensa.

About The Contributors

Vasco Barbosa, Born in Oporto and graduated in Architecture in 2000 at the Faculty of Architecture and Arts, Oporto, Portugal. Since 2018, he is independent expert of European Commission for spatial and urban planning issues. In 2017 finished a Posdoctoral period of 4 years in Brazil, Portugal and UK, about the application of Space Syntax (from University College London) to urban Planning. Ph.D in Spatial Planning and Territorial Development at the University of Santiago de Compostela, 2013. In 2011 completed a Master in "Management in Sustainable Land Use Planning" in the University of Santiago de Compostela. In 2008 completed a postgraduate degree in "Environmental Management and Land Use Planning" in the Superior Institute of Viana do Castelo. Independent expert of European Commission for Urban Planning issues and member of European Science Foundation. Currently, he is researcher at the University Polytechnic of Viana do Castelo, Portugal and associate researcher in the Faculty of Humanities at the University of Johannesburg, South Africa. Current research interests: Urban and rural development; Spatial planning; Land use planning; Space syntax; Urban resilience and inequalities; Architecture, Heritage and landscape; Space Syntax.

Mónica Marcela Suárez Pradilla is a civil engineer from the Universidad Nacional de Colombia, with a Master's and Ph.D. in Urban and Architectural Management and Valuation from the Universitat Politècnica de Catalunya. She is a professor at the Center for Roads and Transportation at the Universidad Escuela Colombiana de Ingeniería Julio Garavito. Her work focuses on sustainable urban transport, territorial development, and the impacts of infrastructure on spatial dynamics. She supervises doctoral and master's theses, contributing to the training of researchers and professionals. Her publications in national and international journals address daily mobility, territorial planning, and equity in infrastructure access. Her research is grounded in methodological development, modeling techniques, and the advanced use of Geographic Information Systems (GIS) to analyze and project urban and territorial dynamics critically and sustainably.

***

Alejandro Acosta-Gonzalez, I hold an undergraduate degree in Microbiology from Universidad de los Andes in Colombia, a Doctorate in Biochemistry and Molecular Biology from Universidad de Granada in Spain, and a Postdoctorate from Universidad de La Sabana. I am currently Associate Professor in the Department of Chemical and Biotechnological Processes at the Engineering Faculty of Universidad de La Sabana in Colombia. My research experience includes environmental remediation and biotechnology, respiratory diseases, and human microbiota. I am also a member of the Young Academy of Sciences (ACCEFYN, Colombia) and a young ambassador of the International Society of Microbial Ecology.

Milena Albrecht Silveira, Master's student in Urban Planning and Policy Design at Politecnico di Milano (POLIMI), Italy, with an MAECI Study in Italy scholarship for 2023/24 and 2024/25. Graduated in Architecture and Urbanism from the University of Passo Fundo (UPF), Brazil, in 2021, with an academic exchange experience at ISCTE – University Institute of Lisbon, Portugal, in 2019.

Oscar Bragos, Architect (Universidad Nacional de Rosario) MSc in Town and Regional Planning (Universidade Federal do Rio de Janeiro) Dr (Universidad de Valladolid) Professor in Town ande Regional Planning - Facultad de Arquitectura, Planeamiento y Diseño - UNR- Researcher (urban expansion, urban policies, urban projects, urban plans, regulatory instruments) - Centro Universitario Rosario de Investigaciones Urbanas y Regionales - CONICET - UNR

Cinthya Butron Revilla, Urban Ecologist Architect. PhD student at the University Pablo de Olavide, Seville-Spain in the Environment and Society programme. Graduated from the Universidad Autónoma de Barcelona Spain from the Master MEISAES specialised in Industrial and Urban Ecology. Architect graduated from the National University of San Agustin Peru - UNSA. Renacyt Research Professor, index H2. Postgraduate and undergraduate lecturer at the Faculty of Architecture and Urbanism FAU-UNSA. Co-investigator in the projects Smartcity Arequipa; Emergency Urbanism in the Colca Valley; Guidelines, planning, actions in peri-urban areas. I am part of the Technical Team of: GEMOTT - Group of Studies of Mobility, Transport and Territory in Barcelona, EOU Colca Valley - Urban Planning Schemes for the Reconstruction of the Ichupampa and Achoma Town Centres in the Colca Valley Peru, PlanMET 2040 - Urban Mobility Team for the Metropolitan Development Plan of Lima. Founding Member of Urbanismo Colectivo Ciudades and Estudio 11 Arquitectura.

Deniz Çam, is a dynamic and young urban planner with a passion for creating sustainable, resilient and liveable cities. He graduated from Mersin University's Faculty of Architecture, Department of Urban and Regional Planning, achieving an honors distinction. He has worked on urban morphology, urban design, walkability, urban heritage, urban regeneration and development, and climate change adaptation. Currently pursuing his Master's degree in Urban Planning and Policy Design at Politecnico di Milano, Deniz Çam's research interests include peri-urbanisation processes, suburbanisation, livability, urban morphology, climate change and urban resilience.

Roger Cardozo is a Civil Engineer with expertise in mobility and transportation. He possesses advanced skills in the analysis of geospatial patterns. His professional experience has focused on identifying and solving issues related to road safety, social development, and territorial planning, providing efficient and strategic solutions. He is particularly interested in the development and urban planning of territories, sustainable mobility, future infrastructure design, and addressing major challenges in mobility and accessibility.

Seyda Emekci received her bachelor's, master and doctoral degrees from Middle East Technical University (METU). Worked as an associate at the Development Agency and the General Director of Nature Conservation and National Parks, in Turkey from 2014 to 2017. Postdoctoral researcher at East London University, in the UK in 2019. Currently teaches in the Architecture Department at Ankara Yıldırım Beyazıt University (AYBU). Has been involved in various change projects at the different architectural levels in public and private sectors and with civil associations in Turkey since 2011. Specialization areas include sustainability, energy efficiency, housing economics.

Mateo Gallardo is a chemical engineer originally from Ecuador, and has Master's degree in Process Design and Management from the University of La Sabana. With an aspiring research career spanning different areas, his work is focused on the development of nanomaterials intended for removal of emergent contaminants from water, especially via electrospinning. However, recently he has also explored the application of this technique for producing biodegradable food packaging materials.

Jaime Hernandez Garcia, Full Professor at the Department of Aesthetics, in the School of Architecture and Design at the Pontificia Universidad Javeriana, in

Bogotá, Colombia. He is Senior Researcher at the Colombian Ministry of Science. He studied architecture at Los Andes University in Bogotá, his Masters at York University, and his PhD was awarded by the University of Newcastle Upon Tyne, in United Kingdom. He completed a Post-doctorate in Conflict and Cities at the University of Missouri Kansas City, with a Fulbright Scholarship. His research interests include informal settlements, public space, nature based solutions and community participation. He has published widely in English and Spanish, articles, chapters and books; among his recent books: "Urban Space: Experiences and Reflections from the Global South", published by Javeriana University; "Ecología de los Paisajes Artificiales", published also by Javeriana University; "Public Space in Informal Settlements, the Barrios of Bogotá", published by Cambridge Scholars Publishing; and "Researching the Contemporary City: Identity, Environment and Social Inclusion in Developing Urban Areas", published by Javeriana University.

Carlos Jimenez, Undergraduate degree in Chemical Engineering (Universidad Nacional de Colombia), M.Sc. in Biotic Product Development (Instituto Politécnico Nacional, Mexico), and Doctor in Food and Nutritional Sciences (University of Reading (England). Associate Professor in the Department of Chemical and Biotechnological Processes, Engineering Faculty (Universidad de La Sabana, Colombia). More than 25 years as a professor in engineering programs, in processes, thermodynamics, bioprocesses, and food. Consulting work in drinking water, wastewater, rheology, and physical properties of materials.

Çağlanur Kösel is a young urban planner with a passion for creating just, cohesive and liveable cities. She graduated from Mersin University, Faculty of Architecture, Department of Urban and Regional Planning with honours. She has worked on urban landscape approaches, urban design, pedestrian mobility, cultural heritage, geographic information systems and urban spatial analyses. Currently pursuing her Master's degree in Urban Planning and Policy Design at Politecnico di Milano, Çağlanur Kösel's research interests include peri-urbanisation processes, antifragility, suburbanisation, urban design, urban ecology approaches and sustainability. She is excited to contribute to projects and publications that aim to shape the future of cities.

Edith Manchego-Huaquipaco, Architect, graduated from the Universidad Nacional de San Agustín de Arequipa, Peru (2014) and Master in Territory, Transport and Urbanism with the specialties of Land Transport and Urbanism at the Polytechnic University of Valencia, Spain (2016), with the Research Project: Public Bicycle System for the City of Arequipa, Peru. Renacyt Research Professor, index H2. Teacher at the Universidad Nacional de San Agustín de Arequipa at undergraduate and postgraduate level. Co-investigator of the research group Urbanismo de Emergencia en el Valle del Colca and Member of the CYTED Network with the project Lineamientos, Planes, Acciones en Áreas Periurbanas (Guidelines, Plans, Actions in Periurban Areas). She is also a founding member of Colectivo Ciudades, an interdisciplinary collective of social innovation and research whose objective is to contribute to the development of more equitable, friendly, inclusive and sustainable cities, through participatory actions seeking to generate citizenship. In addition, he has scientific publications on topics related to Transport Planning, Sustainable Urban Mobility, Teaching in Architecture and Urbanism.

Patricia Orozco Quijano is an Associate Professor at Laurentian University's School of Business Administration, specializing in international marketing and sustainable business, and work-integrated learning (WIL). A trilingual scholar with over 15 years of teaching experience in English, French, and Spanish, she has led pedagogical innovations across undergraduate and graduate business programs. Her research spans international entrepreneurship, sustainable industries, and regional economic development, with publications in peer-reviewed journals and contributions to Ivey Publishing. She has delivered keynote presentations across Latin America and Europe and has served as a visiting scholar in Australia, Peru, and Mexico.

Thaís Rossetto, Master in Architecture, Technology, and the City (PPGATC - FECFAU) from the University of Campinas (UNICAMP), with a CAPES scholarship. Member of the Fluxus Laboratory and part of the Research Group Habitares: Humanizing Living and the City, affiliated with FECFAU and registered with CNPq. Graduated in Architecture and Urbanism from the University of Passo Fundo (UPF - 2020), including a study abroad period through the MARCA program at the Universidad de Concepción del Uruguay - Argentina (2018).

Tapanwita Saha is a Ph.D. scholar (Design) from the Department of Architecture and Design of Lovely Professional University, India.

Absalón J. Salmerón Zapata es Doctor en Ciencias Administrativas por la Universidad Cristóbal Colón, donde actualmente colabora como profesor investigador. Por la misma universidad tiene una Maestría en Administración y la Licenciatura en Psicología. Es teólogo por la Pontificia Universidad Gregoriana. Dirige el Programa DCM, modelo de análisis basado en competencias laborales, en la universidad Cristóbal Colón y es el Vicerrector General de la misma casa de estudios. Su línea de investigación es sobre optimización del talento humano y desarrollo organizacional. Entre sus publicaciones más recientes se encuentran: Conceptual,

Theoretical-Methodological, and Empirical Approaches on the Multidimensional Relationship Between Human Talent Management and Organization.

Bigith V.B., Assistant Professor, Department of Urban Planning, Lovely Professional University

Omar Vargas-González Professor, research assistant and former Head of Computer Systems Department at Tecnológico Nacional de México Campus Ciudad Guzmán, professor at Telematic Engineering at Centro Universitario del Sur Universidad de Guadalajara with a master degree in Computer Systems. Has been trained in Innovation and Multidisciplinary Entrepreneurship at Arizona State University (2018) and a Generation of Ecosystems of Innovation, Entrepreneurship and Sustainability for Jalisco course by Harvard University T.H. Chan School of Health. At present conduct research on diverse fields such as Entrepreneurship, Economy, Statistics, Mathematics and Information and Computer Sciences. Has collaborated in the publication of many scientific articles and conducted diverse Innovation and Technological Development projects.

Index

L

N

P

R

S

T

www.ingramcontent.com/pod-product-compliance
Lightning Source LLC
LaVergne TN
LVHW080341011026
849161LV00009B/2152
9798369360897